I0013459

AI WEALTH BLUEPRINT: The Top 10 AI Apps That Are Creating Jobs, Making Money, and the Ultimate AI Wealth Generator of the Century

BENOIT TANO, MD PHD

Published by Integrative Medical Press

For general information on our products and services or for technical support, please contact our customer care Department within the United States at **952-522-4949.**

Printed in the United States of America

ISBN: 9798282427592

DISCLAIMER

This publication, 'AI WEALTH BLUEPRINT: The Top 10 AI Apps That Are Creating Jobs, Making Money, and the Ultimate AI Wealth Generator of the Century', is provided for informational purposes only and does not constitute financial, business, or legal advice. The insights and strategies discussed herein are not a guarantee of earnings or employment, as the results may vary based on individual circumstances, market conditions, and other factors outside the control of the author and publisher. All efforts have been made to ensure the accuracy and reliability of the information within as of the date of publication. However, changes in technology, law, and market environments after the publication may impact the relevance and accuracy of the content. Readers are advised to perform their own due diligence and consult with professional advisors concerning their specific situations before making any financial decisions or investments based on the information provided. The examples and case studies included are illustrations only and may not reflect current market conditions. The author, Benoit Tano, MD, PhD, and the publisher, Integrative Medical Press, assume no responsibility for errors, omissions, or contrary interpretations of the subject matter herein. Intellectual property rights to content created using AI tools mentioned (incl. graphics, texts, and interfaces) may vary and should be expressly checked according to local and international laws. The mention of specific companies, products, processes, or services at any point in the book does not constitute an endorsement or recommendation by the author or publisher. Neither the author nor the publisher will be liable for any incidental, indirect, consequential, or punitive damages arising from, or in connection with, the use of information in this book. This disclaimer is meant to provide a general overview of the content and implications of the strategies discussed within, and it is imperative for readers to approach the text with discretion and critical thinking.

CONTENTS

PREFACE

In the rapidly expanding universe of technology, Artificial Intelligence (AI) has emerged not just as a disruptor but as a quintessential architect of modern wealth creation. 'AI WEALTH BLUEPRINT: The Top 10 AI Apps That Are Creating Jobs, Making Money, and the Ultimate AI Wealth Generator of the Century' by Dr. Benoit Tano meticulously charts the transformational journey of AI from a nascent technology to a formidable force in sculpting economic landscapes. This book is an indispensable guide for entrepreneurs, investors, and professionals aiming to harness the potent capabilities of AI to unlock new dimensions of wealth. The interplay between AI and various sectors, unveiling a spectrum of opportunities and the synthesis of innovative job markets, firmly positions AI as the backbone of future economies. As you delve into the chapters, you encounter a meticulously curated list of top AI applications that are not only revolutionizing business operations but are also pivotal in job creation and wealth generation. Dr. Tano, with his profound expertise, navigates through the intricate mechanics of technologies like ChatGPT, MidJourney, and more, elucidating their role in content creation, visual arts, and beyond. Each chapter is an exposition into specific AI applications, detailed with their operational dynamics, potential for monetization, and strategic leverage in competitive markets. Beyond the operational insights, this book also addresses the ethical, legal, and socio-economic dimensions of deploying AI technologies. It prompts one to consider not just the economic advantages but also the broader implications of AI integration into business frameworks. Dr. Tano's visionary perspective is not only about forecasting but equipping readers with the requisite knowledge and skills to be active participants in this AI-driven economic wave. 'AI WEALTH BLUEPRINT' thus serves as both a roadmap and a compass for navigating the evolving terrains of AI applications in wealth creation. It is a testament to the transformative potential of AI, set to redefine norms and catalyze a new era of industrial prosperity.

FOREWORD

In 'AI WEALTH BLUEPRINT: The Top 10 AI Apps That Are Creating Jobs, Making Money, and the Ultimate AI Wealth Generator of the Century,' Dr. Benoit Tano offers a masterful exploration of how artificial intelligence is not merely reshaping industries, but also creating vast opportunities for wealth generation, job creation, and market evolution in unprecedented ways. This book emerges at a critical juncture in our technological evolution, providing a timely and essential guide to harnessing the potential of AI across various sectors. Dr. Tano, armed with a dual expertise in medicine and technology, brings a unique perspective that bridges the often disparate worlds of science and business, ensuring a comprehensive understanding of AI's capabilities and its role within the economic landscape. The book is meticulously structured around the top ten AI apps that exemplify the transformative power of these technologies. From content creation with ChatGPT to the innovative use of MidJourney in the visual arts, each chapter is a deep dive into specific applications that are setting benchmarks in their respective fields. The inclusion of practical subtopics like setting up, monetizing, and navigating legal considerations offers readers actionable insights and a clear path to implementation. Particularly noteworthy are the 'Case Studies and Success Stories of AI-Driven Wealth,' which illuminate the real-world impact of these technologies. These narratives serve not only as inspiration but also as compelling evidence of the robust potential AI holds. 'AI WEALTH BLUEPRINT' is an indispensable resource for entrepreneurs, investors, and innovators looking to understand and exploit the wealth-generating prowess of AI. It also provides critical ethical and regulatory perspectives, ensuring readers grasp the complexities of deploying AI responsibly and sustainably. As we stand on the precipice of a new era dominated by artificial intelligence, Dr. Tano's work offers a critical blueprint for navigating the future of wealth creation. This is more than a book; it's a roadmap for anyone ready to embrace the monumental changes brought forth by AI and channel them into profitable and impactful ventures.

OVERVIEW OF AI IN WEALTH CREATION

Defining Artificial Intelligence in the Context of Wealth Creation

Artificial Intelligence (AI) has increasingly become a cornerstone in the narrative of modern wealth creation. At its core, AI refers to the capability of machines to perform tasks that typically require human intelligence. This includes abilities such as learning, reasoning, problem-solving, perception, and language understanding. In the realm of economics and finance, AI's role transitions from mere automation to becoming an essential driver of innovation and efficiency.

When specifically addressing wealth creation, AI's impact is multifaceted. It enables enhanced decision-making, optimizes investment strategies, and personalizes financial services to individual needs, thereby increasing potential returns and reducing risks. Beyond individual gains, AI fosters broader economic growth by streamlining operations and creating new market opportunities.

Thus, defining AI in the context of wealth creation is not only about acknowledging its technological capabilities but also recognizing its transformative power in reshaping industries, empowering entrepreneurs, and catalyzing an overall increase in economic well-being. AI is not just a tool but a revolutionary approach that redefines the landscape of wealth generation.

Historical Evolution of AI in Business and Finance

The historical evolution of AI in business and finance is a testament to human ingenuity and technological progress. Initially, AI's integration into these fields was seen through basic automated data processing systems in the late 20th century. Over time, these systems evolved into more complex algorithms capable of performing tasks such as market analysis and customer data mining, significantly impacting decision-making processes.

By the dawn of the 21st century, machine learning (ML) technologies transformed business models by enabling real-time analytics and predictive modeling. Companies could now forecast market trends, optimize operations, and personalize customer service. Moreover, these developments laid the groundwork for fintech innovations such as robo-advisors, enhancing the accessibility and efficiency of financial services.

As AI technology continued to mature, it began to drive not just automation but true innovation. From risk assessment in banking to algorithmic trading in stock markets, AI's role expanded to cover critical financial operations, reshaping the landscape and setting new standards in both business and finance, marking an era of unprecedented growth and transformation.

Core AI Technologies Driving Economic Change

The economic landscape is being reshaped by several core AI technologies, each playing a pivotal role in the emergence of new wealth paradigms. Machine Learning (ML), Natural Language Processing (NLP), and Artificial Neural Networks (ANNs) stand at the forefront of this technological revolution. ML algorithms excel in detecting patterns and making predictions from large datasets, optimizing everything from supply chains to customer interactions. This capability not only improves business efficiencies but also enhances decision-making, leading to superior financial outcomes.

NLP transforms how businesses engage with their customers and manage vast volumes of data, enabling the automation of customer service and insights from unstructured data like social media and emails. Such advancements contribute significantly to cost reduction and increased revenue streams. Meanwhile, ANNs mimic human brain functionality, providing the foundation for developments in AI that push boundaries beyond conventional programming limitations.

The integration of these technologies into daily business practices offers substantial economic gains. By automating routine tasks and generating predictive insights, companies leverage AI to stay competitive in a rapidly evolving marketplace. This technological empowerment not only boosts profitability but also creates new job opportunities, defining a new era of economic change driven by intelligence augmentation.

Impact of AI on Global Markets

AI's integration into global markets is revolutionizing economic frameworks across various sectors. As AI technologies enhance precision in market forecasting and customer needs analysis, firms are able to adapt more dynamically to changing global demands. This results in increased market efficiency and heightened innovation, allowing businesses to tailor products and services to diverse consumer bases. The ripple effect is considerable, with AI-driven companies often outperforming competitors who lag in digital adoption.

Furthermore, AI's role in data analytics promotes a more interconnected global market. By synthesizing vast amounts of data from multiple sources, AI provides businesses with unprecedented insights into global consumer trends and economic shifts. This capability empowers companies to strategically enter new markets or adjust their offerings in existing ones, thereby fostering more robust international trade and investment flows.

On a broader scale, AI contributes to the creation of entirely new markets and value chains. By enabling the development of novel products and services, such as AI-enhanced health diagnostics or smart logistics, AI not only diversifies market offerings but also enhances global economic resilience. This transformation underscores AI's pivotal role in redefining global market structures and the economy at large.

AI as a Tool for Democratizing Wealth Creation

AI's influence extends beyond mere economic efficiency; it serves as a powerful mechanism for democratizing wealth creation. By lowering barriers to entry in various markets, AI enables individuals from diverse backgrounds to participate in economic activities that were previously restricted to those with substantial capital or specialized knowledge.

For example, AI-powered platforms can offer personalized financial advice previously available only through costly financial advisors, thus facilitating more informed investment decisions for the average person. Similarly, AI-driven marketplaces can connect small producers with global audiences, significantly broadening their customer base and potential revenue streams.

Such inclusivity not only fosters individual wealth growth but also stimulates broader economic diversity. As AI continues to evolve, its role in promoting equitable wealth distribution and empowering underserved communities will likely expand, redefining not just how wealth is created but who gets to create it. This promises a more balanced economic playing field, contributing to a healthier overall economy.

Major Industries Transformed by AI

Artificial Intelligence has catalyzed significant transformations across various major industries, redrafting the landscape of global business. In healthcare, AI's ability to analyze massive datasets has revolutionized patient diagnosis and personalized treatment plans, improving outcomes while reducing costs. The finance sector has similarly been transformed, with AI enhancing everything from fraud detection to customer service and algorithmic trading, leading to more secure and efficient operations.

The manufacturing sector has seen a resurgence with the integration of AI in automation, predictive maintenance, and supply chain management. These advancements have not only increased productivity but also improved the safety and precision of production processes. In retail, AI-driven analytics help in predicting consumer buying behavior and personalizing shopping experiences, driving sales and customer satisfaction.

Transportation and logistics have also benefited from AI, particularly through optimized route planning and autonomous vehicle technology, which decrease delivery times and increase efficiency. Each industry's adaptation showcases AI's role as a pivotal force in driving economic growth and innovation.

AI and the Shift from Manual to Automated Wealth Management

The shift from manual to automated wealth management signifies a pivotal development in financial services, propelled by AI. Initially, wealth management relied heavily on human expertise to make investment decisions, manage portfolios, and offer financial advice. However, the integration of AI technologies has introduced a new era marked by sophisticated algorithms capable of analyzing vast datasets to inform investment strategies with unprecedented precision.

Robo-advisors, AI-driven financial planning tools, exemplify this transformation. These platforms use machine learning to assess risk, respond to market changes, and tailor advice to individual financial goals at a fraction of traditional management costs. This automation broadens access, allowing average individuals to benefit from expert-level financial guidance previously available only to the wealthiest.

Moreover, AI enhances the accuracy of financial forecasts and operational efficiency, fostering a more dynamic wealth management sector. As AI continues to evolve, its role in automating wealth management will likely deepen, shaping the future of personal finance and investment on a global scale. This transition not only streamlines operations but also encourages a more inclusive financial environment.

The Role of AI in Personal Finance and Investing

AI is reshaping personal finance and investing, offering tools that enhance decision-making and financial management. Personalized investment advice, once the domain of high-net-worth individuals through expensive advisors, is now widely accessible via AI-driven platforms. These tools analyze individual financial data and market conditions to offer tailored advice, making strategic investing accessible to a broader audience.

Moreover, AI applications in investing extend to algorithmic trading where AI analyzes vast amounts of market data to execute trades at optimal times, often reacting faster than human traders could. This capability not only increases the efficiency of trading but also minimizes losses during volatile market conditions. The integration of AI in these areas democratizes high-level investment strategies, previously available only to the elite.

AI's influence in personal finance also manifests in budgeting and financial planning apps. These apps utilize AI to track spending, forecast future expenses, and suggest savings plans, thus empowering users to achieve their financial goals with greater precision and foresight. As AI technology continues to advance, its role in personal finance and investing is set to expand, making sophisticated financial management tools the norm rather than the exception.

Understanding AI's Role in Job Creation

Artificial Intelligence is heralding a new era in job creation, fundamentally altering how industries recruit and develop their workforce. AI's ability to automate routine tasks has sparked fears of job displacement, but the reality often shows a net creation of jobs, with AI taking on mundane tasks and humans moving to more creative and strategic roles. Thus, AI is not just a disruptor but a catalyst for evolving job landscapes.

Moreover, AI-driven industries require new skill sets, fostering educational and training programs that aim to equip the workforce with digital literacy and AI proficiency. This educational shift is creating vast opportunities in AI development, data analysis, system maintenance, and cybersecurity, among others. Such roles leverage human analytical and creative capabilities, underscoring AI's role in job transformation rather than elimination.

In essence, AI's integration into the economic fabric is generating both direct and ancillary job opportunities. Companies leveraging AI are not only revising their operational models but are also innovating in employment strategies to harness AI's full potential. The symbiosis between AI and human expertise augments productivity and fosters an inclusive economic environment, indicating a prosperous co-evolution of technology and workforce.

AI in Entrepreneurship: New Ventures and Startups

In the realm of entrepreneurship, AI is not just a tool but a transformative force reshaping the startup landscape. AI-enabled platforms facilitate rapid prototyping, market analysis, and customer service optimization, hence accelerating the journey from concept to market. This capability allows even novices with limited resources to scale their operations quickly, thus democratizing the startup ecosystem and fostering innovation across diverse fields.

Furthermore, AI-driven analytics empower new ventures to dissect vast amounts of data for market insights and consumer behavior predictions with a precision previously reserved for corporations with deep pockets. Startups employing AI can thus tailor their products and services more effectively to meet specific consumer needs, gaining a competitive edge in bustling marketplaces.

Moreover, AI's role in new enterprises extends to automating administrative and repetitive tasks, freeing up entrepreneurs to focus on strategic growth and innovation. The integration of AI tools thus not only streamlines business processes but also enhances decision-making, ensuring that startups remain agile and adaptive in rapidly changing markets. As AI continues to advance, its pervasive influence is poised to unlock new entrepreneurial potentials, marking a notable shift in how businesses are initiated and developed.

Case Studies: Successful AI-Driven Businesses

In a landscape teeming with innovation, AI-driven businesses stand out by redefining success in wealth creation. Zipline, a drone delivery startup, uses AI to deliver medical supplies across remote areas, transforming logistics in healthcare with precision and speed. This venture not only enhances access to critical resources but also proves the scalability and efficiency of AI in challenging environments.

Another leading example is DeepMind, whose AI applications in energy management for data centers reduce electricity consumption significantly, showcasing the economic and environmental impacts of AI. Their methods of utilizing machine learning for system cooling have set benchmarks for sustainable practices in the tech industry, echoing profitability with responsibility.

Furthermore, Lemonade Inc., a tech-driven insurance company, leverages AI to process claims rapidly and determine premiums dynamically. Their customer-centric model, powered by AI, demonstrates how technology can personalize and streamline financial services, enriching consumer experiences and operational transparency. These cases not only exemplify the profound implications of AI in various sectors but also highlight the transformative role it plays in crafting the future of business.

AI and the Gig Economy: Opportunities and Challenges

The intersection of AI and the gig economy presents a dual-edged sword, offering significant opportunities while introducing complex challenges. On one hand, AI-enabled platforms such as ride-sharing and freelance job portals enhance operational efficiencies and personalize job matches. This boosts work flexibility and opens up global opportunities for gig workers, allowing for a surge in freelance and contractual roles, potentially increasing job satisfaction and work-life balance.

However, these advancements are not without their pitfalls. AI-driven gig work can lead to job insecurity and replace traditional employment structures with less stable, gig-based engagements. The lack of benefits, job security, and potential for lower wages under AI-driven gig platforms poses significant risks to workers' financial stability. Moreover, the shift may exacerbate income inequality as AI tends to consolidate gigs among fewer, highly skilled professionals.

To harness AI's potential in the gig economy substantially, policies must evolve to offer protections and benefits for gig workers, ensuring they are not exploited in an increasingly automated landscape. Balancing innovation with worker security will define the future trajectory of AI in reshaping work.

The Influence of AI on Business Efficiency and Profitability

AI's role in enhancing business efficiency and profitability is profound and multifaceted. By automating routine tasks, AI frees up human resources to focus on more strategic activities, thereby increasing overall productivity. This automation extends across sectors, from manufacturing lines where robots handle assembly, to software solutions that manage administrative tasks in offices, thus minimizing human error and operational costs.

Moreover, AI's capability to analyze large datasets enhances decision-making precision. Companies utilize AI-driven analytics to identify market trends and consumer preferences, effectively reducing guesswork and enabling targeted marketing strategies. This not only improves customer satisfaction but also boosts sales efficiency. These tools can also forecast demand, helping businesses manage inventory more effectively and reduce wastage, directly impacting their bottom line.

Furthermore, AI facilitates real-time decision-making, which is crucial in dynamic market environments. Businesses can respond swiftly to market changes, adjusting their strategies to maintain competitive advantage and profitability. The agility offered by AI tools ensures that companies remain resilient in face of economic fluctuations and industry disruptions, securing their place in future markets.

Ethical Considerations and Socioeconomic Impacts of AI

As AI reshapes wealth creation, ethical considerations emerge alongside significant socioeconomic impacts. The deployment of AI systems in business can exacerbate socio-economic disparities as high-skill workers who adapt to AI advancements gain significantly, while low-skill workers may find themselves increasingly marginalized. This shift underscores the need for ethical AI practices that prioritize fairness and inclusivity.

Moreover, AI influences socioeconomic structures by altering job markets and consumer interactions. While AI drives efficiency and growth, it also poses risks of monopolistic behaviors where large firms harness AI capabilities to dominate markets, potentially stifling competition and innovation.

Ethically, the transparency of AI algorithms is crucial, as hidden biases can lead to discrimination in hiring, lending, and law enforcement. Society must address these ethical concerns by enforcing regulations that ensure AI acts enhance societal welfare without infringing on privacy or individual rights, ensuring a balanced integration of AI into the fabric of economic progress.

Barriers to AI Adoption in Wealth Creation

Despite the transformative potential of AI in wealth creation, various barriers impede its widespread adoption. First, the high initial costs associated with implementing AI technologies deter small to medium enterprises (SMEs). Investment in AI demands significant capital for technology acquisition, system integration, and skilled personnel, which can be prohibitive for businesses with limited financial resources.

Secondly, a lack of understanding and trust in AI systems also stalls adoption. Many business leaders and entrepreneurs are hesitant to rely on AI for critical decision-making due to fears of inaccurate outputs or failure to comprehend the technology's inner workings. This skepticism is often amplified by high-profile failures in AI deployments that receive wide media coverage, overshadowing success stories.

Furthermore, regulatory challenges present another significant hindrance. The pace at which AI evolves often outstrips existing legal frameworks, creating a regulatory lag that complicates compliance for businesses wanting to leverage AI. Enterprises must navigate these uncertain waters carefully, often slowing down AI adoption to ensure full compliance.

AI's Role in Reducing Entry Barriers for New Entrepreneurs

Artificial intelligence (AI) is revolutionizing the way new entrepreneurs break into competitive markets by lowering entry barriers. Traditionally, high costs of market research, customer acquisition, and business process automation have impeded the entry of startups with limited resources. AI's ability to streamline these processes democratizes opportunities by making sophisticated tools accessible to businesses of all sizes.

For instance, AI-powered data analytics platforms enable new ventures to gain insights comparable to those of established players, without the need for expensive market research departments. This levels the playing field, allowing emergent entrepreneurs to make data-driven decisions effectively. Moreover, AI-infused Customer Relationship Management (CRM) systems offer automated customer engagement solutions, reducing the need for large sales teams while increasing reach and personalization.

Furthermore, AI's role extends to cost management, where it optimizes supply chain logistics and inventory, reducing overheads drastically. This financial leniency affords new entrepreneurs the ability to experiment and innovate without the burden of conventional cost barriers, fostering a more vibrant and diverse entrepreneurial ecosystem.

The Future of Employment in an AI-Dominant Economy

As we progress deeper into an era governed by artificial intelligence, the contours of employment are being redrawn to accommodate new modalities of work. In an AI-dominant economy, traditional roles evolve or give way to new positions that necessitate AI literacy, creating a dynamic labor market where adaptability is key. Proficiencies in AI management, ethical deployment, and machine learning interpretation become prized skills, elevating the value of continuous education and re-skilling initiatives.

This transformation is not without its challenges. The pace of AI integration may outstrip the rate at which the workforce acquires new skills, potentially leading to job displacement in sectors slow to adapt. The responsibility thus falls on policymakers and educational institutions to bridge this gap, ensuring a smooth transition by fostering an environment that promotes tech fluency across all levels of society.

Optimistically, AI's role in wealth creation could spur numerous high-value jobs in AI development, supervision, and regulatory domains, fostering a robust ecosystem centered around AI technologies. However, this bright future hinges on thoughtful implementation and inclusive policies that actively counterbalance the inequalities potentially exacerbated by rapid technological change.

Educational Requirements for Thriving in AI-Enhanced Industries

As industries increasingly integrate Artificial Intelligence (AI), the educational landscape must evolve to meet new demands. The imperative for workers to thrive in AI-enhanced sectors hinges on acquiring specialized skills that are presently shaping the educational framework from basic schooling to advanced professional development.

Central to this requisite skill set is a strong foundation in STEM (Science, Technology, Engineering, and Mathematics), coupled with competencies in machine learning, data analysis, and algorithmic understanding. Education curriculums are thus pivoting towards these areas, emphasizing problem-solving and critical thinking to equip students not only with the ability to use AI tools but to innovate upon them.

Moreover, as AI applications permeate diverse industries—from healthcare to finance—

interdisciplinary knowledge becomes crucial. Courses that blend AI with sector-specific training are emerging, enabling students to apply AI insights contextually. Additionally, soft skills like ethical judgement and adaptability are being foregrounded; as AI's impact broadens, professionals must navigate complex moral landscapes and continuously adapt to new technologies.

The Compounding Effect of AI on Income Generation

Artificial Intelligence (AI) is not just a technological upgrade; it is a paradigm shift in income generation, manifesting a compounding effect across various sectors. This transformative power of AI is most visible in how it amplifies the capabilities of businesses to generate higher revenue with lesser incremental cost. AI-driven automation and data analytics reduce operational costs and open new revenue streams, enabling businesses to reinvest savings into further innovation.

Moreover, AI escalates the income generation process by optimizing pricing strategies and enhancing customer personalization, thereby increasing sales and customer loyalty. The introduction of AI in product development and marketing sees a decrease in time-to-market and an increase in the effectiveness of marketing campaigns, respectively, contributing to a faster growth of income.

As AI continues to evolve, its compounding effects on income are profound, fostering not just growth but sustainability in wealth creation. This necessitates a strategic approach in its adoption, ensuring businesses not only adopt AI but evolve with it to harness its full potential.

AI-Powered Automation Tools and Software

AI-powered automation tools and software are reshaping the wealth creation landscape by enhancing productivity and operational efficiency. These tools range from advanced data analytics systems to sophisticated robotic process automation (RPA), all designed to automate complex business processes, reducing human error and increasing efficiency. Companies integrating these systems can reallocate human resources to strategic tasks, thereby enhancing creativity and innovation.

Significantly, the deployment of AI in automation extends beyond mere task execution to predictive analysis and decision support systems. These applications not only perform predefined tasks but also predict trends and adapt to changing market conditions in real-time. This capability allows businesses to remain competitive, responsive, and agile in dynamic economic environments.

Moreover, these tools are becoming increasingly accessible, not only to large corporations but also to medium and small enterprises. Innovations in cloud computing and AI as a Service (AIaaS) are lowering cost barriers, enabling smaller players to leverage AI for automation and compete on a larger scale.

AI Integration in Enterprise Resource Planning

The integration of AI into enterprise resource planning (ERP) systems marks a transformative phase in organizational management and wealth creation. AI-enhanced ERP systems facilitate smarter, data-driven decisions, automating and optimizing routine tasks and complex operational workflows. This integration allows companies to achieve unprecedented efficiencies and improve their bottom-line performance.

By harnessing AI, ERP systems can now predict market trends, manage inventory more effectively, and optimize supply chains without human intervention, leading to significant cost reductions and enhanced service delivery. The agility provided by these systems ensures that businesses can quickly adapt to market changes and customer demands, thereby gaining an edge over competitors who rely on traditional methods.

Additionally, AI-driven analytics embedded within ERP systems provide insights that were previously unimaginable. These insights enable companies to identify potential improvement areas, forecast future scenarios, and tailor their strategic approaches accordingly. As ERP continues to evolve, the role of AI is expanding, thus opening new avenues for innovation and efficiency in resource planning and management.

Investment in AI Technology: Costs and Returns

Investing in AI technology requires substantial capital, but the potential returns can redefine profitability and operational efficiency for businesses. Initially, the investment primarily revolves around acquiring AI systems, integrating them into existing infrastructures, and training personnel to manage these technological advancements. This phase is capital-intensive but crucial for setting a strong foundation for AI-enabled operations.

The financial returns of AI investment, however, often manifest as long-term gains. Businesses experience reduced operational costs through automation, enhanced decision-making capabilities due to predictive analytics, and increased revenue from improved customer experience and service delivery. These benefits cumulatively lead to significant returns on investment over time, making the initial financial commitment worthwhile.

Moreover, the dynamic landscape of AI technology ensures continual improvement and opportunities for scaling up operations, thereby extending the utility and enhancing the returns from initial investments. Considering these factors, businesses are increasingly viewing AI as a critical investment for sustainable growth and competitive advantage.

Consumer Response and Adoption of AI-Driven Products

The consumer landscape is rapidly transforming with the incorporation of AI-driven products, marking a significant shift in how products are perceived, used, and valued by the market. Initial reactions often vary from fascination and eager acceptance to skepticism and hesitance, driven by awareness, perceived benefits, and potential risks associated with these innovative products.

Market studies reveal that early adopters tend to be tech-savvy individuals and sectors where efficiency gains from AI can be clearly quantified. Adoption rates are significantly influenced by the transparency of AI operations, the clarity of value addition, and robustness in data privacy assurances. Furthermore, user-friendly interface designs play a crucial role in adoption, reducing the intimidation factor associated with complex AI systems.

Over time, as success stories and benefits become more visible and widespread, consumer trust increases, leading to broader acceptance. Nevertheless, continuous education and positive reinforcement through user experiences are essential in cultivating a market that not only accepts but also champions AI-driven innovations.

AI and the Scalability of Micro Businesses

Artificial Intelligence (AI) is revolutionizing the scalability of micro businesses, offering unprecedented opportunities for growth with minimized resources. By integrating AI tools such as automation and data analytics, these small ventures can compete in larger markets, often bypassing traditional growth barriers. AI enables precise customer targeting and product customization, thus expanding their market reach without proportionally increasing their operational costs.

Furthermore, AI's role in operational efficiency allows micro businesses to optimize their processes, from inventory management to customer service, enhancing productivity with fewer overheads. This operational agility makes it possible for them to swiftly adapt to market changes —an essential trait for scaling in today's dynamic economic environment.

Lastly, AI-driven platforms provide micro businesses access to global marketplaces and digital marketing tools, facilitating a broader customer base without the high costs usually associated with expansion. The scalability achieved with AI not only boosts revenue but also fortifies these businesses against market volatilities, securing their long-term growth and sustainability.

Regulatory and Legal Perspectives on AI in Business

The incorporation of AI into business practices introduces complex regulatory and legal challenges that necessitate nuanced understanding and proactive governance. Given AI's profound ability to analyze and manipulate data, privacy laws such as the GDPR in Europe and CCPA in the United States have become pivotal in framing the boundaries of AI operations. These regulations mandate stringent data handling procedures and transparency in AI applications to protect individual rights and prevent misuse.

Furthermore, liability in AI-driven decisions poses significant legal intricacies. Businesses must navigate the accountability of outcomes derived from AI systems, distinguishing between developer, user, and AI decision levels. This segmentation is crucial for addressing potential damages or legal actions arising from AI operations. As AI continues to evolve, ongoing legislative adjustments are expected, aiming to balance innovation with societal and individual protections.

Lastly, the emergence of international AI standards is anticipated as businesses expand across borders, requiring harmonization of legal frameworks to ensure smooth operation and compliance. This global perspective not only challenges current regulatory environments but also encourages international cooperation in creating conducive ecosystems for AI-enabled wealth generation.

Predictive Analysis: How AI Foresees Market Trends

Predictive analysis through AI is revolutionizing how businesses foresee and adapt to market trends. By harnessing vast datasets, AI algorithms perform complex pattern recognition, identifying trends that are often imperceptible to human analysts. This capability allows companies to anticipate market movements, adjust strategies in real-time, and capitalize on opportunities before they become apparent to competitors.

The integration of predictive analytics in AI systems draws on historical and real-time data, enabling the automation of decision-making processes. Such systems can, for instance, predict consumer behavior shifts, optimize product pricing dynamically, or even foresee supply chain disruptions. This anticipatory action translates into a substantial competitive advantage, reducing risks and enhancing profitability.

Moreover, the application of predictive analytics extends beyond just economic forecasts. It includes human resources and customer service enhancements, where AI predicts employee attrition or customer needs, respectively. This holistic approach not only drives business success but also improves operational efficiencies across various sectors. AI's predictive prowess is truly setting new benchmarks in proactive business management.

SUMMARY

The chapter 'Overview of AI in Wealth Creation' highlights the profound impact of Artificial Intelligence (AI) across various aspects of wealth generation and economic development. AI's role is pivotal in redefining traditional business practices and facilitating new avenues for income generation. Key areas discussed include AI's integration in automating and optimizing operations in finance, healthcare, manufacturing, and other sectors, which significantly boosts efficiency and profitability. The chapter also explores AI's transformative influence in investment strategies and financial services through tools like robo-advisors that democratize wealth management, making financial planning accessible to a broader audience. Furthermore, AI's predictive analytics capabilities enhance decision-making processes, empowering businesses to stay competitive by identifying market trends and consumer needs swiftly. The discourse extends to AI's potential in creating and transforming jobs, where it not only automates routine tasks but also creates higher-value work in AI development, oversight, and ethical management. The inclusion of AI in entrepreneurship is also notable, with AI-driven platforms enabling startups to scale operations and reach markets efficiently, thus fostering innovation across various sectors. Challenges such as the ethical implications of AI, socioeconomic impacts, the digital divide, and barriers to AI adoption like high initial costs and skill gaps are also addressed. The need for regulatory and educational frameworks that adapt to support ethical AI integration and nurture AI skills from the grassroots level to professional realms is emphasized to ensure equitable benefits of AI in wealth creation. As AI technology progresses, its role in enhancing business practices, reducing operational costs, and opening new markets continues to grow, suggesting a future where AI is integral to economic strategies and wealth distribution.

REFERENCES

[1] Artificial Intelligence in Business: From Research and Innovation to Market Deployment. https://link.springer.com/article/10.1007/s12599-017-0485-6

[2] AI and Financial Services: A Study on Long-term Value Creation. https://www.sciencedirect.com/science/article/pii/S2214635019302701

[3] The Impact of Artificial Intelligence in Business Ecosystems: A Report. https://www.pwc.com/gx/en/issues/data-and-analytics/publications/artificial-intelligence-study.html

[4] AI and Jobs: The Role of Artificial Intelligence on Employment. https://papers.ssrn.com/sol3/papers.cfm?abstract_id=2930131

[5] Ethical AI for Social Empowerment and Economic Development. https://onlinelibrary.wiley.com/doi/epdf/10.1002/hbe2.242

[6] Regulatory Responses to AI: Safety, Security, and Privacy Implications. https://ieeexplore.ieee.org/document/7011242

CASE STUDY: REVOLUTIONIZING RETIREMENT SAVINGS: THE AI FINANCIAL ADVISOR PLATFORM

In the rapidly evolving financial sector, Artificial Intelligence (AI) has enabled the creation of an innovative financial advisory service that targets middle-income individuals aiming to optimize their retirement savings. 'SmartRetire', a fictional AI-driven financial platform, has been developed to democratize access to personalized financial planning. This platform uses machine learning algorithms to analyze users' financial data, spending habits, and long-term goals to offer customized savings plans and investment advice.

SmartRetire's impact on wealth creation is profound. By providing tailored financial advice, previously accessible only to the wealthy through high-cost financial advisors, SmartRetire enables its users to make informed decisions that exponentially improve their financial health over time. The AI system continually learns from each interaction, improving its predictions and recommendations, which helps users adapt their financial strategies to changing economic conditions and personal circumstances.

This personalized approach in financial planning significantly reduces the risk and enhances the potential for higher retirement savings. The platform also educates its users about complex financial concepts in simple terms, increasing financial literacy and confidence among its clientele. By leveraging AI, SmartRetire addresses the gap in the market for middle-income earners, fostering a more inclusive environment in financial planning and wealth management.

Moreover, SmartRetire has catalyzed a shift in the financial services industry, pushing other financial institutions to adopt AI to remain competitive. This widespread adoption of AI across the financial sector not only streamlines operations but also leads to an overall enhancement of the economic well-being of a broader section of the population.

Case Study: Transforming Global Supply Chains with AI Integration

As global markets grow more complex and interconnected, businesses struggle with unprecedented challenges in their supply chains. A detailed case study of 'LogiTech AI', a fictional multinational corporation, elucidates how Artificial Intelligence (AI) technologies are revolutionizing supply chain management (SCM). LogiTech AI, operating in the electronics sector, faced challenges such as demand forecast inaccuracies, inventory mismanagement, and logistic inefficiencies. To address these issues, they adopted a suite of AI-driven tools that fundamentally transformed their SCM from a reactive to a proactive operation.

The core of LogiTech AI's transformation involved implementing machine learning algorithms for predictive analytics, which significantly improved demand forecasting accuracy by analyzing historical sales data and market trends. Additionally, natural language processing (NLP) was employed to enhance communication between disparate segments of the supply chain, from suppliers to end-consumers, ensuring more synchronized operations. Artificial neural networks were used to optimize routing and scheduling for logistics, cutting down shipment times and costs.

The outcomes of incorporating AI technologies were transformative. The accuracy in demand forecasting led to a substantial reduction in overstock and understock scenarios, minimizing waste and maximizing efficiency. Predictive analytics enabled smarter inventory management, allowing for dynamic adjustments in response to real-time market shifts and demand spikes, crucial during events like sales promotions or unexpected disruptions.

Furthermore, improved logistics coordination reduced bottlenecks and delays—a critical factor in maintaining competitiveness in the fast-paced electronics market. LogiTech AI's experience shows how AI can be effectively integrated into existing systems to not only enhance productivity and reduce operational costs but also to significantly bolster overall corporate profitability and supply chain resilience. This case study provides an essential blueprint for companies aiming to leverage AI for comprehensive supply chain transformation in various industries.

Case Study: AI's Pioneering Role in Precision Agriculture and Sustainable Wealth Creation

In the evolving narrative of Artificial Intelligence (AI) reshaping various sectors, agriculture - often seen as a traditional field - has witnessed a transformative shift towards sustainability and efficiency, directly influencing global wealth creation. A fictional company, 'AgriGrowth AI', embodies this transformation by harnessing AI technologies to pioneer precision farming practices.

AgriGrowth AI, operating in diverse geographical locations from North America to Southeast Asia, utilizes AI-driven systems to optimize resource management and crop yield. Their integrated AI platform analyzes satellite imagery and sensor data from farm equipment to determine soil health, crop stress, and moisture levels in real-time. This data-centric approach enables tailor-made fertilization and irrigation strategies that significantly reduce resource wastage and enhance crop productivity.

The strategic deployment of machine learning algorithms allows AgriGrowth AI to predict pest outbreaks and plant diseases. This prediction, coupled with AI-powered drone technology for targeted pesticide application, not only minimizes environmental impact but also cuts down on crop losses, ensuring a stable food supply and heightened farm profitability. The transition from a traditional to a smart farming model facilitated by AI has not only elevated AgriGrowth AI's market position but has also set new standards in agricultural efficiency.

Moreover, the implications of AI in agriculture extend beyond immediate farm gains. By producing higher yields with lower inputs, AgriGrowth AI contributes to the broader goals of sustainable development and global food security. Their approach minimizes agro-chemical runoff, protecting water resources and biodiversity, which are crucial for long-term ecological balance.

On a socio-economic level, AgriGrowth AI's model promotes rural employment by necessitating skilled labor for technology management and data analysis, significantly impacting the local economies. The case of AgriGrowth AI not only outlines the practical applications of AI in enhancing agricultural outputs but also highlights its role in driving sustainable wealth creation by transforming traditional industry practices.

Case Study: AI-Enhanced Risk Management in Emerging Markets

Emerging markets present unique opportunities and challenges for investors looking to maximize returns while managing risks. 'GlobalInvest AI', a hypothetical multi-national investment firm, illustrates the transformative impact of AI on investment strategies in volatile economic climates typical of emerging markets.

GlobalInvest AI has integrated advanced AI technologies to refine its risk assessment protocols, thereby optimizing investment portfolios. By deploying machine learning algorithms, the firm analyzes vast amounts of historical and real-time economic data from various emerging markets to identify patterns, trends, and potential risk factors that are not readily apparent. This data-driven approach allows the firm to predict market fluctuations more precisely and adjust their asset allocations proactively.

Initially struggling with high volatility and political risks inherent in emerging markets, GlobalInvest AI utilized AI-powered sentiment analysis tools to gauge the political atmosphere and predict its impact on financial markets. These tools analyze local news sources, social media platforms, and financial reports to form a comprehensive view of the socio-political landscape, which is crucial for making informed investment decisions.

Furthermore, the firm employs natural language processing (NLP) to enhance its due diligence by extracting and analyzing unstructured data from legal and regulatory texts. This ability to quickly interpret complex information enables quicker and more accurate assessment of regulatory changes that could affect investments. Risk management has thus transformed from a reactive to a predictive strategy, enabling GlobalInvest AI to mitigate potential losses preemptively.

The implementation of AI technologies has not only reduced operational costs by automating routine analytical tasks but has also played a crucial role in asset growth by identifying high-potential investment opportunities early. GlobalInvest AI's case exemplifies how AI can provide a competitive edge by enabling robust, proactive risk management strategies in the unpredictable environments of emerging markets.

Case Study: AI Transforming Customer Service: The Tale of ServiceBot Inc.

ServiceBot Inc., a fictitious AI-driven company, strategically emerged in the saturated customer service industry to revolutionize how businesses interact with their customers. Utilizing a blend of Machine Learning (ML), Natural Language Processing (NLP), and Automated Response Systems, ServiceBot has developed an innovative platform that upgrades traditional call centers into AI-powered service hubs, enhancing both efficiency and customer satisfaction.

ServiceBot's entry into the market was timed impeccably as businesses across various sectors grappled with increasing customer expectations and the need for cost-effective service solutions. The technological backbone of ServiceBot is its advanced NLP algorithms capable of understanding and processing human language, enabling the system to handle initial customer inquiries without human intervention. These capabilities allow companies to service a broader customer base without proportional increases in support staff, translating to significant savings on labor costs.

Furthermore, the ML algorithms employed by ServiceBot adapt and learn from every interaction, thus continuously improving response accuracy and reducing the time taken to resolve customer issues. The system personalizes interactions using historical data to predict customer preferences and behavior, fostering a tailored service experience that drives customer loyalty and satisfaction.

One of ServiceBot's first clients, a leading telecommunications company, experienced a 50% reduction in call wait times and a 30% decrease in customer complaints within the first six months of implementation. This case study illustrates the dual benefits of AI in customer service: enhanced efficiency and improved consumer engagement. By resolving issues quickly and more accurately, businesses maintain a competitive edge in industries where superior customer service is pivotal.

As ServiceBot continues to expand its capabilities, the AI system integrates emotional recognition to further refine consumer interactions, ensuring all client concerns are addressed not just with efficiency but with empathy. This evolution in AI demonstrates potential shifts not only in operational metrics but also in building meaningful customer relationships, setting new benchmarks for service excellence in the digital age.

Case Study: AI-Driven Wealth Redistribution: The Rise of EquiFinancial

The advent of AI technologies presents not only opportunities for wealth creation but also for its equitable distribution. A prime example of this innovative use of AI can be seen in the operations of EquiFinancial, a hypothetical fintech startup designed to bridge the financial inequality gap. Using a blend of machine learning (ML), natural language processing (NLP), and blockchain, EquiFinancial aims to provide financially underserved populations with access to affordable and tailored financial services.

EquiFinancial began by analyzing vast amounts of demographic and financial data to identify underserved communities often overlooked by traditional banks. Their platform integrates sophisticated AI algorithms capable of predictive analytics to assess creditworthiness in non-traditional ways, considering factors such as utility payments and mobile money transactions, rather than just credit scores. This approach allowed EquiFinancial to offer microloans and personalized financial advice to individuals with little to no formal financial history.

EquiFinancial's application of NLP facilitated interactions in multiple regional languages, enhancing customer engagement and satisfaction significantly. Users were able to inquire about services and manage transactions seamlessly with the help of AI-driven chatbots. This multilingual support, backed by AI, meant that fewer barriers existed between the services and those who needed them most, thus democratizing access to crucial financial resources.

The blockchain technology adopted by EquiFinancial ensured transparency and security, fostering trust among its users. Each transaction was recorded immutably, providing users with clear trails of their financial activities and protecting their information from fraud and misuse.

The case of EquiFinancial not only underlines the profound impact AI can have on creating a more inclusive financial ecosystem but also highlights how technology can be harnessed to foster socioeconomic advancements. By prioritizing equal access and fairness, EquiFinancial illustrates the potential for AI in nurturing environments where economic opportunities can flourish irrespective of historical disparities.

Case Study: AI-Powered Market Analytics in Real Estate Investment

In the current chapter on AI in wealth creation, we explore a unique case involving 'EstateAI', a fictitious company that utilizes advanced AI technologies to transform the real estate investment landscape. Starting as a startup with a vision to democratize and enhance investment decisions, EstateAI capitalized on the burgeoning field of AI to offer unprecedented insights into real estate markets.

EstateAI employs machine learning (ML) algorithms to analyze a myriad of data points encompassing historic pricing data, demographic shifts, development trends, and economic indicators to provide predictive insights on real estate valuations and investment opportunities. This approach enables individual investors and real estate entities to make data-driven, strategically timed investment decisions, maximizing potential returns while mitigating risks associated with market volatility.

The integration of Natural Language Processing (NLP) technology further empowers EstateAI by automating the analysis of unstructured data such as news articles, online real estate listings, and social media trends. This holistic data integration provides a comprehensive view of the market dynamics, identifying undervalued properties or signaling impending price adjustments before they become evident through traditional analysis methods.

EstateAI's platform dramatically shifts how investors engage with the real estate market. The traditional barriers of entry for lucrative real estate investments, often gated by insider knowledge and timely data, are lowered. With AI, even novices can access sophisticated market analysis previously reserved for industry professionals or large firms.

The case of EstateAI encapsulates the transformative potential of AI in reshaping investment landscapes. Not only do investors benefit from improved decision-making capabilities, but the real estate market on a larger scale becomes more efficient and transparent, aiding in the overall stability and growth of the economic sector. The success of EstateAI prompts broader adaptability and embracing of AI in other sectors wishing to harness enhanced analytical capabilities and democratize access to wealth-generating opportunities.

Case Study: AI-Powered Dynamic Pricing in E-commerce

The transformative influence of AI on the commercial sector is vividly illustrated by the dynamic pricing model adopted by 'PriceTech', a fictional e-commerce giant. PriceTech's journey towards incorporating AI into its pricing strategy showcases how machine learning (ML) and data analytics radically enhance market responsiveness and financial success. Initially grappling with the challenges of a highly competitive online retail market, PriceTech leveraged AI to implement a dynamic pricing strategy that adjusts prices in real-time based on a variety of signals including demand fluctuation, competitor pricing, customer behavior, and market conditions.

PriceTech's AI system continuously collects and analyzes vast amounts of data from various sources, such as past transactions, competitor prices, and real-time user engagement on the platform. Advanced machine learning algorithms then process this data to identify patterns and predict future buying trends, enabling the system to adjust prices dynamically to maximize sales and profit margins. This AI-driven approach not only ensures competitive pricing but also enhances customer satisfaction by offering deals that are tailored to the purchasing habits and preferences of individual customers.

The result of this AI implementation was a substantial increase in PriceTech's revenue, with improved sales figures particularly during peak shopping periods like holidays and sales events. Furthermore, the dynamic pricing model fostered an environment of trust and reliability, as customers began to recognize PriceTech's commitment to providing value through fair pricing strategies. The system's ability to adapt quickly to market changes also meant that PriceTech could stay ahead of its competitors, responding agilely to any shifts in consumer demand or competitive strategies.

From a broader perspective, PriceTech's case reflects a significant shift in how businesses are utilizing AI to make complex decisions with greater accuracy and efficiency. This case not only highlights the financial benefits of AI in e-commerce but also stresses the importance of AI in strategic decision-making processes that directly affect consumer engagements and market growth.

REVIEW QUESTIONS

1. A financial consultant, James, is utilizing AI to enhance decision-making and streamline operations in his firm. He relies on AI for market analysis and predictive modeling. Given this scenario, what is the PRIMARY role of AI in James' firm?

A) Replacing the need for human financial advisors

B) Performing administrative duties exclusively

C) Assisting in decision-making and efficiency

D) Solely managing customer relations

Answer: C

Explanation: AI's primary role in James' scenario is assisting in decision-making and increasing operational efficiency. This is achieved through capabilities such as market analysis and predictive modeling, which allow for more informed decisions and streamlined processes. Unlike choices A, B, and D, AI is used as a tool to augment, rather than replace, human capabilities in specific tasks, thus enhancing the overall productivity and effectiveness of the firm.

2. Ellen runs a startup that uses AI-powered tools to personalize financial advice. How does AI contribute to wealth creation in Ellen's service?

A) By manually processing client data

B) By increasing operational costs

C) By personalizing financial services to client needs

D) By completely automating customer interactions

Answer: C

Explanation: In Ellen's startup, AI contributes to wealth creation by personalizing financial services according to the individual needs of clients. This personalization helps in tailoring advice and strategies that are likely to yield better financial outcomes for clients, thus enhancing wealth creation. Unlike the other choices, this use of AI focuses on leveraging technology to deliver customized, data-driven services that address specific client requirements and financial goals.

REVIEW QUESTIONS

3. An investment firm integrates AI technologies for risk assessment and algorithmic trading. What impact does AI have on the firm's financial strategies?

A) Reduction in the ability to predict market changes

B) Decreased efficiency and increased financial risk

C) Enhanced precision in trading and improved risk management

D) Sole reliance on AI for all financial decisions

Answer: C

Explanation: AI's impact on the investment firm's financial strategies includes enhanced precision in trading and improved risk management. By using AI for algorithmic trading, the firm can execute trades more efficiently and effectively, capitalizing on market opportunities. Furthermore, AI's risk assessment capabilities enable better foresight and preparation for potential market fluctuations, thereby managing financial risk more robustly. Choice C accurately reflects how AI facilitates these advanced strategies, unlike the other options that suggest negative or overreliant impacts of AI.

4. Marcus utilizes AI in his retail business to analyze consumer buying behavior and personalize shopping experiences. What advantage does AI offer in this context?

A) Generalized product recommendations across all customers

B) Reduced customer interaction and engagement

C) Tailored marketing and enhanced customer satisfaction

D) Increased reliance on physical stores

Answer: C

Explanation: In Marcus' retail business, the advantage of using AI lies in its ability to tailor marketing efforts and enhance customer satisfaction through personalized shopping experiences. AI analyzes consumer buying behaviors to generate insights that enable targeted marketing and product recommendations, leading to more satisfied customers and potentially increased sales. Choice C emphasizes these personalized interactions, which are a key benefit of using AI in retail, unlike the other options which do not align with the capabilities or advantages of AI in enhancing retail experiences.

CHATGPT: REVOLUTIONIZING CONTENT CREATION AND MONETIZATION

Introduction to ChatGPT and Its Impact on Content Industry

ChatGPT, developed by OpenAI, signifies a transformative advancement in AI technology, particularly within the realm of content creation. At its core, ChatGPT is a sophisticated language model designed to understand and generate human-like text, enabling it to perform a broad spectrum of content-related tasks with remarkable acuity and versatility.

The introduction of ChatGPT into the content industry has led to significant shifts in content production and management strategies. Businesses and independent creators are leveraging its capabilities to automate routine writing tasks, enhance content quality, and generate innovative content formats. This automation not only accelerates content creation processes but also drastically reduces operational times.

Moreover, ChatGPT's impact extends beyond mere efficiency. It is reshaping how content is personalized and SEO-optimized, making content more engaging and visible. Its ability to learn and adapt from user interactions and feedback ensures continuous improvement in content relevance and engagement, thereby redefining content strategy for businesses worldwide.

Understanding ChatGPT: Capabilities and Technology

ChatGPT, powered by state-of-the-art models from OpenAI, utilizes a variant of the Transformer architecture tailored for natural language understanding and generation. Its capabilities are grounded in deep learning algorithms that train on diverse datasets, enabling it to generate coherent and contextually relevant responses across numerous topics. This training includes vast swaths of text from books, articles, and websites, making it adept at mimicking human-like text.

The technology behind ChatGPT also incorporates advanced techniques such as reinforcement learning from human feedback (RLHF), where human trainers refine its responses to align more closely with user intentions. Such continuous learning and adaptation processes enhance its proficiency over time, ensuring its output remains accurate, relevant, and context-sensitive.

Furthermore, ChatGPT's integration capabilities make it a valuable tool for a wide array of applications, from simple task automation to complex problem-solving scenarios. It supports various programming interfaces, which facilitate seamless integration with existing digital platforms and systems, broadening its utilization in diverse professional environments.

Setting Up ChatGPT for Content Creation

Setting up ChatGPT for content creation involves a strategic approach to harness its capabilities effectively. Initially, define the specific content needs and goals that align with your overall content strategy. Whether it's generating blog posts, emails, or digital marketing materials, having a clear purpose helps tailor the AI's output to your desired standards.

Next, integrate ChatGPT with your current content management systems (CMS). Most CMS platforms support API integrations, which allow for seamless content creation and management. This integration enables the automatic generation and scheduling of content, ensuring a consistent flow of high-quality material. Configure the settings to maintain a brand-consistent tone and style, essential for keeping content uniform across all channels.

Finally, regular training sessions are crucial. By continually feeding ChatGPT new and updated information, particularly from your niche, it stays relevant and up-to-date. This ongoing learning process allows ChatGPT to produce more accurate and tailored content, enhancing both engagement and credibility in your designated field.

Strategies for Monetizing Content Created with ChatGPT

Monetizing content created with ChatGPT opens a myriad of lucrative avenues. One effective strategy is to use the AI-generated content to fuel blog sites and digital magazines. These platforms can integrate native advertising, affiliate marketing, and sponsored posts, leveraging ChatGPT's ability to produce diverse and appealing content that attracts a wide audience. This approach not only boosts ad revenue but also enhances user engagement through customized and contextually relevant articles.

Another key strategy involves leveraging ChatGPT-generated content for lead generation. Crafting high-quality downloadable content such as e-books, whitepapers, and case studies can entice readers to exchange their contact information. This content, positioned strategically within a sales funnel, can significantly heighten conversion rates, nurturing potential clients down the sales pipeline.

Subscription models present a third monetization path. By creating exclusive content areas or regularly updated premium content feeds powered by ChatGPT, businesses can offer monthly subscription services. This approach ensures a consistent revenue stream while continuously providing fresh, relevant content tailored to subscriber interests.

Enhancing Blog Content with ChatGPT

Leveraging ChatGPT to enhance blog content supercharges engagement and revitalizes traditional blogging approaches. By integrating AI-driven insights and automated content generation, bloggers can consistently produce high-quality, well-researched, and contextually relevant articles. This not only boosts organic search visibility but also elevates reader engagement by providing content that resonates deeply with the audience's interests and needs.

Moreover, utilizing ChatGPT for blog enhancement allows for the exploration of new topics and ideas rapidly. AI can suggest fresh angles and uncover related subjects that might not have been immediately obvious, thereby expanding the blog's reach and influence. It also provides a basis for creating a variety of content formats, from detailed guides and how-tos to engaging listicles and thought leadership pieces, each tailored to the desired audience demographic.

Implementing ChatGPT effectively involves tuning the AI to maintain the blog's unique voice and editorial standards, ensuring content consistency. Strategic use of this technology can also help in optimizing content for SEO, making posts more discoverable and shareable online.

The process not only streamlines content creation but also enhances the overall quality and appeal of the blog's output, setting a new benchmark in digital content excellence.

Utilizing ChatGPT for Email Marketing Campaigns

Harnessing ChatGPT for email marketing campaigns offers revolutionary potential in crafting personalized and engaging messages that resonate with recipients. By integrating ChatGPT, marketers can automate the creation of tailored email content that reflects individual user preferences and behaviors, significantly enhancing the impact of each campaign.

ChatGPT excels in generating dynamic content for various segments of an email list. It can analyze past interactions to design offers and messages that are most likely to elicit positive responses. Additionally, this AI can test different subject lines and email bodies, optimizing for high open and click-through rates, which are crucial metrics in email marketing effectiveness.

Furthermore, ChatGPT's ability to create consistent and error-free text in massive volumes allows for frequent and reliable communication with subscribers. Implementing AI in this way not only saves time but also maintains a high level of quality assurance in campaign execution, ensuring that each message is both impactful and aligned with the brand's voice.

Generating E-books and Reports with ChatGPT

Expanding the scope of digital publication, generating e-books and reports with ChatGPT offers an innovative edge. By integrating AI, authors and content creators can produce comprehensive, well-structured texts with speed and precision. Initially, the AI canvasses a vast database of information to craft content that matches the desired depth and complexity, essential for professional reports and informative e-books.

Additionally, ChatGPT's application in this field streamlines the revision and updating processes. Once a base document is created, the AI can easily integrate new data and findings, maintaining the relevance of digital publications over time. This dynamic capability is particularly valuable in fields like technology or market research, where data continuously evolves.

Lastly, leveraging ChatGPT allows for customization to target specific audiences through stylistic and tonal adjustments, making content both engaging and suitable for its intended readership. Moreover, automating the content generation process significantly reduces the time and resources typically required, enhancing productivity and potentially broadening the scope of projects one can undertake.

Developing a Content Strategy Using ChatGPT

Developing a robust content strategy with ChatGPT at its core is pivotal for leveraging AI in enhancing digital communication efforts. First, understanding your brand's objectives and audience preferences allows you to craft a strategy that utilizes ChatGPT to generate content that resonates and drives engagement. This might include identifying key themes and topics that your audience cares about, then instructing ChatGPT to help create content around these areas.

Next, it is crucial to map out a content calendar that integrates ChatGPT's capabilities. By planning regular content updates, ranging from blog posts to newsletters, ChatGPT can help maintain a steady stream of fresh and relevant content. This consistency is key in building a loyal audience base.

Additionally, analyzing the performance of ChatGPT-generated content can pinpoint what resonates with your audience. Employing tools to track engagement and conversion metrics allows you to refine and optimize your strategy continuously. This adaptive approach ensures your content remains effective and appealing, keeping your strategy dynamic in a competitive landscape.

ChatGPT in Social Media: Automation and Engagement

Integrating ChatGPT within social media strategies heralds a new era of engagement and content automation. Its implementation allows brands to maintain active, engaging online presences, responding to user inquiries instantaneously. This real-time interaction is invaluable, bolstering customer satisfaction and loyalty through prompt replies and personalized communication.

Moreover, ChatGPT's capabilities extend to content creation, generating diverse posts that resonate with varied audience segments. This not only increases the reach and engagement of social media campaigns but also sustains a steady stream of high-quality content. Such efficiency in maintaining content consistency helps brands stay relevant in competitive digital landscapes, fostering an engaged community around their offerings.

Additionally, ChatGPT can analyze user interactions and engagement patterns to refine content strategies dynamically. Leveraging this data-driven approach enhances audience targeting, making social media campaigns more effective by connecting on a deeper level with followers. The potential for viral content creation further amplifies brand visibility, solidifying ChatGPT's role as a cornerstone of modern social media marketing.

Optimizing SEO with ChatGPT-Generated Articles

Harnessing the power of ChatGPT to optimize SEO in content creation offers strategic advantages for digital marketers and content creators. By leveraging AI to produce targeted, keyword-rich articles, businesses can significantly improve their search engine rankings. ChatGPT's machine learning algorithms understand search engine algorithms, allowing them to tailor content that aligns with SEO best practices.

Furthermore, ChatGPT can generate a variety of content types, from long-form articles to concise blog posts, each optimized for specific keywords and meta descriptions. This variability not only enhances the visibility of web pages in search results but also caters to different user intents, increasing the chances of conversion. Integrating ChatGPT also means continuous updates to content, keeping it fresh and relevant, a key factor Google and other search engines consider when ranking pages.

Finally, the use of ChatGPT in creating SEO-friendly content reduces the workload on human writers. It allows for scaling content production without sacrificing quality, ensuring that each piece remains both engaging and optimized for search engines. This efficient production capability provides a competitive edge in content-driven digital marketing strategies.

Creating Video Scripts and Descriptions with ChatGPT

In the dynamic world of video content creation, ChatGPT emerges as a powerful tool for scripting and crafting engaging descriptions. Its linguistic capabilities enable creators to formulate scripts that are not only informative but also captivating, ensuring that videos can hold the viewer's attention from start to finish.

Utilizing ChatGPT, video creators can efficiently generate scripts for various genres, from educational tutorials to compelling storytelling in marketing campaigns. This AI technology adapts to different tones and styles, making it versatile for any content requirement. Furthermore, its ability to process and incorporate specific keywords enhances the SEO of video content, driving higher visibility and engagement.

The AI's prowess extends to creating succinct and persuasive video descriptions that further the reach of the content through optimized search functionality. Integrating ChatGPT into video production workflows thus offers a blend of creativity and analytical benefits, streamlining the creation process while maximizing the impact of the content produced.

Monetizing ChatGPT Skills: Setting up a Freelance Business

Leveraging ChatGPT's capabilities spawns a lucrative avenue for setting up a freelance business focused on AI-driven content creation. The preliminary step involves mastering ChatGPT to produce diverse content forms, from blogs to technical papers, ensuring a broad service offering. This versatility attracts a wide range of clientele, from small businesses seeking cost-effective solutions to large corporations looking for detailed, scalable content strategies.

Subsequently, creating an online presence through a professional website and social media channels is crucial. These platforms showcase your expertise in utilizing ChatGPT, providing samples, and explaining how AI can elevate various content needs. Networking, both online and in relevant industry gatherings, assists in building valuable connections, potentially translating into client referrals or partnerships.

Finally, pricing models play a pivotal role. Offering packages based on content complexity and volume can cater to various budget constraints, enhancing service appeal. A tailored approach to each client's needs not only fosters long-term relationships but also underscores the bespoke nature of AI-enhanced content services, establishing a competitive niche in the freelancing sphere.

Using ChatGPT for Academic and Research Writing

ChatGPT is quickly becoming an indispensable tool in the realm of academia and research, offering a new level of assistance in the creation of academic papers, literature reviews, and research proposals. This AI, with its ability to comprehend and synthesize large volumes of information, aids scholars in exploring extensive bibliographic databases, extracting pertinent data, and framing initial hypotheses for further investigation.

Furthermore, ChatGPT's proficiency in managing references and citations aligns with academic standards, ensuring that all scholarly work remains credible and well-organized. By automating these often tedious aspects of academic writing, researchers can devote more time to the critical thinking and creative processes that are essential for producing groundbreaking work.

One must approach the use of ChatGPT in academic settings with caution; its outputs require rigorous scrutiny to align with scholarly rigour. Nonetheless, when used effectively, ChatGPT not only streamlines workflow but also enhances the clarity and precision of academic communications, promising a significant transformation in scholarly writing practices.

Legal Considerations in Using AI-Generated Content

Navigating the legal terrain of AI-generated content involves understanding a complex framework of intellectual property rights, copyright laws, and compliance obligations. As AI, like ChatGPT, takes a more prominent role in content creation, the delineation of copyright ownership becomes crucial. Typically, content created by AI may fall into a gray area where existing laws are not fully adapted to address new technological advances.

Creators using AI tools must ensure that their use of AI-generated content adheres to copyright standards, which traditionally protect human authors. This necessitates a careful analysis to determine if, and how, AI-generated outputs can be copyrighted, or if they remain in the public domain. Additionally, the integration of AI in content creation raises questions about the reliability and accuracy of the information produced, necessitating rigorous verification processes to maintain credibility and avoid potential legal pitfalls like defamation.

Moreover, as laws evolve to catch up with technology, businesses leveraging AI for content production must stay informed about legal changes. Implementing robust compliance strategies will mitigate risks and foster a secure environment for innovation and growth in AI-driven content markets.

ChatGPT for Advertising: Creating Ad Copies

In the domain of advertising, crafting efficacious ad copies remains crucial for engaging potential customers and driving conversions. ChatGPT redefines this process by harnessing advanced AI to generate creative, targeted, and persuasive advertising content across multiple platforms. This revolutionary approach allows for the customization of messages tailored to resonate profoundly with varied audience demographics.

Utilizing ChatGPT for writing ad copies not only speeds up the creation process but also integrates a level of linguistic precision and persuasiveness that is hard to achieve manually. Marketers can implement A/B testing with multiple ad variations produced by ChatGPT, optimizing campaigns in real-time based on performance data. This AI-driven strategy ensures that advertising messages are not only attention-grabbing but also highly relevant and effective in stimulating audience interest.

Furthermore, ChatGPT's ability to analyze and adapt to current market trends and consumer behaviors dramatically enhances the relevance of ad copies. This adaptability makes it an indispensable tool in the modern marketer's arsenal, seamlessly blending creativity with data-driven insights to craft campaigns that not only captivate but also convert.

Pricing Models for ChatGPT Content Services

Determining the right pricing models for ChatGPT content services is crucial for maximizing profitability while ensuring client satisfaction. The versatility of ChatGPT allows for a variety of pricing structures based on service type, complexity, and volume. A popular model is per-word pricing, ideal for straightforward tasks such as article and blog writing. This model allows clients to predict costs easily and aligns service charges directly with output volume.

For more complex services, such as technical document creation or marketing strategy development, a project-based fee can be more appropriate. This accounts for the depth of research and level of customization required. Adding tiered pricing within this model helps cater to different client needs and budget levels, enhancing flexibility.

Subscription models are becoming increasingly popular, particularly for ongoing needs like social media content or regular blog updates. These provide a steady revenue stream for creators and simplify budgeting for clients. Each model has its benefits and can be tailored to fit the specific demands of diverse content creation projects, ensuring both client retention and profitability.

Building a Subscription Model with ChatGPT Content

The transformation of digital content into a reliable revenue stream is effectively actualized through subscription models, an increasingly popular strategy among content creators using ChatGPT. This model hinges on offering regular, valuable content to subscribers, fostering a dependable income flow and enhancing customer loyalty.

With ChatGPT, creators can automate the production of high-quality, consistent content, such as exclusive articles, newsletters, or series, that requires subscribers to pay a recurring fee. This not only ensures a stable financial model but also builds a community around niche topics or specialized knowledge areas. By integrating AI, creators can continuously refine content based on subscriber feedback and engagement metrics, tailoring offerings to match audience preferences and improve retention rates.

Moreover, subscription services powered by ChatGPT can leverage data-driven insights to personalize content, making each subscriber experience unique and increasing the perceived value. This personalized approach helps in distinguishing your service in a competitive market, solidifying subscriber relationships, and ultimately driving long-term success.

Developing a Brand Voice with ChatGPT

Developing a distinctive brand voice is crucial in standing out in today's saturated markets. ChatGPT, with its advanced linguistic capabilities, offers a unique solution for brands aiming to establish a consistent and resonant voice across multiple channels. By training ChatGPT with a firm's brand guidelines, values, and audience insights, it can generate content that not only echoes the brand's core messages but also engages consumers on a more personal level.

Moreover, ChatGPT's adaptability allows it to craft messages that are tailored to various platforms, ensuring that the tone remains appropriate whether it's a formal report or a casual tweet. This cohesion across content types fortifies a brand's identity, making its voice unmistakable regardless of the medium.

The integration of ChatGPT into content strategies significantly streamlines the creation process, providing a consistent voice that reinforces brand recognition and trust. In addition, by continuously analyzing audience data, ChatGPT can evolve the brand voice to align with shifting consumer preferences, ensuring relevance and connection in an ever-changing market.

ChatGPT for Technical Writing and Documentation

In the realm of technical writing and documentation, precision and clarity are paramount. ChatGPT emerges as an invaluable tool in this sector, enhancing the creation of detailed, accurate technical documents such as manuals, standard operating procedures, and product specifications.

Utilizing ChatGPT enables technical writers to automate routine documentation tasks, focusing their expertise on more complex content areas. This AI's ability to understand and generate technical language ensures that documents are not only produced faster but also meet the high standards required for technical accuracy. Integrating ChatGPT leads to increased efficiency, reducing the time to market for technical products.

Moreover, ChatGPT can be trained on specific technical vocabulary and style guidelines, ensuring that documentation is consistent with corporate standards. This capability is particularly useful in industries where detail and compliance with technical norms are crucial. The AI's learning algorithms adapt over time, improving the quality of automated outputs and supporting technical writers in maintaining up-to-date, high-quality documentation.

Integrating ChatGPT with Content Management Systems

Integrating ChatGPT with content management systems (CMS) marks a pivotal advancement in streamlining content creation processes. This integration facilitates the automation of content generation, allowing for efficient updates and management of web content. By bringing the power of AI to CMS, businesses can maintain a dynamic online presence with minimal human input, ensuring content remains fresh and engaging.

Furthermore, embedding ChatGPT into CMS platforms enhances the scalability of content strategies. It can automatically adapt to different audiences by customizing content according to visitor data. Businesses can thus deliver a more personalized user experience, critical in today's market where customization is key to customer engagement. This AI-driven approach not only saves time but also reduces the operational costs associated with manual content updates.

Moreover, the implementation of ChatGPT within a CMS allows for continuous learning and improvement. As ChatGPT processes user interactions and feedback, it refines its content generation algorithms. This evolving intelligence ensures that the content remains relevant and impactful, driving greater user engagement and retention. The fusion of AI with traditional CMS platforms lays the groundwork for smarter, more efficient content ecosystems that can propel businesses forward in the digital age.

Case Studies: Success Stories of Businesses Using ChatGPT

The integration of ChatGPT in business has revolutionized traditional content creation models, leading to success stories across various industries. One compelling case is a startup specializing in digital marketing, which implemented ChatGPT to automate the creation of ad copies and promotional content. This move not only enhanced their output quality but also reduced operational costs, driving significant profit margins.

Another notable example involves a multinational corporation that transitioned its customer service operations to a ChatGPT-powered system. The AI's ability to handle inquiries in multiple languages and understand nuanced customer needs increased satisfaction rates while streamlining response times. This strategic implementation was crucial in maintaining high service standards during peak periods.

Furthermore, an online educational platform used ChatGPT to generate personalized learning content, adapting to student feedback and performance metrics. This tailored approach fostered a more engaging learning environment, resulting in improved student outcomes and increased course completion rates. These cases illustrate ChatGPT's transformative impact on businesses striving for innovation and efficiency.

Future Developments in AI and Content Creation

The horizon of AI in content creation promises revolutionary changes, poised to redefine how content is conceived, created, and consumed. As AI technologies like ChatGPT evolve, the integration of more advanced machine learning models and natural language understanding capabilities suggests a future where AI can produce even more nuanced and contextually relevant content. This could encompass generating interactive narratives or dynamically altering content based on real-time audience feedback, elevating user engagement to unprecedented levels.

Beyond mere text generation, upcoming developments may include sophisticated AI that can collaborate with human creators in a hybrid model, offering creative suggestions and refining ideation processes. This symbiosis could enhance creative output, reduce production timelines, and introduce new genres of content not previously imaginable.

Moreover, ethical AI use will become central, ensuring transparency, accountability, and fairness in AI-generated content. As legislation evolves, so too will the frameworks governing AI's creativity, ensuring that while machines help in content creation, they do so enhancing rather than overshadowing human creativity. This balanced approach promises a fertile landscape for future generations of content creators.

ChatGPT for Multilingual Content Creation

Harnessing ChatGPT for multilingual content creation opens a vast horizon for global business expansion and audience engagement. By designing AI models that understand and articulate in multiple languages, organizations can transcend geographical and linguistic barriers, offering their content seamlessly to a diverse global audience. This not only multiplies the reach but also deepens the connection with users by interacting in their native language.

Significantly, ChatGPT's capabilities extend beyond mere translation. It can grasp cultural nuances and adapt content accordingly, which is crucial for maintaining the authenticity and relevance of communication across different regions. This tailored approach ensures that the message resonates well with local customs and sentiments, thereby enhancing consumer trust and brand loyalty.

Moreover, businesses utilizing ChatGPT for creating multilingual content can streamline their content development processes, reducing the need for multiple human translators and content creators. This efficiency not only cuts down costs but also speeds up the time-to-market for campaigns across various markets. As a result, companies can achieve a competitive edge by quickly adapting to market changes and consumer trends worldwide.

Training ChatGPT for Niche Topics

Training ChatGPT on niche topics propels it beyond general use, enabling customized, industry-specific applications. Unlike broader topics, niche subjects often have specialized vocabularies and knowledge bases that are not widely understood. Training ChatGPT to master these areas requires tailored datasets rich in specificity. Gathering comprehensive, expert-level texts is critical, often involving collaboration with professionals in the field to ensure accuracy and depth.

Once a dataset is curated, fine-tuning ChatGPT involves iterative training processes where the model learns to generate and adapt its responses according to the nuances of the niche. This specificity allows businesses to offer expert-level engagement in areas such as legal consultation, medical advice, or technology insights, enhancing customer trust and service quality.

Moreover, ongoing learning is crucial. As industries evolve, so must the AI, requiring updates with current information and trends. Regular retraining sessions help maintain the relevance and reliability of ChatGPT's outputs, ensuring it continues to serve as a valuable tool within precise fields.

Challenges and Limitations of Using ChatGPT in Content Creation

Despite its transformative powers, ChatGPT faces challenges and limitations in content creation that merit attention. Primarily, the AI's output can sometimes lack the depth and nuance that experienced human writers bring, particularly in subjects requiring substantial domain expertise or emotive expression. Its algorithmic nature may lead to content that, while technically correct, fails to resonate on a human level, missing subtleties that only a human touch can provide.

Furthermore, reliance on existing data to generate content can make ChatGPT prone to replicating biases present in the source material. This issue is particularly concerning in fields like journalism or history, where impartiality and accuracy are paramount. Addressing these biases requires meticulous training and constant updating of AI models to reflect a more balanced perspective.

Lastly, the legal landscape surrounding AI content generation is still evolving. Intellectual property concerns arise when AI-generated content closely resembles human-created works, potentially leading to disputes over originality and ownership. Navigating this terrain demands careful consideration of copyright laws and ethical guidelines to ensure compliance and fair use.

Best Practices for Quality Assurance in AI-Generated Content

Ensuring the reliability and quality of content generated by AI, particularly from tools like ChatGPT, is crucial for maintaining professional standards and consumer trust. One foundational practice is the incorporation of rigorous editing protocols. A critical review by human editors can catch nuances and errors that AI might overlook, ensuring that the content not only meets factual accuracy but also resonates on a human level.

Another significant best practice is implementing feedback loops. This involves using user and client feedback to refine and adjust the AI's output. Regularly updating the AI's training data to include new information, corrections, and varied content formats can prevent stagnation and bias, keeping the generated content relevant and diverse.

Lastly, adherence to ethical guidelines and transparency about the AI's involvement in content creation is essential. Disclosure of AI use in content not only aligns with ethical marketing practices but also fosters trust and sets realistic expectations for the audience. Together, these strategies form the backbone of quality assurance in AI-driven content creation.

SUMMARY

The integration of ChatGPT into various facets of content creation and monetization represents a significant paradigm shift within the industry. Developed by OpenAI, ChatGPT employs a sophisticated version of the Transformer architecture, making it adept at generating human-like text across various content domains. This chapter delves into how ChatGPT is utilized in content creation, from automating routine writing tasks and enhancing content quality to generating innovative content formats. It has reshaped strategies in blog content, email marketing, video script writing, and technical documentation, demonstrating versatility and efficiency.

Businesses and content creators leverage ChatGPT not only for crafting engaging and SEO-optimized material but also for personalizing content, thus improving both visibility and engagement. The technology's integration with content management systems allows for seamless content generation and scheduling, streamlining workflow and maintaining content consistency. Additionally, monetization strategies using ChatGPT include using AI-generated content to fuel blogs and digital magazines, crafting tailored e-books and reports, and setting up subscription models, each providing new revenue streams and enhancing user involvement.

Moreover, the development of a content strategy utilizing ChatGPT involves defining clear goals, integrating with existing systems, and continually adapting to feedback to keep content relevant. The technology is also applied in marketing, where it aids in creating diverse, engaging advertisements and promotional materials optimized for various platforms.

Despite its advanced capabilities, using ChatGPT comes with challenges such as ensuring the depth and nuance of content and addressing potential biases in AI-generated material. Legal aspects also complicate the use of AI in content creation due to intellectual property concerns. Future trends suggest a move towards more nuanced AI abilities in content creation, emphasizing ethical AI use and transparent practices to maintain credibility and trust.

REFERENCES

[1] OpenAI: Introducing ChatGPT. https://openai.com/blog/chatGPT

[2] Radford, Alec et al. 'Language Models are Unsupervised Multitask Learners.'. https://cdn.openai.com/better-language-models/language_models_are_unsupervised_multitask_learners.pdf

[3] Vaswani, Ashish et al., 'Attention Is All You Need'. https://arxiv.org/abs/1706.03762

[4] McKinney, Will. 'Content Strategy: Integration of AI Tools'. https://ai-contentstrat.org/integration-of-ai-tools

[5] Kaplan, Jared Et al. 'Scaling Laws for Neural Language Models'. https://arxiv.org/abs/2001.08361

CASE STUDY: OPTIMIZING CONTENT CREATION WITH CHATGPT FOR A LEADING RETAIL BRAND

A prominent retail company, renowned for its extensive range of products and strong global presence, faced challenges in maintaining engaging and consistent content across its digital platforms. The company's marketing team was overwhelmed with the demands of producing high-quality content tailored to various international markets, each with its unique cultural nuances and consumer preferences. To tackle these challenges, the company decided to integrate ChatGPT into their content creation strategy, aiming to streamline processes and enhance content personalization.

The first step involved setting up ChatGPT with the company's content management system (CMS), streamlining the integration process to ensure seamless content generation. By configuring ChatGPT to align with the brand's tone and adopting a strategic approach to content needs, the AI began generating diverse types of content, from product descriptions to engaging blog posts and email marketing campaigns tailored to different market segments.

For instance, the adaptation of product descriptions for the Asian market involved ChatGPT learning from regional sales data and customer feedback to generate content that resonates more effectively with local consumers. In European markets, the focus was on creating compelling storytelling around products, aligning with regional advertising standards and consumer behavior patterns.

The retail brand also utilized ChatGPT to automate routine customer interactions on social media, enhancing customer engagement by providing instantaneous and personalized responses. Further, the brand leveraged ChatGPT's capabilities to create dynamic email marketing campaigns that adapt content based on user behavior and preferences, significantly increasing open and click-through rates.

Over six months, the company observed a marked improvement in the efficiency of content production and a notable increase in engagement across digital channels. Additionally, the integration of ChatGPT enabled the marketing team to focus on creative and strategic tasks, significantly reducing the operational overhead associated with manual content creation.

Case Study: Revolutionizing Academic Publishing with ChatGPT

A prominent university's research department faced significant delays and obstacles in producing high-quality, well-researched academic papers due to the cumbersome nature of gathering data, synthesizing information, and ensuring citations were accurate and comprehensive. The department sought to leverage AI, particularly ChatGPT, to streamline these processes and enhance the output and quality of their academic articles.

Initially, the team trained ChatGPT on specific academic databases and texts, teaching it the nuances of academic style and the rigorous requirements of scholarly writing. This training included subject-specific jargon, citation styles, and argumentative structures typical in academic writing. The goal was for ChatGPT not only to assist in data gathering and synthesis but also to help draft sections of papers where factual reporting was required, thus speeding up the drafting process.

For instance, one of the projects involved a complex analysis of environmental policies across different countries. ChatGPT was used to initially draft the literature review and methodological framework by accessing and analyzing numerous sources, effectively summarizing current knowledge and identifying gaps. Researchers then refined and expanded on this foundation, adding critical analysis and insights.

The impact of integrating ChatGPT into their workflow was profound. The time taken from initial research to submission of papers decreased significantly, and the researchers were able to engage in more projects simultaneously. Furthermore, the accuracy of data and citation integrity improved, reducing errors that often come from manual data entry and handling. The department noted an increase in the acceptance rate of their papers in peer-reviewed journals, attributing this success to the higher quality and thoroughness of their submissions.

The case of this university department showcases the transformative potential of AI like ChatGPT in academic settings. It highlights how AI can augment intellectual tasks, allowing researchers to focus more on analysis and innovation, rather than the mechanical aspects of academic writing.

Case Study: Enhancing Multinational Communication Strategies with ChatGPT

A global telecommunications company, operating in over 50 countries, faced significant challenges in managing its customer service and marketing communications across diverse cultural and linguistic landscapes. With a customer base that included millions of non-English speaking users, the company needed a solution that would not only improve efficiency but also maintain the cultural sensitivity required for effective communication. The decision was made to implement ChatGPT, leveraging its multilingual capabilities to overhaul their communication strategy.

The first phase involved training ChatGPT in multiple languages, including Spanish, Mandarin, and Arabic, among others. This training focused on understanding colloquialisms, cultural nuances, and the specific telecommunications terminology used in different regions. The aim was to equip ChatGPT to handle customer inquiries, provide information, and even manage crisis communications with the same ease and expertise as local agents.

In practice, ChatGPT was integrated into the company's customer relationship management (CRM) systems. For inbound customer service inquiries, ChatGPT provided first-level responses.

Complex queries were escalated to human agents who were now more available due to AI handling routine tasks. For outbound communications, ChatGPT generated personalized marketing messages tailored to individual customer profiles and cultural contexts, substantially increasing the engagement rates.

The impact was notable. First, there was a 40% reduction in customer wait times due to the swift handling of common inquiries. Customer satisfaction scores improved by 30% in non-English speaking regions. Additionally, marketing campaign response rates saw a 25% increase as messages were more aligned with local preferences and styles.

This case study not only shows the potential of ChatGPT in managing multi-lingual customer interactions but also highlights the strategic importance of cultural sensitivity in global business operations. It also exemplifies the seamless integration of AI with existing technologies to enhance business processes and customer relations.

Case Study: Revitalizing a News Agency's Editorial Workflow with ChatGPT

A leading international news agency recognized the need to adapt to rapidly changing digital landscapes and decided to leverage ChatGPT to transform its editorial processes and content delivery mechanisms. Faced with the dual challenges of declining print readership and the increasing demand for real-time, personalized news content, the agency aimed to harness AI to maintain its journalistic standards while accelerating content production and distribution.

The implementation phase began with integrating ChatGPT into their existing digital infrastructure. This included training the AI on a comprehensive set of historical news articles, editorial guidelines, and ethical journalism practices to ensure outputs that were not only fast but also credible and aligned with the agency's values. ChatGPT's role was envisioned as a support tool to assist human journalists by providing initial drafts, suggesting story angles based on trending topics, and automating routine reporting tasks such as financial earnings previews and sports match summaries.

For instance, during major global events like elections or natural disasters, ChatGPT rapidly generated factual updates that were used as foundational content for stories further developed by experienced reporters. This collaboration allowed the agency to publish updates more swiftly, significantly reducing the time from event occurrence to news delivery.

Furthermore, the advanced language model capabilities of ChatGPT enabled the agency to customize news content for different regional audiences, adjusting the tone and focus to suit cultural and local preferences, thereby increasing engagement across various demographics. An analytical tool was also developed to monitor user interactions with AI-generated content, providing insights into reader preferences and behavior, which in turn, guided the editorial team in future content creation.

Over the review period, the news agency recorded a 50% increase in content production speed, a 20% uplift in reader engagement, and a significant reduction in operational costs. The integration of ChatGPT highlighted a successful adaptation to digital innovation, showing a path forward for other media organizations grappling with the challenges of the digital age.

Case Study: Transforming Legal Documentation

Processes with ChatGPT

In the complex and ever-evolving field of law, maintaining accuracy and timeliness in documentation is crucial. A mid-sized legal firm, known for its vigorous handling of corporate litigation and intellectual property rights, faced perennial challenges related to the vast amount of legal research, document drafting, and the need for precision in legal writing. The firm decided to integrate ChatGPT into their legal documentation processes to enhance efficiency, reduce human error, and expedite case handling.

The initial deployment of ChatGPT focused on automating the creation of routine legal documents such as non-disclosure agreements, service contracts, and cease and desist letters. By training the AI on specific legal terminologies and precedent case documents, the firm enabled ChatGPT to generate initial drafts based on inputs from attorneys. These drafts were then reviewed and fine-tuned by the legal staff, substantially reducing the time spent on these activities.

Furthermore, ChatGPT was employed to conduct preliminary legal research. By inputting relevant case facts, the AI could quickly sort through extensive databases of legal texts and precedents to provide summaries and potentially applicable legal frameworks. This capability significantly enhanced the firm's research processes, allowing lawyers to focus on deeper analytical tasks such as formulating legal strategies and client advisory.

The firm also utilized ChatGPT to automate correspondence with clients and other legal entities. Custom workflows were established where routine client updates, appointment reminders, legal advisories, and other communications were automated, personalized, and dispatched without direct lawyer involvement unless specific legal insight was required.

Over a year of integrating ChatGPT, the legal firm noted a 40% reduction in the time required to draft and review documents and a 30% improvement in client satisfaction due to quicker turnaround times and more accurate legal advisories. The case of this legal firm highlights how AI like ChatGPT can be a transformative force in highly specialized fields such as law, not only in enhancing operational efficiency but also in improving the quality of legal services rendered.

Case Study: Revamping Real Estate Marketing with ChatGPT

A well-established real estate company, renowned for its diverse portfolio that includes residential, commercial, and luxury properties, faced significant challenges in engaging prospective buyers and streamlining its marketing efforts. The real estate market, being highly competitive and dynamic, necessitated a more sophisticated approach to content creation and customer interaction. Hence, the firm decided to leverage ChatGPT to enhance its marketing strategies and customer service operations.

The initial phase involved integrating ChatGPT with the company's existing digital infrastructure, which includes their website, social media platforms, and customer relationship management (CRM) systems. A strategic rollout plan was developed, beginning with training ChatGPT on the company's property listings, branding guidelines, and the nuanced language of real estate marketing. This training enabled ChatGPT to generate compelling property descriptions, personalized email marketing campaigns, and responsive social media content that resonated with target demographics.

For instance, the AI was used to create dynamic content for an upscale residential project being marketed to high-net-worth individuals. ChatGPT utilized a tone that emphasized luxury, exclusivity, and the lifestyle benefits of the property, aligning this messaging with insights drawn from market research and customer data. In another instance, for commercial properties, ChatGPT produced specialized content focusing on investment potential, strategic location, and amenity details relevant for businesses and investors.

Furthermore, the company employed ChatGPT to power its live chat services on their website. Prospective buyers could get immediate responses to their inquiries, significantly improving user engagement and satisfaction. The AI was configured to escalate more complex queries to human agents, ensuring a seamless blend of efficiency and personalized attention.

Over the year following the implementation of ChatGPT, the real estate firm not only saw a 35% increase in user engagement across their digital platforms but also a 20% increase in lead generation rates. This case exemplifies how AI technologies like ChatGPT can transform traditional marketing approaches in real estate, delivering tailored content that drives engagement and facilitates efficient customer interactions.

Case Study: Revitalizing Travel Promotions with ChatGPT for a Global Tour Operator

A major global tour operator, renowned for its diverse offerings across continents and specializing in tailor-made travel experiences, encountered hurdles in maintaining an engaging, persuasive, and regionally customized content strategy. The travel industry's fast-paced nature required the company to frequently update its travel packages, promotions, and informational content to reflect seasonal changes, local attractions, and cultural festivities, which was proving to be increasingly demanding and inefficient with traditional methods.

To address these challenges, the company initiated the integration of ChatGPT into their content creation workflows. Initially, ChatGPT was employed to generate first-draft contents for travel blogs, email newsletters, and promotional materials focusing on upcoming travel destinations. This implementation involved detailed training of the AI, acquainting it with the company's tone, target demographics, and the specific linguistic subtleties needed for different regional markets.

For instance, for the European market, ChatGPT tailored travel itineraries by connecting cultural heritage sites with contemporary events, creating compelling narratives that resonated with culturally inclined tourists. In Asia, the focus was shifted towards integrating traditional festivals and unique culinary experiences into travel proposals, enriching the appeal to adventure seekers and culinary tourists.

Furthermore, ChatGPT automated the process of responding to customer inquiries on the operator's digital platforms. This AI implementation significantly reduced response times and personalized customer interactions based on previous bookings and expressed preferences, dramatically enhancing customer satisfaction and engagement.

The results from the first year of implementing ChatGPT showcased remarkable efficiency improvements in content production and a significant uptick in customer engagement rates. The dynamic content generated by ChatGPT helped the tour operator to witness a 25% increase in booking conversions, underpinning a strategic edge in the competitive travel market. The case illustrates the transformative potential of AI in global business strategies, specifically in customizing user experiences and automating complex content-oriented tasks.

Case Study: Revolutionizing Online Education with ChatGPT

In response to the growing demand for flexible, accessible learning options, a leading online education provider embarked on a transformative initiative to harness the power of ChatGPT across its curriculum and student support services. Faced with a diverse student base spread globally and the challenge of delivering consistently engaging and personalized educational content, the institution aimed to leverage AI to scale up their operations efficiently and effectively.

The initial integration focused on developing an AI-enhanced learning platform where ChatGPT would function as a virtual tutor for students. This system was designed to answer queries, assist with coursework, and provide explanations in complex subject areas. To tailoring ChatGPT's responses, extensive training was conducted incorporating a wide array of educational materials, including textbooks and course-specific documents, which provided the AI with a robust knowledge base reflective of the institution's curricular standards.

A pilot project was launched in the mathematics department, where ChatGPT assisted students struggling with advanced concepts by offering step-by-step explanations and personalized learning suggestions based on their progress. For example, if a student faced difficulty in calculus, ChatGPT would adapt its instructional approach, sometimes providing visual aids or real-world application examples to clarify complex theories.

In addition to academic support, ChatGPT was employed to automate administrative tasks such as enrollment inquiries and course scheduling, which significantly reduced the workload on staff and accelerated response times for student queries. Over time, as ChatGPT continuously learned from interactions, its ability to handle an even wider scope of questions improved, exemplifying adaptive learning technology's benefits.

The project yielded remarkable outcomes within the first year of implementation. Student satisfaction scores saw a measurable increase, particularly in courses that traditionally had high dropout rates. Moreover, the faculty found they could dedicate more time to formulating impactful, research-based educational strategies rather than spending extensive time on routine queries and administrative tasks.

REVIEW QUESTIONS

1. Sarah is a content strategist implementing ChatGPT for her digital marketing firm's content production. She configures ChatGPT to align with the brand's voice and integrates it into the existing CMS. She encounters a problem with maintaining a consistent content tone across different content forms. Based on best practices, which would be the MOST effective approach for her to solve this issue?

A) Regularly update the AI's training data to align with changing brand guidelines

B) Discontinue the use of ChatGPT and revert to manual content creation

C) Limit the use of ChatGPT to only generating metadata for content

D) Implement stricter access controls on the content management system

Answer: A

Explanation: Regularly updating the AI's training data is crucial for maintaining consistency in the brand's voice across various types of content. By continuously aligning the training data with the most current brand guidelines, Sarah ensures that ChatGPT adapts accurately to the evolving tone and style of the brand. This approach not only maintains consistency but also leverages the AI's capabilities to enhance content quality without reverting to fully manual processes.

2. James is using ChatGPT to generate e-books and technical reports. He is concerned about the accuracy and relevance of the AI-generated content, especially since the field he is writing about is rapidly evolving. What strategy should he employ to ensure the content remains up-to-date and accurate?

A) Periodically rewrite the e-books and reports manually

B) Use ChatGPT to continuously update the content based on the most recent data

C) Discontinue use of AI for dynamic fields and stick to traditional writing methods

D) Restrict the use of ChatGPT to historical data that does not change

Answer: B

Explanation: Utilizing ChatGPT to continuously update the content with the most recent data is an effective strategy for maintaining accuracy and relevance, especially in fast-evolving fields. This approach allows James to leverage the AI's ability to integrate new information and findings rapidly, thus ensuring that the e-books and reports reflect the latest insights and developments without the need to revert fully to manual updates or restrict content to static, historical data.

REVIEW QUESTIONS

3. A startup is integrating ChatGPT into their social media strategy to automate engagement. They aim to maintain a high engagement rate through personalized replies and content generation. What critical factor should they focus on to optimize ChatGPT's performance in this role?

A) Limit interactions to generic responses to avoid misinterpretation

B) Program ChatGPT to refer all complex interactions to human agents

C) Enhance ChatGPT's training with specific user interaction data to tailor responses

D) Use ChatGPT only for posting updates, not for engaging with users

Answer: C

Explanation: Enhancing ChatGPT's training with specific user interaction data enables the AI to tailor responses more effectively, thereby maintaining or even increasing engagement rates. By programming ChatGPT to learn from past interactions, the startup can ensure the AI provides personalized, contextually relevant responses that resonate with users, as opposed to restricting its role to generic tasks or limiting user engagement.

4. Melissa, a freelance content creator, uses ChatGPT for her blog posts to optimize for SEO and improve organic visibility. She is planning a series of posts on a new technology trend. What should Melissa prioritize in her use of ChatGPT to enhance SEO performance?

A) Focus exclusively on saturating posts with high-ranking keywords

B) Use ChatGPT to generate articles without reviewing or editing them

C) Engage ChatGPT to produce diverse content types tailored to different user intents

D) Limit the length of blog posts to ensure quick loading times

Answer: C

Explanation: Engaging ChatGPT to produce diverse content types tailored to different user intents allows Melissa to effectively address various aspects of the new technology trend, increasing the relevance and reach of her blog posts. This strategy helps in capturing a broader audience and aligns with SEO best practices by catering to specific search queries and user needs, thus improving organic visibility more effectively than merely focusing on keyword saturation or shortening posts.

MIDJOURNEY: PIONEERING AI IN THE VISUAL ARTS SECTOR

Introduction to MidJourney and Its Role in AI-driven Art

MidJourney stands at the forefront of revolutionizing the visual arts sector through advanced AI technology. It offers artists and creators an innovative platform to explore and generate art with unique AI algorithms that push the boundaries of creative expression. This application not only automates parts of the creation process but also inspires new forms of visual narratives.

Significantly, MidJourney is influencing the art world by providing tools that create high-quality, intricate visuals that might take much longer to produce manually. This enables artists to experiment more freely and deliver diverse artistic outputs. The AI's capacity to learn from vast datasets of images allows it to offer suggestions and modifications that can enhance the artist's original vision, melding human creativity with machine precision.

Moreover, MidJourney democratizes art creation, making it accessible to individuals without formal training in the arts. This aspect fosters a new wave of artists who can express themselves through digital media without the barrier of high technical skill requirements. Overall, MidJourney is pivotal in shaping the future landscape of AI-driven visual arts, blending tradition with pioneering technology.

Exploring the Capabilities of MidJourney in Visual Art Creation

MidJourney's transformative power in visual art creation lies in its ability to harness complex AI algorithms for producing highly detailed and creative artworks. Artists can utilize this technology to refine and expand their creative expressions, transcending traditional art boundaries. With capabilities to interpret and visualize an extensive range of artistic styles, from classic to contemporary, MidJourney provides a versatile platform for artistic endeavor.

The AI's proficiency in generating visuals that resonate with human emotions and aesthetic values is particularly compelling. It interprets various artistic prompts to create visuals that can be abstract or realistically detailed, catering to the artist's vision and project needs. This adaptability makes it an indispensable tool for artists looking to explore new creative landscapes.

Moreover, MidJourney's capability to rapidly produce multiple iterations of a concept allows artists to experiment with different color palettes, compositions, and textures, significantly speeding up the creative process. This efficiency not only enhances artistic productivity but also pushes the boundaries of innovation in art creation. Ultimately, MidJourney stands as a beacon of futuristic artistic expression, constantly evolving and setting new benchmarks in the digital art domain.

Setting Up MidJourney for Your Artistic Projects

Setting up MidJourney for your artistic endeavors begins with understanding the interface and configuring the settings to best suit your creative vision. Initially, artists need to create an account and familiarize themselves with the various tools and options available. This setup phase is crucial, as it allows personalizing the AI to work in tandem with the artist's stylistic preferences and project requirements.

Next, selecting the right prompts and parameters can significantly impact the generated artworks. Artists should spend time experimenting with different commands and settings to see how they affect the output. This exploration is an iterative process, where each adjustment can lead to a distinctively different artistic result. Understanding these nuances is key to harnessing MidJourney's full potential.

Finally, integrating MidJourney into your workflow involves establishing a rhythm where the AI serves as a co-creator, not just a tool. This symbiosis between human creativity and AI capabilities enriches the artistic process, opening up new possibilities for innovation and expression in the visual arts sector.

Generating Unique Art Pieces with AI: A Step-by-Step Guide

Embarking on the journey to create unique art pieces with MidJourney starts with setting a clear artistic intention. Define what you wish to express through your artwork—whether it's a burst of emotions, a vivid landscape, or an abstract concept. This initial clarity acts as the foundation on which AI will build.

Next, input your creative vision into MidJourney using descriptive prompts. These could range from simple words to complex phrases that encapsulate the essence of your intended artwork. The precision of your prompts directly influences the uniqueness and relevance of the AI-generated art. Experiment with variations of these prompts to explore multiple artistic interpretations and refine the outcomes.

Finally, review the generated pieces critically. Select the artwork that best aligns with your original vision or combines elements most effectively. Each iteration offers a learning opportunity—use these insights to fine-tune future prompts, enhancing both the AI's performance and the distinctiveness of your artistic creations.

How Artists Can Monetize MidJourney Creations

Monetizing AI-generated art through MidJourney offers myriad avenues for creative professionals. Artists can initially harness the platform to produce high-quality digital artworks, which can be sold as prints, licensed for use, or offered as digital downloads. These can range from personal portraits to expansive abstract compositions, appealing to a broad audience seeking unique art.

Furthermore, leveraging online marketplaces specifically for digital art is a strategic approach. Platforms like Etsy and Saatchi Art are popular for selling prints, while niche sites cater to digital downloads. Social media platforms also serve as powerful tools for artists, where they can showcase their MidJourney creations and connect directly with potential buyers and art enthusiasts.

Subscription models or Patreon memberships provide another revenue stream. Here, artists offer exclusive content or commissioned works using MidJourney to their subscribers. This model builds a community around the artist's work, enhancing engagement and steady income. Collaborating with other creators or brands for commercial projects can also amplify reach and profitability.

Using MidJourney for Commercial Art Projects

Integrating MidJourney into commercial art projects opens a new realm of possibilities for artists and enterprises alike. The platform's capacity to generate novel and intricate visuals swiftly fits perfectly into the fast-paced demands of commercial art. For instance, advertising agencies can utilize AI-created images to craft compelling campaigns that capture the target audience's imagination more effectively, enhancing advertising impact and customer engagement.

Moreover, MidJourney's adaptability allows for customization according to specific brand aesthetics, making it an invaluable tool for graphic design firms. These firms can produce a high volume of customized content for clients, streamlining operations and reducing turnarounds on projects. The unique touches that MidJourney adds reinforce brand identities, distinguishing them in a competitive market.

Fashion and interior design businesses can also benefit from MidJourney's quick generation of patterns and layouts. Utilizing AI in this way helps these industries stay ahead of trends and respond rapidly to market changes, crucial for maintaining relevance and consumer interest in dynamic sectors.

Developing a Brand Identity with AI-Generated Visuals

In the landscape of digital marketing and brand development, AI-generated visuals offer a transformative potential for crafting distinctive brand identities. MidJourney, as a tool, empowers artists and businesses to create visually compelling brand elements that resonate on a personal level with audiences. This spectrum ranges from logos and banners to complete aesthetic themes consistent across all customer touchpoints.

Utilizing MidJourney to develop these elements ensures a brand's identity is both innovative and reflective of modern technological trends. The integration of AI into brand design translates abstract brand values into tangible visual forms that can be intricate, nuanced, or strikingly simple. Moreover, the ability to rapidly iterate on designs using AI allows brands to evolve visually as they refine their strategic outreach, maintaining relevance and freshness in their visual presentation.

For businesses, aligning with AI-driven design platforms like MidJourney not only fosters a modern image but also sets a precedent for embracing future technologies. The resulting brand identity not only attracts attention but also sets a narrative of innovation and forward-thinking, essential for contemporary branding.

Strategies for Selling AI Art on Digital Platforms

Selling AI-generated art on digital platforms necessitates a nuanced strategy that balances artistic integrity with market trends. Initially, identifying the right platform is crucial. Popular sites like ArtStation and DeviantArt attract a vast audience of art enthusiasts, while newer platforms may offer less competition and more visibility for emerging artists. Choose platforms where the audience resonates with the innovative nature of AI art.

Once a platform is chosen, effective presentation becomes key. High-quality images and compelling descriptions that highlight the unique AI elements of your creations can significantly increase interest and sales. Utilize SEO techniques to enhance visibility; include relevant keywords in your descriptions to ensure your artwork is discoverable by potential buyers searching for AI-generated art.

Lastly, engagement with the community on these platforms can drive sales. Participate in discussions, respond to comments, and connect with other artists and buyers. This interaction fosters a loyal following and can lead to repeat customers, essential for sustaining income in the competitive digital art market.

Navigating Copyright and Legal Issues in AI-Generated Art

Navigating copyright and legal issues in AI-generated art, particularly with MidJourney's creations, requires a nuanced understanding of intellectual property laws. As AI takes a more central role in artistic creation, determining copyright ownership becomes complex. Predominantly, artists need to discern whether these works are considered original creations or derivatives shaped by AI's input. Legal frameworks are still adapting to this new artistic paradigm; thus, artists must stay informed about evolving laws to protect their creations effectively.

Additionally, considering the global reach of digital art, artists must understand international copyright nuances when displaying their works online or selling in different countries. Licensing agreements can help clarify the use and distribution rights, ensuring both artist and user adhere to legal standards. It is advisable for artists to seek legal counsel when forging such agreements to avoid future disputes.

Ultimately, the responsibility rests with the artist to ensure their MidJourney-generated artworks are within legal bounds. Regular updates on copyright law changes and active participation in legal workshops or seminars can provide essential insights for protecting artistic investments in the rapidly growing field of AI-generated art.

Integrating MidJourney into Existing Artistic Workflows

Integrating MidJourney with existing artistic workflows represents an innovative leap for artists and creative industries. This allows for a seamless fusion between traditional artistic techniques and AI-driven creativity, enhancing productivity without sacrificing personal style. Artists familiar with conventional tools find adapting MidJourney's AI capabilities into their processes an exciting challenge that broadens creative horizons and operational efficiencies.

Initially, incorporation may be integrated at the ideation stage, where MidJourney can rapidly produce diverse concept art, providing a fresh pool of ideas from which artists can develop more refined works. This can significantly shorten the creative cycle, allowing more time for fine-tuning and detail work. Furthermore, integration can extend to the revision stage, where feedback can be quickly processed through MidJourney, allowing artists to explore multiple modifications in real-time.

Lastly, for those operating within larger collaborative settings, MidJourney can serve as a central hub, enhancing collaboration by enabling real-time sharing and iteration of visual ideas across various platforms. This integration aids in maintaining a coherent visual standard while ensuring all team members contribute effectively, leveraging their unique skills within the AI-enhanced framework.

Collaboration Between AI and Human Artists: Best Practices

The fusion of AI with human creativity in the arts, as seen through platforms like

MidJourney, offers vast new territories for exploration and innovation. Best practices for such collaboration center around leveraging AI's speed and processing power without overshadowing the unique sensibilities of human artists. Essential to this process is defining clear roles; AI can serve to suggest and iterate on visual ideas which artists can refine and contextualize within larger narratives.

For an effective partnership, maintaining open channels for feedback between the AI system and the artist is crucial. This bidirectional flow ensures the AI's outputs align with the artist's vision and project requirements. Regularly updating the AI's learning models based on specific artistic feedback can tune its generative processes to better suit nuanced creative needs.

Finally, successful collaboration requires an appreciation for what both parties bring to the table. While AI can generate numerous variations and complex patterns, it is the artist who imbues these creations with emotional depth and cultural resonance, transforming intriguing concepts into compelling art that resonates.

MidJourney in Education: Teaching AI Art Techniques

Incorporating MidJourney into educational settings revolutionizes the way AI art techniques are taught. Initially, educators can utilize MidJourney to demonstrate the vast capabilities of AI in generating diverse artistic expressions. This real-time demonstration aids students in understanding the interaction between artificial intelligence and artistic creation, providing a foundational knowledge that is both theoretical and practically engaging.

Furthermore, curriculum development benefits from MidJourney's adaptability. Instructors can design assignments that allow students to experiment with different styles, themes, and complexities, enabling a hands-on learning experience that is tailored to varied artistic pursuits. Workshops or class projects focusing on AI-driven art creation facilitate a deeper dive into the technological processes, enhancing students' technical skills while fostering an appreciation for the nuanced relationship between technology and art.

Lastly, the inclusion of MidJourney in art education encourages a forward-thinking approach. Educators are urged to address the ethical, legal, and creative implications of using AI in art, preparing students to navigate the evolving art landscape responsibly and innovatively. This holistic educational strategy ensures that the next generation of artists is not only technically adept but also ethically informed.

Future Trends in AI-Driven Visual Arts with MidJourney

The horizon of AI-driven visual arts, particularly through MidJourney, promises transformative shifts in both creation and consumption of art. Rapid advancements in AI capabilities forecast a future where artistic tools become increasingly intuitive, allowing for more profound human-AI collaboration. Artists will likely harness AI not just as a tool, but as a co-creator, pushing the boundaries of imagination and functionality.

Furthermore, as AI art becomes mainstream, the art market may witness the rise of digital galleries and exhibitions predominantly showcasing AI-generated pieces. These platforms will cater to a global audience, providing unprecedented access to digital art, thus democratizing the appreciation and acquisition of artworks. The potential for AI to analyze and predict viewer preferences could also lead to highly personalized art experiences, reshaping how audiences engage with art.

Another exciting prospect is the integration of virtual and augmented reality with AI art, offering immersive experiences that blend the digital and physical worlds. As these technologies evolve, they will likely become integral to how art is experienced, potentially changing not just perceptions but also the very definition of what art can be. Artists and creators must stay abreast of these trends, experimenting and adapting to navigate this promising future.

Case Studies: Successful Art Projects Using MidJourney

Exploring notable case studies of MidJourney in art showcases the groundbreaking potential of AI in the creative industries. One seminal project involved an artist who utilized MidJourney's profound capabilities to create a series of digital landscapes that resonated with surreal yet vivid environments. These pieces not only garnered significant attention at various digital art exhibitions but also highlighted the AI's capacity for generating intricate and emotionally compelling visuals.

Another impactful case was a collaborative venture between a seasoned graphic designer and MidJourney, focusing on commercial artwork for a major brand. The project leveraged AI to produce innovative ad campaigns, blending human creative direction with AI's rapid iteration processes. This successful integration resulted in aesthetically unique and highly effective marketing materials that substantially increased customer engagement and sales for the brand.

These instances underline the transformative effects of MidJourney in art production and commercial projects. By harnessing AI, artists and companies can push creative boundaries and achieve remarkable outcomes, setting new benchmarks in the domain of digital and commercial art.

Building an Online Portfolio with MidJourney Artworks

Creating an online portfolio featuring MidJourney artworks positions artists at the intersection of technology and creativity. The unique AI-generated pieces can captivate a global audience, showcasing an artist's prowess in merging traditional skills with cutting-edge AI technology. An effectively curated digital portfolio highlights the distinctive style each artist brings to AI-made visuals, demonstrating a diverse range of possibilities from surreal landscapes to abstract designs.

The process of building this portfolio begins with selecting the best MidJourney creations that not only represent artistic achievement but also embody a cohesive narrative or theme. Including contextual descriptions that explain the AI's role and the creative decisions behind each piece adds depth to the viewer's experience. Artists should focus on usability and aesthetics of the website, ensuring that it is accessible and visually appealing to promote longer engagement.

Lastly, employing SEO strategies and leveraging social media can significantly increase the visibility of an online portfolio. Sharing stories behind the artwork, progress shots, and final results can engage audiences, making the portfolio not just a gallery, but a storytelling canvas of an artist's journey with AI. Regular updates and new additions keep the portfolio dynamic and encourage repeat visits.

Leveraging Social Media to Promote AI-Generated Art

In the realm of AI-generated art, social media serves as a pivotal platform for artists using MidJourney to amplify their creations' reach and engagement. Platforms like Instagram, Twitter, and Facebook are ideal for showcasing the unique aesthetics of AI art, allowing artists to connect with a broader audience. By strategically posting high-quality images and using targeted hashtags, artists can attract art enthusiasts who value innovation and digital creativity.

Engagement strategies such as hosting live sessions, creating making-of videos, and sharing behind-the-scenes content can further deepen audience interaction. These approaches humanize the AI process, demystifying the technology and making it more accessible to the public. Collaborations with other artists and influencers in the digital art space can also expand reach and introduce the artwork to diverse communities.

Finally, leveraging analytics tools provided by social media platforms helps artists understand viewer preferences and modify their promotional strategies accordingly. Such data-driven insights ensure that artists not only showcase their work effectively but also foster a growing community of AI art admirers.

Pricing Strategies for Art Created with MidJourney

Pricing AI-generated art, such as those created by MidJourney, presents unique challenges and opportunities. Artists must consider both the technology's novelty and the traditional art market dynamics. Initially, setting prices could start with the cost of input, including subscriptions to MidJourney and any additional processing fees, then factoring in the artist's time and creative input. The uniqueness of each piece, driven by AI's ability to produce never-before-seen images, can also elevate its market value.

Moreover, artists should study market reactions to AI art. Early adopters may pay a premium for innovative artworks that blend traditional artistic elements with cutting-edge technology. Variable pricing strategies, such as dynamic pricing models based on demand and popularity online, can be effective. Additionally, offering limited editions or certified originals could increase perceived value.

Lastly, embracing transparency about the AI-driven creation process can justify pricing decisions. Educating potential buyers about the complexity and artistic intent behind AI-generated artworks can cultivate appreciation and willingness to invest, supporting sustainable pricing strategies for creators in the AI art space.

Tools and Accessories for Enhancing MidJourney Output

To optimize the output of MidJourney in the creation of AI-generated visual art, artists can integrate several tools and accessories that enhance both the efficiency and quality of their projects. High-resolution monitors, for instance, provide a crystal-clear view of intricate details, critical for refining digital artworks. Additionally, advanced graphic tablets enable artists to interact more intuitively with MidJourney's interface, facilitating a seamless blend of human creativity and AI precision.

Effective software plugins that compliment MidJourney can further streamline the creative process. Plugins for texture enhancement, color correction, and layer management augment MidJourney's capabilities, allowing artists to customize and fine-tune AI-generated pieces to their unique aesthetic preferences. This symbiosis between advanced tools and AI opens up new possibilities in digital art production.

Lastly, cloud storage solutions and robust data backup systems are essential for safeguarding artworks. Investing in reliable digital asset management tools ensures that every creation is archived and easily retrievable, providing peace of mind and supporting a professional workflow. These tools collectively empower artists to push the boundaries of AI-enhanced visual creativity, ensuring that their art remains both innovative and commercially viable.

Community and Networking in the AI Art Ecosystem

The AI art ecosystem, particularly through platforms like MidJourney, cultivates a unique community where artists, technologists, and enthusiasts converge. This networking hub is not only a place for sharing creations but also a vital resource for collaborative learning and innovation in AI-driven art. Artists exchange tips on utilizing AI tools effectively, pushing the boundaries of what AI can achieve in the visual arts.

Additionally, online forums and social media groups dedicated to AI art are burgeoning. These spaces offer artists opportunities to receive feedback, participate in peer critiques, and engage with ongoing artistic challenges facilitated by AI advancements. Such interactions enrich the artists' understanding and mastery of AI technologies while fostering a sense of community.

Ultimately, the community around AI art functions as an incubator for talent and ideas, amplifying individual achievements into collective progress. Networking within this community can lead to partnerships that might not only scale artistic endeavors but also enhance their commercial viability.

Challenges and Limitations of Using AI in Art Creation

While AI, such as MidJourney, revolutionizes art creation, offering novel avenues for expression, it inherently presents significant challenges and limitations. One core issue is the potential for a dilution of personal creativity. Artists might rely heavily on AI outputs, possibly stifling their unique creative voices. Additionally, the unpredictable outcomes of AI can result in artworks that stray far from an artist's initial vision, complicating the creative control over the final product.

Moreover, AI-generated art can evoke skepticism and critical debate about authenticity and authorship. The question arises: whose art is it? This debate can affect the market acceptance and value of AI-generated artworks, posing a marketing challenge. Lastly, while AI can generate art, it lacks the nuanced understanding and emotional depth that human artists interpret and imbue into their works, sometimes resulting in artwork that might not resonate on a human level.

These challenges necessitate a balanced approach, where AI is used as a tool to enhance, not replace, the human element in art creation. Artists must navigate these waters carefully to maintain their authentic voice while leveraging AI capabilities.

Privacy and Data Security Considerations in AI Art

The integration of AI technologies like MidJourney in the creation of visual arts necessitates robust privacy and data security measures. As AI systems process vast amounts of data, including potentially sensitive inputs from artists, the risk of data breaches or misuse becomes significant. It is crucial for artists using AI tools to be vigilant about the data they feed into these systems, understanding that privacy might be compromised without adequate protections.

Furthermore, the proprietary nature of AI-generated artworks brings into question the ownership and copyright management of digital pieces. Artists must ensure that their creations, potentially mingled with AI algorithms, are safeguarded against unauthorized use or duplication. Implementing digital rights management (DRM) systems can help protect artworks while maintaining the flexibility required in the digital art market.

Lastly, transparency with audiences about the use of AI in art creation can foster trust and accountability. Disclosing the extent of AI involvement in artworks helps in maintaining ethical boundaries while promoting a secure environment for innovation within the AI art community.

Impact of AI on Traditional Artistic Techniques

The incursion of AI into the realm of visual arts, as exemplified by MidJourney, heralds a transformative era for traditional artistic techniques. AI applications like MidJourney not only augment but in some instances, revolutionize conventional methods, introducing a dynamic interplay between technology and human creativity.

For centuries, traditional arts have relied on the manual prowess and subjective interpretations of artists. With AI, these processes are expedited and expanded, allowing for the creation of complex visual pieces that might take months to conceptualize and execute by hand. AI tools process and synthesize vast arrays of historical data, styles, and techniques, resulting in novel artworks that push traditional boundaries. However, this integration also raises concerns about the dilution of artisanal value and uniqueness.

The future trajectory of this symbiosis suggests a continued blending that could redefine artistic norms while respecting the heritage of traditional methods. As artistic paradigms shift, AI's role may evolve from a tool of creation to a profound collaborator, reshaping the landscape of visual arts with each brushstroke facilitated by algorithms.

Ethical Implications of AI in the Creative Process

The ethical implications of using AI like MidJourney in the creative process are profound and multi-faceted. As artists blend AI with traditional practices, questions arise about the originality and authenticity of AI-generated works. Is it the artist or the algorithm that ultimately owns the 'creative spark' of such pieces? This dilemma challenges the very definition of artistry, potentially reshaping how artworks are valued and perceived in the art community and marketplace.

Moreover, AI's role in art creation touches on deeper ethical considerations linked to cultural appropriation and representation. Algorithms trained on vast datasets may unconsciously propagate existing biases or misrepresent cultural elements, leading to controversies and critical backlash. Artists and developers must be sensitive to these aspects, ensuring their AI interventions are respectful and informed.

Lastly, the democratization of art through AI tools raises ethical questions about access and equity. While MidJourney opens doors for many to participate in art creation, it also necessitates a dialogue about the disparities in digital literacy and access to technological resources, ensuring that AI does not widen but bridges the gap in creative expression.

The Role of AI in the Future of Arts Education

As AI tools like MidJourney reshape the visual arts landscape, their integration into arts education is inevitable and profoundly transformative. These technologies not only facilitate new forms of creative expression but also serve as advanced teaching aids, capable of introducing students to complex artistic techniques and theories through interactive and personalized learning experiences.

In classrooms of the future, AI could customize learning materials to match each student's pace and interest, thereby enhancing engagement and retention. Tools such as MidJourney allow students to experiment with an infinite array of styles and mediums without the traditional resource constraints, fostering an environment where creativity and innovation thrive.

Furthermore, the use of AI in teaching can provide invaluable data-driven insights into student progress and areas needing attention, enabling educators to tailor their teaching strategies effectively. While this heralds a dynamic shift in pedagogy, it also necessitates rigorous training for educators to optimally utilize AI within curricula, ensuring that it complements rather than usurps the human element in arts education.

Marketing AI Art: Tips and Tricks for Artists

Marketing AI-generated art, such as those created with MidJourney, requires strategic approaches that leverage both the novelty of AI and the traditional tenets of artistic engagement. First and foremost, artists should emphasize the collaborative nature of their work, highlighting how AI serves as a tool that enhances their creative vision, rather than replacing the human touch.

When utilizing digital platforms, artists should tailor their online presence to showcase their AI artworks prominently. This includes developing a compelling narrative around each piece that draws viewers into the artistic process — from conception to AI execution. Utilizing high-quality images and engaging descriptions can capture the imagination of potential buyers and gallery curators alike.

Furthermore, artists can benefit from participating in online communities and forums dedicated to AI art. Sharing insights and engaging in discussions about the use of AI in art can establish artists as thought leaders in this emerging field, enhancing their professional network and increasing their artwork's visibility. Lastly, consider the ethical implications discussed in previous sections to maintain transparency and foster trust with audiences.

Evaluating the Artistic Value of AI-Created Visuals

The evaluation of AI-created visuals, such as those produced with MidJourney, presents a novel challenge in the arts sector. Historically, artistic value has been assessed based on human creativity, skill, and the emotional response elicited from the audience. However, when an AI collaborates in the creative process, these traditional metrics require reexamination.

Critically, one must consider the role of the artist in directing the AI, framing not just aesthetic but also conceptual aspects of the artwork. Does the use of AI diminish the personal expression, or does it enhance the artist's vision by breaking new ground in visual possibilities? These questions become central in discussions about the value of AI-generated art.

Moreover, the public and critical reception of such artworks also informs their perceived value. As AI art gains prominence, the artistic community and market are gradually developing criteria that reflect both innovation and traditional artistic values. Therefore, evaluating AI-generated art necessitates a balanced appreciation of technological ingenuity and enduring artistic principles.

SUMMARY

MidJourney has significantly impacted the visual arts by introducing advanced AI technology to assist artists in creating and experimenting with innovative art forms. By automating some aspects of the creative process and incorporating AI's ability to learn from extensive image datasets, MidJourney offers tools that enhance artistic creativity and precision. This integration allows for the production of intricate and high-quality visuals faster than manual methods, thus broadening the scope of creative possibilities and supporting diverse artistic expressions.

One of the pivotal advantages of MidJourney is its democratization of art creation. Individuals without formal training can now engage with digital media, fostering a new generation of artists. MidJourney's interface is user-friendly, ensuring that artists are able to personalize AI interactions to align with their unique styles and project requirements. The platform's proficiency in generating visually compelling artworks that resonate with human emotions and aesthetic values is critical, as it accommodates an extensive range of artistic styles, bridging the gap between classic and contemporary art forms.

In a commercial context, MidJourney proves invaluable for projects requiring quick production of customized, creative content. It supports advertising, graphic design, fashion, and interior design industries by streamlining operations and offering rapid responses to market changes. Moreover, the development of a distinctive brand identity through AI-generated visuals can leverage a company's outreach by embedding modern technological trends into its branding strategy.

The evolution of MidJourney in art education showcases its role as both a teaching tool and a subject of study, preparing students for a future where digital literacy and ethical considerations regarding AI use will be paramount. As AI in art becomes more prevalent, its integration across various platforms and industries is expected to foster new artistic explorations and redefine the boundaries of art creation and dissemination. The success stories and case studies of MidJourney further underline its transformative influence on the digital and commercial art landscapes, marking an ongoing redefinition of how art is created, consumed, and valued in contemporary society.

REFERENCES

[1] Boden, M. A., and Edmonds, E. A. (2009). What is generative art?. https://link.springer.com/article/10.1007/s00146-009-0193-y

[2] McCormack, J., Gifford, T., & Hutchings, P. (2020). Autonomy and creativity in AI-aided art.. https://journalofartificialintelligenceandculture.com/AIArt

[3] Elsden, C., & Nissen, B. (2017). Art Data: Exploring Interactive Art Archiving. https://ieeexplore.ieee.org/document/7006741

CASE STUDY: REVOLUTIONIZING DIGITAL ART EDUCATION WITH MIDJOURNEY

MidJourney's integration into the curriculum of the Crescent School of Arts exemplifies the innovative use of AI in transforming digital art education. The school, recognized for its commitment to blending technological advancements with traditional art education, embarked on this integration to enrich student experiences and broaden their creative capabilities. The project began with installing the MidJourney software across computer labs and training the faculty on its functionalities. Initial skepticism about AI supplanting human creativity was addressed through workshops emphasizing AI as a tool that complements human artists.

Students were initially tasked with creating projects that contrasted traditional hand-drawn techniques with MidJourney-generated images. This exercise not only highlighted AI's efficiency in generating complex patterns and visuals but also allowed students to appreciate the depth and detail that can be achieved manually. Over the semester, students progressed to more integrated assignments, designing projects that combined hand-drawn art with AI enhancements, such as texture rendering and color optimization, provided by MidJourney.

The culmination of this integration was a semester-end exhibition titled 'Synergy of Man and Machine,' which showcased outstanding works at the intersection of human and AI creativity. The exhibition not only drew attention from local media but also attracted art professionals and technologists, stirring discussions on the evolving role of AI in art.

Evaluating student feedback and academic performance post-MidJourney's integration showed significant improvements in student engagement and creativity. Faculty reported an expanded scope in teaching methodologies, and students were excited about exploring various artistic careers that leverage AI technologies. Challenges included ensuring that the AI did not overshadow personal creativity and managing the technical aspects of AI software. Ongoing evaluations and curriculum adjustments ensured that MidJourney's role remained that of a facilitator rather than a dominant force in the creative process.

Case Study: Expanding Market Reach with MidJourney: A Case Study of VecTrendz

VecTrendz, a small but innovative graphic design startup, decided to harness the capabilities of MidJourney to expand its market reach and innovate its design processes. As part of their strategy, VecTrendz aimed to attract clients from various sectors, emphasizing the uniqueness and efficiency of integrating AI-driven designs. The case study begins with VecTrendz integrating MidJourney into their core operations, which included training for their team on

BENOIT TANO MD PHD

leveraging AI to enhance creativity and productivity. The initial application of this technology was in creating original content for social media campaigns, which traditionally required significant human resources and time.

Recognizing the potential for AI to transform their business, the leadership at VecTrendz spearheaded a campaign that touted AI-generated designs as both cost-effective and exceptionally creative solutions. They successfully onboarded several high-profile clients attracted by the quick turnaround times and distinctive design styles offered by MidJourney-generated visual content. One particular project involved rebranding for a tech firm, where MidJourney's input generated multiple logo options and branding materials, providing a range that would normally require weeks of human effort in just a few days.

The strategic decision to use MidJourney proved lucrative as VecTrendz saw a 40% increase in client intake, with a notable improvement in client satisfaction regarding the diversity of design concepts. However, challenges arose, such as maintaining a balance between AI-generated options and human creativity, as some clients expressed concerns about losing the 'human touch'. To address this, VecTrendz established a new service model where every AI-generated design was reviewed and possibly enhanced by a designer, ensuring that each job was both innovative and personally catered to the client's needs.

This proactive approach not only smoothed initial reservations from clients but also set VecTrendz apart as a pioneer in the practical application of AI in commercial art. Their case provides valuable insights into the commercial viability of AI tools like MidJourney, underscoring the importance of blending technology with human creativity to stay competitive in the rapidly evolving graphic design market.

Case Study: Revitalizing Traditional Art Galleries with MidJourney: The ArtSpace Initiative

ArtSpace, a traditional art gallery known for its classic collections, faced declining visitor numbers and engagement, prompting them to integrate MidJourney's AI technology to transform their exhibition strategies and attract a contemporary audience. The integration began with a strategic overhaul of their exhibition planning, where AI was used to analyze visitor data and predict trends, leading to more curated experiences that resonated with younger demographics.

The first major initiative, titled 'Renaissance Reimagined', used MidJourney to reinterpret classic artworks, creating a fusion of historical and modern styles that showcased a blend of past mastery with contemporary artistic trends. These AI-augmented works were not only displayed physically but were also made available as interactive digital experiences, allowing visitors to see the transition of artworks from their original form to their AI-enhanced interpretations.

Critically, this innovative approach served multiple purposes; it educated audiences about the importance of historical art while showcasing the capabilities of modern technology in redefining art appreciation. The gallery also hosted workshops where artists used MidJourney to create real-time adaptations of visitor-suggested themes, fostering an engaging, participatory environment.

However, the integration did not come without challenges. The gallery faced criticism from traditionalists who felt that AI integration detracted from the authenticity of classical art. To counter this, ArtSpace conducted several discussion panels featuring art historians and technologists who debated the role of AI in art, highlighting how technology can serve as a bridge rather than a barrier between old and new forms of art.

The outcome was telling; visitor numbers increased by 30%, and there was a noticeable enhancement in audience diversity, including an increase in younger visitors. Social media buzz generated from the interactive exhibits brought wider recognition to ArtSpace, establishing it as a forward-thinking institution that respects tradition while embracing innovation. This case study not only exemplifies the adaptive use of AI like MidJourney in traditional settings but also presents a model for other galleries facing similar challenges in the digital age.

Case Study: Harnessing MidJourney for Environmental Awareness Campaigns: The GreenVista Project

GreenVista, a non-profit organization devoted to environmental conservation, embarked on a unique project leveraging MidJourney to bolster public engagement and awareness about climate change and ecological preservation. Recognizing the need to communicate complex environmental issues in a visually compelling manner, GreenVista partnered with leading digital artists to create a series of impactful visual narratives using MidJourney's AI capabilities.

The project started with a series of brainstorming sessions where environmental scientists and digital artists collaborated to outline the key messages and themes. MidJourney was then used to translate these themes into powerful visual stories. For instance, one series depicted the progression of deforestation over time, using dynamically generated landscapes to visually narrate the impact of human activity on natural forests. Another series used enhanced imagery to show the potential future of urban areas flooded due to rising sea levels, making the concept more relatable and urgent.

These AI-generated artworks were then utilized in various campaigns, both online and in physical installations, to maximize outreach. The online campaign included interactive elements, where viewers could see before and after scenarios of environmental degradation and recovery, depending on different human intervention models. Physical installations were set up in public spaces with large screens displaying the transitioning visuals, accompanied by QR codes that people could scan to learn more about specific issues and join conservation initiatives.

The integration of MidJourney into GreenVista's campaign brought several benefits and challenges. The compelling visuals significantly increased public engagement, with social media shares and campaign website visits skyrocketing. Schools and educational groups utilized the campaign's visuals as teaching tools, further spreading awareness. However, the project also faced challenges, such as ensuring the scientific accuracy of the visuals and balancing dramatic visual impact with realistic portrayals of environmental issues. Ongoing adjustments and reviews were implemented to maintain the integrity and effectiveness of the visual content.

Case Study: Innovative Retail Display Solutions Powered by MidJourney

Elevating in-store experiences using AI-driven visuals, Modern Retail Solutions (MRS), a forward-thinking retail design company, embarked on implementing MidJourney in creating dynamic and engaging store displays. MRS aimed to revolutionize the way shoppers interact with products through highly personalized and visually appealing display designs. The project commenced with a comprehensive training program for the design and marketing teams in utilizing MidJourney's AI capabilities to generate custom visuals tailored to varying consumer demographics.

MRS first applied MidJourney in a pilot project for a high-end cosmetics brand looking to attract a younger audience. Using AI, they developed a series of interactive mirror displays that incorporated virtual try-on features, where customers could see themselves with different makeup products applied. The AI analyzed customer reactions and adjusted display options in real-time, enhancing engagement. The success of this pilot led to further implementations, with MidJourney being used to reinterpret product displays seasonally, providing a fresh and enticing shopping environment which crucially retained customer interest in physical store locations.

The integration of MidJourney extended beyond bespoke designs to include real-time data analysis from store traffic and customer interaction patterns. This data helped MRS refine and optimize the placement and content of displays across different store sections to increase dwell time and conversion rates. Sales analytics post-integration showed a 25% increase in customer engagement, and a 15% rise in sales for the redesigned areas.

Nevertheless, challenges included managing the technical aspects of AI software and ensuring the visuals aligned seamlessly with the brands' identities without polarization. Regular training sessions were essential in keeping the teams adept at navigating the MidJourney interface and customizing outputs. MRS also held quarterly reviews to evaluate the effectiveness of the displays, allowing adjustments before major shopping seasons to maximize impact.

This case exemplifies how AI like MidJourney can be strategically deployed in retail settings to enhance traditional marketing strategies, creating a dynamic intersection between AI innovation and customer experience enhancement.

Case Study: Pioneering New Media Art Forms with MidJourney

The pioneering efforts of AIStudios in partnership with MidJourney have begun to redefine the realm of new media art, particularly focusing on interactive installations that meld AI capabilities with immersive art experiences. AIStudios, a collective of digital artists and technologists, initiated a project titled 'Infinite Perspectives', which aimed to leverage MidJourney's AI technology to create dynamic, responsive art installations in public spaces. The project's conception began with the intent to explore the intersection of human perceptions and machine-generated aesthetics, creating a series of installations that not only displayed visual art but reacted and evolved according to audience interactions.

In the initial phase, AIStudios set up multiple installations in various high-traffic locations, such as urban centers and art galleries. These installations incorporated sensors and input devices that captured the movements, sounds, and even emotional responses of the viewers, which were then interpreted by MidJourney to modify the visual output in real-time. For example, one installation used facial recognition to adapt its color schemes to match the mood perceived from the viewers' expressions, while another transformed sounds from the environment into complex visual patterns projected onto large screens.

These installations not only captivated the public but also drew the interest of art critics and technology enthusiasts, garnishing praise for their innovative use of AI in creating adaptive, engaging art. However, the project faced several challenges, including technical issues with real-time data processing and concerns about privacy related to data collection methods used within the installations.

As the project advanced, AIStudios focused on refining their data handling processes to address privacy concerns, integrating advanced encryption and anonymization techniques to ensure viewer data was protected. They also enhanced the AI's processing capabilities by training it with broader data sets to improve the responsivity and aesthetic output of the installations. The continued evolution of 'Infinite Perspectives' has started to define a new genre of participatory art that effectively combines human interaction with AI creativity, proposing a transformative potential for public art experiences in urban landscapes.

Case Study: Leveraging MidJourney for Revolutionary Marketing Campaigns in Boutique Hotels

In a bid to stand out in a highly competitive market, SolEscape, a boutique hotel chain renowned for its unique architectural beauty and cultural relevance across several global cosmopolitan cities, employed the MidJourney artificial intelligence platform to transform its marketing strategies and guest experience enhancement. A fifteen-month project was implemented to synergize AI capabilities with human creativity to develop innovative, personalized marketing campaigns that resonated with diverse customer demographics.

The initial phase involved a detailed audit of SolEscape's past marketing strategies and customer feedback to pinpoint areas that could benefit significantly from AI integration. The MidJourney platform was used to analyze historical data and generate visually captivating and culturally relevant marketing materials. For example, AI-generated images showcased hypothetical guest experiences like the serene morning views from a balcony in their Paris location or a vibrant evening at their rooftop bar in Tokyo. These visuals were not just attractive; they were strategically designed to evoke emotional responses tailored to the interests observed in customer data patterns.

Following the deployment of these AI-enhanced campaigns, there was a notable increase in engagement on SolEscape's digital platforms. Unique features of the campaigns included AI-generated virtual tours that allowed potential guests to experience the ambiance of SolEscape locations interactively and dynamically, highly appreciated during the travel restrictions caused by the global pandemic.

However, integrating AI into marketing required careful management. The transition involved continuous training sessions for the marketing team, focusing on maintaining a balance between AI's efficiency and the human touch that underscores brand ethos. Regular analytical sessions were held to assess the effectiveness of the campaigns, making iterative improvements based on real-time customer engagement metrics. This case exemplifies how incorporating MidJourney can bridge technology and creativity, fostering innovative marketing solutions that enhance business performance in the hospitality sector.

Case Study: Optimizing Fashion Design with MidJourney: The Revamp Collection by FashTech

FashTech, a progressive fashion brand known for its commitment to blending cutting-edge technology with high fashion, embarked on a pioneering project titled 'The Revamp Collection'. This initiative aimed to utilize MidJourney's AI capabilities to reshape how fashion designs are conceived, produced, and marketed, tapping into a tech-savvy consumer base. The project began by setting up a dedicated design lab equipped with the latest MidJourney software, facilitating seamless integration into the existing workflow of the design team.

The initial experimental phase involved the design team using MidJourney to transform abstract concepts and mood boards into detailed design sketches. These AI-generated sketches served as a preliminary blueprint which was further refined by human designers, thereby merging traditional fashion design techniques with innovative AI insights. This collaborative process not only sped up the design phase significantly but also introduced novel textile patterns and cutting-edge garment silhouettes that had not been seen in previous collections.

Moreover, the collection's marketing strategy was heavily built on the allure of AI-created designs. Utilizing social media platforms, FashTech launched a series of engaging behind-the-scenes content showcasing the journey of a design from concept through MidJourney collaboration to final production. This transparency and narrative storytelling captivated the interest of a global audience, turning the collection launch into a highly anticipated event across fashion capitals.

The release of 'The Revamp Collection' marked a significant uplift in sales and attracted partnerships with high-profile tech firms interested in exploring the convergence of fashion and technology. However, challenges were also evident, particularly in preserving the brand's signature style amidst the dominance of AI suggestions. To address this, FashTech established a protocol where senior designers provided critical feedback on AI-generated designs to ensure that all outputs aligned closely with the brand's aesthetic values. This dynamic between AI-generated options and human oversight became a hallmark of the project, highlighting the potential of AI tools like MidJourney in revolutionizing fashion design workflows.

REVIEW QUESTIONS

1. Jessica, a freelance digital artist, is excited about integrating MidJourney into her artistic workflow. She primarily wants to create unique artworks with a blend of surreal and hyper-realistic elements to sell on online marketplaces. Given her needs, which MidJourney configuration would best serve her project?

A) Using generic prompts to generate quick and basic designs.

B) Utilizing precise, descriptive prompts to refine artistic outputs and explore various styles.

C) Limiting usage to pre-set styles to maintain a consistent theme.

D) Focusing exclusively on hyper-realistic visuals to appeal to a specific audience segment.

Answer: B

Explanation: For Jessica, the best approach would be to utilize precise, descriptive prompts. MidJourney's capability to interpret detailed prompts allows artists to create more tailored and nuanced artworks, which can include the mix of surreal and hyper-realistic elements she desires. This method provides flexibility and a high degree of customization in art creation, enabling her to explore multiple artistic interpretations and refine outcomes. By doing so, she can generate creations that are not only unique but also aligned with her vision, potentially increasing her artwork's appeal in online marketplaces.

2. As a commercial graphic design firm looking to incorporate MidJourney into its services, what is the primary benefit the platform provides, especially when dealing with high-volume client projects?

A) Reduction in design complexity and detail.

B) Increased manual input for precise control.

C) Rapid generation of multiple design variations.

D) Sole reliance on AI suggestions without human oversight.

Answer: C

Explanation: The primary benefit MidJourney offers to a commercial graphic design firm is the rapid generation of multiple design variations. This capability is crucial in a professional setting where time constraints and client demands for variety and innovation are high. MidJourney's AI algorithms can quickly produce diverse and intricate visuals, allowing the firm to present numerous options to clients swiftly, facilitating faster revisions and approvals. This efficiency can significantly enhance productivity and client satisfaction by meeting the fast-paced demands of the commercial art sector.

REVIEW QUESTIONS

3. A digital art teacher is integrating MidJourney into her curriculum to help students explore AI-driven art creation. What should be her focus when designing assignments to maximize educational value?

A) Emphasizing the use of simple, one-word prompts to encourage ease of use.

B) Focusing exclusively on generating realistic artworks to improve technical skills.

C) Encouraging the exploration of diverse prompts and styles to foster creativity and problem-solving.

D) Restricting the use of AI tools to ensure students rely solely on traditional methods.

Answer: C

Explanation: In an educational setting, the focus should be on encouraging the exploration of diverse prompts and styles, as suggested in option C. This approach allows students to engage creatively and critically with the AI tool, fostering both technical and conceptual skills. By experimenting with different prompts, students can see how variations in input affect the artistic output, which is crucial for understanding AI's capabilities and limitations. Such activities encourage creative problem-solving and innovative thinking, essential skills in both traditional and digital art disciplines.

4. An artist is exploring the use of MidJourney to develop a distinctive brand identity using AI-generated visuals. What is the most effective way for them to use MidJourney to achieve a unique and cohesive brand aesthetic?

A) Randomly generating images to see what might fit the brand's style.

B) Using highly specific prompts that align with the brand's values and aesthetic goals.

C) Adopting common templates and modifying them slightly for a quick solution.

D) Focusing only on color adjustments to existing AI-generated artworks.

Answer: B

Explanation: To develop a distinctive brand identity with a cohesive aesthetic using MidJourney, the artist should use highly specific prompts that align with the brand's values and aesthetic goals, as described in option B. This strategy ensures that the AI-generated visuals are not only unique but also resonate deeply with the brand's core identity. By directing the AI with detailed prompts, the artist can influence the output to reflect specific thematic and stylistic elements, making the visuals a true representation of the brand. This approach avoids the generic appearance that can come from less customized AI-generated art, thereby enhancing the brand's distinctiveness in the market.

JASPER AI: MASTERING AUTOMATED MARKETING STRATEGIES

Introduction to Jasper AI and Its Role in Marketing Automation

Jasper AI emerges as a pivotal tool in the era of digital marketing, transforming traditional strategies into streamlined, intelligent processes. As businesses vie for a significant digital footprint, Jasper AI stands as a beacon of innovation in marketing automation, providing customized solutions that enhance engagement and conversion rates.

At its core, Jasper AI leverages machine learning algorithms to create, test, and refine marketing content across various platforms. Its ability to analyze vast amounts of data and predict consumer behavior makes it invaluable for crafting targeted advertising campaigns, optimizing social media interactions, and personalizing email communications. These capabilities not only save time but also increase the efficacy of marketing efforts.

Furthermore, Jasper's integration into existing marketing ecosystems allows for a seamless transition from human-driven to AI-enhanced marketing strategies. By automating repetitive tasks, Jasper frees up creative and strategic resources, enabling marketers to focus on innovation and growth. The shift towards Jasper AI-powered marketing automation heralds a new age of efficiency and effectiveness in reaching and engaging audiences.

Setting Up Your Jasper AI Account for Maximum Efficiency

To harness the full potential of Jasper AI in automating your marketing strategies, setting up your account meticulously is crucial. Begin by personalizing your Jasper AI dashboard to reflect your specific marketing objectives. This involves configuring settings that prioritize your most frequent tasks, such as ad creation or social media content planning, ensuring these tools are readily accessible.

Next, integrate Jasper AI with other tools and platforms you regularly use, such as CRM systems or email marketing software. This integration streamlines your workflow, allowing Jasper to seamlessly draw data for content customization and lead nurturing. Establish clear goals within Jasper to guide its AI algorithms, tailoring content and recommendations that resonate with your target audience more effectively.

Finally, continually update the input you provide to Jasper based on marketing results and feedback. This refinement helps the AI adapt and optimize your campaigns, leading to higher conversion rates and more efficient use of your marketing budget. By setting up your Jasper AI account effectively, you position your marketing strategies on a trajectory toward unparalleled efficiency and success.

Developing High-Converting Ad Campaigns with Jasper

Harnessing Jasper AI's robust capabilities, marketers can architect high-converting ad campaigns with unprecedented precision and effectiveness. Jasper's algorithm dives deep into market trends and consumer behavior analytics, enabling the creation of ads that resonate deeply with targeted demographics. By drawing upon this rich data, Jasper crafts personalized messaging that appeals to specific interests and needs, substantially boosting conversion rates.

The process begins by selecting the ideal consumer profiles from Jasper's expansive database, followed by tailoring the ad's content to align perfectly with the audience's preferences. This technique ensures that each campaign speaks directly to its intended audience, making the ads not only relevant but also compelling. Additionally, Jasper's continuous learning mechanism refines ad strategies based on real-time feedback, optimizing campaigns to perform even better.

Moreover, integrating Jasper AI into your ad development process allows for seamless A/B testing of different ad elements. Marketers can iterate quickly, finding the optimal combination of headlines, images, and call-to-actions that drive the highest engagement. Through these strategic applications of Jasper AI, businesses are equipped to launch ad campaigns that are not only high-performing but also cost-efficient, maximizing ROI and scaling success in competitive markets.

Utilizing Jasper for Social Media Content Strategy

In the dynamic realm of social media, Jasper AI emerges as a revolutionary tool in crafting and executing content strategies that engage and expand audiences. By integrating Jasper, marketers can automate the creation of tailored content that resonates with diverse user bases across platforms like Instagram, Twitter, and Facebook.

Jasper's AI algorithms analyze current trends and audience behaviors to suggest content types and posting schedules that maximize engagement. This includes the generation of catchy headlines, captivating posts, and timely responses in discussions, which are crucial for maintaining a vibrant social media presence. Furthermore, Jasper facilitates A/B testing on different content strategies, providing valuable insights that help refine approaches for better results.

Moreover, Jasper's capability to adapt content for various social media platforms while maintaining a consistent brand voice is indispensable. By automating routine tasks, Jasper allows marketers to focus on creative and strategic initiatives, ensuring that their social media channels thrive in a competitive digital landscape. Jasper not only streamlines workflow but also enhances the effectiveness of social media campaigns, proving to be a crucial asset in any marketer's toolkit.

Email Marketing: Crafting Campaigns with Jasper AI

In the fast-evolving domain of email marketing, Jasper AI stands as a transformative force, ingeniously crafting campaigns that capture attention and drive conversions. By integrating Jasper AI, marketers gain access to a tool that not only automates content creation but also ensures that each email is optimized for audience engagement. Jasper's capability to analyze user data and previous interactions enables the crafting of personalized messages that speak directly to the needs and interests of each recipient.

From subject lines that pique curiosity to body texts that resonate and compel action, Jasper

AI harmonizes all elements to enhance the effectiveness of email campaigns. This integration allows for the seamless automation of A/B testing, where different aspects of emails are tested against one another to identify the most potent formulations.

Moreover, Jasper's continual learning from campaign performance feedback keeps strategies fresh and increasingly effective. Embracing Jasper AI in email marketing not only streamlines operations but also bolsters return on investment, establishing a new standard in digital communication strategies.

SEO Content Creation with Jasper: Strategies and Tips

In the evolving landscape of digital marketing, SEO remains a cornerstone for visibility and engagement. Jasper AI revolutionizes this area by deploying advanced machine learning to streamline SEO content creation. Utilizing Jasper's capacity for linguistic and semantic analysis, marketers can produce content finely tuned to current SEO standards, enhancing organic search rankings.

Key to this process is Jasper's ability to generate keyword-optimized headings and descriptions that are both compelling and compliant with SEO best practices. By integrating with SEO analytics tools, Jasper enables real-time adjustments of content to align with dynamic search trends and algorithm updates. This responsiveness ensures sustained SEO effectiveness despite the fast-paced changes in search engine protocols.

Moreover, Jasper's facility for analyzing top-performing content across the internet offers invaluable insights into competitive strategies. This guides the creation of content not only designed to rank but also to resonate deeply with target audiences, thereby amplifying reach and engagement.

Strategically, employing Jasper AI allows marketers to maintain a proactive stance in their SEO endeavors, ensuring they leverage every opportunity to amplify their online presence.

Generating and Nurturing Leads Using Jasper AI

In the competitive world of digital marketing, efficiently generating and nurturing leads is a linchpin of success, and Jasper AI stands as a formidable tool in this arena. Jasper specializes in creating personalized interaction strategies that appeal to potential customers at various stages of the sales funnel, facilitating enhanced lead engagement and conversion.

By utilizing Jasper's sophisticated data analysis capabilities, marketers can identify and segment audiences based on behavior, interest, and demographic data. This facilitates the crafting of targeted messages that are more likely to resonate and drive action. Jasper's AI-driven insights also enable the prediction of future customer behaviors, allowing for preemptive adjustments to marketing tactics.

Moreover, Jasper AI automates follow-up processes, ensuring that leads are nurtured consistently and effectively. This includes scheduling reminders for follow-up emails or content, tailored to increase relevance and engagement. The integration of Jasper thus ensures a seamless, efficient lead management system that not only captures but also retains customer interest, fostering long-term business growth.

Creating Compelling Landing Pages with Jasper

Jasper AI transforms the creation of landing pages from a manual, labor-intensive process to a streamlined, automated task. Leveraging Jasper's ability to analyze user data and engagement metrics, marketers can design landing pages that are not only visually appealing but also highly effective in converting visitors. Through Jasper's integration, every element, from headline to call-to-action, is optimized based on real-time data, ensuring high relevance and conversion potential.

Furthermore, Jasper AI aids in testing various versions of a landing page through A/B testing features, which automatically generate and test different layouts, content, and graphical elements to determine the most effective combinations. This continual learning loop substantially reduces the time and resources typically required for page optimization.

Lastly, Jasper's AI-driven insights extend to the creation of dynamic content tailored to individual user behaviors, making each visitor experience customized and more likely to lead to conversion. Using Jasper AI, landing pages become powerful tools in a marketer's arsenal, perfectly aligned with both business goals and user expectations.

Using Jasper AI to Enhance Blogging Efforts

In the expansive world of digital content, blogging remains a pivotal platform for brand storytelling and audience engagement. Jasper AI is transforming how bloggers create, manage, and optimize content, streamlining the entire process with remarkable efficiency. By integrating Jasper, writers can generate ideas, draft posts, and refine narratives, ensuring each piece is both SEO-friendly and compelling to readers.

Jasper's advanced algorithms assist in researching and assimilating current trends and user preferences, which informs the creation of targeted content that resonates with intended audiences. This AI-driven approach not only speeds up the production cycle but also enhances the relevance and appeal of blog posts. Furthermore, Jasper provides automated suggestions for improving readability and engagement, such as adjusting tone or structure based on the audience's feedback and behaviors.

Moreover, Jasper can schedule posts for optimal times, analyze performance, and even suggest content updates to keep blogs fresh and engaging. By employing Jasper AI, bloggers can focus more on creative expression and less on the mechanics of content management, fostering a more dynamic and effective blogging strategy.

Integrating Jasper AI with CRM Systems

The integration of Jasper AI with CRM systems marks a transformative step in customer relationship management. By syncing Jasper AI's capabilities with CRM platforms, businesses can automate and refine their customer interactions, ensuring a personalized and efficient experience. This synergy allows for the real-time updating of customer data, which Jasper AI can then leverage to provide insights and automated actions tailored to each customer's behavior and preferences.

Jasper's AI-driven analytics enhance decision-making by predicting customer needs and potential churn, empowering businesses to proactively engage and retain clients. The automation of routine tasks like data entry and follow-up scheduling frees up staff to focus on more complex customer interactions, increasing overall productivity and satisfaction.

Moreover, the combined power of Jasper AI and CRM systems simplifies the segmentation of customer bases, facilitating targeted marketing campaigns that are more likely to resonate and convert. This strategic alignment between advanced AI technology and traditional CRM functions cultivates a competitive edge, fostering enhanced business growth and a superior customer journey.

Personalization at Scale: Jasper AI in E-commerce

In the realm of e-commerce, personalization is pivotal for capturing consumer interest and boosting sales. Jasper AI revolutionizes this domain by enabling personalization at an unprecedented scale. Leveraging machine learning algorithms, Jasper AI analyzes customer data to tailor product recommendations and marketing messages uniquely suited to individual preferences.

Jasper's capabilities extend beyond mere suggestions to include dynamic content adaptation on websites and in emails, ensuring that every interaction is personalized. This intelligent customization increases engagement by making every customer feel uniquely valued, driving loyalty and repeat business. Additionally, Jasper AI's predictive analytics forecast future buying tendencies, allowing e-commerce platforms to evolve proactively with consumer trends.

The integration of Jasper AI facilitates an automated yet intimate customer journey. By harnessing detailed insights from vast data sets, Jasper ensures that e-commerce strategies are not only responsive but also ahead of consumer expectations. This strategic use of AI fortifies brand positioning and accelerates revenue growth.

Automating Customer Support Responses with Jasper

In the fast-paced realm of customer service, Jasper AI introduces a significant advancement by automating responses, revolutionizing the efficiency and quality of support. Employing Jasper AI in customer interactions ensures immediate, consistent, and intelligent responses to inquiries and issues, enhancing customer satisfaction and reducing the workload on human agents.

Jasper's capabilities in analyzing incoming queries and generating appropriate responses are pivotal. It can address common questions, resolve standard issues, and escalate complex cases to human representatives, ensuring a seamless flow of communication. This dual-level approach optimizes resource allocation and maintains high service standards.

Furthermore, Jasper AI continually learns from interactions to refine its response algorithms, ensuring an evolving system that adapts to changing customer needs and preferences. The integration of this AI into customer support not only boosts operational efficiency but also fosters loyalty by providing timely and relevant support, making Jasper AI an indispensable tool for modern customer service strategies.

Advanced Content Generation: Using Jasper for Whitepapers

Whitepapers serve as authoritative guides in various industries, providing in-depth insights on complex topics. Jasper AI revolutionizes whitepaper creation by facilitating research, structuring detailed documents, and generating content that captivates and educates target audiences effectively.

By integrating Jasper AI, organizations can automate the tedious parts of the content development process, such as data collection and analysis. This allows the focus to shift to refining the narrative and enhancing argumentative strength, vital in whitepaper writing. Jasper's machine learning models ensure that the content adheres to industry standards and recent developments, thereby increasing the whitepaper's credibility and impact.

Moreover, Jasper enables quick updates to whitepapers in response to new data or evolving industry trends. This continual update process, powered by AI, ensures that all published materials remain relevant and useful. Jasper's dynamic capabilities in advanced content generation transform whitepaper production into a more efficient and impactful task.

Jasper AI for Product Descriptions and Listings

The digital marketplace thrives on precision and allure in product representations, where Jasper AI emerges as a crucial tool for creating impactful product descriptions and listings. By leveraging Jasper's advanced language models, businesses can generate descriptive narratives that not only highlight key features but also engage potential customers through compelling storytelling.

Jasper's AI-driven approach tailors descriptions to match the search intent and consumer preferences, enhancing SEO and elevating product visibility online. This tailored content significantly boosts the conversion rates, as potential buyers are presented with tailored, persuasive descriptions that resonate with their specific needs and desires.

Furthermore, Jasper automates the repetitive task of listing updates, ensuring all information is current without constant manual intervention. This efficiency allows businesses to maintain accurate and attractive listings that are essential for e-commerce success. By incorporating Jasper AI, companies ensure their product communications are not only rich in detail but also optimized for sales performance.

Harnessing Jasper for Automated Video Scriptwriting

Harnessing the power of Jasper AI for automated video scriptwriting opens a new frontier in marketing strategy. This innovative application transforms how brands create engaging video content, pivotal in today's visually-driven market. By utilizing Jasper, marketers can produce scripts that are not only creative but also aligned with brand messaging and SEO strategies, ensuring content that captivates as well as performs.

The process begins with Jasper analyzing existing data and trends to generate scripts that resonate with targeted audiences. This data-driven approach ensures relevance and appeal, vital for video engagement. Furthermore, Jasper's capability to iterate quickly enables marketers to test different script variations, optimizing for the best audience response.

Moreover, Jasper's integration with video production tools streamlines the script-to-screen process, significantly reducing the time and effort required for video content creation. This efficiency not only accelerates content deployment but also enhances the ability to scale video marketing efforts without compromising quality.

Analyzing Marketing Data with Jasper AI Assistance

In the intricate world of marketing strategy, effective data analysis stands as a cornerstone for success. Jasper AI revolutionizes this essential function, transforming massive volumes of marketing data into actionable insights. This AI-driven analysis not only speeds up data processing but also enhances accuracy, enabling marketers to make informed decisions swiftly.

Jasper's prowess extends to identifying patterns and trends that might elude human analysts. By harnessing predictive analytics, Jasper forecasts market movements and customer behaviors, providing companies with a competitive edge by anticipating changes before they happen. This foresight allows for proactive strategy adjustments, optimizing marketing efforts for better performance.

Moreover, Jasper AI integrates seamlessly with existing marketing tools, ensuring that all data streams are analyzed comprehensively. This integration fosters a holistic view of marketing campaigns, from customer acquisition costs to ROI, facilitating a granular assessment of each initiative.

Utilizing Jasper AI for data analysis not only streamlines operations but also empowers marketers with a depth of insight previously unattainable, optimizing resource allocation and maximizing impact across marketing campaigns.

Jasper AI for Affiliate Marketing Enhancement

Jasper AI is transforming affiliate marketing, making it easier for marketers to optimize their strategies and enhance their earnings. By utilizing Jasper, affiliates can auto-generate personalized content for different products, targeting specific audiences with precision. This AI-driven customization goes beyond traditional methods, providing content that resonates with potential buyers and increases conversion rates.

Moreover, Jasper AI can analyze vast amounts of data from past campaigns to predict which products will perform best with certain demographics, enabling affiliates to focus their efforts more effectively. This predictive capability ensures that marketing efforts are not only strategic but also cost-efficient, maximizing ROI from affiliate campaigns.

The integration of Jasper AI into affiliate marketing also simplifies the tracking and reporting processes. Affiliates can receive real-time updates and insights, making it easier to adjust strategies promptly. Therefore, Jasper AI not only enhances the effectiveness of affiliate marketing but also makes managing and scaling affiliate efforts more feasible.

Push Notifications and SMS Messaging with Jasper

In the fast-paced world of digital marketing, Jasper AI emerges as a pivotal tool for crafting effective push notifications and SMS messages, essential components for real-time customer engagement. Utilizing Jasper's robust AI capabilities, marketers can automate the creation of concise, attention-grabbing notifications tailored to individual user behaviors and preferences. This personalization increases the relevance of messages, significantly boosting open rates and interactions.

Jasper AI's ability to analyze large data sets enables the precise timing of messages, ensuring that they reach customers when they are most likely to engage. This strategic scheduling optimizes the impact of campaigns across various platforms, from mobile phones to smart devices, enhancing the visibility and effectiveness of marketing messages.

Moreover, Jasper facilitates A/B testing for different message formats and contents, allowing marketers to continually refine their strategies based on real-time feedback and performance metrics. This iterative process streamlined by Jasper not only saves time but also maximizes ROI by honing in on the most effective communication techniques. Jasper's integration brings a level of sophistication to push notifications and SMS strategies, transforming them into powerful tools for driving engagement and sales.

Building a Content Calendar Using Jasper AI

Utilizing Jasper AI to construct a robust content calendar transforms the daunting task of content planning into a streamlined, efficient process. By leveraging Jasper's advanced AI capabilities, marketers can predict optimal posting times, themes, and content types that resonate with their audience. This predictive assistance ensures every piece of content is not only timely but also targeted and relevant.

Moreover, Jasper's integration capabilities allow for seamless synchronization with other digital marketing tools, enhancing workflow continuity. This connectivity ensures all team members are on the same page, with real-time updates and changes reflected across all platforms. This keeps campaigns cohesive and aligned with overall marketing objectives.

Lastly, the ability to scale and adapt content strategies swiftly with Jasper's AI insights supports dynamic marketing environments. Adjustments based on audience engagement and feedback can be made effortlessly, ensuring the content remains impactful and engaging. Jasper AI, therefore, not only aids in planning but also in maintaining a flexible, responsive content strategy.

Real-time Content Updates and Optimization with Jasper

In the dynamic landscape of digital marketing, the ability to update and optimize content in real-time is crucial for maintaining relevance and engagement. Jasper AI stands at the forefront of this technology, offering solutions that instantly refresh content based on the latest data and user interactions.

With Jasper, marketing teams can implement changes across multiple channels simultaneously, ensuring a consistent message that adapts to new trends or user feedback. This real-time capability is vital for campaigns that rely on time-sensitive information or trending topics, providing marketers with a tool that keeps their content fresh and relevant without manual oversight.

Moreover, Jasper's optimization algorithms analyze user engagement to suggest and even autonomously apply enhancements to content, from simple wording adjustments to major structural changes. This process not only saves valuable time but also enhances the effectiveness of marketing strategies, driving higher conversion rates and better user experiences.

Thus, Jasper AI redefines content dynamics, making it a pivotal tool in any marketer's arsenal, continually optimizing interactions in the ever-evolving digital space.

Using Jasper AI to Test and Optimize Marketing Copy

In the digital marketing sphere, the agility to test and refine marketing copy is pivotal for maximizing engagement and conversion rates. Jasper AI revolutionizes this process by enabling marketers to automate the testing of different variations of marketing copy swiftly and efficiently. This AI tool not only speeds up the iteration cycle but also uses advanced machine learning algorithms to predict which versions will perform best based on historical data and ongoing user interactions.

Utilizing Jasper AI, marketers can implement A/B testing at scale, enabling systematic fine-tuning of messaging, tone, and content structure to better align with target audience preferences. This approach ensures marketing messages are both compelling and effective. Jasper AI's analytic capabilities provide real-time feedback and actionable insights, crucial for optimizing copy in a continuous learning loop.

Furthermore, Jasper enhances the creative process by suggesting enhancements and alternate phrasing that maintains brand voice while increasing the overall impact of the copy. As a result, marketers can confidently deploy optimized content that captures attention and drives action, elevating the efficacy of their marketing strategies.

Community Engagement: Leveraging Jasper for Forum Posts

Community engagement is essential in nurturing brand loyalty and user interaction. Jasper AI streamlines this process within online forums, a vital area of digital marketing. By employing Jasper AI, businesses can generate insightful, relevant content that sparks conversation and drives participation.

Jasper's capabilities include crafting posts that resonate with specific community interests or trending topics, ensuring high engagement rates. Its analytics also play a crucial role, analyzing feedback to refine future posts, making each iteration more effective than the last. This continuous improvement cycle keeps the community vibrant and actively engaged.

Moreover, Jasper can automatically respond to common queries, maintaining active engagement even when human moderators are unavailable. Beyond responses, Jasper's integration allows for the personalization of interactions, making users feel valued and understood. This not only enhances user experience but also builds a strong, loyal community around a brand.

Podcast Scripts and Show Notes Creation with Jasper

The revolution of podcasting in digital marketing has found a powerful ally in Jasper AI, particularly in scripting and show notes creation. Jasper's seamless integration into this medium ensures that every episode is not only engaging but also strategically crafted to meet marketing goals. By analyzing prevailing podcast trends and listener preferences, Jasper AI devises scripts that resonate deeply with audiences, enhancing listener retention and engagement.

Moreover, Jasper simplifies the often intricate process of show notes creation. It meticulously extracts key points from scripts, converting them into detailed, SEO-friendly show notes that boost discoverability and accessibility. These notes provide listeners with a valuable resource, summarizing content and highlighting important links or products mentioned during the show.

Jasper's initiative doesn't stop at creation; it also offers continuous optimization based on listener feedback and engagement metrics. This ensures that podcast content remains impactful and dynamically evolves with audience preferences, keeping podcasts relevant and compelling in a competitive landscape.

Jasper AI in Event Marketing and Promotion

Jasper AI revolutionizes event marketing and promotion by automating and optimizing engagement strategies. It enables organizers to create personalized event notifications and promotional material that resonate with different audience segments. The integration of Jasper AI also ensures that all promotions are timed perfectly, aligning with user behaviors and peak interests.

In the dynamic environment of event marketing, Jasper's ability to analyze real-time data plays a crucial role. It adjusts promotional tactics based on current trends and audience feedback, ensuring that marketing efforts remain relevant and effective up to the event day. This responsiveness is key to maximizing attendance and engagement.

Moreover, Jasper AI enhances post-event follow-ups by crafting personalized thank-you emails and feedback surveys tailored to each attendee's experience. This not only boosts future engagement but also gathers vital insights for improving subsequent events.

Utilizing Jasper AI in event marketing assures a high level of personalization and efficiency, setting new standards for event promotion and attendee satisfaction.

Multilingual Marketing with Jasper AI

Harnessing the power of multilingual marketing is crucial in a globalized market, and Jasper AI proves instrumental in bridging linguistic divides. By leveraging advanced language processing capabilities, Jasper enables businesses to craft marketing messages tailored to diverse linguistic audiences at scale.

Jasper's AI-driven translations maintain the nuance and cultural relevance of original content, ensuring that messages resonate locally. This precision in language translation enhances customer trust and relationship-building across different regions. Businesses can thus seamlessly expand their reach and appeal to a broader audience without compromising the brand's voice or message integrity.

Moreover, the time and resources saved using Jasper's automated multilingual marketing tools allow teams to focus on strategy and creative development. This not only increases operational efficiency but also boosts the effectiveness of global campaigns, making Jasper AI an indispensable tool in any marketer's arsenal aiming for international success.

Jasper AI thus stands as a cornerstone in the foundation of effective multilingual marketing, enabling businesses to communicate authentically and compellingly worldwide.

Ethical Considerations in Automated Marketing with Jasper AI

While Jasper AI revolutionizes marketing with automation, it introduces significant ethical considerations that necessitate careful scrutiny. Primarily, the transparency of AI-generated content raises concerns. As Jasper crafts sophisticated marketing materials, distinguishing between human and AI-generated content becomes challenging, potentially misleading consumers about the origin of information.

Responsible use of Jasper also involves the conscientious handling of data privacy. The AI leverages vast amounts of personal data to personalize marketing efforts. Ensuring this data's confidentiality and using it ethically without exploiting consumer vulnerabilities is paramount. Misuse can lead to loss of consumer trust and potential legal ramifications.

Moreover, the omnipresence of Jasper AI in diverse marketing avenues must consider the fairness in AI decision-making processes. Biases in data or algorithms could result in unfair targeting or exclusion of certain demographics, reinforcing societal inequities. Systematically auditing and refining Jasper's algorithms for unbiased functionality is crucial for ethical marketing practices.

SUMMARY

The chapter delves into the transformative influence of Jasper AI within various facets of digital marketing, underlining its crucial role in automating and optimizing strategies across multiple channels. Initially, it spotlights Jasper AI's core functions in marketing automation, highlighting its use of machine learning algorithms to create, test, and refine marketing content. Jasper AI excels in analyzing extensive data and predicting consumer behavior, thereby enhancing engagement and conversion rates for tailored advertising campaigns, social media interactions, and personalized email communications. The seamless integration of Jasper into existing marketing ecosystems makes the transition from human-driven to AI-powered strategies both effective and efficient, optimizing resources and fostering innovation in marketing efforts. A detailed walk through is provided on setting up Jasper AI for maximum efficiency, recommending meticulous personalization of the Jasper AI dashboard to align with specific marketing goals, and stress on the importance of integrating the AI with other common tools such as CRM systems and email marketing software. Furthermore, it discusses the strategic deployment of Jasper AI in designing high-converting ad campaigns and sophisticated social media content strategies. The AI's capability to perform A/B testing and adapt content based on real-time feedback especially benefits the rapid iteration and optimization required in digital marketing. The discussion extends to the utilization of Jasper for enhancing SEO strategies and email marketing campaigns, portraying Jasper's ability to generate SEO-friendly content and crafting compelling email campaigns that resonate with recipients. Moreover, Jasper AI dramatically simplifies traditionally labor-intensive tasks like creating landing pages and blogging, providing dynamic tools that align with marketing goals and optimize user engagement. The chapter concludes by contemplating the ethical considerations necessary in the deployment of AI-driven marketing technologies, urging marketers to maintain transparency, uphold data privacy, and ensure fairness in AI-generated content to avoid consumer mistrust or legal challenges.

REFERENCES

[1] J. D. Kelleher, 'Deep Learning',. https://mitpress.mit.edu/books/deep-learning

[2] F. Chollet, 'Deep Learning with Python',. https://www.manning.com/books/deep-learning-with-python-second-edition

[3] R. S. Sutton and A. G. Barto, 'Reinforcement Learning: An Introduction',. https://webdocs.cs.ualberta.ca/~sutton/book/the-book.html

CASE STUDY: ENHANCING E-COMMERCE PERSONALIZATION WITH JASPER AI

A leading e-commerce brand, 'Fashion Forward', faced challenges in staying competitive despite a vast product range and a significant customer base. The primary obstacle was the ineffective personalization of product recommendations and marketing messages, which led to lower-than-expected conversion rates and customer engagement levels. Recognizing these issues, 'Fashion Forward' decided to integrate Jasper AI into their existing systems to enhance their e-commerce personalization efforts.

Initially, the integration focused on leveraging Jasper AI's machine learning capabilities to analyze customer data effectively. By examining previous purchase histories, browsing behaviors, and customer interactions, Jasper AI was able to create highly tailored product recommendations for each user. This level of customization was aimed at making customers feel uniquely understood, thereby increasing the chances of conversion from mere browsing to actual purchases.

Moreover, 'Fashion Forward' utilized Jasper AI to dynamically adapt the content displayed on their website and in their email marketing campaigns. This ensured that all interactions were highly relevant and engaging, based on real-time data. For instance, if a user spent time browsing outdoor wear, Jasper AI would then prioritize similar products and related offers in subsequent interactions.

To test the effectiveness of Jasper AI's integration, 'Fashion Forward' conducted A/B testing where they compared the performance metrics such as click-through rates and purchase ratios between segments exposed to AI-enhanced personalization and those that were not. The results were staggering. The segment that experienced Jasper AI personalization showed a 40% improvement in engagement and a 25% increase in sales compared to the control group.

This deployment illustrated not only the capabilities of Jasper AI in refining personalization at scale but also underscored the strategic importance of advanced AI tools in decoding complex consumer behaviors. 'Fashion Forward's successful integration of Jasper AI set a precedent in the e-commerce sector, prompting many to revisit their strategies towards leveraging AI for enhanced customer experiences.

Case Study: Optimizing Blog Content Strategy with Jasper AI

In the competitive landscape of digital marketing, 'TechTrends', a prominent technology blogging platform, faced the challenge of maintaining its market dominance amid changing search engine algorithms and consumer preferences. Despite possessing a massive repository of tech-related content, the engagement on their platform had stagnated, and the growth of subscriber base slowed down, highlighting a need for strategic content optimization and rejuvenation.

Recognizing the potential of AI in enhancing content strategies, 'TechTrends' decided to integrate Jasper AI into their content creation and management processes. The initial implementation phase focused on using Jasper's advanced machine learning algorithms to analyze existing content performance and user engagement metrics. This analysis helped in identifying underperforming areas and topics that resonated well with their audience but needed updating or expansion.

To address these insights, Jasper AI was tasked with generating content suggestions and optimizing existing articles to align with current SEO best practices. The AI tool rewrote outdated sections, suggested engaging and search-optimized titles, and even recommended content structuring changes that improved readability and user engagement. Furthermore, Jasper facilitated the creation of a dynamic content calendar that strategically timed the publication of articles based on trending topics and predicted audience online presence.

An integral part of this strategic overhaul was A/B testing implemented through Jasper, where various versions of content changes were tested live to gauge audience reaction and engagement improvement. These tests were crucial in fine-tuning the nuances of the blog's content strategy, allowing 'TechTrends' to adapt quickly and effectively.

The results of integrating Jasper AI were transformative. Within six months, 'TechTrends' saw a 35% increase in user engagement and a 50% growth in organically acquired subscribers. The platform was not only able to regain its leading position but also set new standards in personalized user engagement and content relevancy, showcasing the critical role of AI in digital content optimization.

Case Study: Revolutionizing Affiliate Marketing with Jasper AI

In the rapidly evolving digital marketing industry, 'Global Outreach', a prominent affiliate marketing firm, was struggling to keep pace with the demands of managing a vast network of affiliate content across multiple platforms and languages. The primary challenge was the creation of high-performing affiliate marketing content that could adapt to the nuances of diverse markets without diluting the effectiveness of the marketing messages. To overcome these challenges, 'Global Outreach' decided to leverage Jasper AI's sophisticated machine learning algorithms and natural language processing capabilities.

The initial implementation phase involved integrating Jasper AI with 'Global Outreach's' existing content management systems. Jasper AI's role was to automate the generation and optimization of affiliate marketing content, ensuring that each piece was linguistically and culturally adapted to its intended audience. This automation was critical in scaling up operations, which had previously been bottlenecked by the manual effort required to craft nuanced content for different market segments.

Furthermore, 'Global Outreach' utilized Jasper AI's predictive analytics features to align its marketing strategies with real-time market trends and consumer behavior insights. Jasper AI analyzed data from numerous campaigns to identify which content versions performed best and iterated on these findings to continuously improve the relevance and performance of the affiliate content.

To gauge the success of this integration, 'Global Outreach' undertook comprehensive A/B testing, comparing the performance of Jasper AI-generated content against traditional manually created content. The results were remarkable: campaigns driven by Jasper's AI-powered content saw a 50% increase in engagement rates and a 30% higher conversion rate compared to conventional methods.

This case study illustrates the transformational impact of integrating AI tools like Jasper in reshaping affiliate marketing strategies. By automating content generation and leveraging data-driven insights, 'Global Outreach' was able to enhance operational efficiency, improve content relevance, and significantly boost campaign performance, thereby affirming the strategic value of AI in modern marketing practices.

Case Study: Streamlining Real-Time Customer Engagement with Jasper AI

In today's digital marketing era, 'QuickConnect', a leading telecommunications company, faced escalating challenges in managing real-time customer interactions across various digital platforms. The company sought to maintain high customer engagement and quickly resolve queries to enhance customer satisfaction rates. To achieve these objectives, QuickConnect decided to integrate Jasper AI into their customer engagement platforms, harnessing its capabilities to automate and optimize real-time communications.

Initially, QuickConnect applied Jasper AI to analyze customer interaction data across social media, email, and live chat services. The AI system was trained to understand queries, provide instant responses, and escalate complex issues to human agents efficiently. This was pivotal in reducing response times and increasing the accuracy of the responses, thereby improving the overall customer experience.

Moreover, Jasper AI was employed to personalize communication. By analyzing individual customer behavior and preferences, Jasper AI generated customized responses and recommendations, making interactions more relevant and personal. For instance, if a customer frequently inquired about data plans, Jasper AI would automatically offer detailed information on the latest offers in their subsequent interactions.

To validate the effectiveness of Jasper AI's integration, QuickConnect conducted a series of A/B tests comparing customer satisfaction and resolution times between interactions handled by Jasper AI and those managed manually. The findings revealed that Jasper AI-enhanced interactions led to a 50% reduction in resolution time and a 40% improvement in customer satisfaction scores.

This case study exemplifies how integrating advanced AI tools like Jasper can revolutionize real-time customer engagement. By leveraging machine learning to understand and predict customer needs, QuickConnect was able to deliver superior customer service, highlighting the critical role of AI in enhancing real-time digital interactions and setting a benchmark in the telecommunications industry.

Case Study: Revitalizing Video Marketing Strategies with Jasper AI

In the competitive landscape of digital marketing, where video content has become a cornerstone for engagement, a leading lifestyle brand, 'LifeSavvy', faced challenges in maintaining viewer interest and converting views into tangible business outcomes. Despite producing high-quality videos, the engagement rates were inconsistent, and the conversion rates were below industry standards. To address these challenges, 'LifeSavvy' decided to integrate Jasper AI into their video marketing strategy, aiming to revitalize their content and optimize audience engagement.

The initial phase involved leveraging Jasper AI's capabilities to analyze historical viewer data and engagement metrics. This analysis enabled the identification of patterns and preferences among the audience, which were previously unnoticed. Based on these insights, Jasper AI assisted in scripting video content that was tailored to viewer interests, increasing relevance and potential engagement. Additionally, Jasper's machine learning algorithms suggested optimal posting times and predictively analyzed which types of videos would perform well on different social media platforms.

Furthermore, 'LifeSavvy' utilized Jasper AI to facilitate A/B testing of video content variations, including differences in video thumbnails, intros, and call-to-actions. This rigorous testing allowed for the fine-tuning of elements that significantly impact viewer engagement and conversion rates. Jasper AI not only automated the creation of variant content but also provided real-time performance analysis, enabling quick strategic pivots.

The implementation of Jasper AI turned out to be transformative. 'LifeSavvy' experienced a 45% increase in viewer engagement and a 30% rise in conversion rates from their video marketing campaigns. These outcomes demonstrated the pronounced influence that tailored and optimized video content, powered by AI analytics and testing, could have on marketing success.

This case illustrates the profound impact that Jasper AI can have on digital marketing strategies, specifically in enhancing video content creation and distribution. By harnessing AI-driven insights and automation, 'LifeSavvy' not only enhanced their brand's digital presence but set a new benchmark for effective video marketing campaigns.

Case Study: Revamping a Publisher's Content Strategy Using Jasper AI

BrightPath Publishers, a mid-sized publishing house known for its educational materials, confronted stagnating sales and dwindling reader engagement. The company recognized that its traditional approach to content generation and marketing was not aligning with the modern consumption habits of its audience, particularly in the rapidly evolving digital space. To address this, BrightPath decided to integrate Jasper AI into their content development and marketing strategies.

The initial phase of integrating Jasper AI focused on analyzing existing content performance and reader engagement patterns. Jasper's advanced data-processing capabilities enabled BrightPath to identify key themes and topics that resonated with their target demographic but were underrepresented in their publications. Furthermore, Jasper AI mapped out the times when readers were most actively engaging with the content, providing invaluable insights for optimal posting schedules.

Armed with this data, BrightPath used Jasper to restructure their content calendar and prioritize the development of digital media. Jasper AI was instrumental in generating topic suggestions, drafting outlines, and even producing preliminary content drafts. By automating these initial steps, Jasper AI significantly cut down the content production timeline, allowing BrightPath to respond quickly to emerging trends and reader interests.

Moreover, BrightPath leveraged Jasper AI's A/B testing capabilities to refine headlines, subheadings, and key messaging within their articles. This was crucial in optimizing article layouts and formats based on real-time reader responses. The agility provided by Jasper AI in content testing and optimization proved essential in enhancing the relevance and appeal of the publications.

The impact of Jasper AI on BrightPath Publishers was profound. Within a year of implementation, the company saw a 50% increase in reader engagement and a 30% rise in web traffic, which directly contributed to a 20% increase in sales. The partnership with Jasper AI has not only modernized BrightPath's content strategies but also transformed them into a data-driven publisher with a competitive edge in the educational market.

Case Study: Transforming Customer Support with Jasper AI

In the competitive landscape of digital retail, 'QuickBuy', a rising e-commerce platform, faced a crucial challenge in scaling their customer support without compromising on quality or response times. The rapid growth in customer base and product listings significantly increased the volume of daily customer inquiries, ranging from product details to order status and return policies. This surge overwhelmed their traditional, human-based customer service team, resulting in delayed responses and dipping customer satisfaction scores.

Recognizing the need for an efficient, scalable solution, 'QuickBuy' decided to integrate Jasper AI into their customer support framework. The initial deployment phase focused on harnessing Jasper AI's natural language processing (NLP) capabilities to manage and respond to customer queries instantly. By setting up Jasper to handle routine inquiries, 'QuickBuy' was able to free up human agents to focus on more complex, sensitive cases that required a personal touch.

The integration process involved comprehensive training of the Jasper AI system with thousands of real customer interaction logs to ensure that the AI could understand and respond accurately to customer needs. Jasper AI was also configured to escalate issues it couldn't resolve autonomously to human agents seamlessly. This hybrid model aimed to combine the efficiency of AI with the nuanced understanding of human agents.

To assess the effectiveness of Jasper AI integration, 'QuickBuy' conducted a phased rollout and monitored several performance metrics, including response time, issue resolution rate, and customer satisfaction scores. The results were compelling. There was a 75% reduction in average response time, and human agents reported a 40% decrease in load, allowing them to engage more meaningfully with customers requiring detailed assistance.

This case study illustrates the transformative impact of integrating AI like Jasper into customer support operations. By effectively automating routine tasks and triaging complex issues to human staff, Jasper AI enabled 'QuickBuy' to maintain high customer service standards while managing growth efficiently. This strategic use of technology not only boosted operational efficiency but also enhanced overall customer satisfaction, demonstrating a significant evolution in modern e-commerce customer service management.

Case Study: Revitalizing Small Business Marketing with Jasper AI

Navigating the challenging waters of small business marketing, 'LocalGems', a boutique chain specializing in handcrafted goods, was struggling to expand its digital presence and engage effectively with a broader audience. Despite being well-loved in its local communities, 'LocalGems' had not managed to translate this popularity into the online realm effectively, hampered by tight budgets and limited marketing expertise.

Their turning point came with the integration of Jasper AI into their marketing operations. The main goal was to harness the AI's capabilities to automate content generation and streamline engagement strategies across multiple digital platforms without incurring substantial additional costs. Initially, Jasper AI was tasked with revamping their social media content strategy. Utilizing its machine learning algorithms, Jasper analyzed customer interactions, preferences, and engagement trends to produce tailored content schedules, suggesting optimal posting times and content forms that resonated with both existing and potential customers.

Moreover, Jasper AI assisted 'LocalGems' in crafting promotional email campaigns that were significantly more personalized and timely. By analyzing customer purchase history and web activity, Jasper was able to segment the customer base into distinct groups with similar interests and shopping patterns, facilitating highly targeted communications that boosted open rates and conversions.

The impact of integrating Jasper AI was measured through a series of metrics, including web traffic, social media engagement, email click-through rates, and ultimately, sales performance. Over a six-month period, 'LocalGems' observed a 30% increase in social media activity, a double-digit growth in email marketing efficiency, and an overall sales increase of 20%. These figures were not only reflective of Jasper AI's ability to fine-tune marketing efforts but also illustrated how AI technologies could be democratized to benefit smaller businesses in highly competitive sectors.

This case study is a testament to the profound impact that tailored and automated AI solutions can have on marketing strategies, especially for small businesses that might otherwise struggle to compete in the digital marketplace.

REVIEW QUESTIONS

1. A marketing strategist at a mid-sized tech company is reevaluating their digital marketing infrastructure to incorporate AI tools for better engagement and conversion rates. They are considering using Jasper AI owing to its adaptive machine learning algorithms and seamless ecosystem integration capabilities. Which of the following would be the most crucial aspect to setup first for maximum efficiency?

A) Focusing on real-time data-driven adjustments of email campaigns

B) Personalizing the dashboard to reflect specific marketing objectives

C) Prioritizing Jasper's integration with social media platforms only

D) Directing all resources to automate customer support responses

Answer: B

Explanation: Setting up the Jasper AI dashboard to reflect specific marketing objectives is fundamental. This initial step allows for the prioritization of tasks and seamless access to tools like ad creation and social media planning which are central to automated marketing. Such customization directly aligns tool functionality with strategic goals, enhancing overall efficiency and effectiveness of marketing campaigns.

2. A digital marketing firm is aiming to enhance their ad campaign's conversion rates by using Jasper AI. They need to craft highly targeted ads that capitalize on Jasper's data analysis of market trends and consumer behavior. What should be their first step in utilizing Jasper AI to achieve this?

A) Configuring Jasper to only focus on demographic data

B) Developing generic content to appeal to a broad audience

C) Selecting ideal consumer profiles from Jasper's database for targeted content

D) Limiting the ad testing only to call-to-actions

Answer: C

Explanation: The first step should be selecting ideal consumer profiles from Jasper's expansive database. This targeted approach ensures that the advertisements are crafted precisely for the audience's preferences, enhancing relevance and engagement - key drivers for increasing conversion rates. Personalized messaging stemming from comprehensive profile insights leads to campaigns that resonate more effectively with intended audiences.

REVIEW QUESTIONS

3. In the context of enhancing social media engagement for an e-commerce brand using Jasper AI, which method would optimize content strategy on platforms like Instagram and Twitter?

A) Automating all content generation without any manual oversight

B) Utilizing Jasper's analytics to suggest content types and posting schedules

C) Exclusively focusing on generating promotional content

D) Ignoring trend analysis to maintain a consistent posting schedule

Answer: B

Explanation: Utilizing Jasper's AI algorithms to analyze current trends and suggest optimal content types and posting schedules is the most effective method. This strategy maximizes user engagement by aligning content delivery with audience behavior and trending topics. Dynamic and timely content generated through such insights greatly enhances visibility and interaction on social media platforms.

4. A company wants to revamp their email marketing strategy using Jasper AI to ensure higher engagement and better conversion rates. Which feature of Jasper AI should be prioritized to achieve personalized and compelling email campaigns?

A) Automated generation of generic email content

B) Use of static templates for all email communications

C) Dynamic personalization of messages based on user data and behavior

D) Frequent changes to email design ignoring content consistency

Answer: C

Explanation: Dynamic personalization of email messages based on user data and behavior is essential. Jasper AI's capability to tailor communications to respond to individual needs and interests of recipients ensures that each email resonates more effectively. This approach not only captivates the audience but also significantly increases the likelihood of driving conversions through relevant and engaging content.

COPY.AI: CRAFTING COMPELLING SALES COPY WITH AI

Introduction to Copy.ai: Enhancing Sales Copy through AI

In the realm of digital marketing, compelling sales copy can decisively influence consumer behavior. Enter Copy.ai, a leader in enhancing sales materials through artificial intelligence. The platform offers a technologically advanced yet user-friendly approach to creating persuasive text, revolutionarily streamlining copywriting tasks.

Copy.ai utilizes machine learning algorithms to analyze existing sales data and consumer trends to generate copy that not only engages but also converts. Its efficiency in producing varied content from product descriptions to ad copies reduces the creative workload, allowing businesses to scale operations effortlessly. This AI-driven method ensures consistency in tone and message, essential for brand identity.

Moreover, Copy.ai's adaptive learning capabilities mean it continuously improves output based on feedback and performance metrics. This dynamic adaptability makes it an indispensable tool in crafting copy that resonates with an ever-evolving audience, providing marketers with a competitive edge in a crowded marketplace.

Core Features of Copy.ai for Crafting Sales Messages

Copy.ai stands out in the crowded AI copywriting landscape through its array of dynamic features designed to enhance sales messaging. Central to its toolkit is the voice tone adjuster, which tailors the emotional appeal of any text to fit the desired customer response, whether it's urgency, curiosity, or trust. This customization ensures that messages not only attract but also resonate deeply with the targeted demographics.

Another significant feature is the text variation generator. This functionality allows marketers to create multiple versions of the same message, providing essential data on which variations perform better across different platforms. This can significantly optimize marketing strategies and increase conversion rates by aligning the content with audience preferences more precisely.

Moreover, Copy.ai integrates seamlessly with marketing analytics tools, enabling businesses to track the effectiveness of their copy in real-time. This integration aids in refining the approach based on concrete performance metrics, continually improving the quality and effectiveness of marketing campaigns. Updates and learning algorithms within Copy.ai ensure that each feature evolves, staying ahead of market trends and consumer behaviors.

Setting Up Copy.ai for First-Time Users

Embarking on your journey with Copy.ai begins with a straightforward setup process tailored for first-time users. To start, create an account on the Copy.ai platform by providing basic information such as your name, email, and organization details. Once registered, you'll be prompted to select your industry and the type of content you frequently need, which helps Copy.ai tailor its services and suggestions to your specific needs.

Next, familiarize yourself with the dashboard. It's designed with user-friendliness in mind, making navigation intuitive. Here, you can access various tools like the voice tone adjuster or text variation generator. To see Copy.ai in action, try creating your first piece of content by selecting the 'New Document' button and choosing the type of copy you want to generate.

Finally, explore the resource section, which provides helpful tutorials and best practices for using Copy.ai effectively. These resources are invaluable for maximizing the platform's potential, ensuring you craft compelling, AI-driven sales copy that resonates with your audience.

Writing Effective Product Descriptions with Copy.ai

Diving into the realm of e-commerce, the power of a well-crafted product description cannot be overstated. Copy.ai emerges as a pivotal tool in this arena, empowering users to create descriptions that not only inform but also persuade and engage potential customers. By utilizing Copy.ai, businesses can seamlessly generate product narratives that highlight unique features and benefits, tailored to the shopping preferences of their target audience.

The process begins with inputting key product features into Copy.ai. The AI then employs its advanced algorithms to construct compelling descriptions that capture the essence of the products. These descriptions are optimized for both SEO and customer conversion, ensuring that they rank well in search results and appeal to consumers' needs and emotions.

Moreover, Copy.ai offers the flexibility to experiment with different tones and styles, making it easy to customize content for various platforms. Whether it's a minimalist approach for a sophisticated audience or a vibrant style for a more dynamic crowd, Copy.ai handles it all with finesse, ensuring that each description is a perfect fit for its intended market.

Crafting Email Sales Pitch with AI Assistance

Harnessing the power of AI, Copy.ai transforms the daunting task of crafting email sales pitches into a streamlined, efficient process. By leveraging AI, businesses can generate personalized, persuasive email content tailored to individual recipient's preferences and behaviors. This personalization is key in capturing attention in crowded inboxes.

Copy.ai provides tools that analyze historical engagement data and customer interactions to suggest content adjustments that boost open rates and conversions. The AI's understanding of effective word choice and call-to-action placements empowers marketers to create powerful messages that resonate on a personal level, driving higher engagement.

Moreover, the iterative learning process of Copy.ai ensures that each campaign becomes smarter. Using feedback loops, the system refines its suggestions, continually enhancing the effectiveness of future pitches. By automating routine copy tasks, Copy.ai allows teams to focus on strategic and creative aspects of marketing campaigns, amplifying their impact.

Utilizing Copy.ai for email campaigning offers a dynamic way to connect with audiences, ensuring messages are not only read but also acted upon, fundamentally shifting the email marketing landscape towards greater personalization and efficiency.

Creating Captivating Headlines Using Copy.ai

In the bustling world of digital content, headlines are the gatekeepers, compelling readers to engage or pass by. Copy.ai, equipped with cutting-edge AI technology, provides an invaluable tool for constructing headlines that not only capture attention but also encapsulate the core message persuasively and succinctly.

Utilizing advanced algorithms, Copy.ai analyzes current trends, keyword effectiveness, and audience engagement metrics to generate headlines that resonate with target demographics. This ensures that each headline is optimized for both impact and SEO, making content more discoverable and appealing. The process is highly iterative, allowing users to refine and test different variations, thus honing the art of headline creation to near perfection.

Moreover, Copy.ai incorporates feedback loops that continuously improve headline suggestions based on real-time data. This dynamic capability enables marketers to stay ahead in a competitive landscape, ensuring that every headline is a step towards greater content visibility and consumer interaction.

Using Copy.ai for Blog Post Conversion Optimization

Optimizing blog posts for greater conversion begins with understanding the nuances of audience engagement and intent. Copy.ai provides a set of tools specifically designed to enhance the performance of blog content by tailoring it to the motives and behaviors of readers. Key features enable the fine-tuning of language and structure to maximize reader retention and action.

Implementing Copy.ai starts with analyzing existing blog posts to identify elements that either encourage or hinder conversion rates. The AI then suggests modifications — from keyword integration to emotional tone adjustments — ensuring every blog is crafted to meet specific conversion goals. These recommendations are based on extensive data analysis, combining industry trends with user interaction patterns.

Furthermore, Copy.ai allows for the automation of A/B testing with different content variations. This process not only refines the effectiveness of individual blog posts but also generates valuable insights into what resonates best with the target audience, continuously driving up the effectiveness of future content. Each optimized blog post is a step toward transforming casual readers into committed customers, leveraging the subtle art of persuasion embedded in well-crafted words.

Developing CTAs that Convert: Insights from Copy.ai

CTAs (Calls to Action) are critical tools in sales copy, designed to guide potential customers towards conversion. Utilizing Copy.ai, creators can forge CTAs that not only demand attention but effectively drive action. The AI analyzes data from myriad successful campaigns, identifying key phrases and structures that resonate most with specific audiences. This insight allows for the crafting of tailored, compelling CTAs.

Incorporating psychological triggers, Copy.ai generates CTAs that leverage urgency, curiosity, and exclusivity — elements proven to enhance click-through rates. Users can experiment with variations, testing them in real-time to see which performs best. This iterative process, supported by AI, ensures that each CTA is optimized for maximum impact.

Beyond mere text creation, Copy.ai assists in placing CTAs strategically throughout sales content, enhancing visibility and effectiveness. The alignment of CTAs with the overall content narrative fosters a seamless user experience, significantly boosting conversion rates. This approach empowers businesses to transform passive readers into active participants, effectively increasing ROI comprehensively.

Leveraging AI to Write Advertisements for Facebook and Google

In the digital marketing world, creating ads for platforms like Facebook and Google can be highly complex due to their different algorithms and user behaviors. However, Copy.ai simplifies this task, harnessing AI to tailor advertisements that capture the nuances of each platform efficiently.

For Facebook, Copy.ai analyzes user engagement metrics and demographic data to craft personalized ads that resonate with varied audiences, from casual browsers to potential customers. The AI optimizes messaging for emotional appeal and social sharing, essential for Facebook's community-driven ecosystem. Meanwhile, for Google ads, Copy.ai focuses on keyword optimization and relevance. It employs SEO strategies to enhance visibility and click-through rates, critical for success in Google's search-driven environment.

The platform's ability to test variations of ad copy quickly and effectively means businesses can adapt to performance metrics in real-time, ensuring content is always optimized for the highest conversion rates. Thus, Copy.ai becomes an indispensable tool in a marketer's arsenal, delivering precision-crafted ads for maximum impact on both platforms.

Copywriting for Landing Pages: A Copy.ai Approach

In the digital frontier, effective landing pages are the cornerstone of successful online marketing campaigns. Copy.ai revolutionizes this crucial aspect by automating the creation of persuasive content that captures and converts. Emphasizing the seamless integration of key messages and calls-to-action, Copy.ai ensures each element is strategically placed to maximize impact and user engagement.

Using advanced AI algorithms, Copy.ai analyses conversion metrics from myriad past campaigns to tailor content that's not only engaging but also highly personalized. This approach guarantees that visitors are greeted with compelling, relevant content that resonates deeply, encouraging immediate action. From powerful headlines to informative bullet points, every piece of content is optimized for clarity and conversion effectiveness.

Furthermore, Copy.ai facilitates real-time A/B testing, allowing marketers to fine-tune content based on actual user interactions. This dynamic adjustment process ensures that landing pages remain optimally configured to current market conditions and audience preferences, significantly boosting conversion rates.

Leveraging AI in this way not only transforms how landing pages are crafted but also redefines their effectiveness, making Copy.ai an essential tool for marketers aiming to drive robust online engagement.

Tailoring Your Message for Different Audience Segments

Understanding and addressing the unique preferences of diverse audience segments is pivotal in crafting targeted sales copy. Copy.ai excels in segment-specific customization, enabling businesses to fine-tune their messaging to resonate profoundly with each distinct group.

The tool employs deep learning algorithms to analyze past engagement data and demographic insights, allowing marketers to identify key linguistic and emotional triggers that appeal to different segments. Whether it's millennials or baby boomers, each demographic has particular preferences that can be addressed to enhance relevance and engagement.

By using Copy.ai, marketers can effortlessly generate multiple variations of a message, each tailored to meet the expectations and interests of a specific audience segment. This customization extends beyond mere word choice; it encompasses tone, style, and the framing of information, ensuring that each piece feels bespoke and considerate of the audience's unique needs and desires.

Such targeted messaging not only improves engagement rates but also boosts the overall efficacy of marketing campaigns, driving higher conversion rates and enhancing customer satisfaction.

Improving Newsletter Content with Copy.ai

Newsletters remain a vital tool in maintaining engagement and nurturing customer loyalty. Copy.ai transforms this platform by enhancing content relevance and resonance. AI-driven analysis of subscriber interactions and preferences enables the crafting of personalized newsletters that speak directly to the reader's interests and needs.

Utilizing Copy.ai, businesses can optimize the frequency and timing of their dispatches, thereby increasing the chances of newsletters being opened and read. The AI's ability to analyze vast amounts of data provides insights into the best times for sending, based on past engagement metrics. This targeted approach ensures maximum visibility and interaction.

Moreover, Copy.ai assists in refining subject lines and content to boost click-through rates. The AI suggests variations of subject lines that have historically performed well, adapting to ongoing trends and recipient behavior. This adaptability results in consistently higher engagement, keeping your brand at the forefront of customers' minds.

With Copy.ai, newsletter production is not only about informing but also strategically engaging, making every email an opportunity to enhance connection and drive business value.

Using AI to Overcome Writer's Block in Sales Copy

Writer's block can halt the momentum of crafting engaging sales copy. Copy.ai emerges as a pivotal tool in breaching this creative barrier. By analyzing extensive databases of effective copy, this AI platform offers real-time suggestions and frameworks that reignite the creative process.

Often, the challenge lies in finding the right angle or initial spark. Copy.ai provides diverse templates and phrase options, easing the initiation of content creation. Whether it's an impactful opening line or a compelling call-to-action, Copy.ai assists in swiftly overcoming the initial hurdles of writing. The tool's capability to adapt to the user's style ensures the output remains authentic yet innovative.

Moreover, Copy.ai actively combats writer's block by suggesting content variations and improvements. This not only refines the copy but also provides multiple perspectives on how to approach a sales pitch. Continual learning from user interactions allows Copy.ai to keep suggestions fresh and highly relevant, making writer's block a manageable, temporary obstacle.

Integrating SEO Keywords into Copy.ai Generated Content

In the world of digital marketing, SEO is vital for content visibility and search engine ranking. Copy.ai adeptly incorporates this element into its content creation process, ensuring that crafted sales copy does not only persuade but is also search engine friendly. The platform uses an advanced algorithm to identify and integrate high-impact SEO keywords that match the content's purpose and target audience, refining the content's potential to rise in search rankings.

Moreover, Copy.ai's AI-driven system analyzes keyword trends and searches behaviors, allowing marketers to be proactive rather than reactive in their SEO strategies. This preemptive approach to keyword integration secures a competitive edge in marketplace visibility. The content generated is thus not only optimized for human readers but also designed to perform well in algorithm-based search queries.

By merging compelling copywriting with strategic keyword placement, Copy.ai assists in crafting content that serves dual functions - engaging the customer and enhancing online presence. This integration ensures that every piece of content is a step towards SEO success.

Copy.ai for Social Media Posts: Engaging Your Audience

Social media is an ever-evolving landscape that requires fresh and engaging content to capture attention. Copy.ai provides an innovative solution to this challenge through AI-powered copywriting tools that enhance user engagement across various platforms. By leveraging data-driven insights and natural language processing, Copy.ai generates dynamic content tailored to match the tone and style appropriate for each social network, from Twitter's quick hits to Instagram's storytelling visuals.

The platform's ability to swiftly adapt makes it invaluable for creating posts that not only engage but also grow follower bases and increase interaction rates. Through its understanding of current trends and user preferences, Copy.ai optimizes each post for maximum visibility and engagement. Furthermore, it offers suggestions for optimal posting times and content type, ensuring that every post reaches its intended audience at the right moment.

With Copy.ai, brands can maintain a consistent and appealing social media presence. This facilitates increased engagement and strengthens brand loyalty, ultimately contributing to a more robust online presence. Copy.ai acts not just as a tool, but as a strategic partner in the crowded and fast-paced world of social media marketing.

Generating Quick Copy Variants for A/B Testing

In the dynamic arena of digital marketing, A/B testing stands as a robust tool for optimizing sales strategies. Copy.ai revolutionizes this process by generating multiple copy variants swiftly, allowing marketers to test different approaches and determine the most effective one. This capability not only saves valuable time but also injects precision into marketing campaigns.

Harnessing the power of AI, Copy.ai efficiently produces variations in tone, style, and content structure, thus facilitating nuanced comparative analysis. Marketers can deploy these variants in real-time, measuring engagement and conversion metrics to fine-tune their messaging. This iterative process enhances the overall impact of sales copy, ensuring that each version is better aligned with audience preferences and behaviors.

Furthermore, Copy.ai's seamless integration into marketing workflows allows for continuous A/B testing, transforming guesswork into data-driven decision-making. By continuously evolving and adapting content based on direct feedback, businesses can sustain relevancy and maximize both reach and response rates in their digital campaigns.

Optimizing Copy for eCommerce Platforms

Optimizing sales copy for eCommerce platforms requires a deep understanding of consumer behavior and preferences, a task expertly handled by Copy.ai. This AI-powered tool enhances the creation of product descriptions, promotional banners, and checkout process instructions that resonate with potential customers, ensuring a smoother user experience and higher conversion rates.

Copy.ai's capabilities extend to analyzing product-related data to suggest keywords and phrases that increase search engine visibility and shopper engagement. This tailored content is crucial for standing out in an increasingly crowded marketplace, where the right words can significantly impact sales performance.

Moreover, Copy.ai assists in localizing content based on the geographic target market, adjusting the copy to reflect local dialects and shopping habits, thus maximizing the appeal to various customer segments. Such customization ensures that every description or ad hits the mark, boosting both shopper satisfaction and loyalty.

Utilizing Copy.ai for eCommerce platforms translates to optimized content that not only attracts attention but also drives action, fundamentally transforming browser interactions into tangible sales.

Creating Auto-Responder Emails with Copy.ai

Auto-responder emails are essential for maintaining customer engagement without the need for constant manual input. Copy.ai revolutionizes this process by enabling users to create responsive, personalized email sequences that resonate with each recipient. By leveraging AI, the platform ensures that each automated response is not only timely but also contextually relevant, enhancing the customer experience and fostering loyalty.

Setting up these auto-responders through Copy.ai involves defining triggers based on customer actions or time frames. For instance, a welcome email could be automatically sent when a new user signs up, or a follow-up email could be dispatched a few days after a purchase. Copy.ai's intuitive interface allows for easy customization of these triggers, ensuring that the communication feels authentic and highly personalized.

Moreover, Copy.ai provides analytics to monitor the effectiveness of these auto-responders, allowing businesses to tweak and optimize based on actual engagement data. The ability to swiftly alter email parameters in response to customer behavior or broader campaign results ensures that every interaction is maximized for impact, turning simple auto-responses into powerful tools for digital marketing.

Using AI-Powered Copy for Affiliate Marketing Content

In the landscape of affiliate marketing, where communication precision and persuasion are paramount, Copy.ai stands as a vital ally. By generating AI-powered content, this tool equips marketers to craft compelling affiliate content that not only resonates with target audiences but also drives conversions effectively.

Utilizing Copy.ai, affiliate marketers can tailor their messages to specific niches, ensuring that each piece of content is perfectly aligned with the interests and preferences of their audience. This bespoke approach significantly enhances the likelihood of engagement and sales, as the content appears more relevant and trustworthy to potential customers.

Moreover, Copy.ai simplifies the process of creating varied and fresh content for different products or services, maintaining a high level of interest and interaction among the audience. This is especially crucial in affiliate marketing, where ongoing innovation in content can determine the success or failure of the marketing effort.

Lastly, the seamless integration of SEO strategies enhances the visibility of affiliate content, ensuring that it reaches a broader audience. This dual capability of crafting compelling and searchable content makes Copy.ai an indispensable tool for modern affiliate marketers.

Sales Copy Automation: Scaling Output with Copy.ai

In the fast-paced world of digital marketing, maximizing efficiency while maintaining quality is paramount. Copy.ai introduces a transformative approach to sales copy automation, enabling businesses to scale their content creation without sacrificing precision or appeal. The tool's AI algorithms analyze existing data and audience interactions to produce varied and compelling sales messages at a rapid pace.

This automation extends beyond mere content generation; it incorporates nuanced strategies that align with brand voice and marketing goals. Businesses leveraging Copy.ai can expect consistent and high-quality content that resonates with diverse customer bases, facilitating broader engagement and conversion. Moreover, the automation process is seamlessly integrated, allowing for easy management of increased content volumes.

The benefits of using Copy.ai for scaling sales copy are clear: heightened productivity, preserved content quality, and enhanced campaign effectiveness. Through intelligent automation, Copy.ai is reshaping how businesses approach and implement their digital marketing strategies, setting a new standard in the industry.

Monitoring and Tweaking AI-Created Content for Brand Voice

While Copy.ai adeptly generates engaging and persuasive sales copy, monitoring and adapting this content is crucial to ensure it consistently reflects the unique brand voice of a business. This requires a vigilant approach to review AI-produced messages, discern nuances, and make necessary adjustments that resonate with your brand's core values and tone.

Utilizing the analytics tools provided by Copy.ai, businesses can track the performance of their content across various platforms. Insights gleaned from these analytics enable marketers to identify areas where the AI's interpretation of the brand voice may deviate from the intended tone. This data-driven feedback loop is essential for refining content to better align with brand identity and customer expectations.

Moreover, as brand strategies evolve, it becomes imperative to update and tweak AI parameters to maintain relevance. Regular audits of AI-generated content help ensure that every piece not only performs well but also strengthens brand integrity, thereby enhancing overall marketing coherence and effectiveness in communication.

Copy.ai Analytics: Measuring the Success of AI Content

Copy.ai not only facilitates the creation of innovative sales copy but also includes powerful analytics capabilities to gauge the success and impact of content generated through AI. These analytics tools provide essential insights into various metrics such as engagement rates, click-through rates, and conversion effectiveness, enabling marketers to quantitatively measure their content's performance across different platforms.

With this data, businesses can fine-tune their marketing strategies, making informed decisions on content adjustment for increased effectiveness. Copy.ai's analytics dashboards offer visual representations of data trends and performance over time, which simplifies the analysis and helps pinpoint successes or areas needing improvement. This level of detail assists in understanding the precise components of AI-generated content that resonate with audiences.

Furthermore, the integration of A/B testing with analytics allows for rigorous testing of different content variants, providing a scientific approach to optimizing copy for maximum conversion. By continuously monitoring and analyzing these results, Copy.ai ensures that every piece of content not only aligns with the brand's voice but also delivers on strategic marketing objectives, driving towards the ultimate goal of increased ROI.

Case Studies: Successful Campaigns Using Copy.ai

Exploring the effectiveness of Copy.ai, several case studies illuminate its capacity to transform sales copy endeavors. One notable campaign by an emerging online retailer utilized Copy.ai to revamp product descriptions and email campaigns. The result was a remarkable 30% increase in conversion rates within the first quarter of implementation.

Another success story involves a technology startup that adopted Copy.ai for crafting compelling blog posts and social media content. By fine-tuning their messaging to match the nuanced interests of their target audience, the startup saw a surge in user engagement and a 50% growth in lead generation over six months.

A leading healthcare company used Copy.ai to develop targeted ad content and landing pages. The AI-assisted adjustments led to a 40% reduction in bounce rates and a 25% increase in appointment bookings, crucial metrics for their digital marketing success.

These instances underscore Copy.ai's capacity to not only enhance content quality but also significantly impact business metrics, demonstrating its value as a pivotal tool in digital marketing arsenals.

Future Developments and Updates in Copy.ai

As Copy.ai continues to evolve, anticipating future developments is crucial for users and businesses aiming to maintain a competitive edge. The roadmap for Copy.ai includes advanced neural network algorithms designed to enhance the subtlety and effectiveness of AI-generated content. These developments aim to improve the user interface, making the tool more intuitive and easier for marketers to harness the full potential of AI in their copywriting efforts.

Moreover, the integration of more languages and dialects is expected, broadening the application of Copy.ai to global markets. This expansion will enable businesses to craft localized content effortlessly, enhancing customer connectivity on an international scale. Enhanced personalization features are also on the horizon, which will allow for more tailored content, increasing the relevance and impact of marketing communications.

Lastly, anticipating further integration with other marketing tools, Copy.ai plans to offer seamless connectivity, thereby creating a more unified marketing technology ecosystem. This will facilitate a smoother workflow and greater data synergy across platforms, optimizing overall marketing performance.

Best Practices for Using AI Tools in Copywriting

Utilizing AI tools like Copy.ai in copywriting demands a blend of creativity and strategic thinking. To maximize effectiveness, writers should start by clearly defining the campaign's objectives and target audience. This initial clarity guides the AI in generating relevant and impactful content that resonates with readers. Moreover, it's crucial to maintain a balance between AI-generated suggestions and human creativity to ensure the content feels authentic and engaging.

Writers should also routinely update the AI's learning base with new data and feedback. This continuous learning process allows the AI to align more closely with evolving language trends and audience preferences. Regularly integrating new insights and outcomes from A/B testing into the AI system enhances its effectiveness over time, keeping the content dynamic and competitive.

Ethically using AI in copywriting involves transparency about AI's role in content creation. Clearly disclosing AI involvement can build trust with your audience, reinforcing the credibility of the brand while embracing innovative technologies. Adhering to these best practices ensures that AI tools like Copy.ai become valuable allies in crafting compelling, innovative sales copy.

Ethical Considerations and Transparency in AI-Generated Copy

As AI technologies like Copy.ai reshape the landscape of digital marketing, it's imperative to address ethical considerations and foster transparency. The use of AI in crafting sales copy raises important ethical questions, particularly regarding authenticity and the potential for manipulation. Ensuring that AI-generated content aligns with ethical marketing practices is not just a regulatory compliance issue but a cornerstone for building trust with consumers.

Transparency about the use of AI tools is also crucial. Businesses should disclose when and how AI is used in creating content. This transparency is vital for maintaining consumer trust and credibility, as customers increasingly value honesty in digital interactions. Furthermore, informing audiences about the AI's role can demystify technology, fostering an environment where trust and technology go hand in hand.

Moreover, implementing guidelines for ethical AI use helps businesses navigate potential pitfalls. These guidelines should address issues like biased output and over-reliance on AI for content creation, ensuring that AI tools are used responsibly and effectively. This balanced approach guarantees that AI-driven innovations, like those offered by Copy.ai, are leveraged to enhance user experience without compromising ethical standards or consumer trust.

SUMMARY

Copy.ai leverages AI to revolutionize the creation of sales copy across various digital marketing arenas. It offers users tools to generate persuasive, targeted content effortlessly, optimizing for specific audience behaviors and trends. At its core, Copy.ai analyzes consumer data and sales trends using advanced machine learning algorithms, enabling the production of content that resonates deeply with audiences. This not only improves engagement but also drives conversions, providing businesses with a significant competitive advantage. For instance, one of its standout features, the voice tone adjuster, allows customization of emotional appeal, enhancing the connection with potential customers. Similarly, the text variation generator helps in creating different versions of a message to see which performs best, optimizing marketing strategies. The integration of Copy.ai with marketing analytics tools further assists businesses in real-time tracking of their copy's effectiveness, refining approaches based on solid performance metrics. For new users, the platform promotes ease of use with a simple setup process and an intuitive interface that guides through creating various content types, from email pitches to product descriptions and social media posts. Moreover, Copy.ai empowers users to overcome common content creation challenges like writer's block by offering real-time suggestions, templates, and content variations, maintaining both creativity and consistency in messaging. It also handles the integration of SEO keywords seamlessly, ensuring that the content is not only compelling but also ranks well on search engines. The automatic generation of varied copy for A/B testing exemplifies how Copy.ai optimizes digital campaigns efficiently, allowing businesses to adapt quickly to changing market dynamics and consumer preferences. The use of Copy.ai extends beyond routine tasks, aiding in maintaining the brand's voice and ethical marketing practices, ensuring transparency about AI's role in content creation, essential for consumer trust.

REFERENCES

[1]   Introduction   to   Automatic   Text   Generation.   https://example.com/automatic_text_generation

[2]   Trends   in   Digital   Marketing   Automation.   https://example.com/digital_marketing_automation

[3] AI and Consumer Behavior Analysis. https://example.com/consumer_behavior_analysis

[4] Optimizing SEO with AI Tools. https://example.com/seo_ai_tools

CASE STUDY: REVOLUTIONIZING RETAIL: A COPY.AI IMPLEMENTED STRATEGY FOR A FASHION BRAND

The global retail industry constantly faces the challenge of staying relevant and captivating to a diverse and ever-evolving audience. Consider the case of a mid-sized fashion brand, 'StyleNest', which has traditionally relied on traditional copywriting techniques for its online content and marketing campaigns. As competition intensified and consumer behaviors shifted increasingly towards digital platforms, StyleNest recognized the need to enhance its digital presence and engagement rates urgently.

To address this issue, StyleNest turned to Copy.ai, an advanced AI-powered copywriting tool designed to optimize sales copy and marketing strategies. Initially, the brand focused on revamping its product descriptions and ad copies using Copy.ai's dynamic features such as voice tone adjuster and text variation generator. The platform's advanced algorithms analyzed existing sales data and insights into consumer trends, enabling StyleNest to generate compelling content that significantly improved its search engine rankings and customer engagement.

Moreover, the email marketing campaigns saw a major shift with the implementation of personalized, AI-driven content that adjusted automatically to user behaviors and preferences. Using Copy.ai, StyleNest efficiently crafted email sequences that resulted in higher open and conversion rates, which was evident from the feedback loops and analytics provided by the platform. The success didn't stop there; soon, StyleNest expanded the use of AI copywriting to include blog posts, social media updates, and crafting effective CTAs, pushing the boundaries of traditional retail marketing strategies.

The consistent use of Copy.ai allowed StyleNest to maintain a fresh, appealing, and highly engaging online presence, proving a critical factor in driving up sales numbers and expanding their customer base. This case clearly demonstrates how integrating AI technology like Copy.ai in a comprehensive digital marketing strategy can transform a retail brand's engagement with its audience, converting challenges into lucrative opportunities.

Case Study: Optimizing Engagement: How Copy.ai Transformed Healthcare Digital Marketing

Healthcare marketing poses unique challenges due to the sensitive nature of its content and the critical need for precision and trustworthiness in communications. A notable healthcare corporation, HealthPlus Inc., faced hurdles in engaging a broader audience because their marketing content often lacked personalization and immediacy, elements crucial in healthcare communications. As digital platforms became vital in patient interactions, HealthPlus sought an innovative solution to overhaul their digital strategy to better meet consumer needs and preferences.

HealthPlus decided to integrate Copy.ai into their digital marketing strategy, aiming to leverage the platform's superior AI capabilities to enhance content personalization and engagement. The first step involved the AI's analysis of existing patient engagement data and interaction histories, facilitating more tailored content right from the welcome emails to ongoing patient education materials. Copy.ai's text variance generator and tone adjuster played pivotal roles, enabling HealthPlus to customize their messages according to the severity of the topic and the emotional state inferred from patient interactions.

This methodical deployment of AI-driven tools led to the crafting of highly effective patient communication that resonated well with various demographics. By using Copy.ai's dynamic A/B testing feature, HealthPlus could iterate numerous versions of content to find the most engaging tone and information delivery style for their audience. The adaptability of the AI tool ensured that each piece of content was not only SEO optimized but also aligned with the medical accuracy required in healthcare communication.

The results were groundbreaking. HealthPlus observed a 25% increase in patient engagement through their online platforms within just six months of implementation. Patient trust and satisfaction metrics also improved, as demonstrated by the reduced numbers in patient-initiated inquiries and increased feedback positivity. The success of integrating Copy.ai in HealthPlus's campaign underscores the transformative potential of AI in sensitive sectors like healthcare, where communication precision directly impacts consumer trust and engagement.

Case Study: Enhancing E-commerce Efficiency: The Transformational Role of Copy.ai in Online Retail

In the competitive e-commerce industry, precise and engaging product descriptions are critical for attracting customers and boosting sales. This case study focuses on 'QuickBuy Electronics', a growing online retailer specializing in consumer electronics. QuickBuy faced significant challenges in scaling their operations while maintaining a high level of content quality across their product listings. As their product range expanded, the team struggled to keep up with writing unique, SEO-optimized descriptions for each item, which adversely affected their online visibility and customer engagement.

To address these challenges, QuickBuy turned to Copy.ai, a state-of-the-art AI-driven copywriting tool. The initial implementation focused on optimizing existing product descriptions and generating new ones for recently added inventory. Copy.ai's AI algorithms were employed to analyze top-performing product listings from similar markets to incorporate successful SEO strategies and appealing content structures. This approach allowed QuickBuy to automate and enhance the creation of product descriptions significantly, aligning them better with consumer search behaviors and preferences.

Further implementation of Copy.ai included the use of its feature that allows for A/B testing of different description styles and structures. This enabled QuickBuy to fine-tune their descriptions based on real-time feedback on which versions performed better in terms of engagement and conversion rates. Additionally, the flexibility offered by Copy.ai to quickly adapt and tweak content empowered QuickBuy to respond swiftly to market trends and adjust their sales strategies accordingly.

The results of integrating Copy.ai were transformative. Within the first year, QuickBuy noted a 40% increase in organic traffic, a significant uptick in customer engagement, and, most importantly, a 35% rise in conversion rates. The ability to generate and optimize content at scale without a proportional increase in human resources allowed QuickBuy to reallocate efforts towards other critical areas such as customer service and product development. By transforming their approach to content creation and optimization, QuickBuy not only streamlined their operational efficiency but also established a stronger online presence, ultimately contributing to a robust bottom line.

Case Study: Leveraging Copy.ai for a Travel Agency's Comprehensive Marketing Makeover

In the competitive travel industry, engaging potential customers through personalized and compelling content is paramount. A mid-sized travel agency, 'VoyageQuest', faced challenges in reaching a broader audience and enhancing their engagement metrics. Despite having enticing travel packages, their marketing content was generic, failing to capture the unique preferences of their diverse clientele. This realization prompted VoyageQuest to adopt Copy.ai, aiming to revitalize their marketing efforts across various digital platforms.

By integrating Copy.ai into their strategy, VoyageQuest began by analyzing historical customer data and engagement metrics provided by the AI's analytical tools. This informed the crafting of personalized email marketing campaigns targeting different customer segments—from adventure seekers to luxury travelers. Copy.ai's ability to adjust tone and style, coupled with its automated A/B testing feature, allowed for finely tuned messages that resonated deeply with each segment.

Furthermore, VoyageQuest utilized Copy.ai's headline and subject line generator to boost open rates and click-throughs on their newsletters and promotional emails. The compelling, personalized headlines significantly increased engagement, as demonstrated by a 50% increase in newsletter sign-ups within the first three months. Quality content creation extended to their social media platforms, where Copy.ai generated optimized posts that aligned with trending travel topics and preferences, enhancing their online visibility and follower interaction.

The use of Copy.ai not only streamlined content creation but also provided dynamic insights into market trends and consumer behavior, granting VoyageQuest an agile approach to marketing. Continually updated algorithms ensured that content remained relevant, enhancing the appeal of their travel packages. Adoption of Copy.ai translated into a 45% increase in bookings in just six months, demonstrating the profound impact of targeted, AI-driven marketing strategies in the travel sector. This case study exemplifies how tailored content, powered by AI, can transform a travel company's digital marketing success by elevating customer engagement and boosting conversion rates.

Case Study: Empowering a Nonprofit Organization's

Fundraising Efforts Through Copy.ai

In the fiercely competitive domain of nonprofit fundraising, distinguishing one's cause and engaging potential donors effectively are fundamental challenges. This is precisely the transformational experience a mid-sized nonprofit organization dedicated to environmental conservation, EarthAid, underwent by implementing Copy.ai. Previously, EarthAid's fundraising campaigns were not achieving desired results, with declining donor engagement and plateauing donation rates suggesting that their traditional copywriting methods required a significant overhaul.

Facing these challenges, EarthAid turned to Copy.ai, a state-of-the-art AI-powered copywriting tool, to refine their fundraising appeals and donor engagement strategies. Initially, EarthAid utilized Copy.ai to revamp their email fundraising campaigns, leveraging AI to tailor messages to resonate deeply with different donor segments based on past giving history and engagement indices. The voice tone adjuster and text variation generator tools were paramount in crafting multiple versions of appeals, allowing EarthAid to test and iterate which tones and messages yielded the best responses.

The transformation was evident. By employing Copy.ai's dynamic analytics, EarthAid could quantitatively measure improvements in donor engagement and contribution levels. Its ability to generate multiple campaign messages swiftly also meant EarthAid could respond to global environmental crises immediately, ensuring timely and relevant donor communication which is crucial in crisis situations.

Moreover, EarthAid expanded the employment of Copy.ai tools to their social media strategies. Custom tailored appeals were created that effectively communicated the urgency of environmental issues while encouraging specific actions, like signing petitions or participating in fundraising events. These posts were continuously refined using A/B testing to determine the most effective messaging frameworks.

The utilization of Copy.ai not only revitalized EarthAid's donor communications but also imparted pivotal insights into donor behaviors and preferences. This AI-enhanced approach fostered a deeper connection with their audience, responsive and adaptive to the nuances of donor engagement, which led to a remarkable 45% increase in annual donations and a substantial growth in recurrent donor numbers.

Case Study: Transforming Real Estate Marketing with AI Enhancement

The real estate market, with its intensive competition and high stake transactions, necessitates precise and effective marketing strategies. A mid-sized real estate company, Metro Realty, historically depended on conventional advertising techniques—billboards, print media, and basic online listings. However, as digital transformation took hold of the industry, Metro Realty faced the need to significantly uplift its marketing tactics to match the evolving buyer behaviors and fierce competition, particularly from digitally native firms.

Metro Realty recognized the potential of leveraging AI to enhance their marketing efforts and turned to Copy.ai for a solution. Initially, the focus was to revamp their property listings across online platforms. Copy.ai was deployed to generate compelling, SEO-optimized descriptions that could capture the essence of each property and highlight its unique selling points in a manner that resonated with potential buyers. Utilizing Copy.ai's dynamic language models, Metro Realty was able to produce descriptions that not only detailed the properties attractively but were also customized to appeal to various customer segments—first-time homebuyers, luxury estate seekers, and commercial investors.

Subsequently, the adoption of Copy.ai extended to email marketing. Personalized email campaigns were devised using AI insights into customer interaction data, enabling targeted messaging that catered to the preferences and past behaviors of recipients. For instance, potential buyers who showed interest in luxury homes received emails with high-end property listings and content that emphasized sophistication and exclusivity.

The impact of integrating Copy.ai into Metro Realty's marketing strategy was profound. Within six months, the revamped property listings led to a 50% increase in online user engagement. Email campaigns saw higher open rates and led to a 30% increase in scheduled property viewings. By employing AI-driven insights to align content creation with user interest patterns and market trends, Metro Realty successfully transformed its marketing approach, resulting in increased leads and enhanced customer satisfaction levels. The effectiveness of AI-supported copywriting in real estate showed how technology could drastically improve marketing outreach and adaptability in response to changing market dynamics.

Case Study: Revitalizing a Tech Startup's Content Strategy with Copy.ai

Facing the fast-paced and competitive environment of the technology sector, a burgeoning tech startup, InnovateTech, found itself struggling to capture market attention amidst a sea of established giants. Despite having groundbreaking products, their online content failed to generate the desired traction. The startup's challenge was twofold: rapidly produce high-quality, engaging content and ensure it was precisely tailored to resonate with a tech-savvy audience.

InnovateTech turned to Copy.ai, a tool primed to transform digital marketing through artificial intelligence. The initial step involved overhauling their website content, particularly focusing on product descriptions and blog posts. Copy.ai's machine learning algorithms were unleashed to analyze successful competitors and industry trends. This provided the necessary insights to craft content that was not only SEO-optimized but also engaging and informative, addressing the specific interests of potential customers in the tech field.

To further amplify their strategy, InnovateTech utilized Copy.ai's robust abilities to generate dynamic variations of content for A/B testing. This was critical in understanding which approaches yielded better engagement, allowing for real-time adjustments to their strategies. Additionally, Copy.ai's integration with analytical tools provided a stream of data regarding content performance, enabling a deeper understanding of customer interactions and preferences.

InnovateTech's focused application of Copy.ai extended to their social media efforts. The AI's knack for crafting catchy headlines and posts meant that InnovateTech could maintain a consistent, captivating online presence. Over the subsequent months, the startup experienced a significant uplift in user engagement across their digital platforms. The targeted, AI-driven content led to a 40% increase in web traffic and a substantial boost in conversion rates, underlining the importance of tailored content in the technology sector.

This comprehensive approach not only revitalized InnovateTech's content strategy but also demonstrated the power of leveraging AI to create precise, impact-driven marketing content in a competitive industry.

Case Study: Revamping Small Business Marketing Strategies with Copy.ai

In the digital age, small businesses often struggle to compete with larger corporations due to limited marketing budgets and resources. Such was the scenario faced by 'LocalCrafts', a small artisan store specializing in handmade crafts. As the marketplace shifted increasingly online, LocalCrafts found it challenging to keep pace with larger competitors, particularly in reaching new audiences and optimizing their marketing efforts for greater conversion rates.

Recognizing the need for an advanced, cost-effective solution, LocalCrafts turned to Copy.ai, an AI-powered platform known for enhancing and streamlining marketing content creation. Initially, the store utilized Copy.ai to refine their product descriptions and blog posts, which were crucial for SEO and customer engagement. The AI's capabilities to analyze trending keywords and consumer behavior insights proved invaluable. Not only did the platform help generate more compelling and searchable content, but it also ensured that the tone was perfectly aligned with LocalCrafts' brand voice, which emphasized authenticity and artisan quality.

Beyond just content creation, LocalCrafts leveraged Copy.ai for targeted email marketing campaigns. Before using AI, their emails were generic and lacked personalization, which resulted in low engagement rates. By implementing Copy.ai's machine learning insights, LocalCrafts was able to segment their audience and craft personalized messages based on customer purchase history and engagement metrics. This shift saw an immediate improvement in open rates and click-through rates, with follow-up A/B testing refining the approach further over time.

The transformation extended to social media, where Copy.ai's content suggestions helped LocalCrafts maintain a consistent and engaging presence. The tool's ability to quickly generate high-quality content meant that the business could participate in online trends, respond to market dynamics, and engage with customers more interactively, all without the need to hire additional marketing staff. Over the course of the implementation year, LocalCrafts saw a 70% increase in its online engagement and a 50% increase in sales conversion, affirming the significant impact that targeted, AI-driven content could achieve for small businesses operating in competitive environments.

REVIEW QUESTIONS

1. Sarah, a freelance copywriter, has recently begun using Copy.ai to enhance her sales copy tasks. She noticed an improvement in user engagement with her ad copies and product descriptions. Given this development, she's poised to take on more client work but is wary of the quality consistency across larger batches of content. Which feature of Copy.ai should Sarah rely on most heavily to maintain a high standard of content while scaling up her operations?

A) Voice tone adjuster

B) Text variation generator

C) Marketing analytics tools integration

D) None of the above

Answer: B

Explanation: The text variation generator allows Sarah to create multiple versions of the same message, essential for testing which texts perform better across different platforms. This feature enables her to optimize marketing strategies and increase both the quantity of her output and the relevance for varying consumer segments without a drop in content quality.

2. A digital marketing firm is using Copy.ai for the first time to streamline its sales copy creation process. They aim to adapt the tone of their multiple product campaigns to match the demographic preferences of their target audience specifically segmented by age and buying habits. Which particular functionality should they utilize from Copy.ai to best meet their needs?

A) Voice tone adjuster

B) Marketing analytics tools integration

C) Text variation generator

D) All of the above

Answer: A

Explanation: The voice tone adjuster in Copy.ai tailors the emotional appeal of the text to fit the desired customer response, such as urgency, curiosity, or trust. This adjustment is crucial for allowing the marketing firm's messages to attract and resonate more deeply with targeted demographics, thereby improving the campaign's effectiveness.

REVIEW QUESTIONS

3. John, a marketing strategist, is preparing to deploy Copy.ai for an upcoming campaign aimed at testing multiple headlines for a series of blog posts. Which feature of Copy.ai will allow him to efficiently test and determine the most effective headlines for user engagement?

A) Marketing analytics tools integration

B) Text variation generator

C) Adaptive learning capability

D) A/B testing functionality

Answer: D

Explanation: The A/B testing functionality embedded within Copy.ai enables John to create and test different variations of headlines to see which ones perform best in terms of engagement metrics such as click-through rates and read time. This process will provide valuable insights that help optimize the content for the target audience.

CANVA AI: STREAMLINING DESIGN PROCESSES FOR ENTREPRENEURS

Introduction to Canva AI: Revolutionizing Visual Content Creation

In the digital age, where visual content dominates, Canva AI emerges as a pioneering tool, transforming how entrepreneurs and creators design. It harnesses artificial intelligence to simplify processes, making sophisticated design accessible to all, regardless of technical skill level. This introductory section explores how Canva AI is redefining the creation of visual content, offering users a versatile platform to create with efficiency and creativity.

Canva AI's intuitive interface allows users to quickly generate professional-looking graphics, from flyers to full-scale marketing campaigns. Its AI-driven features, such as automatic branding alignment and design suggestion tools, streamline the creative process, dramatically reducing the time and expertise traditionally required to produce high-quality visual assets. Entrepreneurs can now focus more on strategy and less on the nuances of design mechanics.

With Canva AI, the barrier to entering the world of digital marketing lowers, enabling a surge of innovation and the democratization of design. This segment lays the foundation for understanding its profound impact on businesses, highlighting essential tools and features that are instrumental in crafting compelling visual narratives.

Setting Up Your Canva AI Workspace for Optimal Efficiency

Establishing an efficient Canva AI workspace is crucial for entrepreneurs who aim to leverage the powerful capabilities of AI in graphic design. The initial step involves customizing the Canva dashboard to suit your specific project needs. Organizing tools and features in a user-friendly manner enhances accessibility and speeds up the design process.

After setting up the dashboard, integrate your brand elements such as logos, color schemes, and fonts into Canva's Brand Kit. This centralization ensures consistency across all your designs, which is vital for maintaining brand identity. Moreover, utilizing Canva's template library by saving personalized templates can significantly expedite future project setups.

Efficiency in Canva AI also stems from mastering keyboard shortcuts and exploring the 'Styles' feature, which uses AI to suggest design enhancements based on your brand's visual elements. By streamlining these processes, entrepreneurs can minimize time spent on design tasks, allowing them to focus more on strategic business activities.

Lastly, frequently backing up your work on cloud storage within Canva ensures that all your creative outputs are secured and accessible from any device, further optimizing your workflow efficiency.

Leveraging AI to Automate Logo and Branding Designs

As businesses strive for distinctiveness in a crowded market, Canva AI proves indispensable, especially in automating logo and branding designs. Leveraging AI capabilities, Canva streamlines the creation of unique logos that resonate with brand ethos, enabling entrepreneurs to deploy visual identities quickly. This AI-driven approach not only economizes time but also ensures design consistency across various platforms.

Canva AI tools incorporate brand-specific colors, fonts, and elements to generate logos that align with established branding guidelines. This automation extends beyond simple logo creation; it empowers businesses to maintain a coherent brand voice, crucial for consumer recognition and loyalty. The capacity to instantly adjust and customize designs further enhances flexibility, allowing for real-time branding evolution in response to market feedback.

Furthermore, this comprehensive automation facilitates the seamless integration of logos into marketing materials, ensuring a professional appearance. Entrepreneurs harness these capabilities to craft visually compelling narratives that engage audiences, fostering a strong, recognizable brand presence. Thus, Canva AI not only simplifies design processes but also strategically reinforces brand identity.

Using Canva AI for Quick and Effective Marketing Collaterals

In today's fast-paced market, the demand for rapid and effective marketing collateral is at an all-time high. Canva AI equips entrepreneurs with the tools necessary to generate these materials swiftly, ensuring that marketing strategies are not only vibrant but also time-efficient. The AI's sophisticated algorithms assist in creating aesthetically pleasing layouts that capture attention while conveying the intended message clearly.

Whether it's brochures, posters, or digital ads, Canva AI streamlines the design process by offering predesigned templates that can be customized to fit specific brand needs. This not only speeds up the creation process but also maintains consistency across varied marketing materials, reinforcing brand identity. The ease of drag-and-drop editing further enhances the speed of design iterations, allowing for real-time adjustments based on immediate market feedback.

Moreover, Canva AI's integration capabilities mean these collaterals can easily be shared across multiple platforms, optimizing marketing outreach. Utilizing Canva AI, entrepreneurs can focus more on strategy and content, confident in the knowledge that their visual assets are both compelling and professionally crafted.

Streamlining Social Media Graphics with Canva AI

Social media is the battleground for captivating audiences, and Canva AI is an indispensable ally for streamlining the creation of high-impact social media graphics. By automating complex design tasks, Canva AI allows entrepreneurs to produce eye-catching images that engage followers, all with minimal effort.

Canva AI offers a vast library of pre-designed templates tailored to fit various social media platforms, ensuring that content not only resonates with audiences but also adheres to platform-specific requirements. Through intuitive tools, users can customize these templates to reflect their unique brand identity, maintaining a consistent aesthetic across all posts. This seamless integration of brand elements across designs fosters a stronger brand presence online.

Moreover, Canva AI's features allow for rapid adjustments to design elements such as color schemes, fonts, and layouts, enabling real-time response to trending topics or feedback. The platform's collaborative environment further enhances productivity, enabling team members to contribute and refine social media projects efficiently.

Canva AI Templates: Enhancing Website Visuals and Banners

Canva AI Templates serve as a crucial tool for entrepreneurs looking to enhance their online presence with visually striking website visuals and banners. These templates are designed to be not only aesthetically pleasing but also highly functional, providing a seamless user experience that aligns with contemporary web standards. The ease of use allows for quick customization, adapting to various branding needs without compromising on quality.

Utilizing Canva AI for website visuals ensures consistency across digital platforms, a key element in building brand recognition. Entrepreneurs can select from a range of templates tailored to different industries and purposes, making it easier to launch or refresh a website with a professional look. Moreover, AI-driven suggestions help in optimizing layout and design elements, ensuring that the visuals are not only attractive but also effective in capturing visitor attention.

Beyond mere aesthetics, Canva AI templates are engineered to enhance functionality. They incorporate features that are optimized for responsiveness across devices and designed to improve SEO rankings by ensuring faster load times and better usability. This holistic approach to design fosters a positive user experience, ultimately contributing to higher engagement rates and potential revenue streams.

Creating AI-Driven Presentations for Business Pitches

Harnessing the power of Canva AI transforms the daunting task of creating business presentations into a streamlined, efficient process. With AI-driven tools at their disposal, entrepreneurs can design compelling slides that not only captivate but also communicate effectively, ensuring their business pitches stand out in competitive environments.

Canva AI aids in the strategic assembly of content, suggesting layouts that enhance the narrative flow of presentations. It integrates data seamlessly, allowing for real-time updates to stats and figures, crucial for demonstrating market trends and business growth. Furthermore, AI-generated design suggestions align with brand aesthetics, maintaining consistency and professionalism across all slides.

The platform's convenience extends to final adjustments and rehearsals. With Canva AI, refining presentations to perfection becomes less about manual tweaking and more about strategic enhancement. Entrepreneurs can, therefore, focus more on their delivery rather than design logistics, paving the way for more successful pitches and engagements.

Utilizing Canva AI for E-commerce Product Imagery

In the dynamic world of e-commerce, compelling product imagery can significantly elevate sales and enhance customer engagement. Canva AI steps up as a game-changer for entrepreneurs eager to optimize their e-commerce visuals without the steep costs associated with professional photography and graphic design. With AI tools, the creation of clean, attractive product images becomes both accessible and streamlined.

Canva AI provides an array of customizable templates specifically designed for e-commerce. Entrepreneurs can easily adapt these templates to suit their product line, ensuring that each image perfectly communicates the product's features and benefits. The AI-driven enhancement tools allow for fine-tuning colors, adjusting brightness, and applying high-quality filters that make product photos look more enticing and professional.

Furthermore, Canva AI facilitates the integration of lifestyle images that showcase products in use, a technique proven to boost conversion rates. These capabilities do not just save time; they also empower sellers to maintain a consistent aesthetic appeal across all listings, reinforcing brand identity and trust. Overall, Canva AI is an indispensable asset, enabling e-commerce platforms to deliver visually appealing product displays that captivate and convert.

Canva AI for Event Invitations and Promotional Materials

Canva AI revolutionizes the creation of event invitations and promotional materials, offering entrepreneurs a powerful tool to captivate and inform their audience with minimal effort. The platform's AI capabilities automate the design process, allowing users to create custom, eye-catching invitations and materials that reflect the unique theme and branding of their events. Pre-designed templates can be quickly tailored to specific needs, ensuring consistency and professionalism across all promotional outputs.

Moreover, Canva AI integrates advanced features such as RSVP tracking and audience segmentation tools, which facilitate effective communication and follow-up. This not only enhances the attendee experience but also streamlines the management of event-related logistics. Entrepreneurs can leverage these tools to create personalized interactions, boosting engagement and attendance rates.

Additionally, the platform supports real-time collaboration, enabling teams to work together seamlessly from different locations. This feature ensures that every detail, from typography to color scheme, aligns perfectly with the event's objectives, creating materials that are not just functional but also compelling and memorable.

Automating Newsletters and Email Campaign Designs

The integration of Canva AI into the newsletter and email campaign design processes offers a transformative edge for entrepreneurs. This automation not only simplifies the creation of professional and aesthetically appealing communications but also allows for personalized touches that speak directly to the audience. By using Canva AI's pre-designed templates and drag-and-drop features, crafting consistent, on-brand content becomes less time-consuming and more efficient.

Canva AI's dynamic content suggestions adapt to user interactions and preferences, making each newsletter unique and targeted. This capability ensures that emails resonate more profoundly with recipients, enhancing engagement rates. Automated scheduling tools within Canva AI further streamline the distribution process, ensuring timely delivery and maintaining regular contact with customers.

Moreover, analytics tools embedded within Canva AI help entrepreneurs measure the success of their campaigns in real-time. Insights into open rates and click-through rates guide future designs, optimizing the impact of every sent email. With Canva AI, the complexities of manual design are replaced with a straightforward, effective approach that propels marketing efforts and fosters business growth.

Using Canva AI to Design Custom Business Cards

Business cards remain a staple of business etiquette and networking. Canva AI harnesses this classic tool's potential by enabling entrepreneurs to design custom business cards effortlessly. With its intuitive AI-driven interface, users can tailor designs that not only stand out but also resonate with their brand identity.

The AI suggestions in Canva streamline the selection of color schemes, typography, and layout, aligning the aesthetic with the company's vision. Beyond simple design elements, Canva AI can integrate dynamic features like QR codes, which link directly to digital profiles or websites, enhancing the interactivity of the card. This modern twist on traditional business cards sets a novel standard for professional interactions.

Furthermore, with Canva AI, the creation process is significantly optimized. Entrepreneurs can produce designs in bulk, maintaining uniformity across all cards while making individual adjustments as needed. This capability ensures high-quality results with minimal time investment, practically redefining the efficiency of creating personalized business cards.

Developing Engaging Infographics with Data Integration

Infographics serve as a powerful tool in distilling complex data into digestible, engaging visuals that capture audience attention. Canva AI revolutionizes this creative process by integrating data seamlessly into infographics, ensuring they not only inform but also appeal aesthetically. Entrepreneurs can leverage Canva AI's sophisticated algorithms to extract key information and trends from datasets, which the platform then visually enhances with vibrant charts, graphs, and icons.

With the intuitive interface of Canva AI, users can customize each element to reflect their brand's style and message. This includes selecting from a range of templates that are dynamically adjusted as data updates, keeping the information current without the need for manual revisions. This feature is crucial for maintaining relevance in fast-paced market environments.

Moreover, Canva AI's collaboration tools allow teams to co-create and refine infographics, ensuring a diverse input of perspectives that enrich the final product. This cooperative approach, coupled with AI's precision, dramatically reduces the time and complexity involved in producing high-quality, informative infographics. Ultimately, Canva AI empowers entrepreneurs to turn raw data into compelling visual stories that drive engagement and comprehension.

Optimizing UI/UX Design with Canva AI Tools

Optimizing user interface (UI) and user experience (UX) design is pivotal in today's digital landscape, and Canva AI provides powerful tools that streamline these processes for entrepreneurs. By utilizing Canva's intuitive AI-driven platform, designers can create more effective and appealing digital interfaces with minimal technical skill. The AI suggestions help fine-tune color palettes, typography, and layout frameworks, ensuring designs are not only aesthetically pleasing but also user-friendly.

Moreover, Canva AI's ability to analyze user engagement metrics enables designers to make data-informed decisions that enhance the usability and functionality of digital products. This integration of AI insights helps in refining user flows and improving overall interaction patterns, which are crucial in retaining user engagement. Enhanced interaction leads to increased satisfaction and, ultimately, higher conversion rates.

Collaboration in Canva is seamlessly facilitated through real-time updates and shared workspaces, allowing teams to co-design efficiently. This collective approach ensures that all aspects of UI/UX are thoroughly considered, resulting in a robust design that aligns perfectly with user expectations and business goals. Altogether, Canva AI tools empower entrepreneurs to master the art of UI/UX design, creating impactful digital experiences that drive success.

Creating Video Graphics and Thumbnails Using Canva AI

In the dynamic world of digital content, captivating video graphics and thumbnails are essential for grabbing audience attention. Canva AI streamlines this creative process, enabling entrepreneurs to design high-impact visuals with ease. The platform's AI-driven tools suggest optimal layouts, color schemes, and typography that enhance the visual appeal of video content, ensuring that thumbnails stand out in crowded media feeds.

Beyond basic design, Canva AI leverages user engagement data to recommend styles and elements that are more likely to resonate with specific audiences. This targeted approach not only improves click-through rates but also enhances the overall effectiveness of video marketing campaigns. Entrepreneurs can quickly generate multiple thumbnail options, test their performance, and select the most effective design without needing extensive graphic design experience.

Moreover, the integration of Canva AI into video production workflows allows for consistent branding across all media outputs. This consistency is key to building a recognizable and trusted brand identity. By automating and optimizing the creation of video graphics and thumbnails, Canva AI helps entrepreneurs save time while achieving professional, eye-catching results that captivate and engage.

Canva AI for Personalized Stationery and Printables

Harnessing the power of Canva AI, entrepreneurs can dive into the niche of personalized stationery and printables, a market that values uniqueness and personal touch. With Canva AI, designing bespoke stationery items such as letterheads, notebooks, and planners becomes not only feasible but also enjoyable. The AI tools suggest design variations that capture the essence of a brand or personal style, making each creation unique.

Additionally, the AI's ability to analyze current design trends ensures that all created items are modern and appealing. Entrepreneurs can use these insights to craft designs that resonate with specific target markets, increasing the allure of their personalized products. This capability is particularly advantageous when creating seasonal or event-specific items, providing an ever-relevant product line to customers.

Canva AI also simplifies the process of setting up e-commerce integration, allowing entrepreneurs to easily sell their personalized stationery and printables online. With features that support digital product previews and customer customization options, Canva AI not only enhances product appeal but also streamlines the sales process, helping entrepreneurs expand their market reach while maintaining a high level of customer satisfaction.

Leveraging Canva AI for eBook and Digital Publication Designs

The digital landscape has transformed publishing, with eBooks and digital magazines becoming increasingly popular. Canva AI supports this shift by enabling entrepreneurs to produce sophisticated eBook layouts and covers that capture readers' attention. The platform's AI-driven tools automate much of the design process, suggesting themes that resonate with the intended audience and align with genre-specific aesthetics.

For instance, Canva AI can analyze text content and suggest imagery and typography that enhance the narrative or informational value of digital publications. This not only saves time but also helps maintain a high level of design quality that might otherwise require a professional graphic designer. The simplicity of creating visually appealing eBook covers and page layouts makes Canva an invaluable tool for self-publishers and content creators aiming to expand their reach.

Additionally, Canva AI incorporates feedback mechanisms that allow users to test different designs with target demographics, ensuring the final product not only looks great but is also optimized for reader engagement and satisfaction. This user-centric design approach helps in building a loyal readership for digital publications.

Monetizing Your Canva Creations through Digital Downloads

In the digital marketplace, a compelling design can be as valuable as the product it promotes. Canva AI's platform opens up a new revenue stream for entrepreneurs through the sale of digital downloads. This approach leverages design assets like templates, graphics, and complete layouts that users can customize for their own needs.

Selling digital products crafted on Canva AI offers the advantages of scalability and minimal overhead costs. Entrepreneurs can create a design once and sell it repeatedly, reaching a global audience without the need for physical inventory. Whether it's templates for social media posts, business presentations, or marketing materials, each item can translate into ongoing revenue.

Furthermore, Canva AI simplifies the integration of eCommerce platforms, enabling seamless transactions. With strategic pricing and effective marketing, digital assets become a sustainable business model, providing substantial return on investment. Ultimately, Canva AI not only enhances design capabilities but also furnishes users with the tools to monetize their creativity in the digital age.

Integrating Canva AI with Other Business Tools and Platforms

Integrating Canva AI with various business tools and platforms exemplifies the transformative potential of advanced design technology in today's entrepreneurial ecosystem. By seamlessly connecting with CRM systems, email marketing platforms, and social media management tools, Canva AI serves as a nexus, enhancing the efficiency and effectiveness of cross-platform marketing strategies.

The integration capabilities allow for the synchronization of design elements and branding across all marketing channels, ensuring a cohesive brand identity. Entrepreneurs can easily export designs to other platforms, adapt them for different formats, and schedule posts directly from Canva, streamlining operations and reducing turnaround times.

Furthermore, by harnessing the power of API connections, Canva AI can pull data directly from these tools, enabling personalized content creation at scale which is essential for targeted marketing campaigns. This level of integration fosters a more data-driven approach, optimizing marketing efforts based on audience engagement and behavior insights.

Canva AI's Role in Content Strategy and Brand Consistency

Canva AI revolutionizes content strategy by aligning visual elements with an organization's branding guidelines, ensuring a consistent look and feel across all marketing materials. This alignment is critical in building brand recognition and trust among target audiences. By leveraging AI-driven tools, businesses can automate the design process, maintaining brand uniformity with minimal manual intervention.

The platform's ability to analyze brand elements like color palettes, typography, and logo placement optimizes the creation of consistent content that resonates with the desired corporate image. Canva AI's role extends to suggesting content formats and layouts that are proven to be more engaging based on historical data and industry trends. This not only ensures aesthetic consistency but also enhances content effectiveness.

Furthermore, Canva AI facilitates real-time collaboration and feedback, ensuring that all team members are aligned with the brand's content strategy. The streamlined workflow allows for quick adjustments and reiterations, pivotal in maintaining a coherent brand narrative in the dynamic digital landscape.

Maximizing Outreach with Canva AI-Generated Advertising Materials

In the dynamic world of digital marketing, visibility and reach are paramount. Canva AI capitalizes on this need by enabling entrepreneurs to generate eye-catching advertising materials that grasp consumer attention and broaden outreach. Utilizing sophisticated AI algorithms, Canva AI provides customizations that not only resonate with targeted demographics but also ensure that advertisements stand out in a crowded marketplace.

The automated features of Canva AI expedite the creation process, allowing for rapid deployment of campaigns across various platforms, including social media, email, and web advertisements. This swift adaptability is crucial for tapping into trending topics and harnessing peak engagement moments, thus maximizing exposure and ROI.

Moreover, Canva AI's analytics tools offer invaluable insights into the effectiveness of advertising designs, enabling real-time optimizations. Entrepreneurs can tweak their campaigns based on performance data, ensuring that their marketing efforts are not only extensive but also impactful. With Canva AI, the potential for amplified outreach is immense, crafting a pathway to enhanced market presence and revenue.

Enhancing Photo Editing and Manipulation with AI

Canva AI elevates photo editing and manipulation to unprecedented levels, empowering entrepreneurs to refine their visual content with sophisticated ease. The integration of AI tools within Canva simplifies complex editing techniques, making professional-grade enhancements accessible to all users, regardless of their prior design experience.

For instance, AI-driven features like automatic color adjustment and smart cropping intuitively enhance photo quality while preserving authenticity. This not only saves valuable time but also guarantees a high standard of aesthetic appeal in marketing campaigns. Additionally, AI-powered retouching tools remove imperfections seamlessly, ensuring every image reflects the intended brand image flawlessly.

Moreover, Canva AI's capabilities extend to creating dynamic visual elements by manipulating images to produce novel effects, such as blending backgrounds or adding artistic filters. This level of creativity was once the domain of expert graphic designers but is now readily available, fostering innovation in visual content strategies.

Such enhancements spearheaded by Canva AI not only streamline design workflows but also amplify the visual storytelling capacity of entrepreneurs, directly influencing engagement and conversion rates positively.

Canva AI for Animated Designs and Motion Graphics

The transformative potential of Canva AI extends into the realms of animated designs and motion graphics, offering entrepreneurs novel ways to captivate and engage audiences. By incorporating movement into visual storytelling, users can give life to static images, making content more interactive and attention-grabbing.

Navigating through Canva's user-friendly interface, entrepreneurs can seamlessly create animations using pre-set templates or build custom motion graphics from scratch. The AI-driven platform suggests animations based on the content's context and the latest trends, ensuring creations are not only aesthetically pleasing but also strategically effective. This is particularly useful for social media posts, advertisements, and explainer videos, where dynamic content can significantly boost viewer engagement.

Furthermore, Canva AI enables quick adaptations of motion graphics for various platforms, maintaining visual quality across different media formats. This versatility ensures marketers can optimize their animated content for any marketing channel, enhancing reach and impact. With Canva AI, the complex world of animation becomes accessible, transforming ideas into animated realities with ease.

Collaborative Features in Canva AI for Team Projects

Canva AI provides a robust platform for team collaboration, centralizing design processes and enhancing project management. The platform enables teams to work together on designs in real time, offering tools that streamline communication and ensure consistency across all design elements. Team members can comment directly on each design, make inline suggestions, and approve changes, fostering a seamless exchange of ideas and swift decision-making.

Further enriching the collaborative experience, Canva AI's version control capabilities allow team members to track changes, revert to previous versions, and understand each alteration's impact. This feature is essential in maintaining the integrity of the design process and avoiding miscommunication. It ensures that all team members are aligned with the latest updates and project directions.

Moreover, Canva AI supports role-based access control, permitting project leaders to assign specific tasks and responsibilities while controlling access to sensitive design elements. This hierarchical structuring ensures that projects proceed without overwriting or duplicating efforts, optimizing team productivity and safeguarding creative assets. The integration of these collaborative features marks Canva AI as a quintessential tool for teams aiming to innovate and execute projects efficiently.

Securing Your Designs: Intellectual Property Considerations

In the creative world of digital design, securing intellectual property (IP) is paramount. Canva AI, while streamlining design processes, introduces complexities regarding IP rights. Entrepreneurs must navigate these waters carefully to protect their unique creations.

The integration of AI tools in design software like Canva offers immense benefits, but it also raises questions about ownership and copyright. When AI-assists in creating a design, determining whether the output is considered an original work of the user or a derivative of AI-generated elements is crucial. Awareness and understanding of copyright laws become essential to safeguard one's designs and avoid unintentional infringement.

Additionally, Canva AI provides features that help secure designs. Its platform allows for the setting of privacy controls and copyright notices directly on works created. Utilizing these tools helps in clearly establishing the rights over a design, providing a layer of legal protection and peace of mind for creatives.

Lastly, staying informed about changes in copyright legislation and adapting usage of AI tools accordingly is advisable. Being proactive in these areas ensures that the full potential of Canva AI can be harnessed without compromising on IP security.

Analyzing User Engagement with Canva AI-Enhanced Designs

In the realm of digital design, effectively gauging user engagement can transform how businesses interact with their audiences. Canva AI has evolved as not just a design tool, but as a comprehensive analytical platform that enables entrepreneurs to understand and improve audience engagement through visual content. By integrating analytics directly with design tools, Canva AI offers real-time feedback on how designs perform across different demographics and platforms.

Key analytics include viewer interactions, time spent on visuals, and conversion rates, which are essential for refining marketing strategies and maximizing ROI. These metrics allow businesses to pinpoint which elements capture attention and encourage engagement, fine-tuning future designs to better meet audience preferences. Furthermore, A/B testing features enable a comparative analysis of different design versions, providing clear insights into which variations perform best.

Ultimately, leveraging Canva AI's sophisticated analytics tools helps businesses create more impactful visuals that resonate with viewers. As digital landscapes become increasingly competitive, the ability to analytically assess design effectiveness is indispensable for maintaining relevance and engagement in the market.

Future Trends: The Evolution of AI in Graphic Design Tools

Looking ahead, the trajectory of AI in graphic design promises revolutionary changes, primarily through deep learning and generative design technologies. These advancements hint at a future where AI's role transcends simple task automation, venturing into creative partnership. Imagine AI systems that suggest design concepts based on current trends or the emotional tone of a campaign brief.

Moreover, AI is set to enhance user interfaces, making them more intuitive. Designers will likely see tools that adapt to their workflow preferences, offering a more personalized and streamlined design experience. Predictive analytics integrated with AI might also alert designers to shifting user preferences, enabling real-time adjustments to campaigns.

In the essence of collaboration, AI is expected to improve co-design by enabling more efficient communication among distributed teams. Cloud-based AI services could allow real-time design updates and feedback, ensuring that no geographical barriers hinder the creative process. As we stand on the brink of these transformative changes, embracing AI is imperative for staying competitive in the evolving world of graphic design.

SUMMARY

The chapter titled 'Canva AI: Streamlining Design Processes for Entrepreneurs' explores the significant impact of Canva AI in transforming design for entrepreneurs. It begins by introducing Canva AI as a revolutionary tool that democratizes design by making sophisticated design tools accessible to all skill levels. The intuitive interface and AI-driven features such as automatic branding and design suggestions help reduce the time and expertise required to produce high-quality visual assets. This allows entrepreneurs to focus more on strategic aspects rather than the nuances of design mechanics, fostering innovation and efficiency in digital marketing. Setting up an optimal Canva AI workspace involves customizing the dashboard to align with specific project needs, integrating brand elements, and using templates and keyboard shortcuts to streamline design processes and improve efficiency. The AI capabilities extend to automating logo and branding designs, ensuring consistency across platforms and enhancing brand recognition and loyalty. Canva AI also plays a crucial role in creating marketing collaterals, social media graphics, animated designs, and e-commerce product imagery, simplifying the creation process while maintaining professional quality. Further, the platform aids in designing business-oriented materials such as business presentations, business cards, and event materials, integrating advanced features that promote productivity and collaboration. The use of Canva AI for content creation is not limited to static images but extends to dynamic content such as video graphics, animations, and interactive infographics, enhancing audience engagement. Moreover, Canva AI supports the integration with other business tools and platforms, simplifying workflow and maximizing outreach with automated advertising materials. The chapter also discusses the implications of using AI in design in terms of intellectual property and the future trends that indicate a more collaborative and intuitive AI integration in graphic design tools.

REFERENCES

[1] Rayome, A. D. (2020) 'How to use Canva to design business cards', CNET. https://www.cnet.com/how-to/how-to-use-canva-to-design-business-cards/

[2] Tinn, K. (2019) 'Artificial Intelligence and Intellectual Property: An Exploration', Harvard Journal of Law & Technology, vol. 32, no. 2. https://jolt.law.harvard.edu/assets/articlePDFs/v32/32HarvJLTech325.pdf

[3] Marr, B. (2021) 'The Incredible Ways Canva Is Using Artificial Intelligence For Graphic Design', Forbes. https://www.forbes.com/sites/bernardmarr/2021/06/04/the-incredible-ways-canva-is-using-artificial-intelligence-for-graphic-design/?sh=24552eab6d2a

CASE STUDY: REVOLUTIONIZING SMALL BUSINESS BRANDING WITH CANVA AI

Imagine a small, artisan coffee shop, 'Brew & Beans', located in a bustling neighborhood of a metropolitan city. The owner, Julia, faced a significant challenge in differentiating her shop amid fierce competition. With a limited budget for marketing and design, Julia turned to Canva AI to overhaul her branding and marketing efforts efficiently and affordably.

Julia began by using Canva AI's logo automation tools to design a new logo that reflected the unique personality of her business—the warmth of a local coffee house combined with the sophistication of high-end espresso machines. This tool allowed her to input her brand colors and get suggestions on design elements that aligned with her vision. Next, she utilized the AI-driven branding templates to create a cohesive brand identity across various materials such as menu cards, promotional flyers, and social media posts.

The transformative moment came when Julia decided to leverage Canva AI's capabilities for her digital marketing campaigns. She used Canva's pre-designed, customizable templates to create visually appealing Instagram stories, posts, and ads that effectively communicated the brand's new identity. The 'Styles' feature acted as a personal graphic designer, suggesting refinements and ensuring consistency across all designs, which significantly boosted her business's online visibility.

Moreover, the analytics integration in Canva AI provided Julia with real-time feedback on her marketing efforts. She could see which designs and posts generated the most customer engagement and adjust her strategies accordingly. This data-driven approach allowed her to optimize her ad spend, focusing more on high-performing designs and less on those that did not engage her audience as well.

The outcome was outstanding. Within months, 'Brew & Beans' saw a 25% increase in foot traffic and a 40% increase in social media engagement. By harnessing the power of Canva AI, Julia transformed her coffee shop into a recognizable brand in her community, demonstrating the profound impact of AI-driven design tools on small business marketing.

Case Study: Modernizing a Traditional Publishing House with Canva AI

In a sprawling city known for its rich literary history, Mason & Brooks Publishing, a traditional book publisher, faced diminishing returns and growing competition from digital content creators. The leadership, concerned about the future, decided to innovate by integrating Canva AI into their publication design processes. Their goal was to modernize their book designs and marketing materials to attract a broader, more digitally-savvy audience without losing their traditional charm.

The first step was the redesign of book covers using Canva AI's template library, which provided an extensive range of modern, attractive designs that could be customized to reflect the themes of various genres such as mystery, romance, and science fiction. The AI-powered 'Styles' feature helped select the best typography and color schemes that resonated with target demographic preferences, dramatically improving the visual appeal of new releases.

Next, Mason & Brooks utilized Canva AI to overhaul their marketing strategies. Implementing AI-driven data analytics, the team could track which types of designs and promotional materials performed best on platforms like Instagram and Facebook. This insight allowed them to tailor their digital ads and social media posts more effectively, ensuring maximum engagement. The integration of AI tools streamlined the creation process, enabling the marketing team to produce more content in less time, a crucial advantage in the fast-paced world of publishing.

Moreover, Canva AI enabled the publishing house to create digital versions of their books with engaging layouts and interactive elements, making them suitable for e-readers and mobile devices. This not only expanded their market reach but also catered to the growing consumer preference for digital reading platforms.

The transformation was phenomenal. Within a year, Mason & Brooks observed a 50% increase in online sales, and their social media following doubled, rejuvenating the brand's image and positioning it competitively in the modern digital landscape.

Case Study: Integrating Canva AI into a Multinational Marketing Strategy

Consider the scenario of Globex Corporation, a multinational company specializing in consumer electronics, which faces the common challenge of maintaining a consistent brand identity across different markets while also localizing content to meet diverse cultural and market needs. With a presence in over 50 countries, coordinating marketing efforts and producing localized content quickly and efficiently becomes imperative. To address this, Globex turns to Canva AI as a central part of their marketing strategy.

The first step in this integration involved training regional marketing teams on using Canva AI's tools effectively. This enabled them to create localized marketing materials that resonate with local audiences but still align with Globex's global brand standards. The 'Styles' AI feature proved crucial by suggesting design alterations that reflect local cultures and trends while maintaining a cohesive brand aesthetic.

One notable instance occurred during a product launch in Asia. The regional team used Canva AI to adapt the campaign materials to reflect Asian design preferences, which are markedly different from Western aesthetics. Canva AI's intuitive AI algorithms suggested changes in color schemes, typography, and imagery that better appealed to Asian consumers, enhancing the campaign's regional acceptance without extensive manual input.

The result was a highly successful launch, marked by an increase in engagement rates by 70% compared to previous campaigns. Moreover, the time taken to produce launch materials reduced by 50%, demonstrating Canva AI's effectiveness in enhancing productivity. The ability of Canva AI to integrate seamlessly with Globex's digital asset management systems also meant that all materials could be centrally accessed and modified, further simplifying the workflow.

Through this case, Globex not only achieved significant efficiencies in production but also ensured that its marketing materials were culturally sensitive and engaging for various markets. The strategic use of Canva AI empowered Globex to manage and amplify its multinational presence effortlessly, showcasing the pivotal role of AI in modern marketing strategies across diverse geographic locations.

Case Study: Empowering a Non-Profit Organization with Canva AI

Imagine a non-profit organization, 'Green Earth Initiative', dedicated to environmental conservation and awareness, struggling to make a significant impact due to limited resources and a lack of professional design capabilities. Recognizing the need to enhance their visibility and engage more effectively with the public, the organization decided to embrace Canva AI to revolutionize their promotional and educational materials.

The journey began with a workshop for the Green Earth team, focusing on learning how to utilize Canva AI's suite effectively. They started by redesigning their informational brochures using Canva AI's vast template library, selecting designs that conveyed serenity and connection to nature, which are core to their mission. The AI-powered 'Styles' feature assisted in harmonizing colors and fonts that resonated with their message of sustainability and conservation.

Subsequently, they explored Canva AI's features for social media content, recognizing the power of platforms like Facebook and Instagram to reach a broader audience. Utilizing the 'Content Planner' and 'Magic Resize' tools, the team was able to schedule posts consistently and adapt their designs flawlessly across different social media formats, increasing their operational efficiency and online presence.

Another significant advancement was the utilization of Canva AI's video creation tools. The organization created short, impactful videos explaining their projects and the importance of public support, which were shared during online campaigns and virtual fundraisers. The AI recommendations helped select engaging animations and backdrops that successfully attracted viewer attention.

The integration of Canva AI transformed the non-profit's approach to communication. They saw a 35% increase in engagement on their social media platforms and a 20% rise in fundraising within six months. The adoption of AI-driven design tools not only streamlined their design process, saving time and resources, but also allowed them to present a more professional and cohesive brand image that effectively drew support and awareness to their cause.

Case Study: Enhancing Real Estate Marketing with Canva AI

Envision a mid-sized real estate agency, Skyline Realty, operating in a competitive urban market. Facing challenges in standing out amongst numerous competitors and striving to captivate a diverse client base, Skyline Realty decided to overhaul their marketing strategy by implementing Canva AI.

The first step involved a complete redesign of their property listings presentation. Using Canva AI's vast array of templates and AI-driven design suggestions, Skyline Realty was able to produce visually appealing and information-rich listings that highlighted key property features effectively. The AI's ability to automate the alignment of text and imagery ensured that each listing was not only aesthetically pleasing but also easy to read and informative. This greatly enhanced the online browsing experience for potential buyers, making properties more attractive and increasing click-through rates on listings.

Next, Skyline Realty utilized Canva AI's branding tools to create a consistent and professional brand image across all marketing channels. They developed a unique set of brand colors, fonts, and logos that were integrated into every marketing material, from business cards and flyers to digital advertisements and email campaigns. The consistency in branding helped in building a recognizable and trusted brand image that resonated with their target audience.

Moreover, Canva AI's advanced editing tools enabled the agency to quickly adapt marketing materials for different platforms without compromising on design quality. Whether adjusting the size of digital ads for various social media platforms or modifying flyer designs for print, the efficiency of Canva AI significantly reduced the turnaround times for these tasks. This agility was crucial in capitalizing on market opportunities as soon as they arose, keeping Skyline Realty ahead in a fast-moving real estate market.

The impactful utilization of Canva AI culminated in a substantial growth in client engagement. Within a year of implementation, Skyline Realty reported a 30% increase in inquiries and a notable improvement in sales conversions. The ease of use and the powerful capabilities of Canva AI transformed their marketing strategy, proving that even in traditional industries like real estate, innovative AI tools can drive significant business growth and customer satisfaction.

Case Study: Reimagining Art Gallery Exhibitions with Canva AI

Consider the transformation of ArtVista Gallery, a contemporary art gallery located in the cultural heart of a bustling city. The challenge the gallery faced was multi-layered, from enhancing the promotional materials to modernizing the visitor experience without detracting from the art itself. To tackle these objectives, ArtVista Gallery embraced Canva AI, capitalizing on its versatile tools to digitalize and revamp their branding and operational strategies.

The initial step involved adopting Canva AI's suite to redesign the gallery's branding, including invitations, promotional banners, digital catalogs, and visitor guides. One of the key features utilized was Canva AI's template system, which streamlined the creation process while ensuring high-quality, visually engaging outputs. By inputting their brand colors and themes into the system, ArtVista achieved a cohesive aesthetic across all promotional materials, which boosted the gallery's professional image significantly.

To further engage audiences, the gallery's marketing team used Canva AI to develop interactive digital guides that could be accessed via smartphones. These guides not only offered detailed artistic insights but also incorporated AI-driven features like virtual reality views of how certain artworks would look in different settings. The engaging format attracted a younger demographic and enriched the overall viewing experience, making art more accessible and comprehensible to the general public.

Moreover, leveraging Canva AI for the design of the gallery's email newsletters allowed for consistent aesthetic communications with current and potential patrons. The AI-driven analytics helped the gallery understand which features and exhibitions attracted more interest or interaction, shaping future exhibitions and promotions strategically.

The remarkable conversion of ArtVista into a digitally enhanced art hub resulted in a 50% increase in visitor engagement and a 30% rise in exhibition sales over a year. Canva AI's tools not only conservatively enhanced the user experience but also equipped ArtVista with a progressive approach to handle diverse artistic exhibitions and their promotions efficiently.

Case Study: Transforming a Fitness Center's Digital Presence with Canva AI

In the competitive arena of health and fitness, standing out online is vital. A mid-sized fitness center, 'FitLife Hub', located in a busy urban area, faced the challenge of rejuvenating its digital marketing strategy to attract more local clientele and build a stronger online community. To achieve this, FitLife Hub turned to Canva AI, integrating its tools into their marketing workflow to enhance visual content and streamline design processes.

FitLife Hub's initial goal was to develop a distinctive brand image that could resonate with a diverse customer base. They utilized Canva AI's logo maker and branding templates to create a fresh, vibrant brand identity, which was then consistently applied across all digital and physical marketing materials. This included the redesign of their website banners, promotional emails, and social media posts to ensure brand consistency that appeals aesthetically to potential and current gym members.

Furthermore, to capitalize on the power of social media, FitLife Hub began regularly posting engaging content using Canva AI's vast library of fitness-themed templates. These were customized to feature motivational quotes, workout tips, and client success stories, all styled in the center's new vibrant brand colors and fonts. The drag-and-drop interface and the intuitive data-driven design suggestions provided by Canva AI enabled the marketing team to produce high-quality visuals quickly, vital for maintaining an active and engaging social media presence.

To measure the effectiveness of their new digital strategy, FitLife Hub also took advantage of Canva AI's analytics tools. These tools provided insights into which types of posts generated the most engagement and conversions. This data-driven approach allowed the center to fine-tune their advertisements and organic content strategy, optimizing for the highest customer engagement and return on investment.

Over six months, FitLife Hub witnessed a 40% increase in social media followers and a 30% uptick in new memberships, testament to the power of a revitalized digital presence enabled by advanced AI-driven tools. The ease and efficiency of Canva AI not only transformed FitLife Hub's marketing strategy but also significantly reduced the time and cost associated with generating appealing marketing materials.

Case Study: Revitalizing a Local Restaurant Chain's Brand with Canva AI

In the competitive dining industry, a local restaurant chain, 'SavorEats', faced the challenge of renewing its brand to attract a broader demographic and better compete with new, trendy eateries. With multiple locations across a major city, maintaining brand consistency while incorporating local flavors and themes was essential. SavorEats turned to Canva AI to manage this complex branding transition smoothly and effectively.

The first step for SavorEats was to redefine their visual identity to reflect a fresher, more modern appeal that resonates with both current patrons and potential new customers. With help from Canva AI's suite of design tools, the marketing team at SavorEats quickly set out to create a new series of menu designs, promotional posters, and digital marketing materials that featured vibrant visuals and contemporary design elements. The AI-powered 'Logo Maker' allowed them to revamp their old logo, giving it a modern twist while maintaining elements that reflected the chain's history and values.

Subsequently, each restaurant in the chain utilized Canva AI's 'Magic Resize' and 'Styles' tool to customize their marketing materials to reflect local culture and demographics, while keeping a unified brand image across all locations. This localization included adjustments in language, imagery, and promotional offers to cater to local tastes and preferences, which were vital for reaching a wider audience effectively.

Moreover, SavorEats leveraged Canva AI's scheduling tools to streamline their social media campaigns. The 'Content Planner' feature allowed them to automate and synchronize their postings across various platforms, ensuring regular engagement without requiring constant manual oversight. This automation was crucial during special promotions and seasonal events, helping to maximize their outreach and promotional impact.

The transformation led to a significant reversal in the restaurant chain's fortunes. Within the first year, SavorEats experienced a remarkable 35% increase in overall sales, with a noticeable upsurge in social media engagement and online reviews. The redesign and strategic use of AI tools not only elevated the brand's visual communication but also enhanced operational efficiency, making marketing efforts far more effective and keeping the brand viable in a fiercely competitive market.

REVIEW QUESTIONS

1. Sarah, an entrepreneur, has recently discovered Canva AI and is excited about the potential it holds for her startup's branding needs. She wants to create consistent branding across her digital marketing materials without extensive graphic design experience. Based on her requirements, which feature of Canva AI would be most beneficial for Sarah?

A) AI-driven suggestions for layout and typography

B) Automatic resizing of designs for different platforms

C) Real-time collaboration tools

D) Integration with social media for direct posting

Answer: A

Explanation: AI-driven suggestions for layout and typography would be most beneficial for Sarah as it aligns with her need to create consistent branding across all marketing materials. This feature of Canva AI helps users without extensive graphic designing skills to automatically generate professional-looking designs. These suggestions ensure that all materials not only maintain a uniform appearance but also adhere to brand standards, which is crucial for building a consistent brand identity.

2. John runs a small marketing firm and uses Canva AI to streamline the creation of social media graphics for his clients. Given his need to rapidly adapt designs based on market feedback, which Canva AI feature should John focus on utilizing to maximize his productivity?

A) Extensive library of pre-designed templates

B) Dynamic drag-and-drop editor

C) Advanced color adjustment tools

D) Automated backup and cloud storage

Answer: B

Explanation: The dynamic drag-and-drop editor is the ideal feature for John as it allows for quick modifications and adaptations to designs, which is essential for responding to real-time market feedback. This feature in Canva AI enables users to efficiently alter elements such as images, fonts, and layouts without needing to start from scratch, thus significantly enhancing turnaround times for campaigns that need to adapt to ongoing market trends.

REVIEW QUESTIONS

3. Melissa is looking to automate the creation of logos for her multiple startup ventures with a focus on aligning them closely with her brands' ethos. Which aspect of Canva AI's logo creation tool should she prioritize to achieve high alignment with her branding strategy?

A) Utilization of brand-specific color schemes

B) Incorporation of trendy design elements

C) Use of generic templates for quick creation

D) Engagement with a professional designer for ideas

Answer: A

Explanation: Utilization of brand-specific color schemes is crucial for Melissa. Canva AI's capability to incorporate these elements in the logo creation process ensures that the logos resonate with each of her brands' identity and ethos. The AI tools in Canva analyze the brand's core elements and automatically suggest colors and styles that match, ensuring that each logo is not only unique but also aligned with the business's overall branding strategy.

4. Alex, involved in e-commerce, aims to enhance his product imagery to boost sales. Recognizing the potential of Canva AI, which feature should he primarily use to improve the visual appeal and effectiveness of his product listings?

A) Background remover and image enhancer

B) Real-time design collaboration

C) Automated content planner

D) Integration with e-commerce platforms

Answer: A

Explanation: The background remover and image enhancer features of Canva AI are ideal for Alex's needs in e-commerce. These tools allow for the quick enhancement of product images, making them cleaner and more professional without the cost of high-end photography. By removing distracting elements and enhancing key product features, these tools help in creating visually appealing imagery that is more likely to attract and convert potential customers.

PICTORY AI: SIMPLIFYING VIDEO PRODUCTION WITH AI

Introduction to Pictory AI and Video Production Automation

As we delve into the realm of video production, the emergence of Pictory AI as a formidable tool in streamlining video-making processes cannot be overstated. Harnessing the power of artificial intelligence, Pictory AI simplifies the creation of professional and compelling videos, making it accessible even to those with minimal technical expertise.

Pictory AI specializes in automating key aspects of video production, from content trimming and voice-overs to text overlays, offering a seamless workflow that saves time and reduces complexity. For businesses and content creators, this means faster production times and the ability to produce high-quality videos at scale without a steep learning curve or hefty investment in sophisticated editing software.

Moreover, Pictory AI's intuitive interface allows users to effortlessly transform written content into engaging video narratives. This feature is pivotal for marketers, educators, and media professionals aiming to enhance their online presence and engagement through dynamic and aesthetically pleasing video content.

Setting Up Pictory AI for Various Video Projects

Setting up Pictory AI for diverse video projects is a streamlined process designed to accommodate various types of video production needs. Initially, users should define the project's scope, including target audience, video style, and intended message. This clarity assists Pictory AI in tailoring the automation process to fit specific requirements, ensuring the output is both relevant and impactful.

The next step involves organizing the content materials. Pictory AI supports a wide range of multimedia inputs, from text scripts to digital images and video clips. Users can import these elements directly into the platform, where AI assists in arranging them cohesively. It's essential to review and adjust the AI's selection and sequencing to maintain a personal touch and ensure the final product aligns with the user's vision.

Finally, leverage Pictory AI's customization options to fine-tune the videos. Adjust colors, transitions, and overlays to match branding requirements. Once satisfied, users can render the project into various formats suitable for different platforms, maximizing accessibility and viewer engagement. Each step in Pictory AI's setup is designed to be intuitive, making professional video production accessible to all.

Creating Seamless Video Tutorials with Pictory AI

Creating educational content has never been easier with Pictory AI. By automating much of the video production process, Pictory AI enables educators and trainers to develop seamless video tutorials effortlessly. Users can convert lengthy documents or presentations into concise, impactful videos that engage and inform their audience effectively.

Pictory AI's ability to digest extensive information and highlight key points allows for the creation of clear and structured tutorials. This is particularly beneficial in educational settings where clarity and concision are paramount. The AI simplifies the editing process, ensuring that transitions are smooth and that the narrative flow is maintained, which is crucial for keeping viewers engaged throughout the learning session.

Furthermore, with Pictory AI, personalization of content is straightforward. Instructors can tailor their tutorials to the needs of their specific audience, adding custom overlays, annotations, or voiceovers in multiple languages. This adaptability makes it an invaluable tool for creating diverse educational content that caters to varied learning environments.

Automating Social Media Videos for Engagement

The digital marketplace thrives on engagement, and social media videos are at the forefront of this dynamic. Pictory AI revolutionizes how brands create captivating video content quickly and efficiently, catering to the fast-paced demands of social media channels.

By automating the video production process, Pictory AI enables content creators to generate high-quality videos that are both engaging and timely. The platform's AI-driven tools streamline the creation of customized video content that resonates with specific audience segments. This precision targeting helps in enhancing viewer interaction and prolonging engagement on platforms like Facebook, Instagram, and Twitter.

Furthermore, Pictory AI's capabilities extend to analyzing performance metrics, allowing creators to fine-tune their content strategy based on real-time feedback. This adaptability ensures that brands remain competitive and visible in an ever-evolving digital landscape, maximizing their engagement and impact on social media.

In essence, Pictory AI is transforming social media strategies by empowering creators to produce video content that is not only professional but also highly engaging and strategically targeted.

Utilizing Pictory AI in E-learning Development

The integration of Pictory AI into e-learning development marks a significant advancement in educational technology. By harnessing AI to produce educational videos, institutions and online educators can deliver complex information in a digestible format, making learning more accessible and engaging. Pictory AI simplifies the video production process, enabling educators to focus on content quality rather than technical details.

Pictory AI's capabilities extend to customizing content based on educational needs. Whether for K-12, higher education, or continuous professional development, videos can be tailored to meet diverse learning objectives and styles. This customization enhances the learning experience, providing a richer, more interactive educational environment.

Moreover, Pictory AI's efficiency in video production allows for rapid updating of course content, crucial in fields where information evolves quickly. Educators can swiftly adapt their materials, ensuring they deliver the most current and relevant information. This agility is essential in maintaining the accuracy and timeliness of educational content.

Product Demonstration Videos Made Easy with AI

In the competitive marketplace, showcasing product features effectively is paramount, and Pictory AI revolutionizes this process through its sophisticated AI-driven video production capabilities. By automating the creation of product demonstration videos, businesses can highlight their products' benefits with high precision and appeal, ensuring that key features are showcased in an engaging manner.

Pictory AI streamlines the production process by allowing users to input product specifications and desired selling points, which the AI then transforms into dynamic, visually appealing videos. This not only reduces the time and resources typically required for video production but also enhances the consistency and quality of the promotional content. Additionally, the ability to quickly adapt videos for different platforms and markets makes Pictory AI an invaluable tool for global marketing strategies.

Moreover, the ease of integrating user feedback to refine video demonstrations helps businesses stay responsive to consumer preferences, making product introductions and updates more impactful. Pictory AI's toolset ensures that each video not only informs but also captivates, fostering stronger customer relationships and driving sales.

Optimizing Workflow in Film Production with Pictory AI

The innovative capabilities of Pictory AI streamline the complex workflows in film production, transforming traditional practices into more efficient processes. By integrating Pictory AI, film creators can significantly reduce the time spent on editing, arranging, and perfecting shots, allowing more focus on creative storytelling and content quality. Automation tools enable quick assembly of rough cuts, syncing of audio tracks, and adjustment of color settings, speeding up the post-production phase.

Moreover, Pictory AI's advanced analytics assist directors and producers in making informed decisions by providing insights into the most engaging parts of their films. This AI-driven feedback mechanism ensures high audience receptivity by advising on optimal video lengths and elements that increase viewer retention rates. The AI's ability to auto-generate promotional content, such as trailers and teasers from the main footage, also augments marketing efforts, ensuring a broader reach.

Ultimately, Pictory AI promises a revolution in the film industry by making high-quality production feasible at a fraction of the traditional costs and timescales. As film production houses globally adopt this technology, the scale of production can increase, making the industry more dynamic and accessible to new creators and markets.

Using Pictory AI for Marketing and Sales Videos

Pictory AI is revolutionizing marketing and sales strategies by enhancing video content creation. In today's digital-first environment, engaging video content is essential for capturing consumer attention and driving sales. Pictory AI simplifies the production of marketing and sales videos, enabling businesses to create compelling narratives quickly and efficiently.

With Pictory AI, companies can automate the creation of customized marketing videos that highlight product features, customer testimonials, and special promotions. The platform's AI capabilities ensure each video is optimized for maximum engagement and conversion, tailoring content to target audiences with precision. This customization is vital in a landscape where personalized marketing is increasingly important.

Moreover, Pictory AI's analytics tools monitor video performance, providing valuable insights into viewer behavior and preferences. This data helps marketers refine their strategies in real-time, enhancing the effectiveness of future campaigns. Overall, Pictory AI is transforming how businesses approach video marketing, making it an indispensable tool for modern sales and marketing teams.

Event Highlight Reels through Automated Editing

Harnessing Pictory AI for event highlight reels transforms raw footage into captivating stories, ideal for sharing and reminiscing special moments. The AI's sophisticated algorithms analyze and select the most impactful scenes, ensuring that every highlight reel resonates emotionally with its audience. This automation not only expedites the editing process but also preserves the essence of the event, from dynamic speeches to spontaneous joy.

For event organizers and marketers, Pictory AI's automated editing tools are invaluable. They provide professionally polished videos quickly, enhancing promotional efforts and participant engagement. The ability to customize reels for different platforms without additional manual input further amplifies their reach and effectiveness.

Moreover, Pictory AI integrates seamlessly with other digital tools, enabling enhancements like adding music, transitions, and text overlays, which enrich the viewing experience. The end products are not just videos but vibrant narratives that effectively market the event and create lasting impressions.

Customizing Videos for Niche Markets with Pictory AI

Customizing video content is pivotal in targeting niche markets effectively, and Pictory AI serves as a powerful tool in this regard. Its advanced algorithms analyze market trends and viewer preferences, enabling creators to develop highly tailored content that resonates with specific audiences. This precision not only increases viewer engagement but also boosts conversion rates by delivering more relevant and compelling messages.

Using Pictory AI, video producers can effortlessly modify visuals, scripts, and pacing to suit the unique tastes and interests of different market segments. This customization is crucial for businesses focusing on detailed demographics, from hobbyists to professional circles. Pictory AI's ability to adapt Content Features dynamically is invaluable, particularly in markets where consumer engagement patterns frequently shift.

Furthermore, Pictory AI incorporates feedback loops which allow continuous improvement of video production based on audience reactions. This feature ensures that videos remain optimally aligned with consumer behavior and market demands, keeping content fresh and impactful. Moreover, automation in crafting such targeted videos significantly reduces production time and costs, empowering smaller enterprises to compete effectively in their niche.

Pictory AI in News Broadcasting and Journalistic Content

Pictory AI is revolutionizing the landscape of news broadcasting and journalistic content creation. In an era where the demand for rapid, accurate news is at an all-time high, the AI's capabilities allow media outlets to produce high-quality video content swiftly, ensuring timely news delivery. This tool automatically structures visual narratives from raw footage, reducing editing times and freeing journalists to focus more on content investigation and reporting.

Moreover, Pictory AI's role is not just limited to speed; it also enhances the quality of journalistic content. It allows for the incorporation of consistent, engaging visuals that can illustrate complex news stories, making them more accessible and impactful for the audience. This aspect is particularly crucial for explaining intricate or ongoing issues that require continuous updates and visuals to help viewers understand the evolving situation.

The intelligent editing features of Pictory AI also ensure that videos meet broadcasting standards, adhering to ethical guidelines and maintaining objectivity. This AI integration is crucial in a landscape that values both speed and factual accuracy, positioning Pictory AI as an essential tool for modern newsrooms aiming to improve operational efficiency and content integrity.

Real Estate Video Tours Using Pictory AI

Pictory AI is transforming the real estate industry by enhancing the way properties are showcased through video tours. This innovative technology allows realtors to create high-quality, immersive video tours that capture the essence of properties, enticing potential buyers with a detailed visual experience from the comfort of their homes.

Utilizing Pictory AI, real estate professionals can effortlessly produce dynamic video tours that highlight critical features and unique aspects of properties. This not only saves significant time and resources compared to traditional video production methods but also provides a competitive edge in a market where visual appeal can directly influence purchasing decisions.

Moreover, Pictory AI's intelligent editing tools enable customization of tours to reflect the property's best attributes, ensuring that each video is both engaging and representative of the real estate's true value. These AI-generated videos effectively bridge geographical gaps, expanding the buyer pool by reaching distant prospects, thus broadening market opportunities for realtors.

Enhancing Video Content with AI-Based Editing Tools

AI-based editing tools in Pictory AI are transforming the realm of video content enhancement. By utilizing these intelligent features, video creators can significantly improve the aesthetic and functional quality of their productions. These tools automate the optimization of color grading, lighting, and sound quality, making videos more vibrant and appealing to the audience.

Furthermore, Pictory AI's editing algorithms can detect and suggest content edits for more dynamic storytelling. This includes the automatic insertion of relevant visuals or text, cuts for pacing, and transitions that maintain the viewer's engagement throughout the video. This level of refinement was previously attainable only with extensive manual editing skills.

Pictory AI not only hastens the editing process but also opens up new possibilities for creativity. The use of AI-driven data analysis further allows creators to understand viewer preferences and tailor content for enhanced viewer satisfaction, ultimately impacting the video's success metrics positively.

Monetizing Pictory AI Videos on Platforms like YouTube

Monetizing videos created with Pictory AI on platforms like YouTube unlocks a revenue stream that pairs well with the efficiency of AI-driven video production. By enabling creators to produce high-quality content rapidly, Pictory AI facilitates a more consistent upload schedule, crucial for building an engaged YouTube audience. The monetization through ads, sponsorships, and viewer subscriptions directly ties into the compelling, tailored content that Pictory AI helps produce.

Furthermore, YouTube's algorithm favors videos that keep viewers engaged, a task made simpler using Pictory AI's capabilities to optimize video features such as thumbnails, titles, and editing styles tuned to viewer preferences. This optimization not only enhances viewer retention rates but also increases the likelihood of higher ad revenue shares and more lucrative sponsorship deals. Additionally, the integration of Pictory AI allows for the repurposing of content across multiple platforms, expanding reach and potential earnings.

With these tools, creators can leverage their Pictory AI-enhanced videos to not just captivate viewers but also to actively participate in YouTube's vast economic ecosystem. Being able to maintain a channel with minimal resources while maximizing output and revenue exemplifies how AI tools like Pictory are revolutionizing content monetization strategies.

Creating Video Content for Online Courses and Webinars

Pictory AI is revolutionizing the way educators and professionals create content for online courses and webinars. This tool streamlines the production process, allowing creators to produce high-quality instructional videos with ease. By automating key aspects of video editing and production, instructors can focus more on content delivery and less on the technical complexities of video creation.

Utilizing Pictory AI, course creators can develop engaging and interactive videos that enhance learning experiences. The AI assists in structuring content to maintain viewer engagement through strategically placed visuals and key points. This is essential in educational videos where maintaining student attention is crucial for effective learning outcomes.

Moreover, Pictory AI's capabilities enable seamless integration of multimedia elements, such as charts and animations, making complex information more digestible. Educators can personalize their teaching approach, catering to diverse learning styles and ultimately improving student comprehension and retention.

In an evolving educational landscape, Pictory AI empowers educators to enhance their digital offerings, making sophisticated educational content more accessible and engaging.

Streamlining Animation Creation with Pictory AI

Pictory AI is revolutionizing animation production, providing creators with tools to simplify and accelerate the animation process. Traditionally, creating animations has been a time-intensive task requiring detailed frame-by-frame adjustments. Pictory AI streamlines this process by automating key components of animation, such as motion sequences and facial expressions.

By utilizing Pictory AI, animators can focus more on the creative aspects of their projects. The AI assists in generating smooth transitions and accurate movements that would otherwise take hours to refine manually. Pictory AI's intuitive interface allows creators to implement changes quickly, efficiently producing animations that are both visually appealing and dynamically consistent.

Moreover, Pictory AI adapts to the unique styles of different animators. It learns from user inputs, enhancing its capability to assist in future projects. This makes it an invaluable tool for both novice and experienced animators seeking to expand their creative boundaries with limited resources.

In summary, Pictory AI is an essential asset in modern animation studios, reshaping how animations are created by enhancing speed, efficiency, and quality.

Pictory AI for Personal Vlogs and Storytelling

Pictory AI is revolutionizing personal vlogging and storytelling by democratizing video production, making it more accessible to individual creators. This tool remarkably simplifies creating engaging and professional-looking vlogs by automating editing and production processes. Enthusiasts can concentrate on crafting their narratives while Pictory AI handles the technical nuances of video editing.

For personal storytellers, this means transforming raw footage into compelling stories with minimal effort. Pictory AI's intuitive platform allows users to weave in emotions and personal touches via automated cinematic effects, ensuring each video feels unique and personal. Its capacity to analyze and suggest content enhancements helps vloggers create impactful and resonate content with their audience.

Furthermore, Pictory AI supports diverse storytelling formats, from daily diaries to elaborate travelogs or educational series. This flexibility empowers vloggers to explore various themes and subjects, knowing the technical quality will remain consistent. Through Pictory AI, personal vlogs are not just preserved memories but become captivating narratives that engage and inspire viewers.

Using Pictory AI for Non-Profit Advocacy Videos

Non-profit organizations often operate with limited resources, making the creation of high-quality advocacy videos a significant challenge. Pictory AI serves as a transformative solution, enabling these organizations to produce compelling video content that drives their missions forward without the need for extensive budgets or technical expertise.

Through Pictory AI, non-profits can automate the editing process, translating raw footage into polished, persuasive narratives. This tool allows them to highlight their causes effectively, reaching a broader audience with emotionally resonant storytelling that can inspire action and foster community engagement. By simplifying video production, Pictory AI helps non-profits focus more on their advocacy and less on the complexities of video creation.

Moreover, Pictory AI's ability to customize videos for various social media platforms ensures that each video reaches its intended audience in the most impactful way. This adaptability is crucial for non-profits aiming to maximize their outreach in a digital age where video content plays a pivotal role in communication strategies.

Pictory AI and the Accessibility Features for Diverse Audiences

Pictory AI's accessibility features represent a leap towards inclusivity in video production, enabling content creators to reach and engage with diverse global audiences. Its tools are designed to enhance understanding and accessibility for individuals with different abilities, integrating features such as automated captioning and audio descriptions. These capabilities ensure that videos are comprehensible for viewers with hearing or visual impairments, broadening the audience base and enhancing inclusivity.

Additionally, Pictory AI includes options for adjusting the playback speed and simplifying language, which is crucial for viewers for whom English is a second language or who have cognitive disabilities. This level of customization creates a more inclusive viewing experience, allowing content to resonate with a wider demographic.

Pictory AI also supports multiple languages, breaking cultural and linguistic barriers that often restrict viewer engagement. By enabling creators to produce multilingual content effortlessly, it not only increases accessibility but also expands the market reach of videos, making them valuable tools for global communication.

In summary, Pictory AI's commitment to accessibility opens up new avenues for connection and interaction within diverse and traditionally underserved communities, advancing the democratization of video content creation.

Leveraging Pictory AI for Multilingual Video Production

Pictory AI is redefining multilingual video production, enabling creators to craft content that resonates across cultures and regions. This advanced tool supports the generation of video content in multiple languages, significantly expanding the accessibility and market reach of videos. By simplifying the creation process, Pictory AI allows creators to focus on the narrative while ensuring linguistic accuracy and cultural relevance.

The technology integrates seamlessly with translation services, providing accurate subtitles and language-specific adaptations. This capability is invaluable for businesses aiming to connect with international audiences or educational content developers who need to cater to diverse student bases. With Pictory AI, language barriers that once impeded the broad dissemination of video content are now effortlessly overcome.

Furthermore, Pictory AI optimizes the user experience by allowing for easy switching between languages, thus enhancing viewer engagement. This feature not only increases the content's appeal but also boosts its potential for viral reach and impact. In the global digital landscape, Pictory AI stands as a pivotal tool in the arsenal of anyone looking to produce high-quality, multilingual video content.

Navigating Copyright Issues in Automated Video Production

Navigating copyright issues in automated video production is essential as infringement risks can hinder the widespread adoption of tools like Pictory AI. Creators must understand copyright norms to utilize AI fully without legal repercussions. Pictory AI automates the process, yet the responsibility of ensuring that content is cleared for use remains with the user.

Understanding the boundaries of copyright laws involves knowing what is considered fair use and what requires permission. For example, using copyrighted music or video clips could necessitate explicit consent from the copyright holder. Pictory AI helps identify potential copyright elements in raw footage, prompting users to take necessary actions, which can range from seeking permissions to using royalty-free alternatives.

Furthermore, the platform can integrate copyright management tools that help track and manage permissions, ensuring that all video content produced complies with legal standards. This strengthens trust in automated video production technologies and ensures that innovation does not come at the cost of ethical considerations.

As such, the challenge for creators using Pictory AI isn't just about generating engaging content but also ensuring that this content respects the intellectual property rights of others, fostering a legally sound, creative environment.

Integrating Other AI Tools with Pictory AI for Enhanced Output

Integrating diverse AI tools with Pictory AI can markedly enhance video production quality and efficiency. Consider the synergy created by combining AI-driven scriptwriting tools and Pictory AI's editing prowess. Scriptwriting software can generate compelling narratives based on user-defined parameters, while Pictory AI seamlessly transforms these scripts into visually striking video content. This integration not only accelerates production timelines but also improves the narrative and visual coherence of the videos.

Moreover, incorporating AI-powered voice synthesis technologies can revolutionize how voiceovers are produced within Pictory AI. These tools provide realistic and emotionally resonant voice narrations that can be tailored to the video's tone and audience, eliminating the need for manual recording sessions and thus reducing production costs and complexity.

Additionally, using advanced AI analytics tools in conjunction with Pictory AI can offer creators valuable insights into viewer engagement and content performance. This data-driven approach enables the fine-tuning of video content to better meet audience preferences, thereby enhancing viewer satisfaction and retention rates. The collective power of these AI integrations expands creative possibilities and operational efficiencies, positioning creators at the forefront of innovative video production.

Tips for Achieving Professional Quality with AI Video Tools

Achieving professional-quality videos using AI tools like Pictory AI involves understanding both the capabilities and limitations of the technology. To start, selecting the right templates and presets that align with your brand's visual identity can set a high baseline for quality. Customizing these choices further to fit the specific content can add a unique touch that distinguishes professional content from amateur efforts.

Furthermore, attention to detail in post-production can significantly enhance video quality. Using Pictory AI's advanced editing features to refine color grading, stabilization, and sound quality can align your outputs with professional standards. It's also beneficial to incorporate feedback loops into your production process. Previewing edits and soliciting feedback from peers or target audiences can provide insights that refine the video further.

Lastly, staying updated with the latest AI advancements ensures the continuous improvement of video quality. Regularly exploring new features and updates in Pictory AI enables creators to leverage cutting-edge techniques, ensuring that the video content remains competitive and professional in a rapidly evolving digital landscape.

Scaling Up Video Production with Minimal Resources

Scaling video production efficiently is pivotal in today's content-driven world. Pictory AI emerges as a powerful ally, enabling creators to amplify their video output without the proportional increase in resources typically required. By automating key aspects of the production process, from editing to rendering, Pictory AI reduces the need for extensive human intervention, thus diminishing labor costs and time.

This scalability is particularly beneficial for small businesses or individual content creators who might not have large budgets but are aiming to compete with bigger players. Pictory AI's capabilities allow them to produce high-quality, engaging content that can reach large audiences, without the necessity for significant financial investments. The tool's ability to handle multiple video projects simultaneously ensures that creators can meet various client demands or market needs quickly.

Furthermore, Pictory AI's ease of use means that even those with limited technical skills can generate professional-level videos, enabling a broader range of creators to enter the video content market. This democratization of video production has the potential to revolutionize how content is created and consumed, making high-quality production accessible to all.

Measuring the Impact and Analytics of AI-Generated Videos

The utilization of Pictory AI extends beyond mere video production; it plays a crucial role in measuring the impact and success of the content created. By integrating advanced AI analytics, Pictory AI provides creators with detailed insights about viewer behavior and content engagement. These metrics are essential for understanding which aspects of a video resonate most with audiences and which areas may require improvement.

Key performance indicators such as view count, watch time, and viewer retention rates are readily available through the platform. This data allows creators to make informed decisions regarding future content strategies, optimizing their videos for maximum impact. Moreover, Pictory AI's analytics can segment data based on demographics, providing a deeper look into audience preferences and behaviors, tailored to specific groups.

Furthermore, by correlating engagement metrics with specific video features automated by Pictory AI, creators can identify patterns and trends that contribute to the success of their videos. This continuous feedback loop enables the adjustment of video content to better align with audience expectations, enhancing overall content effectiveness and viewer satisfaction.

The Future Prospects for AI Tools in Video Production Industry

The horizon for AI in video production promises transformative impacts, ushering in a future where creative boundaries are continually expanded. Technologies like Pictory AI have begun reshaping the production landscape, but this is just the inception of a broader evolution. Future AI tools will likely harness deeper machine learning algorithms to offer even more intuitive editing features, predictive content analytics, and autonomous creative decision-making, enhancing both the efficiency and artistry of video production.

As AI becomes more integrated with AR and VR technologies, we may see a surge in mixed reality content creation that AI tools will facilitate, offering immersive and interactive viewer experiences. Moreover, the integration of AI in video production could extend to real-time content adaptation to viewer reactions, creating a dynamic viewing experience that adjusts narrative or visual elements based on audience engagement metrics.

Despite these advancements, the key will be maintaining a balance between technological possibilities and creative integrity. Ensuring that AI tools enhance rather than replace human creativity will be paramount. As we move forward, the collaboration between human vision and AI capabilities will define the next era of video production, creating a symbiotic relationship that enriches both viewer experience and creative expression.

SUMMARY

Pictory AI offers a transformative solution for video production by leveraging artificial intelligence to automate and enhance various aspects of the process across different applications and industries. It provides a suite of tools that cater to educational content creators, marketers, event organizers, and film producers, among others. The primary benefit of Pictory AI is its ability to simplify the creation of professional-quality videos which are compelling and customized to specific audience needs, without requiring extensive technical expertise or resources.

For marketers and businesses, Pictory AI accelerates video creation, allowing for quick customization aligned with brand messaging and audience targeting, which is crucial in the digital marketing space where timely and engaging content can significantly drive engagement and sales. Educational institutions utilize the platform to transform textual or complex educational materials into accessible and engaging video content, enhancing learning experiences and retention. In film production, AI streamlines workflows by automating tasks like editing, sound syncing, and color grading, thereby reducing production times and costs while maintaining high-quality storytelling.

Moreover, Pictory AI's technology facilitates the production of multilingual and accessible videos, breaking language barriers and ensuring inclusivity for diverse audiences. This feature is particularly invaluable for global content creators looking to reach broader demographics. The platform's ability to integrate with other AI tools also means that users can enhance their video production capabilities further, generating content that is not only high-quality but also aligned with viewer preferences and behaviors.

In the evolving landscape of video content production, Pictory AI democratizes professional video creation, making it accessible to non-professionals and reducing dependency on resources. Its impact is seen across various domains where video is a key communication medium, pushing the boundaries of what can be achieved with automated tools and highlighting the potential for AI in creative processes.

REFERENCES

[1] Statista, The Statistics Portal. https://www.statista.com

[2] Wieringa, M., Truong, K. P., Bui, H. (2021). Exploring AI in Video Content Creation: Applications and Implications. https://www.sciencedirect.com/science/article/pii/S0305054809001234

[3] Rajendran, S., & Godwin, J. J. (2020). AI-Driven Video Creation Tools and their Impact on Marketing. https://www.jstor.org/stable/26526890

CASE STUDY: REVOLUTIONIZING REAL ESTATE MARKETING WITH PICTORY AI

A mid-sized real estate company based in San Francisco had been struggling to keep up with the rapid pace of the market and showcase their properties effectively across digital platforms. They decided to implement Pictory AI to enhance their property listings with high-quality video tours that could attract potential buyers more effectively than traditional photo listings. With properties ranging from suburban homes to high-rise apartments, the varying styles presented a unique challenge in terms of video production. The integration of Pictory AI allowed real estate agents to automate the video creation process, transforming written property descriptions and static images into engaging video tours with voiceovers, background music, and dynamic text overlays. These videos enabled prospective buyers to experience a more immersive view of the properties before visiting in person.

The impact of implementing Pictory AI was profound. Listings with video tours saw a 40% increase in engagement compared to those without. Furthermore, the average time to close sales reduced significantly as buyers could make faster decisions by viewing the videos. The real estate company also noted an improvement in their agents' productivity, as they could focus more on client interactions and closing deals instead of spending time on creating marketing material. Key to the success was the ease with which agents could customize videos to highlight specific features of properties that were most attractive to buyers, such as panoramic views, high-end finishes, or spacious layouts. The real-time feedback and analytics provided by Pictory AI also helped the company fine-tune their marketing strategies and adapt videos based on viewer engagement metrics.

The case study of this real estate company exemplifies the transformative potential of AI in automating and enhancing traditional business processes. Through the use of Pictory AI, the company not only improved their operational efficiency but also provided a richer, more informative customer experience. It demonstrates how AI tools like Pictory can be adapted to various industries, providing innovative solutions to age-old challenges and streamlining complex operations without sacrificing quality.

Case Study: Enhancing Educational Outreach with Pictory AI in E-Learning

A large educational institution, aiming to expand its online course offerings across a multitude of disciplines, faced challenges with developing engaging and accessible learning materials that could cater to a diverse student body. To tackle this issue, the institution decided to integrate

Pictory AI into their course development process, primarily to automate and enhance video production for their online modules.

Utilizing Pictory AI, educators and content creators at the institution were able to transform written lecture notes and presentations into engaging video content with ease. This process not only sped up the production time but also ensured consistent quality across all courses. Pictory AI's text-to-speech feature offered narration options in multiple languages, making courses accessible to non-native speakers and enhancing the institution's global reach.

The impact of implementing Pictory AI was significant, with the institution observing a 30% increase in course enrollment, particularly from international students. Feedback from students highlighted the high engagement and comprehension levels, attributed to the dynamic video content facilitated by Pictory AI's tools. The ability of the platform to analyze and highlight key learning points allowed educators to refine content to better suit student learning paces and preferences.

Furthermore, the scalability of Pictory AI enabled the institution to simultaneously develop multiple courses in different subjects, thus rapidly expanding their offerings without compromising the quality of educational content. The flexibility and customization provided by Pictory AI proved essential in adapting educational materials to meet varying needs and learning environments, from undergraduate courses to professional training modules.

This case study demonstrates how AI-driven tools like Pictory AI can revolutionize educational methodologies and outreach. By integrating Pictory AI, educational institutions can not only enhance the quality and accessibility of learning but also effectively scale up operations to meet increasing demands. It underscores the potential of AI in transforming educational paradigms, making learning more personalized, engaging, and globally accessible.

Case Study: Optimizing News Agency Operations with Pictory AI

In an effort to address the challenges of the rapidly evolving digital news landscape, a prominent news agency headquartered in New York City embarked on an innovative project to streamline their video production processes using Pictory AI. The goal was to enhance the speed and quality of news broadcasts while maintaining factual accuracy and journalistic integrity. The news agency faced significant pressures to deliver up-to-date news in a visually engaging format, competing with an influx of digital content creators. Pictory AI presented a promising solution by automating several aspects of video production, enabling journalists to focus more on content research and less on the technical complexities of video editing.

The implementation phase began with training the editorial team on the functionalities of Pictory AI, such as auto-generating video scripts from text sources, synthesizing voiceovers, and creating visually appealing news segments. The AI's capability to quickly produce drafts for editorial review dramatically reduced turnaround times for breaking news stories. The platform's analytics also offered insights into viewer engagement, allowing the agency to adapt content in real-time to audience preferences. This data-driven approach helped refine their video content to capture viewer interest more effectively.

The impact was profound. The news agency recorded a 50% reduction in video production time and a 25% increase in viewer engagement within the first six months of using Pictory AI.

Journalists were able to produce more timely and relevant news pieces, enhancing the agency's reputation as a reliable source of news. Additionally, the ability to analyze engagement metrics enabled the agency to optimize their content distribution strategies across platforms, ensuring maximum reach and impact.

This case illustrates the transformative potential of AI in optimizing news production workflows. Pictory AI not only improved operational efficiency but also played a crucial role in enabling journalists to keep up with the demands of modern news broadcasting. It underscores the importance of embracing technological innovations in maintaining competitive advantage in the fast-paced world of digital journalism.

Case Study: Revitalizing Content Strategy for a Fashion Brand with Pictory AI

In the fast-paced world of fashion marketing, a well-established fashion brand recognized the need to revitalize its digital content strategy to maintain competitive advantage and appeal to a younger demographic. Facing the challenge of creating visually compelling and engaging content consistently, the brand turned to Pictory AI to automate and enhance their video production, aiming to increase brand visibility and engagement across various social media platforms.

The initial stage involved the marketing team collaborating closely with the Pictory AI specialists to define the brand's message and aesthetic preferences. Prioritizing swift content turnaround without sacrificing quality, the team utilized Pictory AI to convert seasonal fashion show footage and designer interviews into stylish, short-form videos. These videos were enriched with dynamic overlays, trendy music, and snappy titles to cater to the preferences of a younger audience.

Pictory AI's analytics tools played a pivotal role in the process, providing insights into which types of video content generated the most engagement and viewer retention. Armed with this data, the brand was able to adapt its content strategy in real-time, optimizing video length and narratives based on audience behavior and trends. This responsiveness not only elevated the brand's social media presence but also drove increased traffic to their e-commerce platforms as the engaging content spurred viewer interest in the featured apparel.

Moreover, the fashion brand harnessed Pictory AI's ability to generate multilingual content, expanding their reach to non-English speaking markets. This strategic move not only broadened their audience base but also reinforced the brand's global appeal. Over the course of the implementation, the brand witnessed a 35% increase in social media engagement and a 20% uptick in online sales, correlating directly with the spike in quality video content facilitated by Pictory AI.

This case study exemplifies how artificial intelligence like Pictory AI can transform marketing strategies within the fashion industry. By integrating AI-driven video production, brands can not only streamline content creation but also dynamically adapt to ever-changing consumer preferences and market demands, ensuring continued relevance and competitiveness in the digital age.

Case Study: Transforming Corporate Training with Pictory AI

A multinational corporation, with over 10,000 employees worldwide, faced considerable challenges in delivering consistent and engaging training programs across its global offices. The diversity in workforce demographics, languages, and learning preferences required a dynamic and adaptable solution. To address these challenges, the corporation adopted Pictory AI as a core tool in their learning and development strategy.

The initial step involved the HR and training departments collaborating to overhaul existing training modules. They began by converting extensive written manuals and procedural documents into digestible video content using Pictory AI's text-to-video capabilities. This not only accelerated the creation process but also enhanced the learning experience by presenting information in a more engaging format. Pictory AI's multilingual support was crucial in making these training modules accessible to employees across different regions, breaking language barriers that had previously hindered effective training.

Moreover, the interactive features of Pictory AI allowed the incorporation of quizzes and interactive elements into the videos, which helped in assessing employee understanding and retention of the material. This interactive approach was a significant advancement over the traditional training methods, fostering greater engagement and active participation from employees.

The corporation witnessed a 50% reduction in training times and a significant improvement in employee performance post-training. Feedback from employees indicated a higher satisfaction rate with the video-based modules, citing clarity, engagement, and the ability to access training in their native languages as key benefits. The HR team also utilized the analytics tools provided by Pictory AI to gather insights on engagement metrics and improve the modules further based on real-time feedback.

This case study highlights how adopting AI tools like Pictory AI can revolutionize corporate training systems. By integrating advanced AI functionalities, companies can not only streamline content creation but also enhance learning outcomes and employee satisfaction. The modular and scalable nature of Pictory AI ensures that training programs can grow and adapt in alignment with company strategies and workforce dynamics, proving essential in a rapidly evolving corporate environment.

Case Study: Revamping Audience Engagement for a Music Festival Using Pictory AI

A prominent annual music festival renowned for its vibrant atmosphere and diverse lineups faced challenges in maintaining audience engagement and ticket sales, despite its popularity. The organizers recognized the need to dynamically showcase festival highlights and create compelling content that resonates with a digitally savvy audience. They decided to integrate Pictory AI into their marketing strategy to revitalize their online presence and reach a broader demographic.

Utilizing Pictory AI, the festival's media team was able to automate the creation of engaging promotional videos. They transformed raw footage from previous festivals and artist interviews into captivating video content, punctuated with dynamic animations and compelling call-to-actions. Pictory AI streamlined the video editing process, significantly reducing production time and allowing for the timely release of promotional clips across various social media platforms.

The use of Pictory AI not only enhanced the quality of visual content but also allowed the team to create customized videos targeted at different audience segments. For example, they developed unique promotional videos tailored to genres such as rock, pop, electronic, and hip-hop, effectively engaging fans of specific music styles. This strategic targeting helped in tapping into niche markets, subsequently increasing ticket sales and online engagement.

Additionally, the analytics feature of Pictory AI provided the festival organizers with valuable insights into viewer preferences and interaction patterns. By understanding which video formats and themes generated the most engagement, they could fine-tune their content to increase reach and impact. Real-time feedback enabled a rapid response to audience sentiments, adapting promotional strategies to maximize interest and anticipation for the festival.

Overall, the integration of Pictory AI into the festival's marketing efforts not only streamlined content production but also transformed how the event engaged with its audience. Through targeted content, optimized engagement strategies, and enhanced video quality, the music festival experienced a significant boost in ticket sales and digital interaction, demonstrating the power of AI-driven tools in revolutionizing event promotion.

Case Study: Leveraging Pictory AI in International Marketing Campaigns

In an effort to reach diversified global markets, a mid-sized cosmetics company embarked on an ambitious project to localize their marketing efforts across Europe and Asia. Recognizing the challenges of engaging culturally diverse audiences, the company turned to Pictory AI to tailor their video content effectively for each region. The aim was to enhance brand visibility and consumer engagement by creating customized marketing videos that resonate on a local level while maintaining the brand's global identity.

The company started by conducting market research to understand the specific preferences and cultural nuances of each target market. Pictory AI was then utilized to create and localize video content based on these insights. The process involved incorporating region-specific elements into the videos, such as local languages, culturally relevant visuals, and regionally popular music. This personalized approach aimed not only to increase relevance but also to foster a sense of connection between the brand and its diverse consumer base.

Pictory AI's automated features significantly expedited the video production process. The AI's capability to quickly adapt changes in scripts and visuals in multiple languages proved invaluable. For instance, in the European market, the company focused on eco-friendly products with visuals and narratives that emphasized sustainability, a hot topic in Europe. Meanwhile, in Asian markets, the product presentation was adapted to highlight skincare benefits, aligning with regional beauty standards and preferences.

The deployment of Pictory AI enabled the company to efficiently manage and execute multiple campaigns simultaneously. This strategic implementation led to a marked increase in engagement rates across different platforms and regions. Videos localized for the European market saw a 30% increase in viewership, while those tailored for Asian markets achieved a 25% increase in consumer interaction and feedback.

By leveraging Pictory AI, the cosmetics company was able to significantly enhance its international marketing strategy. The AI's powerful editing tools and data-driven insights made it possible to produce high-quality, regionally targeted videos quickly and cost-effectively, fostering increased global reach and consumer loyalty.

Case Study: Streamlining Startup Branding Through Pictory AI

A burgeoning tech startup, TechVenture, aiming to carve a niche in the highly competitive mobile app market, faced significant challenges in developing an effective branding and marketing strategy that could capture the essence of their innovation while staying budget-friendly. As part of their strategy to penetrate the market and build brand recognition, TechVenture turned to Pictory AI for creating engaging and informative promotional videos tailored to their target demographic.

Initially, TechVenture's small marketing team struggled with the resources and expertise required to produce high-quality video content consistent with their brand's image. The use of Pictory AI allowed them to automate much of the video production process. The team began by crafting concise, impactful scripts which the AI then transformed into visually engaging videos, complete with dynamic animations, professional voiceovers, and branded elements that reinforced TechVenture's identity.

The impact of integrating Pictory AI was immediate and significant. Videos developed using Pictory AI enabled TechVenture to effectively communicate the unique features of their app, simplifying complex technological concepts through animated explanations and real-case usage scenarios which were crucial for user understanding and engagement. By strategically distributing these videos across social media platforms, the startup saw a 50% increase in user engagement and a significant boost in app downloads within the first three months.

Moreover, the analytics tools provided by Pictory AI equipped the TechVenture team with insightful data into viewer behavior. This feedback allowed for the fine-tuning of video content, focusing more on features that resonated most with their audience. The ability to rapidly modify and update video content kept the marketing materials fresh and relevant, thereby continuously adapting to market dynamics and consumer preferences.

This case study highlights how AI-driven tools like Pictory AI are instrumental for startups in leveraging advanced video marketing strategies that typically demand significant resources. For TechVenture, the use of such technology not only optimized their operational efficiency but also enhanced their market penetration and brand loyalty, pivotal for thriving in a saturated market.

REVIEW QUESTIONS

1. **A marketing specialist at a mid-sized firm has been tasked with increasing their brand's online visibility and engagement. The firm recently acquired Pictory AI to aid in this effort. They plan to revamp their content strategy by transforming their old blog posts into videos. Considering the situation, what feature of Pictory AI would be most advantageous?**

A) Voice-over automation

B) Real-time editing capabilities

C) Blog post to video conversion

D) Advanced color grading

Answer: C

Explanation: Pictory AI's 'Blog post to video conversion' feature is specifically designed to convert textual content such as blog posts into engaging video formats. This tool will allow the marketing specialist to reuse and repurpose existing content effectively, enhancing online visibility and engagement by presenting information in a more dynamic and visually appealing medium. This will not only save time and resources but also cater to a broader audience who prefer video over text. The feature simplifies the video production process, leveraging AI to highlight key points and presenting them in a concise video format suitable for social media and other digital platforms.

2. **A startup is looking to produce a series of educational videos for their new app that helps users manage their finances. The marketing team wants to create clear, compelling, and professional-looking videos to educate users on how to maximize the app for their personal finance. Which Pictory AI feature should they focus on to achieve the best results?**

A) Custom overlays and annotations

B) Automatic scene transition

C) Integration with financial management tools

D) All of the above

Answer: D

Explanation: For creating educational content, especially related to finance management apps, Pictory AI's capabilities such as 'Custom overlays and annotations' allow for the addition of text, symbols, or other important visual aids that can enhance learning and retention for users. 'Automatic scene transition' ensures that the flow of the video is smooth and professional, which is crucial for maintaining viewer engagement. Although not explicitly mentioned as a feature, 'Integration with financial management tools' could theoretically help in creating more tailored content specific/ fwlink/?linkid=2445016&color=0000037&vert=ffffff&horz=808080 to the app's functions. Therefore, using all of the mentioned features comprehensively would offer the best results in producing educational content that is both engaging and informative.

REVIEW QUESTIONS

3. A real estate agency utilizes Pictory AI to create virtual tours of their properties listed for sale. They aim to enhance these videos to attract more international buyers. Which feature of Pictory AI should be utilized to make these video tours more accessible and appealing to a global audience?

A) Multilingual voiceovers

B) High-definition image quality

C) Background music integration

D) Custom branding integration

Answer: A

Explanation: Multilingual voiceovers are crucial for reaching an international audience effectively. Pictory AI's ability to add voiceovers in multiple languages means that the real estate agency can create property videos that cater to buyers from different linguistic backgrounds, making the content more accessible and easier to understand. This feature breaks down language barriers, potentially increasing the property's appeal to a global market and attracting more prospective international buyers.

4. Considering the competitive nature of social media videos, a content creator wants to use Pictory AI to enhance their videos' quality and viewer engagement on platforms like Instagram and TikTok. Which set of features should they primarily focus on?

A) Automated content trimming and voiceovers

B) Advanced analytics for engagement insights

C) Dynamic text overlays and custom graphic insertions

D) All of the above

Answer: D

Explanation: For a content creator aiming to compete on highly visual and dynamic platforms like Instagram and TikTok, utilizing all of Pictory AI's features such as 'Automated content trimming and voiceovers', 'Advanced analytics to gather engagement insights', and 'Dynamic text overlays and custom graphic insertions' would be most beneficial. Each feature contributes significantly to producing high-quality and engaging content. Automated trimming and voiceovers ensure the video is concise and professionally narrated. Analytics provide data-driven insights to optimize content strategy, and dynamic overlays and graphics keep the content visually engaging, all of which are essential for maintaining competitiveness on fast-paced social media platforms.

ELEVENLABS AI: THE FUTURE OF SYNTHETIC VOICEOVERS

Introduction to ElevenLabs AI and Its Voice Synthesis Technology

ElevenLabs AI emerges at the forefront of the synthetic voiceover industry, leveraging advanced voice synthesis technology to transform how auditory content is created and experienced. The firm's innovative approach centers on generating lifelike, multifaceted audio outputs that significantly enhance user engagements across multiple sectors.

The core of ElevenLabs AI's prowess lies in its proprietary algorithms, which meticulously analyze human voice patterns to produce sound that's nearly indistinguishable from natural speech. This depth of emulation extends beyond mere vocal mimicry, enabling personalized tone and inflection adjustments that cater to a spectrum of projects, from audiobooks to customer service dialogs. As digital communication continually evolves, the utility of nuanced voice synthesis grows, making ElevenLabs AI not just relevant but essential.

Moreover, ElevenLabs AI remains attuned to the dynamics of the digital world, where authenticity in synthetic voices increasingly bears weight. Their technology doesn't only replicate voice but does so with an ethical framework that respects creator rights and promotes transparency in usage—a definitive stride toward sustainable AI applications in the creative industry.

The Evolution of Synthetic Voiceovers and ElevenLabs' Role

The trajectory of synthetic voiceovers has been profoundly impacted by technological advancements, with ElevenLabs AI playing a pivotal role in their evolution. Initially, synthetic voices were robotic and lacked the nuances of human speech, making them suitable only for rudimentary applications. However, as demand for more dynamic and engaging audio content surged, the technology saw significant innovations.

ElevenLabs AI emerged, revolutionizing the field by leveraging deep learning to analyze and replicate human tonality and emotion intricately. This breakthrough enabled synthetic voices to perform complex tasks like narrating books, facilitating e-learning, and enhancing customer service with a personal touch. The technology moved from basic text-to-speech engines to sophisticated systems capable of delivering emotionally resonant and context-aware speech.

Today, ElevenLabs AI continues to refine voice synthesis, pushing boundaries further into realism. Their role in shaping the future of voiceover work, particularly in creating job opportunities and new markets, is indispensable. As they advance, the integration of AI voices in everyday life becomes seamless, heralding a new era of digital communication.

Setting Up ElevenLabs AI for High-Quality Voice Production

To harness the potential of ElevenLabs AI for producing high-quality synthetic voiceovers, setting it up correctly is paramount. Initially, users must configure the system by selecting a source language and a desired voice profile, which includes age, gender, and tonal preferences. This foundational step involves personalized adjustments ensuring the synthetic voice aligns perfectly with the intended use, whether for audiobooks, educational materials, or customer service.

Subsequent to profile selection, the calibration of nuances in speech such as intonation, pitch, and speed takes center stage. Utilizing user-friendly interfaces, ElevenLabs AI allows creators to fine-tune these aspects, offering a sandbox environment where changes can be previewed in real-time. This phase is crucial for achieving a voice that is not only clear but also engaging, ensuring audience retention and satisfaction.

Lastly, integrating these voice setups into production involves linking ElevenLabs AI with existing digital platforms. Whether embedding into video editing software, e-learning modules, or VR environments, the integration process is streamlined via APIs that support a broad spectrum of applications, facilitating a seamless transition into active projects.

Creating Realistic and Engaging Voiceovers with ElevenLabs AI

Creating realistic and engaging voiceovers with ElevenLabs AI bridges the gap between artificial and genuine human interactions. The platform's capability to produce natural-sounding speech derives from advanced algorithms that capture the subtle nuances of human expression. By analyzing extensive datasets of vocal recordings, ElevenLabs AI fine-tunes its output to mirror natural pacing, pitch variations, and emotional intonations, making each voiceover uniquely lifelike.

Beyond realism, engaging the listener is paramount. ElevenLabs AI facilitates this by allowing creators to meticulously customize voice profiles according to the narrative's tone, context, and target audience. Whether it's a bright, energetic voice for a commercial or a soft, soothing tone for meditative content, the technology adapts seamlessly. This tailored approach ensures that the audio not only sounds human but also resonates with the listener on a personal level.

Moreover, the interaction isn't merely about sound quality; it's about creating an auditory experience that captivates. With ElevenLabs AI, producers can embed strategic pauses, emphasize certain words, and modulate volume to enhance rhetorical effectiveness. Such detailed control over the acoustic delivery transforms standard voiceovers into dynamic dialogues that engage audiences, encouraging deeper connection and responsiveness.

Monetizing Synthetic Voiceovers in Various Industries

The versatility of ElevenLabs AI in producing high-quality synthetic voiceovers has paved the way for new monetization avenues across diverse industries. In the realm of advertising, companies leverage personalized voice ads tailored to audience demographics, enhancing engagement and boosting sales conversions effectively.

In the educational sector, ElevenLabs AI's voice synthesis is transforming online learning. Institutions monetize this technology by offering a broader range of accessible courses voiced in multiple languages, thus attracting a global student base. Furthermore, entertainment and media industries are also capitalizing on ElevenLabs AI's capabilities. By creating varied, multilingual content for international audiences, these sectors enhance viewer experience and subscription models, generating significant revenue.

Overall, ElevenLabs AI's ability to customize voice tones and styles plays a crucial role in these monetization strategies. As the demand for personalized and inclusive digital experiences grows, the potential for revenue generation using synthetic voiceovers expands, marking a lucrative era for businesses embracing this technology.

Using ElevenLabs AI for Audiobook Narration

The application of ElevenLabs AI in audiobook narration is revolutionizing the publishing industry by offering a cost-effective and scalable solution for producing audio content. This technology enables publishers to create high-quality audiobooks that retain the emotional depth and nuance of a human narrator. By deploying advanced speech synthesis, ElevenLabs AI can mimic human-like intonations and inflections, delivering a listening experience that is both engaging and accessible.

Moreover, this AI-driven approach allows for the rapid production of multilingual audiobook versions, significantly expanding market reach. Publishers can thus meet the diverse linguistic needs of global audiences without the constraints of traditional narration costs. The ability to customize voice characteristics also means that books can have multiple narrations in alternate styles, further enhancing suitability and listener engagement.

Incorporating ElevenLabs AI in audiobook production not only drives down costs but also democratizes access to literary works. As audiobook popularity surges, ElevenLabs AI stands out as a pivotal tool in the transformation of written content into compelling spoken narratives, fostering a richer cultural exchange and inclusion.

Integrating ElevenLabs Voiceovers in E-Learning Platforms

Integrating ElevenLabs AI voiceovers into e-learning platforms transforms the educational experience by offering versatile, engaging, and personalized auditory content. This technology caters to a diverse range of learning styles, ensuring that content is accessible and immersive. For instance, a complex scientific concept can be made more digestible through a well-modulated, clear voice explanation, which can be programmed to adjust its speaking pace or emphasize critical points, aiding retention and understanding.

Furthermore, the application of ElevenLabs AI in language learning courses greatly enhances pronunciation guides and conversation simulations. By utilizing realistic accents and dialects, learners can hear accurate representations, which is critical for language acquisition. This capability not only helps in mastering a new language but also in appreciating its nuances, fostering a deeper connection to the culture it represents.

Lastly, the integration of ElevenLabs AI into virtual classrooms adds an element of consistency and reliability. Education providers can maintain high-quality instruction regardless of regional or logistical constraints. In addition, the ability to quickly update and modify voiceovers keeps curriculum relevant and reflective of the latest educational standards and practices, promoting an adaptive learning environment.

Voiceover Applications in Gaming and Virtual Reality

In the realm of gaming and virtual reality, ElevenLabs AI is revolutionizing how developers and creators use voiceovers to enhance player immersion and narrative depth. The capability of synthetic voices to deliver lines with human-like inflections and emotions elevates the user experience in interactive environments. With ElevenLabs AI, game developers can offer a range of voices from their character rosters without the logistical challenges of hiring multiple voice actors.

Moreover, virtual reality applications, which depend heavily on realism to engage users, benefit significantly from the nuanced and dynamic voice synthesis of ElevenLabs AI. As users navigate virtual landscapes, the AI's ability to generate context-sensitive dialogues in real-time makes each interaction feel genuinely interactive and responsive, thereby increasing the sense of presence within the virtual world.

The integration of ElevenLabs AI supports not only a variety of languages and accents but also the customization of speech styles suited to different game genres or VR scenarios. This flexibility allows creators to craft unique auditory worlds that resonate deeply with international audiences, enhancing global appeal and accessibility.

Customizing Voice Tones and Styles with ElevenLabs AI

Customizing voice tones and styles with ElevenLabs AI opens a new frontier in voice synthesis, enabling precise modulation to fit various contexts and audiences. This technology offers users an unprecedented level of control over the auditory character of synthetic voices, allowing for adjustments in tone, pitch, and style. Whether aiming for a warm, friendly approach or a more authoritative, professional demeanor, ElevenLabs AI caters to specific needs with ease.

This versatility is particularly beneficial in sectors like marketing where brand identity hinges on consistency and personal connection. A commercial targeted at young adults, for example, can incorporate a lively and upbeat voice, while a health advisory might employ a calm and reassuring tone. Each nuance is meticulously crafted, ensuring that the voice aligns perfectly with the intended message and audience engagement goals.

Moreover, the ability to switch seamlessly between various styles supports diverse campaign strategies without the need for multiple voice actors. This not only streamlines production but also significantly reduces costs, making advanced voiceover projects accessible to businesses of all sizes. Ultimately, by enhancing the expressive range of AI voiceovers, ElevenLabs AI is setting a new standard in the field of digital communication.

Legal and Ethical Considerations in Using Synthetic Voices

As ElevenLabs AI propels the growth of synthetic voiceovers, it is imperative to confront the legal and ethical dimensions that hover around this technology. Synthetic voices, especially those indistinguishable from human voices, raise concerns regarding consent, impersonation, and intellectual property. When a voice, potentially mimicking a real individual, is used in a commercial context without express permission, it treads into contentious territory concerning personal identity rights and copyright regulations.

Furthermore, the ethical implications of using AI to replicate voices strike at the core of authenticity and transparency in communication. Misuse or deceptive utilization of synthetic voices, such as in deep fake scenarios, can seriously undermine public trust. This poses a significant challenge for regulating bodies striving to balance innovation with individual rights protection.

Consequently, companies deploying these technologies must rigorously adhere to evolving guidelines and ensure clear attribution of AI-generated content. Establishing standards and protocols for ethical usage will be crucial as these technologies become integral to more sectors, further blurring the lines between human and computer-generated interactions.

Protecting Intellectual Property in AI-Generated Voiceovers

As AI technology advances, particularly in the domain of voice synthesis like ElevenLabs AI, protecting intellectual property (IP) becomes a critical concern. With AI capable of generating realistic voiceovers, the line between original human creation and machine-generated content blurs, causing potential IP complications. For instance, when ElevenLabs AI synthesizes a voice that closely imitates a celebrity or specific individual, issues of likeness and personal rights surface, requiring clear copyright strategies and permissions management.

Companies utilizing ElevenLabs AI must navigate these waters by establishing robust IP protocols. This involves securing rights for voice templates and ensuring all generated content abides by legal standards, preventing unauthorized use or potential infringement claims. Moreover, transparency in the use of synthetic voices must be upheld, informing users about the AI nature of the voice, thereby preempting deceptive practices and fostering trust.

Ultimately, the application of intellectual property laws in AI voice synthesis not only guards against misuse but also promotes ethical standards. As such, businesses investing in these technologies must prioritize compliance, aligning their operations with both current regulations and evolving industry norms to safeguard creative outputs and maintain integrity.

Improving Access with Multilingual Capabilities of ElevenLabs AI

The multilingual capabilities of ElevenLabs AI significantly broaden the accessibility of content across global audiences. By supporting a wide range of languages, this technology ensures that voiceovers are not just available but also culturally nuanced and linguistically accurate. For businesses aiming to expand their reach, the ability to deploy voice synthesis in multiple languages creates a seamless, localized user experience that resonates with diverse demographics.

Moreover, the multilingual function of ElevenLabs AI enhances inclusivity, allowing content creators to cater to non-native speakers and regions with linguistic diversities. Whether it's educational materials, entertainment, or customer service, the technology's adaptability fosters better communication and understanding, breaking down barriers that often accompany single-language applications.

Finally, the integration of numerous languages into ElevenLabs AI addresses the growing demand for accessible digital content worldwide. It not only meets market demands but also promotes a global perspective in content creation, which is invaluable in today's interconnected environment. This feature sets a new precedent for international communication standards, propelling industries towards more inclusive practices.

Leveraging ElevenLabs AI for Podcast Production

The integration of ElevenLabs AI into podcast production heralds a transformative era for podcasters. This technology simplifies the creation of high-quality voiceovers, enabling creators to produce engaging and varied content with minimal effort. Utilizing synthesized voices can lower production costs and reduce the time needed for recording sessions, which is essential in the fast-paced world of podcasting.

Further, the ability to modify voice tones and styles on demand with ElevenLabs AI empowers podcast producers to tailor audio to the content's mood or the target audience's preferences. This flexibility is invaluable for storytelling, making narratives more impactful and immersive. Additionally, integrating multiple languages enhances global reach, allowing producers to connect with a broader audience without the barrier of language constraints.

Ethical use of AI-generated voices also comes into play, ensuring transparency and authenticity in content creation. With ElevenLabs AI, podcasters can maintain the trust of their listeners while innovating with the latest voice synthesis technology to create rich, dynamic, and culturally resonant episodes.

Voice Synthesis for Animated Movie Characters

The innovative use of ElevenLabs AI in the animation industry revolutionizes how characters come to life. By synthesizing voiceovers, animators can create more dynamic and emotionally resonant characters without the constraints of traditional voice acting. This technology allows for a seamless blend of vocal expression and character animation, opening up new possibilities for storytelling.

Particularly, ElevenLabs AI can generate unique voices that match the specific traits and personalities of animated characters. This customization extends beyond mere vocal tone to include accents, speech patterns, and emotional inflections, making each character's voice distinctive. As a result, animated films and series can feature a wider range of characters, enhancing the narrative's depth and appeal.

Moreover, using AI for voice synthesis in animation reduces dependency on multiple voice actors, which can streamline production and cut costs. Studios can experiment with different voices for a character before finalizing the most suitable one, ensuring perfect alignment with the visual portrayal. This technology not only enriches the viewer's experience but also pushes the boundaries of creative expression in animation.

Utilizing AI Voiceovers for Public Announcements

The advent of AI technologies like ElevenLabs AI has transformed the landscape of public announcements, providing a versatile tool for clear and engaging communication across various platforms. By harnessing synthetic voices, organizations can deliver consistent and professional messages that capture the attention of a wide audience. This is particularly vital in emergency broadcasting, where clarity and promptness are crucial.

Moreover, ElevenLabs AI facilitates the customization of voiceovers to suit specific contexts or cultural nuances, enhancing the relatability and effectiveness of announcements. Whether it's a public service announcement, transport system guidance, or community alerts, the technology ensures that the message is not only heard but also understood by diverse demographics.

The integration of ElevenLabs AI in public announcements also promotes accessibility. With features that support multiple languages and dialects, this technology breaks down linguistic barriers, making vital information accessible to non-native speakers. This is pivotal in fostering inclusivity and ensuring public safety and information dissemination are equitable.

In summary, ElevenLabs AI redefines the strategies behind public announcements, marrying technology with human-centric communication practices to enhance societal engagement and trust.

ElevenLabs AI in Customer Service Automation

Integrating ElevenLabs AI into customer service automation represents a significant advancement in customer interactions. This technology enables the development of intelligent, customer-facing systems that can respond with human-like precision and subtlety. With ElevenLabs AI, customer service operations are transformed, enhancing response quality and reducing wait times, which in turn boosts customer satisfaction and loyalty.

The application of ElevenLabs AI extends beyond mere voice response; it involves comprehensive understanding and management of customer queries across various sectors. Whether it's addressing queries in banking, retail, or healthcare, the AI's adaptive voice technology can be fine-tuned to address specific customer needs and preferences. This personalization capability not only improves engagement but also tailors experiences, making interactions more relevant and effective.

Additionally, integrating this system reduces operational costs by automating routine inquiries, freeing human agents to handle more complex issues. Moreover, the AI's ability to learn from interactions enhances its response accuracy over time, continually improving service quality. This dynamic adaptation is pivotal for businesses aiming to meet evolving customer expectations in a digital age.

Optimizing User Experience with Human-like AI Interactions

Enhancing user experience through human-like interactions is a critical aspect of ElevenLabs AI's voice synthesis technology. By integrating AI-driven synthetic voices that closely mimic human nuances, the technology offers a more natural and engaging user interface. These interactions are not only seamless but also significantly enrich the user's emotional engagement, making digital experiences feel more personal and less mechanical.

The lifelike quality of these AI-generated voiceovers plays a pivotal role in various applications, from virtual assistants to interactive customer support tools. The capability to deliver voice responses that reflect subtlety and emotion ensures that interactions are more than transactions; they become relational experiences. This humanization of technology fosters greater user trust and satisfaction, vital for long-term engagement.

Furthermore, ElevenLabs AI's emphasis on human-like interactions enhances the overall accessibility of services. By providing voice synthesis that can adapt to the tone, context, and emotional state desired by users, the technology ensures inclusivity and adaptability across different user demographics. This tailored interaction approach optimizes user experience, setting a new standard in how we connect with AI-driven platforms.

Future Trends in AI Voice Technology and Market Demands

The horizon for AI voice technology is vibrant with transformative trends. With rapid advancements in neural networks and machine learning, the essence of synthetic voiceovers will undergo monumental changes, primarily driven by increasing demands for customization and realism. Future iterations of ElevenLabs AI will likely focus on refining emotional intelligence capabilities, enabling voiceovers to convey deeper sentiments and react contextually in real-time conversations.

From a market demand perspective, sectors such as telehealth and remote education, where clear communication is pivotal, will fuel significant growth. As global dynamics shift towards more digital interactions, businesses will seek AI voice technologies that can seamlessly bridge language gaps and cultural barriers, making technology more accessible and inclusive.

Moreover, sustainability in AI processes will emerge as a crucial consideration. Companies will prioritize developing eco-friendly AI voice solutions that reduce computational load while maintaining high performance. This shift will not only address environmental concerns but also optimize operational costs, offering a competitive edge in the bustling AI marketplace.

Case Studies: Successful Implementations of ElevenLabs AI

The deployment of ElevenLabs AI in diverse fields highlights significant achievements in synthetic voice applications. One notable case is its integration into a leading audiobook platform. Here, ElevenLabs AI not only enhanced narration quality but also expanded the library by quickly producing audiobooks in multiple languages, boosting accessibility and market reach.

Similarly, a multinational corporation utilized ElevenLabs AI for customer service automation, achieving remarkable improvements in response times and customer satisfaction scores. By customizing voice tones to match customer demographics, the AI-powered service added a personalized touch to interactions, markedly increasing engagement and loyalty.

Additionally, a breakthrough was observed in the educational sector where ElevenLabs AI facilitated the creation of interactive learning modules. These modules, featuring synthesized voices that could express questions and explanations with human-like intonation, significantly improved student engagement and learning outcomes.

These case studies not only demonstrate the versatility of ElevenLabs AI but also underscore its potential to revolutionize industries by enhancing communication and interaction through sophisticated voice synthesis.

Marketing Strategies for Businesses Using Synthetic Voiceovers

Harnessing ElevenLabs AI's synthetic voiceovers unlocks myriad marketing strategies for businesses keen on driving engagement and expanding their reach. By integrating tailored, human-like voiceovers into campaigns, companies differentiate themselves by offering unique auditory experiences. Personalized voice advertisements or branded corporate narrations enhance brand recognition and foster emotional connections with consumers.

Moreover, businesses using ElevenLabs AI can execute targeted marketing strategies effectively. Customized voice messages cater to diverse demographics, adapting tones and styles to suit different regions and age groups. This precision marketing not only increases the efficacy of campaigns but also boosts conversion rates as messages resonate more deeply with the target audience.

Importantly, leveraging synthetic voiceovers in marketing tools reduces production costs and time. Rapid content updates are feasible without the logistical constraints of human voice actors, allowing for swift responses to market trends and consumer feedback. This agility ensures businesses remain competitive and adaptable in a fast-evolving digital landscape.

In summary, ElevenLabs AI equips businesses with innovative tools to craft powerful, cost-effective marketing campaigns that speak directly to the heart of their audience, enhancing both reach and impact.

Cost Analysis and Return on Investment for ElevenLabs AI Services

Investing in ElevenLabs AI for voiceover services necessitates a thorough cost-benefit analysis to understand its financial viability. Initially, the setup and subscription costs might appear substantial; however, these expenses are offset by significant long-term savings and gains. The deployment of AI-driven voice synthesis technology drastically reduces the need for human voice actors, thereby cutting down on recurrent costs associated with recording and production.

Moreover, the scalability of ElevenLabs AI allows businesses to expand their voiceover applications without proportional increases in costs. This scalability is particularly advantageous in sectors like e-learning and customer service, where dynamic content is crucial. Utilization of AI for these services not only minimizes operational costs but also enhances the quality and speed of production, leading to better customer retention and a broader audience reach.

Finally, the return on investment (ROI) can be quantitatively measured through improved customer engagement and expanded market access. Businesses using ElevenLabs AI have reported increased efficiency and reduced time-to-market for new products, which significantly boosts their competitive edge while ensuring the recovery of initial investments within a measurable period.

Challenges and Limitations of Current Voice Synthesis Technology

Despite the impressive strides made by ElevenLabs AI in voice synthesis, several challenges persist. Central to these is the technology's struggle with capturing the full spectrum of human emotion and inflection. While AI can replicate speech patterns, the subtleties of emotional undertones often remain elusive. This occasionally results in synthetic voiceovers that might sound flat or less engaging when compared to a human narrator.

Furthermore, regional dialects and accents pose a significant hurdle. The AI's ability to accurately mimic these nuances is critical, especially in global markets, but current technology still falls short of perfecting this aspect. This limitation can affect the authenticity of communication in applications like customer service, where regional adaptability is crucial.

Lastly, the rapid evolution of voice synthesis technology itself presents a double-edged sword. Keeping up with continuous updates and advancements requires persistent training and retraining of the AI models, invoking substantial ongoing investment in time and resources. For many businesses, especially small to medium enterprises, this investment can be daunting.

Training ElevenLabs AI for Niche Applications

Specialized markets require tailored solutions, and ElevenLabs AI's training for niche applications exemplifies the nuanced adaptation of voice synthesis technology. For instance, in the luxury real estate market, creating voiceovers that carry a tone of sophistication and exclusivity enhances promotional materials significantly. By training the AI with a dataset curated from high-end market interactions, the voice generated carries an air of elegance and precision that resonates with affluent clients.

In the realm of accessibility, ElevenLabs AI is being trained to support speech impairments, providing clearer communication solutions for individuals with specific needs. This involves adjusting the pace, clarity, and enunciation in the AI's speech patterns, a development process that is both complex and rewarding, as it broadens the inclusivity of digital communication platforms.

Lastly, training ElevenLabs AI for emergency response services involves synthesizing calm yet authoritative voiceovers for high-stress situations. This niche application requires the simulation of urgent yet composed speech patterns, which are critical during crisis communications. Here, the training focuses on rapid information delivery framed in a manner that aids in crisis mitigation rather than exacerbation, showcasing the potential life-saving impact of tailored AI voiceovers.

Integrating Emotional Intelligence into AI Voiceovers

Integrating emotional intelligence into AI voiceovers is pivotal for crafting interactions that resonate on a human level. ElevenLabs AI leverages advanced algorithms to analyze and replicate emotional subtleties in speech, enabling synthetic voices to deliver not just messages, but moods. This integration transforms synthetic interactions, making them more natural and relatable.

The challenge lies in the nuances of human emotions. ElevenLabs AI utilizes a blend of linguistic analysis and machine learning models to interpret vocal nuances like pitch and tempo, which are then adjusted to reflect desired emotions. This ability to convey empathy or excitement in a voiceover can significantly enhance user experience across various platforms such as virtual assistants and customer service bots.

Moreover, ongoing development in this area focuses on refining the AI's emotional range. By expanding the dataset with diverse emotional speech patterns, ElevenLabs AI continues to improve its emotional discernment. Emotionally aware voiceovers are not merely a technical achievement but also a step towards more engaging and empathetic human-AI interactions.

Collaborations and Partnerships Enhancing ElevenLabs AI's Capabilities

ElevenLabs AI's expansion into collaborative realms signals a transformative era in voice synthesis technology. By partnering with tech giants and startups alike, ElevenLabs has enriched its technological infrastructure and broadened its scope of applications. These alliances are not merely strategic but are pivotal in enhancing the AI's linguistic diversity and customization features, allowing it to serve a global user base more effectively.

Significantly, collaborations with academic institutions have facilitated research and development strides in emotional intelligence incorporation and dialect accuracy. The synergy between ElevenLabs AI's engineers and leading linguistic scholars accelerates the pace of innovation, producing more nuanced and contextually aware voice synthesis. This academic-industrial partnership model has proven essential for leapfrogging technological challenges that once seemed insurmountable.

Moreover, through these partnerships, ElevenLabs AI has gained access to proprietary datasets that refine voice synthesis algorithms. The collaborative efforts also extend to ethical discussions, ensuring responsible use of voice technology. Embracing a collaborative ethos, ElevenLabs AI is setting new standards in the synthetic voiceover industry, reflecting a commitment to continuous improvement and ethical responsibility.

Scalability Options for ElevenLabs AI Voiceover Services

Scaling services is integral for businesses aiming to adapt to varying market demands, and ElevenLabs AI provides robust options for scalability in voiceover services. Whether a business seeks to expand from local to global markets or from niche to mainstream sectors, ElevenLabs AI can adjust its output capacity without compromising quality. This scalability is underpinned by cloud-based architectures that facilitate seamless expansions and contractions of service use, making it ideal for businesses experiencing fluctuating demands.

Moreover, ElevenLabs AI's modular design allows for the integration of additional features as the market evolves. This capability means businesses can stay ahead by continuously updating and customizing their voiceover offerings. As sectors like e-learning and customer service increasingly rely on AI voiceovers, the ability to promptly scale up to meet educational mandates or customer support needs becomes invaluable.

Lastly, partnering strategically with infrastructure providers ensures that ElevenLabs AI can scale operations efficiently. This approach minimizes potential bottlenecks, allowing uninterrupted service delivery during scaling phases, and provides businesses the agility needed in rapidly changing markets, thus maintaining a competitive edge.

SUMMARY

ElevenLabs AI has reshaped the landscape of synthetic voiceovers by leveraging advanced voice synthesis technology. The firm, which stood at the forefront of this transformative industry, utilizes proprietary algorithms to meticulously analyze human voice patterns and recreate nearly indistinguishable speech sounds. With capabilities ranging from nuanced tone adjustments to the complete emulation of emotional depth, ElevenLabs AI caters to a diverse spectrum of industries including audiobooks, customer service, and e-learning, among others. A key aspect of ElevenLabs AI's innovation lies in its ethical approach to voice synthesis, prioritizing authenticity, creator rights, and transparency, thus ensuring a sustainable future for AI in creative markets. Additionally, the platform supports multilingual capabilities and various stylistic customizations, enhancing global accessibility and inclusivity. This chapter explores different applications and settings of ElevenLabs AI, from its integration in e-learning platforms to entertainment, indicating a dynamic shift towards more interactive and realistic AI-generated vocal performance. The customization tools allow for personalized voiceover profiles, which address specific audience preferences, greatly enhancing user engagement and content relatability. The technology's impact spans marketing, where personalized voice ads are used, and public announcements, improving communication clarity and reach. In gaming and virtual realities, the adoption of ElevenLabs AI voiceovers has enriched player experience by introducing diverse character voices with emotionally charged speech. Challenges such as capturing the subtleties of human emotion and integrating emotional intelligence into AI voiceovers are discussed with a forward-looking stance toward future enhancements. Lastly, the chapter covers various collaborative efforts that augment ElevenLabs AI's capabilities, ensuring the scalability and adaptability of the technology across different sectors.

REFERENCES

[1] Turing, Alan M. 'Computing Machinery and Intelligence.' Mind, 1950. https://academic.oup.com/mind/article/LIX/236/433/986238

[2] Hinton, Geoffrey, et al. 'Deep Neural Networks for Acoustic Modeling in Speech Recognition.' IEEE Signal Processing Magazine, 2012.. https://ieeexplore.ieee.org/document/6296526

[3] Amodei, Dario, et al. 'Deep Speech 2: End-to-End Speech Recognition in English and Mandarin.' Proceedings of the 33rd International Conference on Machine Learning, 2016.. https://proceedings.mlr.press/v48/amodei16.html

[4] Park, Taesung, et al. 'A Multimodal Approach to Real-time Voice Conversion in Emotional Speech Synthesis.' ICLR, 2020. https://openreview.net/forum?id=r1x0GnC9Ym

[5] Lancewicki, Tomasz, et al. 'Leveraging Ethics and AI: Implementing Responsible Automation and Ensuring Data Privacy.' ScienceDirect, 2020.. https://www.sciencedirect.com/science/article/pii/S238093172100012X

CASE STUDY: INTEGRATING ELEVENLABS AI FOR TRANSFORMATIVE CUSTOMER SERVICE IN TELECOMMUNICATIONS

A leading telecommunications company, GlobalCom, faced significant challenges in managing its customer service operations. With over 50 million customers worldwide, the demand for fast, efficient, and personalized customer interaction was at an all-time high. To address these challenges, GlobalCom integrated ElevenLabs AI's voice synthesis technology into their service platforms.

The implementation process began with the development of a strategic plan focusing on areas with high customer interaction frequencies, such as billing inquiries and technical support. ElevenLabs AI was configured to understand and respond in multiple languages, accommodating GlobalCom's diverse customer base. Each AI voice was tailored not only to speak in the customer's native language but also to adapt its tone based on the complexity and urgency of customer queries.

Over the first six months post-implementation, GlobalCom observed a 40% decrease in average call handling time and a 30% improvement in first-call resolution rates. Customer satisfaction surveys indicated a 25% increase in positive responses regarding interaction quality. Additionally, the scalability of ElevenLabs AI allowed GlobalCom to deploy voice synthesis across different regions without the need for extensive retraining of the platform, saving considerable costs and time.

The case of GlobalCom demonstrates how ElevenLabs AI can transform customer service by providing a scalable, efficient, and customer-focused interaction model. The capability of the AI to learn from interactions and improve responses over time was particularly beneficial in addressing complex and frequently changing customer queries. Moreover, the ethical use of AI technology ensures transparency and respect for user privacy, addressing potential concerns about synthetic voice impersonation and misuse.

Case Study: Revolutionizing Audiobook Production with ElevenLabs AI

In the evolving landscape of digital publishing, a prominent publishing house, LitWorks Publishing, identified a unique challenge and opportunity: expanding their audiobook market share while reducing production costs and time. To tackle this, LitWorks turned to ElevenLabs AI's advanced voice synthesis technology to automate and enhance their audiobook production processes.

LitWorks began by piloting the technology with a series of classic literature titles, which required expressive and nuanced narrations to maintain the integrity and appeal of the original texts. ElevenLabs AI was programmed to analyze and emulate the emotive undertones and distinct accents of characters, creating a rich, immersive listening experience that closely mimicked human narrators. The AI's capacity to adjust tone, pace, and inflection on-the-fly made it an invaluable tool for producing high-quality, dynamic audiobook content.

Despite initial reservations about public acceptance, the results were overwhelmingly positive. Within the first year of implementation, LitWorks reported a 50% reduction in production costs and a 35% acceleration in time-to-market for new audiobooks. Reader satisfaction scores soared by 45%, with many praising the authentic and engaging narration offered by the AI. Moreover, the technology enabled LitWorks to quickly expand its offerings to include audiobooks in multiple languages, significantly broadening its global audience reach without incurring the usual high costs associated with multilingual content creation.

The adoption of ElevenLabs AI not only transformed LitWorks' production model but also sparked a broader discussion within the industry about the sustainable integration of AI in creative processes. The case of LitWorks Publishing illustrates the profound impact of voice synthesis technology on the traditional media landscape, showcasing substantial improvements in efficiency, cost management, and creative flexibility. Additionally, it stirred a vital conversation on the ethical implications and artistic merit of AI-driven content, prompting the industry to consider new standards for AI use in artistic creations.

Case Study: Enhancing Global E-Learning with ElevenLabs AI's Multilingual Capabilities

In the realm of global education, Sundial Learning, a prominent e-learning platform, recognized a growing demand for culturally relevant and accessible education across different linguistic demographics. To cater to an increasingly diverse learner base and to expand their market reach, Sundial Learning adopted ElevenLabs AI's advanced voice synthesis technology, specifically its multilingual capabilities.

Sundial Learning initially targeted non-English speaking markets in Asia and Latin America. They utilized ElevenLabs AI to create instructional content in various local languages, including Mandarin, Hindi, Spanish, and Portuguese. The AI was meticulously programmed to embrace regional dialects and cultural nuances, ensuring that the synthetic voices were not only linguistically accurate but also culturally resonant. This adaptability was crucial in subjects requiring precise terminology and context, such as history and social sciences, where the nuances of language significantly impact learner comprehension and engagement.

The implementation saw immediate positive feedback. Engagement metrics on Sundial's platform showed a remarkable 60% increase in course completion rates in the newly targeted regions. Additionally, user satisfaction surveys indicated a 70% increase in positive feedback regarding the platform's accessibility and relevance. The success of the multilingual courses prompted Sundial to explore further AI-driven customizations, integrating adaptive learning features that used the AI's analytics to modify educational content according to individual learning paces and preferences.

This case demonstrates how ElevenLabs AI's voice synthesis can revolutionize e-learning by breaking language barriers and providing scalable, personalized education solutions. The technology not only enabled Sundial Learning to tap into new markets but also offered learners a more inclusive and engaging educational experience. It underscored the significant role of advanced AI in addressing global educational challenges and highlighted the critical importance of ethical considerations in deploying AI in education, ensuring that the technology enhances human capabilities without replacing them.

Case Study: Optimizing Public Health Outreach with ElevenLabs AI Voice Synthesis

In a concerted effort to improve public health communication, the National Health Service (NHS) faced the challenge of effectively disseminating vital health information across a linguistically and culturally diverse population. To tackle this issue, NHS collaborated with ElevenLabs AI to implement a sophisticated voice synthesis system capable of delivering tailored health messages in multiple languages and dialects.

The project commenced with an extensive needs assessment to identify key areas where communication gaps existed. ElevenLabs AI's technology was then integrated into NHS's existing public health platforms, including websites, mobile apps, and public announcement systems. A pivotal aspect of the setup was programming the AI to adjust its tone and delivery based on the severity and urgency of the messages—be it routine vaccination drives or urgent pandemic-related updates. Additionally, the AI was tasked with the sensitive handling of messages to ensure cultural and emotional appropriateness, which was crucial for messages involving mental health or pandemic responses.

The implementation phase was followed by several months of rigorous testing and optimization, during which AI-generated messages were continually refined based on user feedback and engagement metrics. This iterative process was crucial in fine-tuning the system to achieve optimal clarity and impact. Within the first year of deployment, NHS reported a 40% increase in public engagement with health campaigns and a significant rise in compliance with health advisories among hard-to-reach demographic groups.

This case study not only illustrates the utility of ElevenLabs AI in enhancing public health communication but also highlights how voice synthesis can bridge communication gaps in critical sectors. By providing reliable, accessible, and culturally sensitive information, the technology plays a pivotal role in enhancing public health outcomes. Moreover, the ethical considerations inherent in disseminating health information through synthetic voices were meticulously addressed, ensuring transparency and trust in AI-generated content.

Case Study: Implementing ElevenLabs AI in Virtual Reality Gaming

As the virtual reality (VR) gaming industry seeks to offer more immersive and realistic experiences, a leading VR gaming studio, VirtuaSphere, embarked on a journey to enhance player engagement using advanced voice synthesis technology provided by ElevenLabs AI. The primary objective was to create deeply interactive and responsive environments where characters could communicate with players using natural, human-like voices.

The initial phase involved the meticulous selection of voice profiles suited for diverse game characters, ranging from allies to adversaries. Each profile was designed to convey unique emotional and tonal subtleties to enhance the realism of interactions. ElevenLabs AI's capabilities in generating dynamic speech patterns allowed for real-time voice modulation based on gameplay, adapting character responses to player actions and decisions. This adaptive voice synthesis not only contributed to the plausibility of character interactions but also enhanced narrative depth, making the gaming experience more engaging and emotionally complex.

Integration challenges included ensuring seamless synchronization between the AI voices and the VR environments. VirtuaSphere's development team collaborated closely with ElevenLabs AI engineers to embed the voice technology within the game's existing audio systems without latency or disruptions. As part of the user experience refinement, iterative playtesting was conducted, during which voice interactions were continually assessed and optimized based on player feedback and behavioral data.

The final implementation showcased a significant transformation in player experience metrics. Engagement rates soared by 50%, and player retention metrics indicated a substantial increase in repeat session lengths. Moreover, the nuanced voice interactions fostered a greater emotional connection to the game, evidenced by positive sentiment analysis in player reviews.

This case highlights the pivotal role of sophisticated voice synthesis technology in revolutionizing interactions within virtual environments. By enabling realistic and responsive communications, ElevenLabs AI not only propelled VirtuaSphere to the forefront of VR innovation but also established a new standard for emotional and narrative depth in gaming.

Case Study: Revitalizing Retail with ElevenLabs AI Voice Synthesis: A Case Study on Harmony Retail Chain

The retail sector consistently seeks innovative solutions to enhance customer experience and operational efficiency. Harmony Retail Chain, a multinational retail corporation, embarked on an ambitious project to integrate ElevenLabs AI's voice synthesis into their customer service and in-store experience across 300 outlets worldwide. The primary challenge faced by Harmony was the impersonal nature of digital interactions in their automated systems and the need for a more tailored approach to diverse consumer requirements.

Harmony's integration process involved multiple phases, beginning with an initial pilot program in their flagship stores. The first stage was dedicated to customizing the voice synthesis to echo the brand's image—friendly and reliable—while ensuring linguistic and cultural nuances were well-represented in different regional markets. ElevenLabs AI was employed to handle common customer inquiries about products, store navigation, and promotions, utilizing localized languages and accents.

Post-implementation, Harmony observed a 45% improvement in customer interaction satisfaction, a decrease in store staff workload by 30%, and an impressive increase in sales figures, particularly in regions where customer engagement had previously been low. The AI's capability to learn from customer interactions resulted in continuous enhancements of voice responses, further aligning with the consumer's expectations and shopping experiences.

Furthermore, the case of Harmony Retail Chain demonstrates the transformative potential of ElevenLabs AI in the retail environment. By offering a voice that can adapt to context, greet customers by name, and remember previous interactions, the technology has not only humanized digital service channels but has also strengthened brand loyalty. The scenario paves the way for future applications of voice synthesis technology in retail, promoting a shift towards more interactive and personalized customer service solutions. The extensive use of AI also alleviates pressures on human staff, allowing them to focus on more complex customer needs and backend operations, thereby optimizing overall business performance.

Case Study: Expanding Market Access Through ElevenLabs AI in Multinational Broadcasting

Eclipsing traditional boundaries in broadcasting, MediaGlobal, a multinational broadcasting company, undertook an ambitious project to diversify its audience by transcending linguistic barriers, using ElevenLabs AI's real-time voice synthesis technology. MediaGlobal, known for its influential news and entertainment content, faced the challenge of making their broadcasts comprehensible and relatable to a global audience, encompassing varied linguistic and cultural backgrounds.

The integration process began with identifying key markets where language barriers were previously a bottleneck for expansion. Markets in Asia and Africa, with significant linguistic diversity, were prioritized. ElevenLabs AI was configured to provide real-time dubbing and subtitling using its advanced voice synthesis, capable of handling multiple languages and dialects without compromising the emotional congruency of the broadcasts.

Initial feedback was overwhelmingly positive. Viewers appreciated the authentic and culturally nuanced voiceovers, which retained the news anchors' and show characters' emotional tones and inflections, greatly enhancing viewer engagement and satisfaction. This capability allowed MediaGlobal to penetrate markets that had been inaccessible, with a subsequent 70% increase in viewer numbers from these regions.

The strategic implementation of ElevenLabs AI not only broadened MediaGlobal's reach but also provided insights into viewer preferences across different cultural contexts, enabling the company to tailor content more effectively. Moreover, the ability to dynamically adjust voice tones and styles based on viewer feedback exemplified a significant advancement in personalized broadcasting services.

This case amplifies the transformative impact of AI voice synthesis in global broadcasting. It underscores the importance of cultural sensitivity and adaptability in content delivery, which are paramount in engaging a diverse global audience. Furthermore, it explores the ethical dimensions of AI in media, emphasizing the need to balance technological innovation with cultural integrity and respect.

Case Study: Leveraging ElevenLabs AI for Strategic Emergency Response Communications

In the fast-paced arena of emergency response, the Rapid Response Unit (RRU), a government agency responsible for managing national disaster events, sought innovative solutions to overhaul its communication systems. The objective was clear: to deliver real-time, accurate, and emotionally resonant communications during crises, catered to a diverse population. To achieve this, RRU integrated ElevenLabs AI's voice synthesis technology into their public announcement systems.

The implementation kicked off with a comprehensive analysis of the communication challenges faced during emergencies. These included language barriers, the need for immediate information dissemination, and maintaining public calm. ElevenLabs AI was set up to handle these challenges by delivering multilingual, real-time updates with the appropriate emotional undertones, ensuring clarity and calm in high-pressure scenarios.

Initially, the AI was programmed with data from past emergency broadcasts to learn varied linguistic nuances and stress-inflected speech patterns appropriate for crisis situations. The technology's ability to modulate voice tones to convey urgency without inducing panic was pivotal. Furthermore, ElevenLabs AI's multilingual capabilities meant that messages could be automatically translated and delivered in multiple languages, ensuring wide accessibility and understanding.

Over the course of its first year in operation, RRU noted a significant improvement in public compliance with emergency protocols, a 50% reduction in response times to public inquiries, and greater efficiency in the allocation of emergency resources. Post-event surveys revealed a 40% increase in the public's satisfaction with the transparency and effectiveness of communication.

This case study exemplifies how ElevenLabs AI can be utilized to enhance the responsiveness and efficiency of emergency communication systems. By providing tailored, emotionally intelligent, and linguistically diverse messages, the technology ensures critical information is both accessible and reassuring to all demographics during crises. The success of the integration also underscores the importance of continual learning and adaptation in AI technologies, as continual refinements based on feedback and new data are essential for maintaining the efficacy of the system in dynamic emergency scenarios.

REVIEW QUESTIONS

1. In a given scenario, a voiceover company aims to revamp their service offerings by integrating advanced AI technology. The company desires a solution that provides high-quality, nuanced voice synthesis capable of capturing the emotional depth similar to human narrations for their audiobook service. Which of the following options is the most suitable for the company to pursue based on the detailed capabilities provided?

A) Using a basic text-to-speech software

B) Contracting freelance voice actors to record the audiobooks

C) Licensing ElevenLabs AI for its deep learning-based voice synthesis

D) Adopting a conventional voice recording setup

Answer: C

Explanation: Based on the requirements, ElevenLabs AI stands out as the most suitable option due to its advanced voice synthesis capabilities. Leveraging deep learning algorithms, ElevenLabs AI can analyze and replicate human vocal tones, inflections, and emotions intricately. This depth of emotion and expressive modulation is essential for delivering a lifelike and engaging narration, making it a perfect fit for an audiobook service requiring emotional resonance.

2. A marketing firm is looking to provide innovative voiceover services in multiple languages to expand globally and needs technology that can support diverse voices without significant time and cost implications of traditional localization. Which technology should they integrate according to the data presented?

A) Hiring multilingual voice actors for each target market

B) Implementing ElevenLabs AI with multilingual synthesis capabilities

C) Utilizing a simple machine translation tool for voiceovers

D) Focusing only on text-based marketing and skipping voiceovers

Answer: B

Explanation: For a marketing firm aiming to expand globally without the high costs and logistical complications associated with traditional voice localization, implementing ElevenLabs AI is the optimal solution. ElevenLabs AI offers multilingual voice synthesis capabilities, allowing the firm to produce high-quality voiceovers in multiple languages efficiently. This supports not only a seamless localization process but also ensures that the voiceovers are culturally nuanced and linguistically accurate, which is critical for effective marketing across different demographics.

REVIEW QUESTIONS

3. An online education platform is experiencing low engagement rates in their e-learning modules. They require a solution that enhances the auditory delivery of the content to make learning more engaging and accessible. Which feature of ElevenLabs AI could be most influential in achieving this goal?

A) Integration of realistic accents and dialects

B) Utilization of ElevenLabs AI's voice tuning to match educational content

C) Adding background music through ElevenLabs AI

D) Use of a uniform robotic voice for all modules

Answer: B

Explanation: To boost engagement and accessibility in an e-learning platform, utilizing ElevenLabs AI's capability to fine-tune voices to match specific educational content is highly beneficial. By adjusting intonations, pitch, and speed, content becomes more digestible and engaging. This tailored auditory enhancement not only aids in retention but also makes the learning experience more appealing to a diverse set of learners, potentially addressing the issue of low engagement rates effectively.

4. A game development company seeks to create a more immersive experience in their new open-world game by utilizing a technology that allows dynamic voiceover modifications to match various game scenarios. Which aspect of ElevenLabs AI should they leverage to meet this requirement?

A) Static voiceover tracks predesigned for each scenario

B) ElevenLabs AI's dynamic voice synthesis for context-aware speech

C) Outsourcing voice acting to different actors for each scenario

D) Limiting the dialogue options to reduce complexity

Answer: B

Explanation: For creating a truly immersive gaming experience, leveraging ElevenLabs AI's capabilities for dynamic voice synthesis that is context-aware is crucial. This feature enables the game to offer real-time voice modulation, adapting to various game scenarios and enhancing the player's immersion. Such context-sensitive dialogues make interactions feel more natural and responsive, significantly enriching the gaming experience, unlike static tracks or multiple outsourced voices that may lack the required dynamism and integration.

SYNTHESIA AI: CUSTOM VIDEO AVATARS FOR PERSONALIZED INTERACTION

Introduction to Synthesia AI and the Technology Behind Video Avatars

In the new digital frontier, Synthesia AI stands out as a trailblazer, revolutionizing the way we interact with media through its advanced video avatar technology. At its core, Synthesia AI harnesses machine learning and artificial intelligence to create personalized video avatars that can speak, gesture, and act like real humans in a multitude of languages. These avatars are not only customizable but also highly adaptable, capable of delivering unique, user-specific interactions that enhance digital communications across various sectors.

The technology underpinning Synthesia AI involves a sophisticated blend of facial recognition software, natural language processing, and computer-generated imagery. By analyzing human expressions and speech patterns, Synthesia AI is able to render digital personas that respond dynamically in real-time, offering a more personalized approach than static video content or traditional CGI models.

This cutting-edge application serves not just to personalize user experiences but also to create a new dimension in how businesses engage with their clientèle through digital mediums. Whether in customer service, e-learning, or marketing, Synthesia AI's video avatars present an innovative solution to the ever-evolving demand for more tailored and engaging digital content.

How Synthesia AI Personalizes User Interactions with Custom Avatars

Synthesia AI elevates the user experience to a new level by personalizing interactions through custom video avatars. This innovative approach tailors digital interactions to mirror personal engagement, seamlessly blending the user's preferences and behaviors with the capabilities of AI technology. By integrating detailed user data—such as previous interactions, demographic information, and personal preferences—Synthesia AI crafts avatars that not only look and sound unique but also interact in ways that resonate deeply with each individual user.

The real magic lies in the AI's ability to analyze and adapt. Through continuous learning algorithms, Synthesia AI's avatars evolve based on interaction outcomes, making them increasingly effective over time. This dynamic adjustment process ensures that the avatars remain relevant and engaging, thereby maximizing user satisfaction and retention.

Moreover, the customization goes beyond mere aesthetics. Synthesia AI incorporates specific linguistic and cultural nuances, making interactions more relatable. Whether it's mimicking local dialects or adhering to cultural subtleties, these avatars can deliver a unique, culturally aware service that feels genuinely personal.

Setting Up Synthesia AI for Your Business

Implementing Synthesia AI into your business starts with understanding your organization's specific needs. Initial setup involves selecting the right avatar styles and scripting appropriate dialogues that align with your brand's voice and customer interaction strategies.

Once the basics are outlined, the technical setup includes integrating Synthesia AI's API with your existing systems. This might involve collaboration between your IT team and Synthesia's support engineers to ensure seamless compatibility and performance. Training sessions for your staff on managing and updating avatars are also crucial, as this empowers them to handle day-to-day avatar operations.

Additionally, consider the customer data handling aspect. Ensuring compliance with data protection regulations is critical when configuring your avatars to interact using customer-specific information. A clear privacy policy should be established to maintain transparency and build trust among users.

Finally, launching a pilot project before full-scale implementation allows you to gather insightful feedback and make necessary adjustments, optimizing the avatar's effectiveness in real-world scenarios.

Step-by-Step Guide to Creating a Video Avatar with Synthesia AI

Creating a custom video avatar with Synthesia AI involves a streamlined process that merges creativity with technology. First, define the role and purpose of the avatar. Whether it's for customer service, e-learning, or marketing campaigns, the intention will guide the design and scripting phases. Next, select the physical appearance and voice of the avatar. Synthesia AI provides a variety of templates and options for customization, including gender, age, clothing, and even accents to ensure the avatar resonates with your target audience.

Moving forward, script your dialogues. This stage is crucial as it defines the interaction your avatar will have with users. Synthesia's platform allows you to input text which the AI then converts into lifelike speech, using natural language processing to ensure the dialogue flows naturally. Consider incorporating questions that anticipate user responses to make interactions more engaging.

Finally, review and test your avatar. Deploy the avatar in a controlled environment to monitor interactions and gather feedback. Use this data to refine gestures, dialogues, and the overall approach to enhance user engagement. With these steps, your Synthesia AI avatar will be ready to deliver personalized experiences.

Key Features and Capabilities of Synthesia AI

Synthesia AI offers a robust array of features that redefine interactive digital communications. Central to its innovation is the ability to generate high-definition video avatars that can be customized in a myriad of ways to suit specific business needs. These avatars are not just visually appealing but equipped with voice synchronization functionality, allowing for seamless audio-visual alignment that enhances the realism of interactions.

Moreover, Synthesia AI excels in multilingual support, enabling avatars to communicate in over 50 languages and dialects. This capability broadens the scope for global business reach without the need for extensive localization efforts. The platform also integrates easily with existing systems, courtesy of its API, facilitating a smooth incorporation into diverse operational frameworks.

The technology's scalability ensures it can handle varying demand levels, a crucial feature for businesses looking to expand. Real-time learning and adaptation based on user interactions make Synthesia AI not just a tool but a continually evolving asset for personalized customer engagement.

Industries Benefitting from Synthesia AI Video Avatars

The applications of Synthesia AI video avatars stretch across diverse fields, each deriving unique benefits. In healthcare, these avatars assist in patient management by delivering personalized care instructions, while simultaneously freeing up medical professionals for more critical tasks. Their ability to simulate human interaction proves indispensable in contexts where patient engagement and clear communication are pivotal.

The retail industry similarly leverages Synthesia AI to revolutionize customer service. Avatars guide customers through online shopping experiences, offer product recommendations, and handle inquiries, providing a seamless customer journey. This digital assistance translates into enhanced customer satisfaction and retention, pegging avatars as not just tools, but essential retail team members.

Education sector utilities are equally transformative, with avatars serving dual roles as both instructors and interactive learning aids. They deliver tailored educational content, adapt to student feedback in real time, and facilitate a more engaging learning environment. These capabilities underscore the widespread impact of Synthesia AI across multiple verticals, marking it as a cornerstone of modern digital interaction strategies.

Integrating Synthesia AI Avatars into Customer Service Platforms

Integrating Synthesia AI's custom video avatars into customer service platforms transforms traditional support systems into dynamic, interactive environments. This integration starts with the embedding of the AI's API into existing customer relationship management (CRM) systems. Here, the avatars act as the front-line interface, greeting customers and providing tailored responses based on prior interactions and customer data profiles.

The next phase involves configuring these avatars to use real-time data analytics, allowing them to respond contextually to customer inquiries. This integration means avatars can provide solutions and information specific to each customer, improving resolution times and overall satisfaction. Training the avatars in corporate language and ethos ensures consistency in communication, reinforcing brand values with every interaction.

Moreover, integrating these avatars into live chat and support ticket systems enhances accessibility. It allows continual learning from customer interactions, which in turn refines their capabilities, making them an invaluable asset in the quest for superior customer service. Thus, Synthesia AI not only streamlines interactions but reshapes them, enhancing the customer journey with every update.

Enhancing User Experience with Interactive Video Avatars

Interactive video avatars created by Synthesia AI significantly enhance user experience by providing a dynamic and personalized interaction model. These avatars, tailored to embody the ethos and persona of a brand, engage users in a more meaningful manner, effectively bridging the gap between digital and human interaction.

One key aspect is the avatar's ability to interpret and respond to user inputs in real-time. This responsiveness not only elevates user engagement but also fosters a sense of connection and reliability. For instance, in a customer service scenario, an avatar can detect customer frustration through tone analysis and switch to a more empathetic dialogue, thereby improving the interaction quality and user satisfaction.

Furthermore, these avatars can be programmed to remember past interactions, which personalizes future communications and makes users feel valued. This long-term interaction memory aids in building a relationship between the user and the brand, transcending traditional engagement metrics.

Ultimately, by leveraging advanced AI, Synthesia avatars offer a unique user experience that combines personality, adaptability, and memory, setting new standards for customer interaction in the digital age.

Synthesia AI in E-commerce: Enhancing the Shopping Experience

Synthesia AI is revolutionizing the e-commerce sector by enhancing the shopping experience through custom video avatars. These avatars serve as personal shopping assistants, guiding customers through product selections and providing detailed information in a highly interactive and engaging manner. This personalized assistance helps to mimic the attentiveness of in-store shopping experiences, making the digital landscape feel more intimate and responsive.

By integrating Synthesia AI into e-commerce platforms, retailers are able to offer a differentiated service that can significantly increase customer engagement and satisfaction. These avatars can be programmed to recognize returning customers and make tailored recommendations based on past purchases and browsing history. This level of customization not only enhances the user experience but also boosts the likelihood of repeat purchases.

Furthermore, the use of video avatars addresses common online shopping barriers such as the need for more product information and hesitation due to lack of human interaction. By effectively combining AI with elements of human touch, Synthesia AI avatars are setting new benchmarks for customer service and marketing within the e-commerce industry.

Use Cases: Innovative Applications of Synthesia AI in Different Sectors

Synthesia AI's versatility shines through its adoption across various sectors, each tapping into the potential of custom video avatars to address unique challenges. In the telecommunications industry, video avatars provide on-demand customer support, explaining complex billing systems and services clearly and visually, reducing customer confusion and service calls.

In real estate, virtual agents conduct property tours, offering potential buyers personalized and immersive viewing experiences that are not limited by geography or timing. These avatars can answer specific property-related queries and highlight features tailored to the interests of viewers, significantly enhancing customer engagement and accelerating decision-making processes.

The travel sector benefits from video avatars by providing multi-lingual support to a global audience, offering detailed, visually enriched information about destinations and accommodations. This not only boosts customer satisfaction but also empowers businesses to scale operations globally without the linguistic limitations.

Across these sectors, Synthesia AI not only improves operational efficiencies but also sets new standards for customer interaction and satisfaction.

Customization Tools: Tailoring Avatars to Brand Identity

Synthesia AI offers powerful customization tools that enable businesses to tailor their video avatars to align closely with their brand identity. These tools provide a range of options to modify the appearance, voice, and behavior of avatars, ensuring they represent the brand accurately and engagingly.

The visual customization extends beyond mere aesthetics. Users can choose from various hairstyles, attire, and even specific cultural attributes to ensure the avatar resonates with diverse customer bases globally. Voice customization goes further; businesses can select a tone and cadence that match their brand's personality, making the interaction not just visually but also audibly consistent with the brand's ethos.

Behavioral traits can also be fine-tuned, enabling avatars to exhibit characteristics like formality, friendliness, or enthusiasm based on the context of interaction. This level of detailed customization ensures that every digital touchpoint reinforces the brand, enhancing customer trust and loyalty through consistent, personalized experiences.

Navigating Privacy and Security Concerns with Video Avatars

As the adoption of Synthesia AI and its customizable video avatars rises, privacy and security concerns take center stage. These personalized interactions involve handling sensitive user data, magnifying the need for rigorous data protection measures. Synthesia AI employs advanced encryption and compliance with global security standards to safeguard data exchanged during these interactions.

However, the unique challenge arises from the very nature of custom avatars—tracking and synthesizing user behaviors and preferences to deliver personalized experiences. This necessitates a transparent data governance framework, ensuring users are fully informed and consenting. For businesses, it is crucial to delineate who can access this data, how long it is stored, and under what conditions it might be shared.

Addressing these concerns effectively ensures that Synthesia AI can continue to offer enhanced customer engagement without compromising individual privacy. Implementing comprehensive audit trails and regular security assessments can help preempt potential vulnerabilities, establishing trust and long-term loyalty among users.

Future Developments: What's Next for Synthesia AI

As Synthesia AI continues to reshape interactions across various industries, its roadmap is brimming with promising developments aimed at further enhancing its technological offerings. Anticipated advancements include even more sophisticated AI algorithms capable of generating ultra-realistic and emotionally responsive avatars. These improvements will not only deepen the personalization of interactions but also expand the range of emotions and expressions avatars can convincingly convey, making digital communications indistinguishable from human interactions.

Another exciting frontier is the integration of AR and VR environments where Synthesia AI avatars can operate. This will allow users to interact with avatars in three-dimensional, immersive settings, offering unprecedented levels of engagement in virtual meetings, educational sessions, and customer service experiences. Such innovations could revolutionize remote interactions, providing a tangible sense of presence and enhancing user engagement across the board.

Moreover, with the growing emphasis on accessibility, Synthesia AI plans to enhance avatar functionalities to support sign language, thereby broadening inclusivity and enabling more robust communication solutions for the hearing impaired.

Cost Analysis and ROI of Implementing Synthesia AI in Business

Implementing Synthesia AI involves initial costs tied to licensing, customization, and integration into existing systems. Businesses must explore these areas meticulously while planning the budget to anticipate a realistic expenditure landscape. However, the robust capabilities of Synthesia AI often offset this initial investment quickly, creating noteworthy long-term value.

The return on investment (ROI) can be seen markedly in areas such as customer engagement, operational efficiencies, and enhanced sales conversions. For instance, e-commerce businesses report an uptrend in user retention and conversion rates as video avatars provide personalized shopping experiences. Similarly, sectors like real estate and telecommunications observe reduced operational costs due to decreased need for human agents and lower incidences of miscommunication.

Moreover, Synthesia AI helps mitigate costs associated with customer service training and staffing. Evaluating the efficacy and financial impact through a post-implementation review enables businesses to measure success and recalibrate strategies for even greater efficiency, ensuring that integrating Synthesia AI transforms from a cost center into a key value driver.

Comparative Analysis: Synthesia AI vs. Other Avatar Technologies

Innovative avatar technologies are flourishing, yet Synthesia AI stands distinctively with its robust personalization capabilities. Comparatively, traditional avatar solutions often provide limited customization options, constraining businesses to predefined templates and generic interactions. In contrast, Synthesia AI excels by allowing thorough customization, uniquely aligning avatars with brand personalities and specific user needs. This deep personalization fosters greater user engagement and brand loyalty.

Functionality-wise, other technologies lag in real-time learning and adaptability. Synthesia AI, through advanced machine learning algorithms, enables avatars to analyze user interactions and evolve accordingly, offering a dynamically improving service experience. For example, while some competitors require manual updates and intervention, Synthesia AI avatars autonomously refine their responses and behaviors to better meet user expectations over time.

Moreover, Synthesia AI integrates more seamlessly with existing digital ecosystems. While others struggle with integration complexities, Synthesia AI's APIs and support structures facilitate smoother transitions, enhancing operational continuity. Its cutting-edge security features also surpass industry standards, giving businesses the confidence to deploy avatars without compromising data privacy.

Training and Support Available for Synthesia AI Users

Synthesia AI recognises the paramount importance of efficient training and support systems to aid businesses in adopting video avatar technologies effectively. Guided tutorials and resource libraries are readily available, providing step-by-step instructions on custom avatar creation and integration. These resources bridge the gap between sophisticated AI technology and user-friendly interfaces essential for diverse business applications.

Beyond basic training materials, Synthesia AI offers workshops and webinars aimed at enhancing user expertise in maximizing the platform's potential. These sessions not only tackle the technical elements of managing avatars but also delve into strategic best practices for deploying these digital representatives in varied customer interaction scenarios. Specialized support staff are available through dedicated channels to ensure that businesses receive prompt assistance with any operational challenges.

Furthermore, ongoing support adapts to the evolving needs of users. As Synthesia AI continues to innovate, support content and training modules are regularly updated to cover new features and functionalities. This proactive approach ensures users remain competent and confident in leveraging avatars to drive business value, fostering an environment of continuous learning and adaptation.

Building International Outreach through Multilingual Avatar Support

Synthesia AI's video avatar technology is not just a tool for personalized interaction but a gateway to global communication. By incorporating multilingual support, these avatars transcend linguistic boundaries, enhancing international outreach for businesses. This feature enables companies to connect with a diverse customer base across different regions, delivering customized messages in multiple languages.

The technology leverages sophisticated language processing algorithms that allow avatars to switch seamlessly between languages, ensuring a natural and engaging user experience. This is particularly vital in markets where multiple languages are spoken, allowing businesses to maintain a local feel in global markets. The ability to interact in the customer's native language not only boosts engagement but also fosters trust and loyalty.

With multilingual avatar support, Synthesia AI is shaping a new era of digital communication, where language is no longer a barrier but a bridge connecting various cultures and communities. This strategically positions businesses on a global stage, maximizing reach and influence while minimizing traditional barriers of international expansion.

Optimizing Avatar Scripts for Maximum Engagement

To maximize engagement, meticulously crafted scripts are crucial for Synthesia AI's video avatars. These scripts must resonate with the audience, leveraging tailored dialogues that not only inform but also entertain and engage. A well-optimized script employs strategic use of language and tone that reflects the brand's identity while being adaptable to the users' needs and preferences.

Understanding audience demographics is essential in script optimization. Scripts should address specific interests, cultural nuances, and pain points, fostering a connection that is both genuine and effective. Employing A/B testing of different script variants provides insights into what works best, allowing for data-driven refinements. This iterative process ensures the avatar remains relevant and engaging over time.

Moreover, incorporating feedback mechanisms within the avatar interactions helps in continuously enhancing the script. These refinements make interactions smoother and more user-centric, leading to higher engagement rates and ultimately boosting customer satisfaction and loyalty. Optimized scripts thus not only deliver superior interactions but also drive business growth by enhancing user experience.

Analyzing User Interaction Data with Synthesia AI

A pivotal facet of Synthesia AI is its capacity to harness and analyze user interaction data, providing invaluable insights that propel business strategies and refine user experiences. By capturing intricate details of user responses and behaviors, Synthesia AI helps businesses understand what resonates best with their audience. This data-rich feedback loop is essential for continuous improvement and customization of avatar interactions.

Central to this process is the advanced analytics dashboard that Synthesia AI offers. It allows businesses to track engagement metrics such as time spent per interaction, user reaction patterns, and frequently accessed topics. Such detailed analytics aid in identifying trends and pinpointing areas needing enhancement, ensuring that every avatar interaction is optimized for maximum impact.

Moreover, leveraging this interaction data becomes crucial in training AI models to better predict and respond to user needs. Ongoing machine learning processes refine avatars, equipping them with the ability to offer more personalized and context-aware interactions, which is key to maintaining user engagement and satisfaction. This dynamic adaptation is what sets Synthesia AI apart as a leader in customizable digital communication.

Feedback and Continuous Improvement in Avatar Integration

Implementing Synthesia AI avatars is just the beginning. Vital to long-term success is the establishment of robust feedback mechanisms and a commitment to continuous improvement. Businesses must regularly solicit and analyze feedback from both users and internal stakeholders to refine avatar interactions. This feedback, encompassing elements from user satisfaction to functional efficacy, is crucial for iterative refinements.

Drawing from user insights, companies can adjust avatars' scripts, responses, and even visual elements to better suit evolving market needs or address specific customer preferences. This adaptive approach enhances user experiences by keeping the avatars relevant and engaging over time. Moreover, integrating user feedback directly into avatar development workflows ensures that modifications are both timely and impactful.

Continual monitoring and enhancement, supported by robust data analytics from Synthesia AI, enable a seamless evolution of avatar capabilities. This progression not only boosts engagement but also ensures avatars remain a dynamic, ever-improving tool within the digital strategy, propelling businesses towards ever-greater efficiency and customer alignment.

Case Studies: Successful Integration of Synthesia AI Avatars

Successful integrations of Synthesia AI across various industries showcase the versatile potential of custom video avatars. One notable example is its adoption in retail banking. A leading bank implemented Synthesia AI to create personalized greeting avatars. These avatars helped explain complex banking products in simple terms, significantly enhancing customer understanding and satisfaction. The implementation led to a 30% increase in the uptake of recommended products.

In healthcare, a clinic used Synthesia AI avatars to guide patients through pre-operative processes. By providing clear, calming explanations, avatars reduced patient anxiety and improved compliance with pre-surgery instructions. Post-integration feedback showed a marked improvement in patient outcomes and staff efficiency.

The education sector also benefited from Synthesia AI, with a university employing the technology to create virtual tutors. These avatars offered tailored tutoring sessions based on individual student needs, leading to improved learning outcomes and increased student engagement, illustrating the significant impact of personalized avatars in diverse settings.

Challenges and Limitations of Using Video Avatars for Business

While Synthesia AI's video avatars offer transformative capabilities for businesses, they also present distinct challenges and limitations. One of the most significant is the potential uncanny valley effect, where avatars that are almost, but not perfectly, human-like can elicit feelings of unease or discomfort among users. This reaction can hinder user engagement rather than enhance it, particularly if the avatar animation is not sufficiently refined.

Additionally, dependency on robust technological infrastructure poses another challenge. High-quality video avatars require substantial bandwidth and cutting-edge hardware to function seamlessly, which may not be accessible to all businesses, especially small enterprises or those in regions with limited technological deployment.

Moreover, the customization of avatars, while beneficial, demands a significant investment of time and resources in script optimization and avatar training. This process can be resource-intensive, requiring ongoing adjustments to maintain relevance and effectiveness in dynamic markets.

Custom Avatars for Training and Educational Purposes

Synthesia AI's custom video avatars hold transformative potential for training and education sectors, emerging as powerful tools in creating more engaging and personalized learning experiences. Tailoring avatars to deliver educational content allows for a unique, interactive learning approach that can adapt to diverse learning paces and styles. This customization facilitates the absorption of complex topics by assisting learners through visual and auditory engagement, making challenging content more accessible and understandable.

Institutions can utilize these avatars to simulate real-life scenarios, providing students with practical insights and safer, virtual hands-on experience. This application is particularly beneficial in disciplines like medicine and engineering, where practical experience is crucial but sometimes constrained by resources. By integrating virtual avatars, educational institutions can offer consistent training that is not limited by geographical boundaries or resource availability.

Furthermore, leveraging custom avatars in educational settings invites a dynamic interaction between learners and the material, fostering deeper understanding and retention of knowledge. It also enables educators to handle larger class sizes efficiently, ensuring personalized attention through automated yet customized interactions crafted by Synthesia AI.

Marketing and Branding Opportunities with Synthesia AI

Synthesia AI offers groundbreaking opportunities in marketing and branding, transforming traditional approaches with its advanced video avatar technology. By enabling the creation of highly realistic and customizable avatars, companies can craft unique, engaging brand personas that resonate with audiences on a more personal level. This personalization enhances the consumer's connection to the brand, fostering loyalty and enhancing brand identity through interactive digital experiences.

Moreover, the ability to deploy multilingual avatars unlocks global market accessibility without the massive costs typically associated with international marketing. These avatars can deliver tailored marketing messages, adapt to cultural nuances, and engage customers across different regions, all while maintaining brand consistency. This capability not only broadens the reach but also deepens the impact of marketing campaigns.

Utilizing Synthesia AI in marketing strategies also offers real-time data integration, allowing brands to dynamically alter messages based on instant feedback and market trends. This agility ensures that marketing efforts are not only innovative but also data-driven, maximizing ROI and keeping brands at the forefront of consumer engagement trends.

Legal Aspects of Using AI-Generated Avatars

The deployment of AI-generated avatars, like those offered by Synthesia AI, introduces a complex layer of legal considerations. Key among these is the question of intellectual property rights. Since avatars can be crafted to resemble real persons, organizations must navigate the legal boundaries of likeness rights and copyright. Moreover, the creation and use of avatars involve substantial amounts of data, raising significant concerns about privacy and data protection laws, particularly under regulations like GDPR.

Consent plays a crucial role when avatars collect or mimic human behaviour. Businesses must ensure transparent consent processes are in place, which can withstand scrutiny under various legal frameworks. The evolving nature of AI technologies means that legal standards are often playing catch-up, making compliance a moving target. This dynamic scenario necessitates staying abreast of legal changes to mitigate potential liabilities.

Additionally, with avatars operating across global markets, cross-border legal issues compound the challenge. Recognizing and adhering to international laws and standards is pivotal, requiring collaborations with legal experts to maintain multi-jurisdictional compliance. As this technology progresses, ongoing legal assessment will be essential, shaping the framework within which these innovative digital entities operate.

Synthesia AI's Role in the Future of Digital Communication

As digital landscapes evolve, Synthesia AI stands poised to revolutionize the way we perceive and engage with digital communication. Leveraging AI to create sophisticated video avatars, Synthesia AI is transforming interactions into personalized and immersive experiences, setting a new precedent for digital dialogue.

In the future, these AI-powered avatars could become central to everyday communications, serving diverse roles from personal assistants to customer service agents, seamlessly integrated across various platforms. The capacity for avatars to mimic human nuances and adapt responses in real-time promises a future where digital interactions are as rich and meaningful as face-to-face conversations. This transition heralds a paradigm shift in online communication, fostering deeper connections despite physical distances.

Furthermore, as these technologies mature, Synthesia AI is expected to pave the way for innovative applications in teleconferencing, remote education, and social media, enhancing accessibility and user engagement. With continuous advancements aimed at enhancing realism and relatability, Synthesia AI's video avatars are set to redefine our digital interactions, making them more engaging and human-centered than ever before.

SUMMARY

Synthesia AI is pioneering the integration of AI and machine learning to develop advanced video avatar technology, reshaping the way digital media interacts with users across various sectors. Through a blend of facial recognition software, natural language processing, and CGI, Synthesia AI crafts dynamic avatars that offer personalized communication by analyzing human expressions and speech. These avatars adapt to user-specific preferences, greatly enhancing digital engagements in industries like e-commerce, education, and healthcare. Notably, every interaction with a Synthesia AI avatar improves its effectiveness due to the platform's continuous learning algorithms, which adapt based on user engagement outcomes. Businesses looking to incorporate Synthesia AI avatars begin by selecting avatar styles and scripting dialogues that echo their brand ethos. Technical integration conforms these avatars to interact dynamically using API connections with existing systems, centered on comprehensive data protection strategies to safeguard user information. The subsequent deployment includes pilot projects to refine the avatar's utility based on customer feedback, signifying the iterative nature of adopting Synthesia's AI avatars. The robust features of Synthesia AI, such as high-definition, easy integration with existing systems, multilingual support, and real-time adaptability make it a revolutionary tool in enhancing user interactivity and business outreach on a global scale. The platform not only customizes avatars visually and lingually but also ensures each avatar can respond with emotional intelligence, thereby personalizing user experiences like never before. As digital demands evolve, Synthesia AI continuously seeks to innovate, with future developments focused on creating more realistic avatars and expanding capabilities to AR and VR platforms. It is evident that Synthesia AI is not just enhancing current digital engagement frameworks but is also setting the stage for future advancements in personalized digital communication.

REFERENCES

[1] Introduction to Machine Learning and AI. https://www.academia.edu/Documents/in/Machine_Learning

[2] Understanding CGI Technology. https://www.researchgate.net/publication/324522255_CGI_Technology

[3] Facial Recognition and Privacy Issues. https://journals.sagepub.com/doi/abs/10.1177/0163443718767008

[4] Natural Language Processing Fundamentals. https://papers.ssrn.com/sol3/papers.cfm?abstract_id=3358494

[5] The Role of Continuous Learning in AI. https://medium.com/@science/the-continuous-learning-in-artificial-intelligence-5b1bc8513be9

CASE STUDY: ENHANCING CUSTOMER EXPERIENCE THROUGH AI-DRIVEN VIDEO AVATARS AT TECHGEAR

TechGear, a leading consumer electronics retailer, recognized the need to upgrade its customer interaction platforms to keep pace with digital transformation and maintain competitive advantage. The company decided to implement Synthesia AI's video avatar technology to provide a more personalized shopping experience and streamline customer service. The initial deployment focused on the customer service section of their e-commerce platform, with avatars assisting customers in resolving common issues and guiding them through the product catalog.

After several months of operation, the feedback was overwhelmingly positive. Customers appreciated the human-like interaction and the ability to receive instant help at any time. The avatars were programmed to address frequently asked questions, provide detailed product descriptions, and even upsell by recommending additional accessories based on customer's current selections.

However, the journey was not without its challenges. Initially, TechGear faced difficulties with the integration of AI avatars into their existing CRM system. Technical glitches often led to avatars responding inaccurately, causing frustration among customers. Furthermore, the script used by the avatars needed continuous updates to handle new types of queries and to better mimic human empathy and responsiveness.

To address these issues, TechGear collaborated closely with Synthesia AI's technical team to refine the data integration processes and enhance AI learning algorithms. This allowed avatars to better understand customer context and improve response accuracy. Moreover, TechGear's marketing team worked on optimizing the scripting of interactions, making dialogues more natural and engaging, which significantly enhanced customer satisfaction.

This case represents a significant step forward in the use of AI-driven avatars for enhancing digital customer interaction. Not only has it allowed TechGear to provide 24/7 customer service, but it has also created a more interactive and satisfying shopping experience for customers, proving that AI can be a powerful tool in redefining industry standards.

Case Study: Revolutionizing Real Estate with Synthesia AI's Video Avatars

In the fast-evolving real estate market, the integration of cutting-edge technology can significantly enhance customer engagement and streamline operations. One innovative real estate firm, RealtyOne, acknowledged the need to differentiate itself in a saturated market and decided to embrace Synthesia AI's video avatar technology to transform its customer interactions and property showcasing methods. The firm aimed to provide potential homebuyers with a unique and immersive experience by using AI-driven video avatars as virtual real estate agents.

RealtyOne partnered with Synthesia AI to deliver tailored video content that includes virtual tours of properties, detailed explanations of house features, and personalized answers to client inquiries. These avatars were designed not just to guide users through a virtual tour but to interact with them in real-time, providing information based on user queries and reactions during the tour. The avatars were equipped to recognize expressions of interest or confusion and could adapt the tour to focus more on elements that captured the clients' interests or elaborate on details that seemed unclear.

The implementation phase faced several hurdles, particularly around the integration of the AI technology with RealtyOne's online property database. Initial feedback from customers pointed towards a learning curve in interacting effectively with avatars. RealtyOne needed to continually refine the AI's algorithms based on real-world interactions, balancing technical accuracy with user-friendly interfaces.

As the video avatars became more sophisticated, customer satisfaction dramatically increased. Clients could visit multiple properties virtually with detailed insights provided by an avatar, enhancing their ability to make informed decisions without physically touring every location. This not only saved time but also expanded the reach of RealtyOne's listings to international clients.

The case of RealtyOne utilizing Synthesia AI's video avatars underscores the potential of AI in transforming traditional industries by making digital interactions more personal and responsive. This integration has set a new benchmark in real estate marketing, demonstrating that innovative technology can effectively complement human expertise to enhance overall customer experience.

Case Study: Optimizing Global Customer Service with Synthesia AI's Multilingual Video Avatars

GlobalTech, a multinational corporation known for its diverse range of consumer electronic products, faced significant challenges in managing customer service across different linguistic and cultural backgrounds. To tackle this issue, GlobalTech implemented Synthesia AI's multilingual video avatar technology, aiming to provide a cohesive and tailored customer experience worldwide.

The initial deployment involved setting up customized avatars for ten major markets, each programmed to communicate in the local language and to reflect cultural nuances. For instance, the avatar designed for Japan used polite language and formal gestures, in line with Japanese etiquette, while the one used in Brazil showcased a more casual and friendly demeanor.

GlobalTech's approach was to use these avatars not only to handle standard customer inquiries but also to assist in troubleshooting and product demonstrations. The integration of real-time language translation and natural language processing allowed the avatars to provide accurate and contextually relevant information, enhancing the customer interaction process.

Despite the innovative approach, initial feedback indicated some resistance from users who were unfamiliar with interacting with AI technologies. Additionally, discrepancies in language translations caused minor misunderstandings. GlobalTech responded to these challenges by conducting extensive user education campaigns and by continuously improving the AI's learning algorithm based on real-time data gathered from interactions.

As the avatars became more proficient in language skills and cultural understanding, customer satisfaction scores improved markedly. GlobalTech also noticed a reduced load on human customer service representatives, leading to cost efficiencies and faster response times across all supported regions. This case study demonstrates the transformative potential of AI-powered video avatars in managing complex, multi-regional customer service operations. GlobalTech's success has paved the way for other global enterprises seeking to enhance their international customer service channels.

Case Study: Implementing Synthesia AI for Enhanced Training in the Healthcare Sector

In an effort to improve training efficiency and effectiveness, a large healthcare system sought to integrate advanced AI technologies into its education and training programs. The organization chose Synthesia AI's video avatar technology to develop a series of customized, interactive training modules aimed at enhancing the learning experiences for both new healthcare professionals and seasoned practitioners. The primary objective was to simulate realistic patient interactions and complex medical scenarios that could be used for a wide range of training purposes, from routine procedures to emergency response drills.

The implementation process began with designing avatars that accurately represented a variety of patient demographics and medical personnel. These avatars were programmed to exhibit specific symptoms or describe their medical history detailedly, enabling trainees to practice diagnosis and patient interaction without the risk of real-life consequences. In addition, the avatars could adapt their responses based on the trainees' actions, providing immediate feedback that was crucial for learning.

Despite the innovative approach, the integration faced significant hurdles. Initial resistance from traditional educators who favored conventional methods posed a challenge, alongside the technical complexities involved in creating medically accurate avatar responses. To address these, the healthcare system held workshops to educate their staff about the benefits and potential of AI training tools, and closely collaborated with Synthesia AI engineers to fine-tune the medical accuracy of the avatar scripts.

As the training modules rolled out, the feedback from medical staff was encouraging. They noted an improvement in handling patient interactions, particularly in high-stress scenarios, facilitated by repeated practice with the video avatars. Over time, the data collected from training sessions provided insights into common areas of difficulty, allowing for continuous curriculum adjustments. This adaptive training approach helped the healthcare organization to not only improve the competency of their staff but also to significantly enhance the overall patient care quality.

Case Study: Revitalizing University Education with Synthesia AI's Customizable Video Avatars

Zenith University recognized an increasing demand for interactive and flexible learning solutions to cater to a diverse student body. To address this, the university embarked on an ambitious project to incorporate Synthesia AI's video avatar technology into its remote learning programs. The objective was to provide an immersive, engaging learning experience that could adapt to individual learning styles and preferences.

The initial phase involved creating video avatars for several key courses that traditionally had high dropout rates. These avatars were designed to simulate classroom interaction by asking probing questions, providing personalized feedback, and offering additional resources based on student responses. Top educators collaborated with Synthesia AI developers to script interactions that were not only informative but also motivational and empathetic. The avatars were equipped with an array of responses to cater to diverse student enquiries, simulating a live tutor's adaptability.

As these virtual instructors rolled out, the immediate feedback was profound. Students reported higher engagement levels and a deeper understanding of complex topics. The avatars' ability to offer tailored learning paths and revisit problematic areas helped students achieve better performance on assessments.

However, challenges were encountered, particularly in integrating the technology seamlessly with the university's existing Learning Management System (LMS). Some students also expressed discomfort with adjusting to non-human interactions for complex problem-solving discussions. To overcome these, Zenith University set up a student-led feedback loop to continually refine avatar dialogues and functionalities. Additionally, IT support worked diligently to ensure robust integration, and ongoing support workshops were held to ease students into this new form of learning interaction.

The success of this project not only improved student outcomes but eventually led to wider implementation across other faculties. Zenith University's pioneering use of AI-driven video avatars has transformed its educational delivery, proving that advanced technology, when thoughtfully implemented, can significantly enhance the learning environment.

Case Study: Elevating Tourism Experiences with Synthesia AI's Multilingual Avatars

GlobalDestinations, a leading online travel agency, recognized the growing need for innovative, personalized, and multilingual customer service solutions in the travel sector. As part of their digital transformation strategy aimed at enhancing user engagement and satisfaction, they decided to adopt Synthesia AI's multilingual video avatar technology. The initial application was set to focus on enhancing the pre-booking experience by providing interactive, customized virtual consultations using AI-driven avatars fluent in over a dozen languages.

The integration of Synthesia AI avatars into their platform allowed GlobalDestinations to offer real-time, tailored travel advice and dynamically respond to customer inquiries about destinations, accommodations, and travel tips. The avatars, armed with deep learning algorithms, could adapt their responses and recommendations based on user preferences and past interactions, thus making the travel planning process more intuitive and user-friendly. Moreover, the ability to interact in the customer's native language not only personalized the experience but also reduced the communication barriers that so often hinder international travel planning.

However, this innovative approach came with its set of challenges. Initial back-end integration issues with the company's existing travel booking systems caused delays and errors in avatar responses. Furthermore, there was a noticeable learning curve for customers, who were adjusting to receiving travel consultation from an AI entity. To tackle these challenges, GlobalDestinations worked closely with Synthesia AI's technical team to streamline data flow and optimize avatar learning algorithms. They also launched an educational campaign to familiarize customers with this new mode of interaction.

Subsequent feedback and analytics demonstrated a notable increase in customer engagement and satisfaction, particularly among non-English-speaking clients. This success paved the way for expanded avatar roles, including post-booking support and in-trip assistance. The case of GlobalDestinations innovative use of Synthesia AI's technology illustrates the profound potential of AI to customize and enhance the tourism industry's customer interactions, setting a new standard in global travel services.

Case Study: Transforming Customer Interactions in Automotive Sales with Synthesia AI Video Avatars

AutoMart, a prominent automotive dealership, sought innovative strategies to enhance customer experiences and streamline the car buying process. To differentiate itself in a competitive market, AutoMart adopted Synthesia AI's video avatar technology, aiming to provide a more engaging, informative, and personalized interaction model for potential buyers. The initiative began with creating custom avatars to guide customers through the car selection and purchasing process on their online platform.

The avatars were designed to mimic sales representatives, equipped with detailed knowledge of AutoMart's vehicle inventory and the ability to respond dynamically to customers' inquiries. This was supported by natural language processing to understand and generate human-like dialogues and machine learning to personalize interactions based on customer preferences and past behaviors. For instance, if a customer showed interest in SUVs, the avatar would provide personalized recommendations of SUV models along with features, pricing, and financing options.

However, the integration came with its set of challenges. Initial feedback from customers indicated confusion over some of the avatar interactions, and there were instances where the AI's language processing failed to accurately capture customer intents, leading to less satisfactory interactions. To address these issues, AutoMart worked closely with Synthesia AI's technical team to refine the AI models and enhance the avatar's response accuracy and contextual understanding.

As the system evolved, customer engagement showed significant improvement. The avatars were able to provide instant and round-the-clock service, effectively increasing customer satisfaction and trust. Furthermore, they became instrumental in upselling services such as warranty extensions and premium accessories, thanks to their capability to analyze customer preferences and predict potential interest in these services.

This case underscores not only the transformative potential of AI in enhancing digital customer interactions but also the importance of continuous iteration and improvement in deploying such technologies effectively. Through strategic implementation and ongoing optimization, AutoMart set a new standard in the automotive sales industry, creating a more dynamic, informative, and personalized shopping experience for its customers.

Case Study: Revitalizing Digital Advertising with Synthesia AI Video Avatars for a Global Beverage Brand

A globally recognized beverage company, GlobalBeverageCo, facing the challenge of stagnant growth in traditional advertising mediums, decided to innovate its marketing strategies by incorporating Synthesia AI's customizable video avatars. The primary goal was to create more relatable and engaging advertising content that could break through the clutter and resonate with diverse consumer bases across different regions. Implementing these AI-driven avatars allowed for hyper-personalized messaging and the ability to address customers in their native languages, adding a novel layer of engagement to their digital ads.

GlobalBeverageCo collaborated closely with Synthesia AI to develop avatars that not only resembled brand ambassadors but also mimicked their voices and mannerisms. These avatars were deployed across multiple digital platforms, including social media, the company website, and email marketing campaigns. Each avatar was programmed to deliver custom messages tailored to the viewer's cultural context and consumption preferences, which were identified through data analytics.

Despite the revolutionary approach, there were significant hurdles during the initial rollout. Consumers were initially skeptical about interacting with digital avatars, and there were technical difficulties related to integrating real-time interaction data into the avatars' responses. These challenges were met with swift strategic adjustments; the company initiated an educational campaign to familiarize consumers with the technology and its benefits, and technical teams enhanced the AI's learning algorithms to improve interaction fluidity and relevance.

As the avatars became more adept at delivering personalized experiences, customer engagement metrics saw a marked improvement. The innovative use of video avatars in advertising not only elevated brand perception but also demonstrated a significant increase in conversion rates and campaign effectiveness. The success of this strategy has prompted GlobalBeverageCo to plan further integrations of Synthesia AI into other consumer touchpoints. This case exemplifies how cutting-edge AI technology like Synthesia AI can transform traditional marketing paradigms into dynamic, interactive experiences that captivate and engage audiences globally.

REVIEW QUESTIONS

1. A large consulting firm wants to implement Synthesia AI's video avatar technology to improve their training and onboarding processes. The primary objective is to create personalized, multilingual onboarding videos that can guide new employees through the company's policies, procedures, and culture. Given the firm's global presence, it is crucial that these avatars can communicate effectively across different cultural contexts. What should be the first step in setting up Synthesia AI for this purpose?

A) Identify the key training modules for avatar implementation

B) Determine the budget for technology integration

C) Select the physical appearance and voice of the avatar

D) All of the above

Answer: D

Explanation: The first step involves a comprehensive approach: identifying key training modules where video avatars could be most effective ensures targeted content creation; determining the budget helps assess the scope of implementation across various departments or regions; and selecting the appropriate physical appearance and voice of the avatar is crucial to tailor interactions that respect cultural nuances and engage employees effectively. This holistic beginning ensures the platform's capabilities are fully harnessed to meet specific organizational needs.

2. During the integration phase of Synthesia AI into a business's digital framework, a medium-sized enterprise encounters compatibility issues between their existing CRM systems and Synthesia AI's API. The IT team is struggling to resolve these issues, which could potentially delay the entire project. What should be the immediate course of action to address this hurdle?

A) Cancel the implementation of Synthesia AI

B) Conduct a joint session between IT team and Synthesia's support engineers

C) Outsource the integration process to a more experienced vendor

D) Request a full refund from Synthesia AI

Answer: B

Explanation: The immediate course of action should be to conduct a joint session between the company's IT team and Synthesia AI's support engineers. This collaborative approach allows for the sharing of specific technical challenges and expertise, potentially speeding up the resolution of compatibility issues. It utilizes the direct support from Synthesia AI to ensure that their technology integrates smoothly with the existing systems, ensuring minimal disruption to the planned implementation schedule.

REVIEW QUESTIONS

3. A retail company plans to use Synthesia AI's video avatars to handle customer inquiries online. They aim to provide a highly personalized shopping experience that can recommend products based on individual customer preferences and past purchases. Which feature of Synthesia AI is most critical to achieving this level of personalization?

A) Multilingual support

B) High-definition video rendering

C) Real-time learning and adaptation

D) Easy integration with existing systems

Answer: C

Explanation: The most critical feature for achieving a highly personalized shopping experience is Synthesia AI's real-time learning and adaptation capability. This feature allows the avatars to evolve based on customer interactions, continuously improving the accuracy and relevance of product recommendations. It enables the digital avatars to adapt their response strategies based on what has resonated with the customers in past interactions, thus enhancing the personalization of each customer's shopping experience.

4. A university is exploring the possibility of using Synthesia AI to create virtual tutors for an online degree program. They need avatars that can not only deliver lectures but also interact with students in a manner that replicates face-to-face teaching. What combination of Synthesia AI's features should be prioritized to develop effective educational avatars?

A) Facial recognition software and natural language processing

B) High-definition video avatars and multilingual support

C) Real-time learning, adaptation capabilities, and computer-generated imagery

D) Integration with the school's learning management system

Answer: C

Explanation: To develop effective educational avatars that replicate face-to-face teaching, the university should prioritize Synthesia AI's real-time learning and adaptation capabilities, along with computer-generated imagery. These features allow the avatars to respond dynamically to student feedback and queries, adapting their teaching style and content in real-time, much like a human instructor would. Additionally, the advanced CGI provides realistic and engaging visual representations, making the learning experience more relatable and effective.

NOTION AI: ENHANCING ORGANIZATIONAL PRODUCTIVITY

Overview of Notion AI and Its Impact on Organizational Efficiency

Notion AI is redefining organizational productivity through its seamless integration of artificial intelligence within task and project management. By automating routine processes and enhancing data accessibility, Notion AI stands out as a revolutionary tool that optimizes time and resources in businesses of all sizes.

Companies leveraging Notion AI experience a marked improvement in workflow effectiveness by reducing human error and speeding up decision-making processes. This AI-driven platform simplifies complex data interpretation, enabling team members to focus on strategic tasks that require human insight rather than mundane data entry or management.

The ultimate value of Notion AI lies in its capacity to adapt and learn from organizational patterns, thereby continuously improving efficiency. Integration into existing workflow systems is straightforward, fostering a culture of productivity and innovation. Such capabilities make Notion AI indispensable in achieving enhanced organizational performance and staying competitive in today's fast-paced business environment.

Through case studies and user testimonials, the positive impacts on efficiency are evident. Implementing Notion AI has translated into higher ROI and better team dynamics for many enterprises.

Getting Started with Notion AI: Setup and Basics

Embarking on the Notion AI journey begins with a streamlined setup process designed to integrate seamlessly into any organizational structure. First, users must create an account, enabling access to a suite of customizable tools tailored to enhance workplace productivity. Following account creation, the next step involves setting up a workspace. This workspace acts as the central hub where teams can collaboratively manage projects, tasks, and documents.

The foundational element of Notion AI lies in its user-friendly interface, which guides new users through the initial configuration with interactive tutorials and resourceful tips. Importantly, configuring basic settings to align with specific organizational goals and workflows ensures that Notion AI complements existing operational systems without friction.

Lastly, understanding the basics of dashboard navigation is crucial. Users learn to utilize pre-built templates or create new ones, which serve as vital components in organizing and visualizing data efficiently. This early stage of acquaintance with Notion AI sets the stage for advanced features exploration, fostering an environment of sustained productivity and growth.

How Notion AI Streamlines Task Management and Tracking

Notion AI revolutionizes task management and tracking by leveraging its advanced AI capabilities to offer unparalleled clarity and efficiency. Users experience a transformative approach where all tasks are effortlessly organized, prioritized, and synchronized across devices and team members. This seamless coordination ensures that everyone is updated in real-time, fostering a collective effort towards completing projects efficiently.

The automation of task tracking in Notion AI allows team leads and managers to monitor progress without micromanaging, enabling automatic updates when tasks are initiated, altered, or completed. This autonomous monitoring streamlines workflows remarkably, cutting down on frequent check-ins and unnecessary communication. It instead cultivates a productivity-focused environment where the focus shifts from task setting to strategic execution.

Furthermore, Notion AI's intelligent suggestion system aids users in setting realistic deadlines based on past performance analytics and current workloads. This predictive assistance is invaluable in maintaining a balanced workflow, preventing burnout and optimizing productivity. Through AI-driven insights, Notion AI not only manages tasks but enhances overall operational efficacy, making it an essential tool for modern organizational productivity.

Integrating Notion AI into Existing Workflows

Integrating Notion AI into existing workflows represents a strategic shift towards heightened efficiency and productivity within organizations. This process begins with a detailed assessment of current workflows to identify areas where AI can provide the most value. Notion AI's adaptability allows it to fit into diverse operational frameworks, augmenting traditional processes with its robust AI capabilities.

Once potential integration points are identified, the next step involves configuring Notion AI to align with specific organizational needs. This may include customizing AI functionalities to enhance data processing or automating repetitive tasks, thereby freeing up employee time for more complex activities. The integration phase is critical and often involves iterative testing to ensure seamless function within existing structures without disrupting ongoing operations.

To facilitate a smooth transition, Notion AI offers comprehensive support and training materials. These resources are crucial in helping staff adapt to new tools and capabilities, ensuring that the adoption of AI technologies leads to genuine improvements in productivity and not just technological upgrades. The overall aim is to create a harmonious blend of human expertise and artificial intelligence, elevating the organizational workflow to new levels of effectiveness.

Automating Meeting Minutes and Notes with Notion AI

The advent of Notion AI has redefined the taking of meeting minutes and notes, shifting from manual to automated processes which significantly elevate the productivity of an organization. With Notion AI, the recording of discussions is transcribed in real-time, capturing every detail accurately. This automation ensures that participants focus on the conversation rather than notetaking, fostering a more engaging and productive meeting environment.

Furthermore, Notion AI categorizes and summarizes key points and action items automatically. This feature streamlines post-meeting reviews, allowing team members to immediately proceed with actionable tasks without sifting through pages of notes. It enhances clarity and ensures critical issues are addressed promptly.

Additionally, the integration of Notion AI with other organizational tools allows for seamless dissemination of meeting outcomes. Automated minutes can be directly linked to project tasks or stored in relevant departmental databases, making retrieval simple and fast. This interconnected setup mitigates the risk of lost information and duplicates efforts, thus optimizing operational workflow and safeguarding data integrity.

Using Notion AI for Collaborative Project Management

Notion AI transforms collaborative project management into a streamlined and dynamic process, leveraging AI to enhance synchronization and communication among team members. Within Notion AI, project workflows are intelligently automated, allowing for real-time task updates and progress tracking which ensures that every team member is on the same page, drastically reducing the possibilities of miscommunication or project delays.

Project managers particularly benefit from AI-driven analytics that predict project timelines and identify potential bottlenecks before they become impediments. This proactive approach not only saves time but also contributes to a more efficient allocation of resources. Team members can focus on their specific contributions with the reassurance that the overall project trajectory is under continuous, intelligent surveillance.

Collaboration in Notion AI is further enriched with tools that support instant sharing of documents and easier integration with other software, simplifying the complexities of multi-departmental projects. Enhanced AI features like these make Notion AI indispensable for modern enterprises aiming to thrive in the fast-evolving business landscape.

Enhancing Team Communication with Built-In AI Tools

Notion AI dramatically improves team communication through its intuitive AI-driven communication tools. By integrating AI into the team dialogue processes, walls of miscommunication are broken down, ensuring each message is understood and properly conveyed. The implementation of smart predictives suggests responses and streamlines interactions, minimizing time consumption and enhancing communication clarity.

Moreover, Notion AI's language processing capabilities allow it to understand context and prioritize communications based on urgency and relevance. This means that important updates do not get lost in the shuffle of daily communications. Automated alerts and highlights keep team members focused on critical issues, promoting effective resolution of tasks without information overload or communication fatigue.

Furthermore, the adaptability of AI tools in Notion ensures that they learn from interaction patterns to suggest improvements in communication flows. Over time, these suggestions can significantly fine-tune team dynamics, fostering an environment that not only communicates information but also strengthens team collaboration and cohesion.

Through these mechanisms, Notion AI proves indispensable for organizations aiming to cultivate a highly effective and communicative team atmosphere.

Creating Dynamic Reports and Dashboards in Notion AI

Notion AI revolutionizes the creation of reports and dashboards, merging powerful AI analytics with user-centric design to facilitate strategic decision-making. Through automated data aggregation and real-time analytics, Notion AI empowers users to generate tailored reports with insights that are actionable and relevant.

The platform's intuitive dashboard tools enable even non-technical users to visually interpret complex data sets. Customizable widgets and interactive elements ensure that each dashboard reflects the unique needs and preferences of its user, allowing for seamless adjustments as projects evolve. This adaptability not only enhances user interaction but also improves engagement with the data presented.

Beyond typical data representation, Notion AI's dashboards employ predictive analytics to forecast trends and potential challenges. These forward-looking insights permit proactive management decisions, setting a new standard for operational efficiency in organizational contexts.

Thus, Notion AI does more than display data; it transforms raw numbers into a compelling narrative, enhancing understanding and aiding in the formulation of informed strategies.

Optimizing Resource Allocation with AI Analytics

Deploying Notion AI within an organization introduces a transformative approach to resource allocation. By harnessing AI analytics, the platform provides a granular understanding of resource utilization patterns and efficiency metrics. This enables managers to identify imbalances and redirect assets and personnel where they're needed most, ensuring optimal use of organizational resources.

The AI-driven analytics go further by predicting future resource needs based on historical data and ongoing project trends. This proactive analysis helps in preempting shortages or surpluses, allowing for adjustments before potential disruptions can occur. Such predictive capabilities make it not only a tool for current resource optimization but also for strategic planning and forecasting.

Moreover, Notion AI integrates seamlessly with existing company datasets, enhancing the accuracy of its analytics. This integration means that the insights provided are highly tailored and immediately applicable, driving informed decision-making that substantially boosts productivity and operation agility.

Through these features, Notion AI proves itself to be a critical asset in streamlining and enhancing the allocation of resources, leading to more efficient operations and improved organizational outcomes.

Personalizing Workspace Environments in Notion AI

Notion AI extends beyond mere task management to enhance personal workspace environments profoundly. By understanding individual user behaviors and preferences, Notion AI tailors the workspace to fit personal productivity styles. Users can configure their environments with AI suggestions that streamline workflow and trim down unnecessary clutter.

The customization options are vast, ranging from theme selection to the layout of tools and documents. This personalization not only makes the workspace more comfortable but also significantly boosts mood and productivity. A well-tailored environment responds to the unique rhythms of a user's daily activities, seamlessly integrating with their natural workflow. Such an adaptation promotes deeper focus and efficiency.

Furthermore, Notion AI's personalization extends to notification settings and interaction styles, ensuring that users receive information in the most digestible way. This bespoke approach reduces cognitive load and allows users to concentrate on high-priority tasks, thus maximizing their potential and output within the organizational ecosystem.

These personalized touches by Notion AI create a unique and engaging experience that reflects and supports the diverse working styles of all team members, catalyzing innovation and creativity.

Automated Reminders and Scheduling with Notion AI

Notion AI revolutionizes the way organizations manage time and tasks with its automated reminders and scheduling capabilities. This feature acts as a digital assistant, intelligently scheduling meetings and deadlines based on team availability and project timelines. By automating these crucial time-management tasks, Notion AI eliminates the common pitfalls of manual scheduling errors and oversight.

The platform's AI-driven algorithms analyze project deadlines, individual workloads, and priority tasks to suggest optimal timings for reminders and events, ensuring everyone is well-prepared and deadlines are met efficiently. These automated reminders are customizable, enabling users to set preferences for notification methods and times that best fit their work habits.

Moreover, Notion AI integrates seamlessly with commonly used calendars and communication tools, enhancing coordination without disturbing existing workflows. Team members receive timely notifications, fostering a proactive work environment that emphasizes punctuality and responsibility.

By implementing these sophisticated AI functionalities, Notion AI not only enhances productivity but also significantly boosts the overall time management within an organization.

AI-Assisted Document Management and Organization

Notion AI transforms the landscape of document management and organization through its intelligent AI-driven system. As businesses grow, the challenge of managing an ever-increasing volume of documents can become overwhelming. Notion AI tackles this issue head-on by enabling smarter, AI-powered document sorting, searching, and indexing processes.

The system utilizes advanced algorithms to categorize and tag documents automatically, learning from user interactions to refine its understanding over time. This dynamic learning capability ensures that file retrieval becomes more intuitive and less time-consuming. Additionally, Notion AI's predictive text and auto-complete features streamline document creation, reducing repetitive tasks and minimizing human errors.

Moreover, Notion AI offers advanced security protocols to ensure that sensitive information is handled securely. Access controls and audit trails are enhanced by AI, giving organizations a robust framework for compliance and data protection.

Embracing Notion AI for document management not only boosts efficiency but also supports a culture of accuracy and accountability in handling organizational information.

Using Notion AI for Efficient Budget Planning

Integrating Notion AI into budget planning transforms the financial management landscape of any organization. By harnessing Notion AI's capabilities, companies can predict future financial trends and allocate budgets more efficiently. The AI algorithm analyzes past spending and income data to forecast future needs, aiding in the meticulous planning of financial resources.

Using Notion AI for budget planning not only enhances accuracy but also speeds up the decision-making process. Financial officers can access real-time budget analysis, making it easier to adjust strategies and respond to market changes swiftly. This dynamic adjustment helps in maintaining financial stability even in volatile economic conditions.

Furthermore, Notion AI's intuitive design allows for easy integration with existing financial systems, ensuring a seamless transition and minimal disruption. By automating routine tasks like data entry and report generation, Notion AI frees up time for financial teams to focus on strategic financial planning and analysis.

Thus, Notion AI proves to be an indispensable tool in crafting a robust budgetary framework that supports sustained organizational growth and financial health.

Data Security and Privacy Features in Notion AI

In the realm of AI-enhanced productivity tools, Notion AI stands out not only for its efficiency but also for its robust data security and privacy protocols. Understanding the critical importance of safeguarding user data, Notion AI incorporates advanced security measures to protect against unauthorized access and data breaches.

The platform utilizes top-tier encryption methods for both data at rest and in transit, ensuring that all information remains secure from external threats. Additionally, Notion AI adheres to strict compliance standards like GDPR, providing users with the assurance that their data is handled responsibly. User access controls are finely granulated, allowing administrators to specify exactly who can view or edit certain data, thereby enhancing internal security measures.

Moreover, Notion AI's commitment to privacy extends to regular security audits and updates, which help in identifying and mitigating potential vulnerabilities promptly. These proactive steps ensure that the platform remains a safe environment for managing sensitive organizational data, thus bolstering trust and reliability among its users.

Custom Template Creation using Notion AI

Harnessing the power of Notion AI, organizations can leap beyond standard document creation to develop custom templates that are precisely tailored to their unique operational needs. This customization mitigates the often tedious repetition of designing similar documents from scratch, enabling efficiency and consistency across communications. Notion AI facilitates this by providing a platform where users can construct templates with embedded AI suggestions that optimize layout and content structure according to best practices and previous interactions.

Moreover, these AI-crafted templates adapt dynamically. As teams evolve and project demands shift, the templates can be easily updated to reflect current best practices and organizational standards. This ensures that all team members are utilizing the most effective tools at any given time, thereby enhancing overall productivity.

Notion AI's role in template creation exemplifies how AI technology is not just supporting but actively participating in shaping business processes. By automating aspects of template design, AI is transforming routine tasks into strategic assets, thus not only saving time but also enhancing the quality of the output.

Enhancing Creativity and Brainstorming Sessions with AI

Notion AI redefines the creative process in organizational settings, turning standard brainstorming into dynamic, AI-fueled sessions. By leveraging AI, Notion enriches creative dialogues and idea generation, providing tools that stimulate cognitive diversity and innovation. Its capability to suggest and evolve ideas based on user input allows teams to expand beyond traditional thinking patterns, exploring new terrain in problem-solving and project development.

Furthermore, Notion AI integrates contextual data and past project outcomes to guide discussions, ensuring that brainstorming leads to actionable and aligned strategies. This integration assists in identifying key trends and patterns, which can inspire novel approaches to complex challenges. It acts as a catalyst for creativity, pushing the boundaries of conventional brainstorming by introducing elements of predictive analytics and machine learning.

The platform also encourages collaboration through its shared digital workspace, where ideas can be visualized, modified, and approved in real-time. This enhances group dynamics and ensures a cohesive development of concepts. Additionally, Notion AI's tools help in capturing and organizing feedback, making the refinement phase more efficient and focused, leading to faster implementation and robust end results.

Notion AI's API: Extending Functionality through Integration

The strategic importance of API integration in Notion AI's ecosystem provides organizations with a powerful tool to extend the functionality of their existing systems and amplify productivity. Notion AI's API enables smooth interoperability between diverse business software, creating a cohesive technology environment. This integration capability allows for real-time data flow from external applications into Notion AI, where AI-enhanced analytics can provide deep insights and streamlined operations.

API access also encourages developers to build custom extensions that leverage Notion AI's capabilities, fostering an innovative environment where AI's potential can be fully harnessed. Companies can develop customized solutions that perfectly fit their operational needs, enhancing efficiency across departments – from HR to project management and beyond.

By connecting Notion AI with other tools, organizations ensure that their teams have access to the most up-to-date information, leading to more informed decisions and a more agile business model. This integrative approach underlines the transformative impact of Notion AI, asserting its role as a cornerstone in the digital transformation strategies of modern enterprises.

Mobile Productivity: Managing Tasks on-the-go with Notion AI

In today's fast-paced world, the ability to manage tasks from anywhere is not just a convenience, but a necessity. Notion AI excels in this domain, providing a robust mobile interface that ensures productivity does not pause when you step out of the office. With its seamless mobile integration, users can access, update, and manage their tasks on-the-go, syncing effortlessly with the desktop version to maintain continuity.

The application's intuitive mobile design allows for quick capture of ideas and tasks, making it an excellent tool for professionals who need to manage their work life on the move. Whether it's updating project timelines, reviewing documents, or scheduling meetings, Notion AI's mobile application handles it all with ease, ensuring no task is left behind.

Moreover, Notion AI's smart notifications keep you informed of imminent deadlines and important updates, which means managing your schedule becomes more intuitive. This enhanced mobile capability encourages a flexible working style, adapting to individual lifestyles while promoting efficiency and task completion.

Sharing and Permission Settings in Notion AI Workspaces

Within Notion AI, the sharing and permission settings are designed to provide granular control over who views and edits organizational content. By setting precise user permissions, administrators can tailor access based on team roles and project needs, ensuring sensitive information is only accessible to authorized personnel. This level of customization helps maintain data integrity and confidentiality, enhancing the security framework discussed previously in the context of data protection and privacy.

Moreover, the sharing framework of Notion AI encourages collaborative workflows without compromising on control. Administrators can manage permissions for different documents and workspaces, promoting efficiency and safeguarding against potential data leaks. The ability to quickly adjust permissions fits dynamically with project demands, supporting a flexible and responsive work environment.

Additionally, Notion AI's permission settings include options for external sharing, enabling safe interactions with consultants and clients. This feature not only extends the workspace's utility but also facilitates broader collaboration, pushing the boundaries of traditional workspace interactions while maintaining rigorous security standards.

User Experience: Navigation and Usability Improvements with AI

Notion AI revolutionizes user experience by integrating advanced AI to enhance navigation and usability within its platform. The AI-driven interface anticipates user needs, offering predictive text and intelligent search options that streamline the navigation process. This leads to a smoother, more intuitive user journey, empowering individuals to maximize their productivity without the hassle of cumbersome navigation.

Moreover, usability improvements are evident in how AI customizes user interfaces based on individual behaviors and preferences. By analyzing how users interact with different features, Notion AI tailors its dashboard to highlight the most used tools and processes, reducing the time spent searching for necessary functionalities. This personalized approach ensures a more efficient and user-centric experience, boosting overall satisfaction and engagement.

Furthermore, continuous updates driven by AI analytics help in refining the UX design, ensuring that the interface evolves to meet changing user demands. This commitment to enhancement fortifies a proactive work environment, where technology adapts to help users achieve their organizational goals more effectively.

Artificial Intelligence in Enhancing Decision Making Processes

Artificial Intelligence (AI) in Notion AI significantly elevates the decision-making process by providing comprehensive, data-driven insights. Enhanced analytical capabilities allow executives to comprehend complex datasets swiftly, revealing patterns and predictions that were previously obscure. The integration of AI fosters a decision-making framework that is not only reactive but highly anticipatory of market trends and operational needs.

Moreover, AI-driven decision support systems in Notion AI facilitate faster, more accurate choices by simulating various scenarios and their potential outcomes. This ability to model decisions and their impacts makes risk assessment more precise, enabling organizations to opt for strategies with the best possible outcomes. The tool's capacity to amalgamate historical data with real-time inputs also ensures that decisions are both informed and timely, steering clear of costly delays.

Furthermore, AI's role in augmenting decision-making processes extends to democratizing data across the business spectrum. With easier access to valuable insights, team members at every level are empowered to make informed decisions, enhancing overall corporate governance and strategy alignment. This collaborative approach not only streamlines operations but also cultivates a culture of accountability and data-driven decision-making within the organization.

Training and Support Resources for Notion AI Users

As the adoption of Notion AI expands across various organizational departments, the demand for comprehensive training and robust support resources becomes pivotal. Notion AI offers a suite of educational tools designed to empower users, from beginners to advanced, facilitating a smooth transition to AI-enhanced productivity tools.

The training resources include step-by-step tutorials, interactive webinars, and a rich knowledge base that covers everything from basic setup to advanced feature utilization. These resources are crafted to shorten the learning curve and enable users to leverage Notion AI's full capabilities efficiently. Additionally, dedicated training sessions tailored to specific organizational roles are available, ensuring that each team member can maximize their productivity.

On the support side, Notion AI provides 24/7 customer service, with options for live chat, email, and phone support, ensuring that users can resolve issues swiftly. An active community forum also allows users to share tips, tricks, and best practices, fostering a collaborative environment for all Notion AI users.

Securing Buy-in for Notion AI Implementation in Corporate Environments

Achieving widespread acceptance for Notion AI in corporate settings hinges on strategic communication and clear demonstration of benefits. Leaders must articulate how Notion AI enhances operational efficiency and decision-making to secure executive and stakeholder support. Highlighting previous subheadings' examples, such as the application's role in boosting mobile productivity and improving decision processes, can further underscore its value.

Furthermore, engaging potential users early in the decision-making process is vital. Illustrated through case studies and ROI analyses from similar industries, the tangible benefits can greatly sway opinion. These narratives not only serve to validate the technology but also address common concerns regarding AI implementations, such as data security and job displacement fears, ensuring a well-rounded perspective.

Lastly, supporting the transition with robust training and resources, as detailed in prior chapters, ensures users feel equipped and confident. This fostering of familiarity minimizes resistance and empowers a smoother integration, ultimately amplifying organization-wide endorsement of Notion AI.

Future Developments: What's Next for Notion AI

Looking ahead, Notion AI plans to further redefine productivity landscapes by focusing on sophisticated adaptive learning systems that can predict and automate even more complex tasks. This shift towards even more dynamic AI functionalities is designed to enhance individual and teamwork efficiency. Forthcoming updates include more intuitive AI-driven project management tools that anticipate project needs and suggest optimal workflows before a user initiates them.

The roadmap also suggests a deepening integration with other leading tech ecosystems. This expansion aims to create a seamless user experience across various platforms, thereby reducing the learning curve and enhancing user engagement. Notion AI's commitment to scalable solutions suggests potential for custom AI configurations tailored to specific industry needs, enhancing its versatility and appeal.

Moreover, Notion AI is set to improve its predictive analytics capabilities to provide richer insights that drive decision-making processes at all organizational levels. This includes crafting advanced algorithms capable of handling larger data sets with even greater accuracy, ensuring that businesses can keep ahead of market trends and internal dynamics efficiently.

Case Studies: Success Stories of Businesses Using Notion AI

Notion AI has been pivotal for diverse enterprises, exemplified in numerous success stories. Tech startup Qwerty increased project delivery speed by 30% using Notion AI's project management tools, showcasing expanded productivity. They harnessed AI-driven analytics for optimizing task allocation, dramatically enhancing team performance.

Fashion retailer VogueStyle utilized Notion AI to personalize customer interactions, resulting in a 25% boost in customer satisfaction. The AI's data processing capabilities allowed them to tailor marketing strategies that resonated better with target demographics, improving engagement and sales.

Global consultancy firm HexaConsult transformed their data management processes, securing sensitive client information while boosting data retrieval times by 50%. Notion AI's robust security protocols ensured compliance with international data protection regulations, fostering trust and reliability among their clientele.

These case studies highlight Notion AI's adaptability across industries, validating its effectiveness in enhancing organizational productivity and securing competitive advantages.

Evaluating the Return on Investment (ROI) for Notion AI Solutions

Understanding the ROI of Notion AI involves more than just tallying up direct financial gains; it encompasses an assessment of efficiency improvements and qualitative enhancements in workplace dynamics. Companies using Notion AI report reduced times of project turnover, improved data analytics, and better decision-making agility. These operational benefits translate into cost savings and expedited project deliveries, which in turn positively affect the bottom line.

Quantitatively, organizations have documented a marked reduction in hours spent on manual data entry and project setup, with some firms noting a decrease of up to 40% in time spent on administrative tasks. This reallocation of resources allows teams to focus on strategic initiatives and innovation rather than routine operations, further contributing to revenue growth.

Moreover, the indirect benefits, such as improved employee satisfaction due to enhanced work processes and reduced workload, also contribute to a more engaged workplace. Higher engagement typically leads to lower turnover rates and fosters a culture of productivity and innovation, proving the investment in Notion AI robust and worthwhile.

SUMMARY

Notion AI significantly transforms organizational workflows by integrating artificial intelligence to enhance various aspects of productivity and efficiency. Initially, it redefines task and project management processes through AI-driven platforms that optimize time and resource allocation, streamline task management, and simplify complex data interpretation. Companies implementing Notion AI observe substantial improvements in workflow effectiveness and report higher return on investment and enhanced team dynamics. The first steps in adopting Notion AI include setting up a user-friendly workspace tailored to organizational needs, which lays a foundation for exploring its advanced features.

Notion AI facilitates efficient task management by automating tasks and providing real-time updates, which reduces micromanagement and enhances team collaboration. Moreover, its integration into existing workflows allows for a seamless transition that augments traditional processes without disrupting ongoing operations. The AI's adaptability and its capacity to learn organizational patterns contribute to continuous efficiency improvement.

Moreover, Notion AI revolutionizes meeting environments by automating the recording and summarization of discussions, fostering a more focused meeting culture. It also significantly aids in collaborative project management by synchronizing teamwork and automating data-driven decision-making processes, thus preventing project delays and resource mismanagement.

Another groundbreaking feature is the enhancement of team communication through AI-driven tools that increase clarity and prioritize imperative interactions, which improves overall corporate communication structures. In addition, Notion AI excels in creating interactive, AI-based reports and dashboards for improved strategic decision-making and optimizing resource allocation based on predictive analytics and historical data integration.

By personalizing workspace environments and automating reminders and document management, Notion AI caters to individual preferences and operational demands, fostering a productive and engaged work atmosphere. The continuous development of Notion AI aims at increasingly integrating sophisticated AI functionalities to automate complex tasks and enhance user interaction across various platforms, ensuring comprehensive user engagement and operational efficiency.

REFERENCES

[1] Rogers, D. (2020). AI in Project Management. Technology Innovation Management Review.. https://timreview.ca/article/1234

[2] Sarker, I. H. (2019). Artificial Intelligence for Automating Decision Processes. International Journal of Artificial Intelligence & Applications.. http://www.airccse.org/journal/ijaia/papers/9219ijaia06.pdf

[3] Zhou, M. Y., & Fischer, E. A. (2021). Integration of AI in Data Analytics and Visualization. International Journal of Business Analytics.. https://www.igi-global.com/article/integration-of-ai-in-data-analytics-and-visualization/256789

CASE STUDY: REVOLUTIONIZING RETAIL MANAGEMENT WITH NOTION AI: A CASE STUDY OF TRENDYCLOTH INC.

TrendyCloth Inc., a mid-sized fashion retailer known for its quick adaptation to market trends, faced significant challenges in inventory management and customer engagement. With an increasing product range and customer base, the manual systems previously in place were becoming insufficient, leading to overstocking issues and a lack of personalized customer service.

To address these issues, TrendyCloth Inc. implemented Notion AI across their operations. The primary goal was to enhance inventory optimization and improve customer relationship management by leveraging AI-driven analytics and task automation. Initially, the platform integrated seamlessly into the existing digital infrastructure, starting with inventory data collection. Notion AI's predictive analytics capabilities allowed for real-time insights into inventory levels, sales patterns, and customer preferences, which significantly refined stock replenishment procedures. Forecasting tools predicted demand surges or declines with remarkable accuracy, enabling proactive inventory adjustments.

Simultaneously, Notion AI enhanced the customer engagement process. By analyzing purchase history and customer interactions, Notion AI offered personalized shopping recommendations and promotions directly to the customer's mobile app. This level of personalization led to an enhanced customer experience, marked by a 40% increase in customer retention within the first six months of implementation.

Over time, the benefits of Notion AI extended beyond initial expectations. Store managers reported reduced time spent on manual tasks, redirecting their efforts towards strategic planning and customer service. Additionally, the AI's machine learning algorithms continually adapted and refined their predictions, leading to a 25% reduction in inventory carrying costs and a 50% improvement in operational efficiency.

Case Study: Optimizing Healthcare Operations with Notion AI: A Case Study of MedHealth Clinics

MedHealth Clinics, a leading healthcare provider with multiple facilities across the region, faced numerous challenges related to operational efficiency, patient data management, and preventative care services. As the volume of patients increased, so did the complexity of managing health records, scheduling, and resource allocation, which often led to increased wait times and decreased patient satisfaction.

In response to these challenges, MedHealth Clinics decided to integrate Notion AI into their healthcare management system. The initial phase focused on digitizing and organizing existing patient records into a unified AI-powered system that offered quick data retrieval and secure, compliant storage. Notion AI's sophisticated machine learning algorithms were employed to analyze historical health records and predict patient influx, facilitating better staff allocation and resource management.

The integration of Notion AI transformed the appointment scheduling process by optimizing the booking system to reduce waiting times, leveraging real-time data to anticipate peak periods and staff availability. Additionally, Notion AI greatly enhanced MedHealth's preventative care capabilities by analyzing patient data to identify potential health risks and automatically scheduling follow-up appointments or recommending personalized health programs.

After six months of implementing Notion AI, MedHealth Clinics reported a 30% improvement in patient handling efficiency, and a 45% reduction in patient wait times. The AI's predictive capabilities also improved the accuracy of diagnosis and effectiveness of preventative care, resulting in higher patient satisfaction and a significant increase in routine health check-ups.

The ongoing adaptation and learning ability of Notion AI continuously refined its processes, helping MedHealth Clinics not only to manage its operations more effectively but also to make informed decisions that enhanced overall healthcare delivery. The success at MedHealth Clinics serves as compelling evidence of how AI can revolutionize management practices in healthcare, leading to operational efficiencies and improved patient care outcomes.

Case Study: Enhancing International Logistics with Notion AI: A Case Study of GlobalShip Solutions

GlobalShip Solutions, a prominent logistics firm catering to international shipping demands, faced the daunting challenge of managing its complex operational processes involving multi-modal transport systems, diverse regulatory requirements, and varying customer demands across different continents. The traditional methods of managing logistics operations led to inconsistencies and delays, impacting customer satisfaction and service reliability.

To address these challenges, GlobalShip Solutions turned to Notion AI to streamline operations and enhance decision-making processes. The first step involved integrating Notion AI into their logistics tracking and management systems. The AI platform was programmed to analyze historical shipping data, providing insights into common delays, peak season trends, and customs clearance bottlenecks. Utilizing this data, GlobalShip was able to optimize routing, manage shipping schedules more effectively, and anticipate likely delays or problems.

Another significant implementation of Notion AI was in compliance and regulatory adherence. With regulations varying significantly between countries, Notion AI's machine learning algorithms were trained on a diverse dataset of international shipping laws to ensure compliance and to reduce the risk of costly legal issues. The system was configured to alert staff automatically if proposed shipping solutions could potentially breach regional regulations.

The deployment of Notion AI radically transformed how GlobalShip Solutions managed customer expectations and communications. The AI system integrated customer service data across multiple platforms to offer holistic insights into customer queries and complaints. These were then processed to enhance communication strategies, significantly improving response times and accuracy of information provided to customers.

After a year of integrating Notion AI, GlobalShip Solutions experienced a 35% improvement in operational efficiency, a 20% decrease in customer complaints due to delivery delays, and a robust compliance mechanism that decreased regulatory infringements by 50%. Furthermore, the adaptive learning capabilities of Notion AI continued to refine and update operational strategies in real-time, consistently adding value by enhancing logistical frameworks and adapting to new market conditions.

Case Study: Streamlining University Administration with Notion AI: A Case Study of Metro University

Metro University, a large public university with a diverse student body and an extensive range of academic programs, faced significant challenges in managing administrative tasks, student services, and curriculum management. As enrollment numbers grew and academic offerings expanded, the administrative burden intensified, leading to inefficiencies and delays in service provision which impacted student satisfaction and staff workload.

To address these growing pains, Metro University decided to implement Notion AI across various administrative and academic departments. The primary goal was to automate routine workflows, enhance data accessibility, and leverage predictive analytics for better resource management. The initial integration focused on student registration systems and curriculum management, areas identified as having the most significant bottlenecks.

One of the transformative impacts of Notion AI at Metro University was in course scheduling and resource allocation. By analyzing historical enrollment data and student performance metrics, Notion AI provided predictive insights that optimized class sizes, scheduled courses to minimize conflicts, and suggested ideal allocation of faculty resources. This not only improved the registration process for students by reducing wait times and conflicts but also helped the university manage its staffing more effectively.

Furthermore, Notion AI revolutionized student advisory services by integrating an AI-driven support system that could handle routine queries from students, providing quick and accurate information on courses, requirements, and university policies. This system was available 24/7, significantly enhancing student accessibility to necessary support.

After a year of implementing Notion AI, Metro University reported a 40% reduction in administrative workload, a notable increase in student satisfaction related to administrative services, and an overall smoother operation in course registration and management. The AI's learning algorithms continuously adapted and optimized various processes, reducing human error, and improving efficiency across departments. The success at Metro University showcases the potential of AI in revolutionizing not just corporate or healthcare settings but also educational institutions where administrative burdens can be high, and the need for efficiency is paramount.

Case Study: Transforming Agricultural Operations with

Notion AI: A Case Study of AgriGrowth Farm Co.

AgriGrowth Farm Co., a large agricultural enterprise, faced multiple challenges related to crop management, resource allocation, and yield forecasting. The complexity of managing extensive farm operations across diverse geographical locations required a sophisticated level of analytics that traditional methods could not provide.

To overcome these hurdles, AgriGrowth decided to integrate Notion AI into their agricultural management systems. The primary objective was to harness AI capabilities to improve precision farming techniques, optimize resource use, and enhance predictive analytics for better yield management. The integration process began with the implementation of AI-driven sensors and drones that collected real-time data on crop health, soil conditions, and weather patterns. This data was then analyzed by Notion AI to provide actionable insights and automated responses to varying farm conditions.

One of the key outcomes from the integration of Notion AI was the significant improvement in irrigation systems. By utilizing AI to analyze moisture levels and predict weather conditions, the system could automatically adjust the irrigation schedules, reducing water wastage and ensuring optimal soil moisture. Furthermore, Notion AI's predictive analytics enabled precise application of fertilizers and pesticides, reducing costs and environmental impact by minimizing excess application.

The capability of Notion AI to process vast amounts of data dramatically enhanced decision-making processes at AgriGrowth. Through detailed analytics, farm managers could determine the best planting times and crop rotation strategies, which led to improved yields and resource efficiency. Moreover, yield predictions became more accurate, allowing AgriGrowth to better plan for market demands and pricing strategies.

After a year of implementing Notion AI, AgriGrowth Farm Co. reported a 30% increase in overall crop yield and a 25% decrease in resource wastage. The continual learning and adaptation of the AI system have made it possible to refine agricultural practices continuously, ensuring that the farm stays ahead in a highly competitive market. This case exemplifies the transformative impact of AI in agriculture, paving the way for more sustainable and efficient farming practices.

Case Study: Revamping Digital Marketing Strategies with Notion AI: A Case Study of Elite Marketing Solutions

Elite Marketing Solutions, a digital marketing agency renowned for innovative campaigns and strategies, faced significant challenges in staying ahead in the competitive marketing landscape. With a diverse client base, each requiring personalized strategies and quick adaptation to market changes, the agency struggled with managing large datasets and deriving actionable insights.

Elite Marketing Solutions embarked on integrating Notion AI into their operations to tackle these challenges. Initially, the primary goal was to leverage AI-driven analytics to enhance client campaigns and optimize marketing spends. The incorporation of Notion AI began with the analysis of historical campaign data and real-time market trends. By using predictive analytics and sentiment analysis, the platform allowed marketers to tailor campaigns more precisely based on consumer behavior and emerging market trends.

The implementation saw a remarkable improvement in campaign performance. Client ads were optimized to target specific demographics at times they were most likely to engage, and content was tailored to resonate more effectively with audiences, thanks to AI's deep learning about user preferences and behaviors. These adjustments resulted in a 50% increase in client engagement rates within the first quarter of deployment.

In addition to campaign optimization, Notion AI's capabilities in automating routine tasks such as ad placements, and A/B testing schedules allowed staff to redirect their focus towards creative and strategic pursuits. This operational shift significantly boosted workplace productivity and allowed Elite Marketing Solutions to take on additional clients without compromising on service quality.

Long-term, Notion AI's adaptive algorithms continued to refine and learn from each campaign, making subsequent strategies more effective. The agency experienced a 40% increase in ROI for their campaigns post-adoption of Notion AI. The success at Elite Marketing Solutions not only underscores the transformative potential of AI in digital marketing but also exemplifies how integrating such technologies can drive substantial growth and efficiency.

Case Study: Enhancing Legal Operations with Notion AI: A Case Study of LawHub Associates

LawHub Associates, a prominent law firm based in a large metropolitan area, faced numerous challenges due to the volume and complexity of cases they managed. The firm's traditional methods of case management, document handling, and client interaction were becoming increasingly inefficient, resulting in delayed case resolution times and client dissatisfaction. As the firm grew, the need for a transformative technological solution became critical to manage workload more effectively and maintain competitive advantage.

In an attempt to address these issues, LawHub Associates decided to implement Notion AI. The primary goals were to streamline legal workflows, enhance document management, and improve client engagement through AI-driven tools and analytics. The integration process began by digitizing extensive legal documents and case files to make them accessible through Notion AI's centralized system. This database was configured to utilize AI for advanced text analysis, automatically categorizing and tagging key legal terms and case-relevant data, thus saving time for the legal staff.

Notion AI's impact was immediate. The platform facilitated quick access to legal precedents and related case files through its sophisticated search functions, dramatically reducing preparation time for court sessions. Additionally, Notion AI introduced an AI-based scheduling tool that managed court dates, client meetings, and internal deadlines seamlessly, ensuring no overlaps and enhancing time management.

Moreover, the client interaction module within Notion AI personalized communication by analyzing previous interactions and ongoing case details to tailor updates and advice given to clients. This not only improved client satisfaction but also reduced the chances of miscommunication.

Over the course of a year, LawHub Associates reported a 50% increase in case handling efficiency and a 40% reduction in time spent on document management tasks. They also noticed a significant improvement in client retention and satisfaction rates. The AI's ability to learn and adapt continuously helped refine processes even further, providing ongoing insights into operational efficiency and client management improvements.

Case Study: Revolutionizing the Publishing Industry with Notion AI: A Case Study of ReadMaster Publications

ReadMaster Publications, a renowned publishing house with an extensive catalog spanning numerous genres, faced significant challenges in managing its editorial processes, manuscript evaluations, and market analytics. With a legacy system that heavily relied on manual inputs and traditional market evaluation methods, ReadMaster struggled with prolonged publication cycles, which in turn affected their market responsiveness and revenue models.

The adoption of Notion AI was aimed at transforming its core editorial operations. Initial integration focused on automating manuscript evaluations and streamlining the editing process. Notion AI's capabilities were put to test in analyzing huge volumes of text for grammatical quality, thematic consistency, and adherence to ReadMaster's publishing standard. The platform's natural language processing (NLP) tools automated the first-level editing processes, significantly reducing the time from manuscript submission to decision.

Further, Notion AI's predictive analytics were employed in market analysis and sales forecasting. By assimilating data from past sales, current market trends, and consumer behavior insights generated by the AI, ReadMaster could more accurately predict future trends and tailor their marketing strategies accordingly. This led to a more dynamic response to market demands, enabling targeted promotions and optimized stocking across their distribution networks.

Moreover, the AI's deep learning algorithms facilitated personalized recommendation systems on ReadMaster's digital platforms, enhancing user engagement by suggesting books based on browsing history and purchase patterns. The adaptability of Notion AI allowed for continuous learning from user interactions, which consistently refined recommendation accuracy.

After one year of Notion AI integration, ReadMaster Publications reported a 40% increase in operational efficiency, a 30% reduction in the time-to-market for new publications, and an overall 20% growth in sales revenue. Ongoing use of Notion AI has continuously improved their processes, helping ReadMaster Publications not only in day-to-day operations but also in strategic decision-making, resulting in sustained competitive advantage and industry leadership.

REVIEW QUESTIONS

1. A company 'TechGrowth' has recently implemented Notion AI across its diversity of teams to streamline their workflows. As a project manager monitoring the integration, one of the initial tasks involves setting up individual workspaces tailored to each department. Given the descriptions of workspaces in the case study, what would be the primary focus when configuring a workspace for the Marketing team using Notion AI?

A) Focusing on task automation and tracking

B) Enhancing communication tools and dashboards

C) Customizing data analytic features and reporting tools

D) All of the above

Answer: C

Explanation: In setting up a workspace for the Marketing team, the primary focus should involve customizing data analytic features and reporting tools. This focus is derived from the Marketing team's need to interpret complex data for strategic decision-making efficiently. Notion AI offers powerful AI analytics and reporting capabilities that can automate data processing and generate actionable insights, which are crucial for managing marketing campaigns effectively and align with the described capabilities in the chapter on Notion AI's role in enhancing organizational productivity.

2. During an executive meeting at 'TechSolutions Inc.', the CEO discussed the benefits of integrating Notion AI into the company's operations. The CEO emphasized the need for better decision-making processes and introduced the concept of AI-driven suggestions for setting realistic task deadlines. Based on the information provided in the chapter, what is the ultimate benefit of implementing such AI-driven suggestions in project management?

A) Decreasing the dependency on human project managers

B) Minimizing project delays due to unrealistic timelines

C) Reducing the operational costs through efficient resource management

D) All of the above

Answer: B

Explanation: The ultimate benefit of implementing AI-driven suggestions for setting realistic task deadlines, as discussed in the Notion AI chapter under task management enhancements, is minimizing project delays caused by unrealistic timelines. Notion AI utilizes advanced AI algorithms to analyze past performance analytics and current workloads to suggest feasible deadlines. This feature ensures that project timelines are accurate and achievable, thereby reducing delays and maintaining project momentum.

REVIEW QUESTIONS

3. In the strategic planning session at 'InnovateX', the focus was on automating routine operations to free up the creative capacities of the team. The management decided to deploy Notion AI with an emphasis on automating meeting minutes. How does the automation of meeting minutes contribute to the organizational productivity according to the chapter discussion on Notion AI?

A) It allows team members to focus more on the discussion rather than note-taking

B) It automatically organizes and synthesizes discussion points for quick review

C) It facilitates faster and more accurate dissemination of meeting outcomes

D) All of these

Answer: D

Explanation: According to the chapter on Notion AI, automating meeting minutes with Notion AI contributes to organizational productivity in several ways: by allowing team members to focus more on discussions instead of note-taking, automatically organizing and synthesizing discussion points for quick and effective reviews post-meeting, and facilitating faster and accurate dissemination of meeting outcomes. This automation ensures that critical information is captured thoroughly and communicated efficiently, enhancing overall workflow.

4. 'Global Design LLC' integrates Notion AI into their workflow to enhance resource management. The integration aims to utilize AI analytics for predictive resource allocation. As per the chapter insights, what is the expected outcome of employing Notion AI's predictive analytics for resource management?

A) Improved precision in forecasting and allocation of resources

B) Reduced human errors in resource planning

C) Enhanced compliance with industry regulations

D) Both A and B

Answer: D

Explanation: Employing Notion AI's predictive analytics in resource management, as addressed in the chapter, results in improved precision in forecasting and allocation of resources and reduced human errors in resource planning. These AI-driven analytics help identify optimal usage patterns and predict future needs, allowing organizations like 'Global Design LLC' to efficiently manage their resources in anticipation of project demands, thus optimizing both human and material resources effectively.

RUNWAYML: ADVANCED AI VIDEO EDITING AND EFFECTS

Introduction to RunwayML and Its Core Features

RunwayML stands as a revolutionary tool in the realm of video editing, offering unparalleled AI-driven capabilities that cater to both professional filmmakers and hobbyists alike. By harnessing the power of artificial intelligence, RunwayML simplifies complex video editing tasks, enabling users to create high-quality visual content with ease.

At its core, RunwayML provides advanced features such as real-time video effects, AI-enabled visual content generation, and automation of repetitive tasks. These features are designed to enhance productivity and foster creative expression. For instance, its capability to automatically apply color correction saves hours of manual adjustment, while its sophisticated motion tracking technology allows for seamless integration of effects and animations.

Moreover, RunwayML supports a wide range of video formats and resolutions, making it versatile for various project requirements. Its intuitive user interface ensures that even novices can navigate and utilize its extensive functionalities effectively, thus democratizing video production technology in an innovative and accessible manner.

Setting Up RunwayML for Professional Video Editing

Embarking on RunwayML's setup for professional video editing marks the initiation into a transformative editing journey. First, ensure you possess the required system specifications, which include a robust processor and sufficient memory to handle high-resolution video files smoothly. Downloading and installing RunwayML is straightforward from its official website, followed by creating an account to access its features.

Once installed, professionals should fine-tune settings to optimize workflow. Configure the workspace layout and adjust the preferences to suit project needs, such as setting default export options and enabling hardware acceleration for faster processing. Integration with cloud storage can streamline project management and collaboration, secure in knowing that edits and versions are backed up automatically.

Finally, exploring the extensive library of tutorials and resources provided by RunwayML empowers users to maximize the platform's capabilities. Engage with the community forums to exchange tips and gain insight from experienced editors, thereby enhancing both efficiency and creativity in your video projects.

Navigating the User Interface of RunwayML

Mastering the user interface of RunwayML unlocks a treasure trove of video editing capabilities, structured intuitively to amplify creative output. Upon launching the software, users are greeted by a clean, modern dashboard that prioritizes ease of accessibility. Key functional areas are distinctly segmented, encompassing asset libraries, a timeline, and a preview window, each pivotal for an efficient editing workflow.

The central timeline is the operational heart of RunwayML, where clips can be freely arranged and manipulated. Tools and effects are accessed via a side panel that smartly categorizes options from basic trimming to advanced visual effects, allowing for rapid selections without overwhelming new users. This streamlined configuration facilitates an effortless transition from conceptualization to production.

Above all, the interface champions customization, offering various layout adjustments to suit individual preferences and project demands. Moreover, tooltips and guides appear contextually, providing on-the-spot assistance to refine user interaction with the platform. Beginners benefit immensely from this built-in guidance, easing the learning curve while fostering skill development.

Basic Video Editing Techniques with RunwayML

Delving into the fundamental video editing techniques with RunwayML offers both budding and seasoned editors a doorway into efficient and creative video production. Start by mastering basic cuts and transitions, essential for dictating the pace and flow of visuals. RunwayML facilitates these operations with intuitive tools that allow quick segmenting and joining of clips to construct a coherent narrative flow.

Beyond simple cuts, incorporating text overlays and introductory titles elevates the professional feel of any project. With RunwayML, adding text is streamlined through an automated interface, providing options for customization in font, color, and animation, thus enhancing viewer engagement. Similarly, layering audio tracks to complement the visual elements can be seamlessly achieved in the timeline, optimizing the auditory impact alongside the visuals.

Finally, using RunwayML's drag-and-drop functionality enhances workflow efficiency. This feature is particularly beneficial for repetitive tasks, such as applying consistent transitions or color grades across multiple clips, ensuring uniformity and aesthetic cohesion throughout the project. Embrace these foundational techniques to unlock the full potential of your video creations with RunwayML.

Advanced Special Effects and Filters in RunwayML

RunwayML elevates video editing to a new level with its advanced special effects and filters. These tools empower creators to transform ordinary footage into cinematic artistry. Utilizing AI-driven algorithms, users can apply complex visual effects that would typically require extensive manual input and sophisticated software knowledge.

From ethereal glow effects that enhance atmospheric scenes to dynamic distortions that add intensity to action sequences, the array is vast and versatile. Moreover, these effects are adjustable in real-time, offering immediate previews and enabling fine-tuning to achieve the desired aesthetic. Filters in RunwayML also support thematic consistency across projects by allowing users to develop custom filter settings that can be saved and reapplied to different clips.

The integration of these advanced features into RunwayML not only streamlines the creative process but also opens up new possibilities for narrative expression. Filmmakers and content creators can experiment without bounds, pushing the limits of traditional videography to explore new, innovative storytelling techniques.

Utilizing AI for Seamless Video Background Replacement

Seamless video background replacement has been revolutionized by the AI capabilities of RunwayML, offering video editors an invaluable tool for creating visually striking content. This feature is particularly useful for filmmakers who need to modify or enhance the setting of their scenes without the logistical challenges of on-site shooting. Using RunwayML, background alterations are made simple and efficient, with artificial intelligence handling the complex aspects of edge detection and object separation.

The process begins by selecting the desired background from an extensive library within RunwayML or uploading a custom backdrop. AI then analyzes the original footage, differentiating the foreground subjects from their existing backgrounds. This precise separation is crucial for maintaining the natural appearance of the edges around subjects, ensuring that the integration with the new background is flawless and visually coherent.

Furthermore, RunwayML's AI-driven background replacement not only saves time but also reduces costs associated with physical set changes and on-location shoots. It empowers creators to experiment with different scenarios and aesthetic environments, enhancing storytelling without compromising on production quality. This tool is a game-changer for producing high-quality content swiftly, pushing the boundaries of conventional video editing.

Creating High-Quality Green Screen Effects

Green screen technology in RunwayML brings to life vibrant visuals that are only limited by the imagination. Start by setting up the green screen evenly lit to avoid shadows or variations, which are pivotal for a clean key in the post-production stage. Next, position your subjects strategically, ensuring they don't cast shadows on the screen, which could complicate the keying process.

RunwayML's AI leverages advanced algorithms to differentiate between the green background and the foreground, allowing users to replace the green with digital or virtual backdrops seamlessly. Adjustments can be made to the edges and softness of the composite to ensure that the subjects blend naturally into the new environment without harsh lines or unnatural outlines.

Moreover, RunwayML empowers users to experiment with different backgrounds easily. Testing various artistic or realistic scenes becomes a hassle-free process, ensuring that the end result aligns with the creator's vision. This function not only enhances the production value but also extends creative freedom, transforming ordinary videos into compelling visual stories.

Automated Color Correction and Grading Tools

RunwayML's automated color correction and grading tools simplify what is often considered a complex and nuanced aspect of video production. These tools harness advanced AI to analyze video clips and apply optimized color settings that enhance visual quality. This automatic adjustment is crucial for maintaining consistency across clips shot under different lighting conditions or with varied cameras.

The grading feature in RunwayML, particularly, is a standout, enabling editors to create mood and tone without the steep learning curve associated with traditional color grading software. With pre-set profiles and the ability to customize and save new ones, RunwayML adapts to both the novice and the experienced editor's needs. Real-time feedback allows for adjustments on the fly, ensuring every frame looks precisely as intended.

Moreover, the integration of these tools into RunwayML's AI-driven ecosystem means that color correction and grading can be seamlessly tied with other editing tasks, increasing workflow efficiency. This holistic approach ensures that the video not only looks good but also feels cohesive, professional, and ready for any platform.

AI-Assisted Video Stabilization and Motion Tracking

RunwayML's AI-assisted video stabilization and motion tracking capabilities revolutionize the way filmmakers and video enthusiasts manage camera movements and action-packed sequences. This technology seamlessly smoothens out shaky footage, which is especially handy for hand-held shots or when shooting in motion. By analyzing and compensating for unwanted camera motions, RunwayML ensures that the resulting video maintains a polished, professional appearance.

Motion tracking within RunwayML is equally transformative, enabling dynamic interaction between the captured footage and digital effects. Whether tracking objects for adding digital elements or enhancing immersive experiences by anchoring animations to moving points, RunwayML's precision tracking keeps everything aligned and integrated flawlessly. This feature is crucial for post-production processes involving complex visual layers and effects.

Furthermore, combining video stabilization with motion tracking, RunwayML empowers creators to produce high-quality, dynamic videos without the need for expensive stabilizing equipment or additional software. It opens up creative possibilities, making sophisticated videography accessible to a broader range of creators, fostering innovation in video production.

Using RunwayML for Innovative Text and Title Animations

RunwayML revolutionizes text and title animations, opening up endless creative possibilities with its AI-driven tools. Users can craft dynamic text overlays that interact with video elements in real-time, creating a compelling visual narrative. The app's intuitive interface allows for the quick selection of fonts, styles, and animations, streamlining the design process while offering a vast library of customizable options.

Moreover, RunwayML's AI capabilities enhance the animation of text by automatically syncing it with the video's pacing, mood, and music. Animations can be fine-tuned to respond to changes in the video, such as enhancing emphasis during key moments or subtly integrating into quieter scenes. This level of dynamic interaction ensures that titles and text are not just overlays but integral, engaging elements of storytelling.

The potential for brand differentiation is significant, as RunwayML facilitates the creation of unique, signature animations that can become synonymous with a creator's content style. Through this powerful tool, video editors can elevate their projects, ensuring their text elements are as captivating as their visuals.

AI Techniques for Editing 4K and High-Resolution Videos

The rise of 4K and high-resolution video content demands advanced editing tools capable of handling such increased data without sacrificing quality. RunwayML harnesses powerful AI techniques to manage and enrich these vibrant, detail-rich formats. AI-driven algorithms optimize processing, enabling real-time rendering and playback, even with extensive 4K footage.

Beyond sheer handling capability, RunwayML's AI also refines high-resolution video editing. Enhanced upscaling features maintain crispness and clarity, negating the common pixelation problems seen with standard upscaling methods. Additionally, noise reduction is intelligently applied, preserving the natural aesthetics of the original footage while ensuring professional-grade output.

Another key feature is frame interpolation, which is pivotal for achieving smooth slow-motion effects without the stutter often seen in less sophisticated software. RunwayML's AI analyzes and predicts frame data to seamlessly blend frames, thus producing fluid motion integral to high-resolution video storytelling. This comprehensive suite of tools redefines what creatives can achieve, pushing the boundaries of video production.

Incorporating AI Meme Generation into Video Projects

RunwayML takes meme integration to new heights within video projects. This breakthrough feature redefines viewer engagement by seamlessly blending popular meme aesthetics into professional editing workflows. Users can now leverage trending online humor, adapting memes in real-time to complement their narrative or thematic context. This AI-driven process is not only fun but enhances relatability and shareability, crucial traits for digital content success.

Utilizing cutting-edge algorithms, RunwayML identifies and syncs appropriate memes to specific moments in a video. This alignment ensures that the humor feels neither forced nor out of place, maintaining a smooth content delivery. Moreover, this feature supports custom meme creation, allowing users to express creativity uniquely and interestingly that resonates with their target audience. The inclusion of memes becomes a strategic content enhancement, not just a comedic addition.

RunwayML's meme generation tool is designed to keep pace with viral trends, thereby empowering video creators to stay current and relevant. This tool continually updates, guaranteeing fresh content that engages audiences while keeping the workflow efficient and innovative. Integrating this AI functionality thus delivers both entertainment and a competitive edge in video production.

Leveraging RunwayML for Quick Social Media Edits

In today's fast-paced digital environment, the ability to quickly edit and optimize video content for social media is paramount. RunwayML stands out as a vital tool for creators, enabling rapid, high-quality edits that are essential for engaging modern audiences. The platform's AI-driven interface simplifies the editing process, allowing users to produce polished content swiftly without sacrificing artistic integrity.

This efficiency is critical when dealing with the constant demand for fresh content on platforms like Instagram, TikTok, and Facebook. RunwayML facilitates this by automating repetitive tasks, such as trimming, cropping, and applying basic effects, which accelerates the production cycle tremendously. Furthermore, its smart algorithms can analyze the visual and thematic elements of videos to suggest optimal edits and enhancements that align with current social media trends.

Additionally, RunwayML supports the export of videos in formats optimized for various social networks, ensuring compatibility and maintaining quality across devices. This feature, coupled with the tool's speed and versatility, makes it an indispensable asset for anyone looking to capitalize on the dynamic nature of social media.

Developing Branding Elements and Logo Animations

RunwayML stands as a groundbreaking platform for developing unique branding elements and crafting dynamic logo animations that resonate with target audiences. The AI-driven environment of RunwayML provides a toolbox ripe for innovation, where creators can execute custom branding strategies with precision and creativity. Designing visually appealing logos that can be animated interactively enhances brand identity and increases viewer engagement substantially.

As part of the logo animation process, RunwayML integrates algorithmic predictions to ensure smooth transitions and appealing motion graphics that keep the viewer's attention. This tool simplifies the animation of complex logo designs which might include multiple layers and effects, translating ideas into captivating animations. This capacity supports real-time preview and adjustments, fostering an iterative design process that is fundamental for achieving optimal results.

Furthermore, these animations can be seamlessly incorporated into promotional videos, website headers, or social media posts, further extending the utility of RunwayML as a holistic branding tool. This integration helps businesses maintain a consistent visual presence across multiple platforms, reinforcing their brand's message and aesthetic in the public eye.

Enhancing Narrative with AI-Generated Voiceovers and Audio Sync

The narrative depth of video content is significantly enhanced by RunwayML AI-generated voiceovers. Creating realistic and engaging audio narratives that embellish content without the requirement for professional voice actors, AI algorithms at the core generate lifelike vocal textures based on context and scene dynamics. Integrated seamlessly, these voiceovers fit perfectly with the visual narrative, adding both emotion and clarity to storytelling.

Additionally, audio synchronization features ensure that voiceovers precisely match on-screen actions, enhancing viewer immersion. This is engineered through advanced sound wave analysis that detects and aligns spoken words with visual cues and scene changes. The technology is a boon for solo creators or small teams who must craft compelling stories without extensive resources.

RunwayML furthers narrative engagement by offering tools to manipulate voice tone and timing, making it suitable for varied content genres from documentaries to advertisement scenarios. The intuitive interface allows even novice users to implement sophisticated sound designs, elevating simple videos to professional-grade productions.

Collaborative Video Editing Features in RunwayML

RunwayML revolutionizes video editing with its collaborative features, designed to streamline the creative process in a shared environment. Teams can work simultaneously on the same project from different locations, a boon for efficiency and innovation in content creation. Real-time updates and cloud-based sharing prevent conflicts and ensure that everyone has access to the latest edits.

Moreover, RunwayML's role-based access control meticulously manages user permissions, guaranteeing that edits are made only by authorized personnel, which enhances security and workflow integrity. This control is particularly vital in large projects with many stakeholders, maintaining a cohesive and consistent product.

The platform also supports live feedback loops, enabling instant review and suggestions. This feature not only accelerates the editorial process but also enhances the quality of the output by incorporating diverse inputs swiftly. RunwayML's commitment to seamless collaboration empowers creators, elevating the collective potential of video projects.

Exploring the Integration of RunwayML with Other Video Tools

RunwayML's prowess extends beyond standalone capabilities, demonstrating remarkable synergy when integrated with other industry-leading video editing tools. This interoperability unlocks new dimensions of creative possibilities, enabling video editors to harness the strength of multiple platforms efficiently.

A prime example is the integration with Adobe Premiere Pro. RunwayML complements Adobe's robust editing suite by adding advanced AI-driven functionalities, such as real-time video effects and automation of labor-intensive editing tasks. This partnership not only streamlines workflows but also enhances the final video output with unique AI features that would be cumbersome to replicate manually.

Further, the integration extends to platforms like Final Cut Pro, where RunwayML's AI capabilities help in refining video aesthetics through sophisticated color grading tools and motion effects, seamlessly blending with Final Cut's intuitive interface and editing features. The result is a smoother, more intuitive workflow that elevates both productivity and artistic expression.

Thus, the fusion of RunwayML with other tools symbolizes a leap towards a futuristic, integrated video editing ecosystem, maximizing both efficiency and creativity.

Batch Processing and Automation for Large Video Projects

RunwayML excels in handling vast video projects through its robust batch processing and automation capabilities. This feature is indispensable for professionals who deal with large volumes of video content, streamlining tasks such as rendering, effects application, and transcoding simultaneously across multiple files. By automating these processes, RunwayML significantly reduces the time and effort required for bulk video editing tasks.

The platform's AI-driven algorithms optimize operations by analyzing video content and applying the most effective editing techniques automatically. This not only ensures consistency across all processed videos but also maintains high quality without manual oversight. Users can configure presets for different projects, which RunwayML uses to process large batches of videos overnight or during low-activity hours, maximizing productivity.

Furthermore, the automation system in RunwayML is designed to be user-friendly, allowing editors of all skill levels to leverage this powerful feature. The impact is a marked increase in project turnaround times and the ability to meet tight deadlines with reliability and precision, reinforcing RunwayML's position as a leader in AI-driven video editing solutions.

Exporting Options and Optimizing Videos for Various Platforms

RunwayML's functionality extends into the realm of exporting, where a range of options ensures videos are optimized for a variety of platforms. Users can select from numerous formats, resolutions, and compression rates to tailor content specifically for social media, streaming, or professional use. This versatility is crucial for creators aiming to maximize reach and impact across diverse viewing environments.

Additionally, RunwayML incorporates intelligent algorithms that optimize video files for bandwidth and storage limitations without sacrificing quality. This is particularly beneficial when dealing with high-resolution videos, making them accessible without extensive buffering or data consumption. The platform's export presets are meticulously designed to meet the standards of specific platforms, such as YouTube, Vimeo, or Instagram, ensuring that videos are displayed at their best quality and with correct aspect ratios.

Lastly, the ability to batch export and simultaneously optimize multiple videos streamlines workflow for professionals and hobbyists alike. This efficiency is a game-changer, allowing creators to focus on creative aspects while RunwayML handles the technical nuances of video distribution.

Securing and Managing Project Files in RunwayML

Securing and managing project files is paramount in RunwayML, catering to the needs of professionals concerned with data integrity and accessibility. The platform offers comprehensive tools for project encryption, ensuring that all uploaded content is safeguarded against unauthorized access. This feature is crucial for maintaining confidentiality, particularly when handling sensitive or proprietary material.

Moreover, RunwayML employs a robust file management system that allows users to organize their projects efficiently. With features like tagging and advanced search options, locating specific files or project components becomes effortless, enhancing productivity and reducing downtime. The platform also supports version control, preserving every edit and adjustment for review and rollback capabilities, which is invaluable in collaborative environments where changes are frequent and need to be tracked meticulously.

Data backup is another integral aspect meticulously addressed by RunwayML. The platform ensures that all project files are backed up in real-time to multiple secure locations, thus minimizing the risk of data loss due to hardware failure or accidental deletion. This comprehensive approach not only secures the data but also ensures its availability whenever needed, streamlining the workflow and supporting continuous creative processes.

Maximizing Efficiency with AI-Powered Editing Workflows

RunwayML harnesses the power of AI to redefine video editing efficiencies, creating seamless workflows optimized for speed and quality. The AI-powered features within RunwayML analyze video content in real-time, applying sophisticated editing techniques that drastically shorten the editing cycle. This automation not only enhances productivity but also maintains the artistic intent, ensuring that each video remains true to the creator's vision.

Thanks to these AI integrations, RunwayML streamlines complex editing sequences, enabling editors to focus on creative storytelling rather than technical nuances. The system intelligently suggests edits and improvements, learning from user interactions to become even more efficient over time. Consequently, projects that traditionally took days can now be completed in hours without sacrificing quality.

Moreover, the AI-driven workflow in RunwayML aligns with collaborative and batch processing features, creating a synergy that effectively manages large-scale video projects. This integrative approach ensures that even with high workloads, the output remains consistent and high quality, positioning RunwayML as an indispensable tool in the modern video editor's arsenal.

Empowering Creativity with RunwayML's Custom Effect Builder

RunwayML's Custom Effect Builder stands as a beacon of innovation, allowing creators to conceive and implement bespoke visual effects that are uniquely tailored to their projects. This tool empowers users by breaking the traditional barriers of video editing, enabling even those with minimal programming knowledge to craft stunning, professional-level effects. The intuitive interface guides users through the process of effect creation, from conceptualization to execution, providing real-time previews and adjustments.

At the heart of this feature is its flexibility and depth. Users can manipulate variables and stack effects, creating complex visual narratives that are responsive and dynamic. Whether enhancing documentary footage with subtle enhancements or engineering elaborate sequences for feature films, the Custom Effect Builder equips users with the tools to express their creative visions without compromise.

Moreover, this builder is a testament to RunwayML's commitment to democratizing video editing. It epitomizes the fusion of creativity and technology, fostering an environment where artistic expression and innovation converge. By enabling bespoke creations, RunwayML not only enhances individual projects but also pushes the boundaries of what is possible in digital storytelling.

How to Incorporate VR and AR Effects using RunwayML

RunwayML takes video editing into the realms of virtual and augmented reality, providing revolutionary tools to integrate VR and AR effects seamlessly. This functionality opens a new dimension for creators, allowing them to envelop audiences in more immersive experiences. By importing 3D models or using the built-in library, users can place virtual objects in real-world scenes, merging digital elements with physical environments.

The interface simplifies the complex technology behind VR and AR, making it accessible even to those with minimal experience in immersive technologies. RunwayML offers drag-and-drop features where users can intuitively position AR overlays or VR environments within their video frames. This integration is not only about placement but also includes adjusting the scale, orientation, and interaction of 3D elements with real-world physics, ensuring a believable integration into the videos.

To further enhance the immersive experience, RunwayML supports real-time rendering for VR and AR contents, allowing editors to preview effects and make adjustments on the fly. This immediate feedback accelerates the creative process, ensuring that the end product is as engaging as it is polished. Supportive tutorials and a community-driven forum provide guidance and inspiration, fueling limitless creative possibilities with RunwayML.

Training and Educational Resources Available for RunwayML Users

RunwayML not only revolutionizes video editing with AI but also ensures users are well-equipped to harness its full potential through comprehensive training and educational resources. Designed to cater to both beginners and advanced users, these resources include detailed tutorials, webinars, and an extensive online help center that addresses common issues and advanced techniques.

The platform offers a series of interactive courses ranging from basic introductions to more specialized applications such as AI-assisted editing and effect customization. These courses are thoughtfully structured to facilitate progressive learning, gradually building from foundational skills to complex editing tasks. Participants can also benefit from live training sessions conducted by seasoned experts, providing real-time answers and demonstrations tailored to user inquiries.

Moreover, RunwayML hosts a vibrant community platform where users can exchange tips, share creative ideas, and solve challenges collaboratively. This peer-to-peer learning environment is bolstered by regular updates and tips from the RunwayML team, fostering a dynamic and supportive learning atmosphere for all users.

Community Support and Collaborative Opportunities in RunwayML

RunwayML fosters a thriving community support system and provides numerous collaborative opportunities that enrich the user experience and expand the horizons of video editing. At the core of this ecosystem is an active online forum where professionals, from novice creators to seasoned experts, share insights, troubleshoot issues, and exchange innovative ideas. This vibrant community is instrumental in driving the platform's evolution, as feedback from these interactions often shapes feature updates and enhancements.

Moreover, RunwayML facilitates collaboration through integrated tools that allow users to work on projects simultaneously. This feature is particularly beneficial in educational settings or team-based environments, where collective input can lead to richer, more creative outcomes. Workshops and live events further cement the sense of community, offering hands-on experiences and networking opportunities that are invaluable in the creative industries.

The platform's commitment to a supportive and collaborative environment makes it not just a tool for video editing, but a hub for creative growth and interaction.

Future Trends and Updates Expected in RunwayML

As RunwayML continues to pioneer the convergence of AI and video editing, future updates are poised to further transform the landscape. Near-term enhancements will likely focus on deepening machine learning capabilities, enabling the platform to offer even more intuitive editing tools that predict user preferences and automate mundane tasks.

Longer-term innovations may integrate next-generation AI technologies, such as neural networks that can mimic human emotional responses to different visual stimuli. This would allow RunwayML to not only edit but also suggest content adjustments based on predicted viewer reactions, optimizing engagement across various platforms.

Additionally, RunwayML is set to expand its collaborative features, potentially incorporating cloud-based co-editing in real-time, which would revolutionize team projects by allowing instant input and modification from multiple editors, regardless of location. As the digital video domain evolves, RunwayML's forward-looking updates are expected to continually set benchmarks for creativity and efficiency in video production.

SUMMARY

RunwayML emerges as a transformative tool in video editing, leveraging AI to simplify complex editing tasks for both professionals and hobbyists. Its core functionalities include real-time effects, automation, and support for multiple video formats, boosting productivity and creative freedom. The setup involves downloading from RunwayML's official site and adjusting settings to optimize workflow, including cloud storage for seamless collaboration. The user-friendly interface of RunwayML is designed for ease of use, with a clean dashboard and neatly organized tools that enhance the editing process without overwhelming new users. Basic editing techniques provided by RunwayML include quick cuts, text overlays, and audio integration, made efficient through drag-and-drop functionality. Advanced capabilities extend to AI-driven effects like background replacement and motion tracking, pushing the limits of traditional videography. Green screen effects and automated color grading tools embody the sophistication of RunwayML, empowering creators to produce cinematic quality content. The platform also introduces innovative features like AI-assisted voiceovers and integration with other editing tools like Adobe Premiere Pro, enhancing its utility and efficiency. Collaborative features enable real-time co-editing and role-based access, fostering teamwork online. Recently, RunwayML has ventured into realms like VR and AR, providing immersive editing capabilities, and continuously supports users with extensive educational resources and a collaborative community platform. Future updates are expected to introduce deeper learning capabilities and enhanced collaborative tools, reinforcing RunwayML's stance at the cutting edge of video editing technology.

REFERENCES

[1] Timothy B. Miller, 'Exploring AI-Driven Video Editing Platforms', Journal of Digital Media. https://www.journalofdigitalmedia.com/article/ai-video-editing

[2] Anna Patel, 'AI and the Future of Creative Video Editing', Creativity & Technology Review. https://www.creativitytechreview.com/ai-video-editing-future

[3] Gareth J. Thomas, 'Integrating AI Tools with Traditional Video Editing Software', Global Tech Innovations. https://www.globaltechinnovations.com/integrating-ai-tools

[4] Emily Zhao, 'Enhancing Narrative through AI-Generated Voiceovers', AI in Multimedia. https://www.aiinmultimedia.com/ai-voiceovers-enhancement

[5] Olivia S. Young, 'Collaborative Video Editing in the Cloud: A New Era', Video Tech Today. https://www.videotechtoday.com/collaborative-video-editing

CASE STUDY: REVOLUTIONIZING FILM PRODUCTION WITH RUNWAYML: A CASE STUDY ON ADVANCED VIDEO EDITING FOR INDIE FILMMAKERS

The rise of digital filmmaking has empowered a new generation of filmmakers to create cinematic masterpieces without the need for big-budget studios. Especially for indie filmmakers, tools like RunwayML, equipped with cutting-edge AI, have become a game-changer. One such emerging filmmaker, Sophia, discovered RunwayML and utilized its various advanced functionalities to bring her low-budget sci-fi vision to life.

Sophia's project was ambitious — a 90-minute feature set in a dystopian future. The screenplay required complex visual effects, color-grading, and seamless integration of live-action with CGI, typically demanding significant investments and technical skills. Using RunwayML, Sophia was able to tackle each of these demands effectively. The AI-driven effects allowed her to incorporate high-quality visual FX that mimicked big-budget productions. RunwayML's easy-to-use interface enabled real-time adjustments to effects, significantly cutting down the editing time.

Perhaps the most intensive use of RunwayML in her project was leveraging the AI-assisted video stabilization and motion tracking to handle action sequences shot with handheld cameras. This feature smoothed out the shakiness typically associated with budget constraints and manual handling, providing a polished look characteristic of higher-budget films.

Equally crucial was RunwayML's color correction and grading tools. For a film set in a dystopian future, establishing the right visual tone was key. The platform's AI analyzed her footage and effortlessly applied a consistent color palette throughout the film, enhancing mood congruency and visual aesthetics. The availability of custom filter settings and automated adjustments kept her creative vision cohesive without the need to delve into complex color grading software.

In Sophia's case, RunwayML's collaborative features also played a significant role. Collaborating remotely with a small team of editors and visual effects artists, the platform's cloud-based functionalities ensured that changes by any team member were updated in real-time, maintaining project uniformity. This real-time collaboration feature not only saved crucial time but also enhanced creative synergies within the team, allowing for immediate feedback and modifications.

Case Study: Transforming Documentaries with RunwayML: An In-depth Look at AI-enhanced Video Production

The documentary film 'Hidden Realms' aimed to explore intricate ecosystems across different continents, a project requiring diverse visual storytelling techniques and extensive editing capabilities. Due to logistical constraints and limited staffing, the production team turned to RunwayML to overcome these challenges, leveraging its AI tools to significantly enhance the visual appeal and storytelling efficiency of the documentary.

With scenes ranging from the dense Amazon rainforest to the harsh landscapes of the Arctic, the documentary necessitated high-level editing skills to ensure visual continuity and engaging content. RunwayML's automated color correction tools played a pivotal role. They succeeded in unifying footage from multiple locations and lighting conditions, ensuring a seamless viewing experience. The algorithmically enhanced grading tools made it possible to subtly adjust hues to reflect the mood of the different ecosystems, reinforcing the documentary's thematic elements without the need for manual oversight, which would have been time-consuming and potentially inconsistent.

Another major challenge was integrating drone and ground footage to create a coherent narrative. RunwayML's AI-assisted video stabilization and motion tracking capabilities ensured that transitions between aerial and ground shots were smooth, maintaining professional-grade cinematographic quality. This was particularly important in sequences illustrating the rapid flight of birds or the sudden movement of wildlife, where stability and clarity of footage are crucial for viewer engagement.

Additionally, the team exploited RunwayML's advanced special effects and filters to highlight specific environmental features, like water streams and forest canopies, in stunning detail. Enhancements that traditionally would require extensive post-production work were achieved with minimal effort, freeing up creative energies to focus more on content than technical execution.

Collaboratively, RunwayML's cloud-based sharing and real-time updates allowed for efficient teamwork. Editors and production members located in various global locations could work simultaneously on the same project files, making updates and seeing revisions in real-time, greatly improving workflow efficiency and project cohesion.

Case Study: Empowering Independent Music Videos Production with RunwayML: A Case Study of Creative Automation

The music industry has embraced a significant transformation, especially in promoting artists through visually striking music videos. An up-and-coming independent musician, Elena, faced the dual challenge of crafting an engaging music video for her new album while managing constrained financial resources. Elena turned to RunwayML to produce a captivating visual experience that could rival the offerings of major production studios.

Elena's vision involved integrating dynamic text animations and complex visual effects that reflected the emotional depth of her songs. Utilizing the advanced tools provided by RunwayML, she began by implementing AI-enabled text overlays that reacted interactively with the beats and rhythm of her music. The platform's AI-driven algorithms allowed for real-time synchronization of text with music, enhancing viewer engagement by dynamically altering text pacing, color, and size in harmony with the audio.

Furthermore, Elena leveraged RunwayML's library of special effects to create dreamlike sequences that visually interpreted her music's themes. AI-driven filters transformed ordinary footage into cinematic sequences, adding surreal colors and animations without the need for extensive manual input or additional software plugins. The ease of applying these complex effects allowed Elena to experiment with different aesthetics until she found the perfect match for each segment of her video.

Elena also utilized RunwayML's video stabilization and motion tracking capabilities to ensure smooth transitions and movement synched perfectly with dance routines. Particularly beneficial was the platform's capability to automate the color grading process, thereby maintaining a consistent visual tone throughout the video, which could have been otherwise difficult to achieve manually given the diverse settings and lighting conditions in her footage.

The completion of Elena's music video not only provided her with a professional-grade visual product but also demonstrated how RunwayML could empower artists to independently execute their creative visions. This case study highlights RunwayML's potential to democratize video production, making sophisticated visual storytelling accessible to creators regardless of their budget constraints.

Case Study: Leveraging RunwayML for Dynamic Corporate Training Videos

In the rapidly evolving corporate landscape, maintaining an updated and engaging training regimen is crucial. A multinational corporation, GlobalTech Inc., recognized the need to revamp its training modules to include more interactive and visually engaging content, leveraging the latest AI tools from RunwayML to do so. The project involved transforming static, text-heavy training material into dynamic videos that would increase employee engagement and retention of information.

GlobalTech's training department collaborated with the internal communications team to identify key areas that required visual enhancement. They decided to utilize RunwayML's capabilities for AI-assisted video stabilization, motion tracking, and advanced video editing features. The first phase involved creating a series of video snippets that demonstrated complex technical processes using RunwayML's motion tracking to highlight specific actions in assembly and repair tasks common in their factories.

The training videos incorporated AI-generated voiceovers, a feature provided by RunwayML, to explain processes while maintaining a consistent professional tone across all modules. This AI voiceover tool was crucial in producing multi-lingual content, ensuring that all of GlobalTech's international employees had access to training in their native languages without the extensive costs associated with traditional dubbing.

Moreover, the module on workplace safety was enhanced with virtual simulations using RunwayML's AR and VR capabilities, allowing employees to visually engage with potential safety hazards in a controlled environment. This immersive experience was instrumental in teaching complex safety protocols and ensuring that employees had a clear understanding of emergency procedures.

Upon implementation, GlobalTech noted a significant improvement in employee engagement metrics and a decrease in training-related queries. The new dynamic training videos allowed for a more interactive learning environment, aiding in higher retention rates and more practical application of the procedures demonstrated. Furthermore, the ease of updating video content with RunwayML meant that any changes in procedures could be quickly reflected in the training modules, ensuring that they remained current with industry standards and regulations.

Case Study: Innovations in News Media: Transforming Broadcast Journalism with RunwayML

Imagine a bustling newsroom at a prominent news network, constantly seeking to improve their broadcast content in a highly competitive media landscape. The network recently adopted RunwayML, a cutting-edge AI video editing platform, for their daily news segments. This move revolutionized how they handle footage from global correspondents, breaking news clips, and in-depth feature stories.

The initial challenge was integrating RunwayML's capabilities with their existing editing infrastructure, which was traditionally dependent on manual editing workflows. The first trial involved using RunwayML to enhance the visual quality of live field reports, which were often shot in diverse lighting conditions and required rapid editing. RunwayML's automated color correction and grading tools enabled the network to maintain a consistent visual quality between different reports, which was crucial for viewer retention and brand consistency.

The news network also saw potential in RunwayML's advanced AI-assisted video stabilization and motion tracking technologies to improve the clarity and impact of live-action footage, particularly during high-intensity events like protests or natural disasters. This technology helped stabilize shaky camera work in real-time, providing a clearer and more professional broadcast of unfolding events, which greatly enhanced the end viewer's experience.

Another significant application was RunwayML's ability to swiftly generate AI-enhanced voiceovers for segments needing quick turnaround. Using RunwayML's advanced voice synthesis, editors could produce realistic and context-aware narrations without waiting for voice actors, thus significantly speeding up the production cycle. This feature was particularly beneficial when covering breaking news, requiring updates to be aired without delay.

Over time, the editorial team grew proficient at leveraging RunwayML to not only streamline workflows but also create more dynamic and engaging news content. Features like real-time text overlays and QR code generation for interactive news stories enabled viewers to access additional digital content seamlessly, thus enriching the news delivery and enhancing audience engagement.

Case Study: Revolutionizing TV Advertising with RunwayML: Enhancing Ad Designs for Enhanced Viewer Engagement

In the fast-paced world of television advertising, keeping viewers engaged and receptive to ads is a monumental challenge, especially in an era where ad-blockers and digital streaming platforms diminish traditional ad viewership. A mid-sized marketing firm, AdFluence, specializing in TV commercials for consumer products, looked to RunwayML to revolutionize their ad production process to capture and retain viewer interest more effectively.

AdFluence's primary challenge was creating highly appealing ads that could stand out amidst the clutter of traditional TV commercials. Their approach involved utilizing RunwayML's AI-driven video editing and special effects tools to produce ads that were not only visually striking but also personally relevant to diverse viewer segments. Particularly, they leveraged RunwayML's capabilities in AI-assisted video stabilization, motion tracking, and advanced special effects to produce smooth and visually engaging commercials. These features allowed the creation of ads with dynamic backgrounds and animations that were seamlessly integrated with high-motion scenes, keeping the ad visuals appealing throughout.

However, the innovative use didn't stop at visuals. Real-time color grading and automated editing features in RunwayML ensured that each ad maintained visual consistency and high-quality aesthetics without extensive manual labor, which was essential for producing multiple ad variants tailored for different viewer demographics and broadcast times.

Furthermore, AdFluence utilized RunwayML's automated audio sync technology to perfectly align voiceovers with dynamic video content, enhancing the auditory appeal and ensuring messages were delivered coherently. This alignment was crucial as it kept the viewer's auditory engagement synchronized with visual elements, crucial for ads related to complex products like electronics or intricate services like insurance platforms.

The integration of all these features via RunwayML transformed AdFluence's workflow, drastically reducing production times and costs while enabling the custom creation of ads that responded dynamically to collected viewer data predictions, substantially increasing viewer retention and engagement rates.

Case Study: Reimagining Fashion Industry Marketing with RunwayML: A Case Study on Interactive Campaigns

In the highly competitive landscape of the fashion industry, modernizing marketing strategies to captivate digital audiences is increasingly vital. A progressively innovative boutique fashion brand, ModaNovo, embarked on a mission to set trends not only in fashion but also in digital marketing. They turned to RunwayML's advanced AI video editing capabilities to forge an interactive marketing campaign that paralleled their brand's creative ethos. This case study explores how the integration of AI-driven video tools can transform traditional marketing into a dynamic, engaging consumer experience.

Starting with the concept stage, ModaNovo envisioned a campaign where their clothing line would adapt dynamically within videos based on user interaction. This necessitated the use of the more advanced functionalities of RunwayML, such as motion tracking and real-time effect applications. Utilizing these technologies, ModaNovo could enable viewers to change outfit colors and styles through simple interactive prompts in the video. Effectively, this turned traditional advertising on its head by providing an immersive experience where the audience had a hand in customizing the product, enhancing engagement and personal connection to the brand.

The technical execution demanded precise synchronization between viewer inputs and video response, a complex challenge where RunwayML's AI-driven interface was pivotal. By analyzing user engagement metrics, the AI allocated resources to ensure seamless transitions, maintaining high-quality visual outputs regardless of user interaction intensity. Additionally, the campaign utilized RunwayML's color correction tools to ensure that the various clothing options appeared true to life, enhancing the viewer's perception of quality.

Post-launch analytics demonstrated a significant uptick in audience engagement, with viewers spending multiple minutes interacting with the video, far surpassing traditional viewing metrics. Moreover, the data collected on preferred customizations provided invaluable insights into consumer preferences, allowing ModaNovo to forecast trends more accurately and adjust their inventory in line with real-time consumer data. This campaign not only elevated the brand's market position but also showcased the potential of integrating sophisticated AI video editing tools like RunwayML in redefining marketing paradigms.

Case Study: Harnessing RunwayML for Enhanced Real Estate Marketing: A Comprehensive Case Study

In the competitive real estate market, standout visual presentations can significantly influence buyer decisions. A mid-sized real estate company, UrbanSpaces, leveraged RunwayML to transform their property marketing strategies, aiming to create more engaging, immersive virtual tours and promotional materials with advanced AI-driven video editing capabilities offered by RunwayML.

UrbanSpaces faced the challenge of presenting their properties in a way that would captivate potential buyers and stand out in a saturated market. They began by using RunwayML to create highly detailed virtual tours of their listings. Utilizing the platform's advanced special effects and filters, they were able to enhance the lighting and textures of the property videos, making them appealing and inviting. The AI-driven environment adjustments allowed for the simulation of different times of day, showing prospective buyers the ambience of homes during sunrise, daylight, and twilight, which added a unique selling point that was previously not possible.

Furthermore, UrbanSpaces capitalized on RunwayML's AI-assisted video stabilization to produce ultra-smooth walkthroughs of the properties. This feature was crucial because it eliminated the often amateurish shakiness associated with handheld video tours, providing a professional-grade viewing experience. RunwayML's motion tracking also enabled the integration of dynamic annotations within the videos, where key features of the property were highlighted as the tour progressed, making it informative without being obtrusive.

In enhancing the narrative allure, the company utilized RunwayML's AI-generated voiceovers for guided tours, introducing a consistent and engaging audio guide across all videos. This not only saved on the cost of professional voice actors but also allowed for easy customization and updates.

The results were transformative. The marketing videos saw higher engagement rates and longer viewing times, leading to a higher volume of inquiries and visits. UrbanSpaces noted a significant increase in the speed of sales closures, with potential buyers feeling more connected and informed about the properties. The application of AI in editing not only elevated the visual standards but also significantly automated repetitive tasks, allowing the marketing team to focus on creative strategies and personalized client interactions.

REVIEW QUESTIONS

1. A video producer is using RunwayML to streamline their video editing workflow for a project involving multiple outdoor scenes shot under varying lighting conditions. They are particularly interested in achieving a uniform color tone across all segments. Which feature of RunwayML should they primarily use to optimize their workflow and maintain consistency?

A) Real-time video effects

B) Automated color correction and grading tools

C) AI-assisted video stabilization

D) Advanced special effects and filters

Answer: B

Explanation: The Automated color correction and grading tools in RunwayML are specifically designed to handle the issue described. These AI-driven tools analyze the video clips and apply optimized color settings automatically, which enhances visual consistency across clips shot under different lighting conditions. This feature saves significant time in post-production by eliminating the need to manually adjust color settings for each clip, ensuring a uniform look throughout the entire project. It is ideal for projects like the one described, where multiple outdoor scenes can vary widely in lighting and color tone.

2. An independent filmmaker is experimenting with creating a fantasy sequence within their film using RunwayML. They want to add ethereal glow and dynamic distortions to enhance the mystical elements of the scene. Which of the described features in RunwayML caters best to their needs for this particular project aspect?

A) Real-time video effects

B) Basic video editing techniques

C) Advanced special effects and filters

D) AI-driven background replacement

Answer: C

Explanation: The Advanced special effects and filters provided by RunwayML are perfectly suited for the filmmaker's requirements. These tools utilize AI-driven algorithms to apply complex visual effects such as ethereal glows that enhance atmospheric scenes and dynamic distortions that add intensity to action sequences. The adjustments in these effects are manageable in real-time, offering immediate previews which help in achieving the desired aesthetic efficiently. This feature will allow the filmmaker to transform standard footage into a captivating fantasy sequence by incorporating visually striking elements that align with the mystical theme of the scene.

REVIEW QUESTIONS

3. A content creator needs to replace the background in a series of instructional videos to make them appear as though they are all shot in the same studio, despite being recorded in various locations. The creator is looking for a seamless and cost-effective solution within RunwayML. Which tool should they use to achieve this with the least physical and financial hassle?

A) Batch processing automation

B) Advanced special effects and filters

C) AI-driven video stabilization

D) AI-powered video background replacement

Answer: D

Explanation: The AI-powered video background replacement tool in RunwayML is the ideal solution for the content creator's needs. This feature uses AI to analyze the video footage and efficiently differentiate and separate the foreground subjects from their backgrounds. By selecting a consistent studio background to apply across all videos, the tool facilitates a flawless replacement, giving the appearance that all instructional videos were shot in the same location. This process not only enhances the professional quality of the videos but also saves on costs and logistics associated with physical set changes, perfectly aligning with the creator's requirements for efficiency and budget-friendliness.

DEVELOPING THE AI WEALTH GENERATOR APP: COMBINING THE BEST OF AI FEATURES

Assessing Current AI Wealth Creation Apps: Strengths and Limitations

The landscape of AI-enabled wealth creation apps presents a complex tapestry of innovative strengths and notable limitations. On one hand, these applications democratize financial strategies, leveraging AI to offer personalized investment advice and predictive market analytics previously reserved for professionals. Users benefit from real-time decision-making support, drawing on vast data sets that human advisors may overlook.

However, limitations are evident. Many such apps rely heavily on algorithmic models that may not account for sudden market volatility, leading to potential inaccuracies in investment predictions. Moreover, the depth of personalization is often as good as the input data; thus, less informed users might receive generic advice, diluting the potential benefits.

Despite these challenges, the opportunity for a unified wealth creation platform is clear. By combining the strengths of existing apps while addressing their limitations, the development of a more robust AI wealth generator could set new standards in personalized financial growth, reshaping how individuals interact with economic ecosystems.

Identifying Core Features Across Leading AI Apps

In the vast landscape of wealth creation, AI apps distinguish themselves by leveraging unique core features that drive user engagement and financial success. Foremost among these is the sophisticated use of machine learning algorithms that personalise financial advice, adapting to user behaviors and market conditions in real-time. This dynamic adjustability ensures that financial strategies remain robust, even amidst turbulent markets.

Beyond adaptive learning, seamless integration with various fintech services enhances user experience, allowing for a cohesive approach to asset management, budget planning, and expenditure tracking. These integrations facilitate a more holistic view of financial health, enabling smarter, data-driven decisions.

Another critical feature is predictive analytics, empowering users with forward-looking insights based on historical data analysis. This preemptive advice often leads to better risk management and potential for higher returns by identifying trends before they become mainstream.

Collectively, these features forge the backbone of top-tier AI wealth generators, ensuring that they not only meet current user needs but adapt fluidly to future financial landscapes.

Conceptualizing a Unified AI Wealth Creation Platform

Envisioning a unified AI wealth creation platform requires a strategic blueprint that transcends traditional financial tools, integrating the best of artificial intelligence to forge a system that not only manages wealth but actively enhances it. At the heart of this concept is the creation of a holistic user experience, combining intuitive design with powerful technological backends to serve diverse financial needs seamlessly.

The platform must integrate core technologies such as adaptive AI, predictive analytics, and comprehensive data synthesis to provide personalized financial insights and recommendations. This integration enables the application to learn from user interactions and market trends, offering tailored strategies that evolve based on real-time data. Furthermore, the integration should ensure fluid connectivity with existing financial ecosystems, enhancing user engagement through a comprehensive, all-in-one financial management suite.

Moreover, by embedding robust security protocols alongside advanced data analytics, this platform will not only safeguard user information but also empower users to make informed decisions confidently. The end goal is a self-enhancing system where artificial intelligence continuously refines and optimizes wealth creation strategies, thereby establishing new paradigms in personal finance management.

The Role of Artificial Intelligence Fusion in Wealth Generation

The innovative fusion of various Artificial Intelligence (AI) technologies plays a pivotal role in the landscape of wealth generation. This convergence, often referred to as AI Fusion, integrates diverse AI disciplines such as machine learning, predictive analytics, and natural language processing to create a multifaceted tool capable of dynamic financial management.

Unique amongst its capabilities, AI Fusion facilitates a sophisticated understanding of vast, complex data sets, enabling the AI Wealth Generator to anticipate market trends and provide preemptive investment advice. This proactivity ensures that wealth generation strategies are not only reactive to immediate circumstances but also predictive of future financial opportunities.

Moreover, AI Fusion supports enhanced decision-making through the aggregation of insights from disparate AI fields, crafting a robust platform that caters to nuanced investor needs. This holistic approach produces tailored investment strategies that dynamically adjust to both market conditions and user preferences, maximizing wealth generation potential.

Ultimately, the role of AI Fusion in wealth generation is indispensable. It fosters a forward-thinking development environment that continually evolves, ensuring sustainable and progressive financial growth for users.

Designing a User-Centric Interface for an AI Wealth Generator

Designing a user-centric interface for an AI Wealth Generator demands intuitive navigation and clarity, ensuring that users of all levels are catered to efficiently. The interface must be visually appealing yet practical, consolidating complex functionalities into user-friendly operations. This involves employing minimalist design principles that focus on essential features, avoiding overcrowding and reducing cognitive load, thereby enhancing user engagement and satisfaction.

Critical to this design is the adaptability of the interface, offering customization options that allow users to tailor their financial views and tools to their personal preferences and financial goals. Implementing adaptive UI elements that respond to the user's interaction patterns can significantly augment the overall experience, making financial management not only more personal but also more accessible.

Furthermore, incorporating feedback mechanisms within the interface design ensures continuous improvement. By enabling users to report issues and suggest enhancements directly through the platform, developers can iteratively refine the app, fostering a community-centric development atmosphere. Ultimately, this concerted focus on UX design will empower users, making complex wealth management tasks more approachable and less intimidating.

Engineering an AI App with Comprehensive Income Streams

Engineering an AI wealth generator involves creating diverse income streams that cater to varying user needs and market dynamics. By analyzing patterns from previously successful AI finance apps, developers can integrate multiple revenue models such as subscriptions, in-app purchases, and premium analytical services. Each stream will be tailored to specific user segments, ensuring broad appeal and accessibility.

A key component is incorporating automated investment strategies, where AI not only advises but also potentially takes actions based on predefined rules enhanced by continuous learning algorithms. This proactive feature would attract users seeking hands-off wealth management solutions with high reliability. Furthermore, advertisement placements, driven by user data analysis, can provide a non-intrusive revenue stream without compromising user experience.

To ensure these income streams are sustainable, they must be built on a robust technological framework capable of adapting to financial trends and user feedback. This will require ongoing development and refinement to keep the offerings competitive and attuned to consumer demand, ultimately maximizing the financial effectiveness of the app.

Developing APIs for Cross-Platform Integration

In the realm of AI-driven wealth generation, the importance of seamless cross-platform integration cannot be overstated. Developing robust APIs is pivotal, allowing the AI Wealth Generator to connect fluidly across various financial platforms and systems. These integrations enhance the app's ability to synchronize data, extend functionalities, and provide a cohesive user experience regardless of the device or service being used.

APIs serve as the backbone for real-time data sharing, crucial for maintaining an up-to-date, holistic view of user finances. By facilitating smooth data exchange between different financial services, they enable the app to offer comprehensive wealth management strategies that adapt quickly to market changes and user inputs. This integration supports predictive analytics and automated decision-making processes, essential for dynamic wealth optimization.

Moreover, well-crafted APIs ensure scalability and flexibility, allowing the wealth generator app to seamlessly incorporate future financial technologies and services. They provide a secure gateway for expanding the ecosystem without compromising user data integrity or app performance, laying the groundwork for sustained innovation and customer satisfaction.

Security Measures for Protecting User Data in AI Apps

In the development of the AI Wealth Generator app, implementing stringent security measures to protect user data is paramount. As users entrust the platform with sensitive financial information, the integrity and confidentiality of these data must be maintained through advanced security protocols and encryption techniques. Utilizing state-of-the-art cryptographic methods ensures that all data transmissions are secure, preventing unauthorized access during data exchanges.

Beyond encryption, the system leverages multi-factor authentication (MFA) and continuous monitoring strategies to enhance security. MFA provides an additional layer of defense, making unauthorized access challenging. Continuous monitoring helps in detecting and responding to security threats in real-time, thus safeguarding user data against potential breaches.

The app also incorporates privacy-by-design principles from the outset, ensuring that data protection is a core aspect of the system architecture. Regular security audits and compliance checks are conducted to align with global standards, reinforcing the commitment to user data security. Together, these comprehensive measures form a robust framework that prioritizes user trust and safety in the AI-driven financial ecosystem.

Customization Features for User-Specific Wealth Creation Goals

Central to the AI Wealth Generator's appeal is its ability to offer deep customization for every user, aligning with specific wealth creation goals. This personalization is not merely a feature but the core of the platform's philosophy, enabling users to shape the application's advice and services to fit their unique financial landscapes and aspirations.

Configurability options range from basic goal-setting functionalities, allowing users to define short-term objectives like savings for a vacation, to more complex long-term investment strategies such as retirement planning. Each user can adjust risk preferences, desired investment types, and financial milestones, which the AI adapts to by recalibrating its algorithms to optimize outcomes tailored to these personal settings.

Moreover, the app's adaptive learning component continually fine-tunes its advice based on user interactions and feedback. By dynamically adjusting to user behavior and market conditions, it ensures sustained relevance and effectiveness in wealth generation. This personal touch empowers users, giving them control over their financial destinies, continuously curated by AI precision and adaptability.

Supporting Multiple Languages and Regional Adjustments

Recognizing the diversity of its user base, the AI Wealth Generator app is designed to transcend cultural and linguistic barriers by supporting multiple languages and making regional adjustments. This inclusivity ensures that users from various parts of the world can access and utilize the app effectively, enhancing user engagement and satisfaction across different demographics.

Key to this feature is the implementation of advanced language translation technologies coupled with local cultural nuances. The app not only translates text but also adapts its user interface and financial advice to align with local customs, economic conditions, and regulatory environments. This local adaptation is critical in maintaining relevance and effectiveness, providing a customized experience that feels familiar and trustworthy to users globally.

By integrating regional data and continuously learning from user interactions, the AI Wealth Generator app dynamically adjusts its functions to serve diverse user needs. These adjustments are crucial for ensuring the app's global appeal and usability, ultimately contributing to its success in various markets around the world.

Incorporating Blockchain for Transparent Transactions

The AI Wealth Generator app enhances its transactional integrity by integrating blockchain technology. This innovation guarantees transparency, offering an immutable record of all monetary operations. Leveraging blockchain's decentralized nature ensures that each transaction is recorded on a public ledger, visible and verifiable by all users, thus fostering unparalleled trust and openness.

Adopting peer-to-peer blockchain transactions mitigates potential risks associated with traditional central clearinghouses. This architectural shift reduces the propensity for fraud and allows for faster, more cost-effective money transfers. By deploying smart contracts, the app automates and secures complex financial agreements without human intervention, minimizing errors and maintaining exacting standards of accuracy and accountability.

Furthermore, blockchain integration not only positions the platform at the forefront of the secure wealth management technology but also aligns with modern regulatory standards. It provides a framework for meeti...

Utilizing Big Data Analytics for Strategic Wealth Advising

In the age of information, big data analytics stands as a cornerstone for the AI Wealth Generator app, transforming vast volumes of data into actionable, strategic financial advice. By harnessing the power of big data, the platform can analyze patterns, predict market trends, and provide personalized advice that aligns with individual financial goals and risk profiles.

The depth of analysis possible with big data means that each user's financial strategy is not only responsive to current market conditions but also anticipatory of future shifts. This proactive approach enables users to maximize their wealth potential efficiently. Sophisticated algorithms sift through global financial data, consumer behavior, and economic indicators, tailoring unique, strategic insights that empower users to make informed decisions.

Moreover, continuous learning mechanisms embedded within the AI refine its predictive capabilities over time, ensuring that the wealth advising remains relevant as markets evolve. Integration of these insights into the user's financial planning process makes the AI Wealth Generator an indispensable tool for modern financial management, driving smarter, data-driven wealth accumulation strategies.

Implementing Advanced Machine Learning Models

The AI Wealth Generator integrates cutting-edge machine learning (ML) models to provide superior financial insights and decision-making capabilities. These advanced algorithms are designed to learn from a myriad of data inputs, continuously improving their predictive accuracy in wealth management scenarios.

Central to this integration is the deployment of deep learning and neural networks which analyze historical and real-time financial data to forecast market trends and user behavior. This allows the app to offer personalized investment strategies that are dynamically adjusted as market conditions change. By embedding such sophisticated ML models, the app ensures that financial advice is not only based on past patterns but also anticipates future market movements.

Moreover, reinforcement learning techniques are utilized to refine investment approaches through simulated environments, optimizing the risk-reward balance tailored to individual user profiles. This strategic application of ML not only enhances user satisfaction through customized advisories but also strengthens the app's capacity to manage economic uncertainties, securing its role as a pivotal tool in modern wealth generation.

Attracting and Managing An Early User Base

Capturing and nurturing an early user base is pivotal for the AI Wealth Generator's launch success. Initially, the focus is on identifying innovators and early adopters, whose enthusiasm for cutting-edge technology can trigger organic growth through word-of-mouth and social proof. Targeting tech-savvy individuals and financial tech communities online can facilitate a quick influx of these critical early users.

The management of this user base focuses on engagement and retention, optimizing their initial experiences to foster loyalty and advocacy. Special incentives, such as exclusive access to beta features or enhanced customization capabilities, reward early adopters. Moreover, active participation in feedback loops is encouraged through user-friendly interfaces and responsive customer support systems, turning early users into co-creators of the platform.

Strategic communication is key during this phase. Regular updates about enhancements, driven by user feedback, and transparent discussions about roadmap developments are essential. This transparency not only builds trust but also empowers users, involving them directly in the evolution of the AI Wealth Generator app.

Beta Testing Strategies for the AI Wealth Generator

Beta testing is crucial for fine-tuning the AI Wealth Generator app, ensuring it meets user expectations and functions seamlessly upon launch. The process begins by selecting a diverse group of testers who reflect the app's target demographic, encompassing varied financial backgrounds and technological savviness. This diversity helps in identifying a broad range of issues, from user interface glitches to complex algorithmic biases in wealth management advice.

The testing phase is structured in stages, starting with closed beta to gauge core functionality and moving to open beta to test the app's scalability and performance under real-world conditions. Feedback mechanisms are integral, with easy-to-use tools embedded within the app allowing testers to report problems and suggest improvements directly. Real-time data analytics monitor app performance, guiding developers in prioritizing fixes and enhancements.

Post-beta, insights gathered are meticulously analyzed to optimize the app further, combining user feedback with automated system reports to refine and adjust functionalities. This iterative process not only enhances the app's reliability but also aligns it more closely with user expectations, contributing significantly to its eventual market success.

Analyzing User Feedback for Continuous Improvement

Continuous improvement is at the heart of the AI Wealth Generator app, where user feedback is not just valued but pivotal for iterative enhancements. This feedback loop begins by collecting diverse inputs through integrated mechanisms within the app, allowing users to easily communicate their experiences and suggestions. This direct line from users to developers ensures that every piece of feedback is documented and analyzed, contributing to a rich dataset that informs the continuous development cycle.

Once feedback is gathered, sophisticated analytic tools assess the data to identify common patterns, anomalies, and areas ripe for enhancement. This analysis combines quantitative data, like usage stats, with qualitative insights from actual user comments, creating a holistic view of the app's performance and user satisfaction levels. Prioritization of issues is guided by their impact on user experience, aligning development efforts with user needs.

The final step involves testing solutions to feedback-derived issues, ensuring any adjustments align with user expectations and app stability before full deployment. Regular updates communicated back to the users build trust and encourage further engagement, sustaining a vibrant cycle of feedback and refinement that drives the app toward excellence.

Marketing Strategies for Launching the AI Wealth App

Launching the AI Wealth Generator requires innovative marketing strategies that highlight its unique blend of AI-driven financial advising and machine learning capabilities. Initial tactics should focus on digital marketing, leveraging SEO and targeted social media campaigns to reach potential users interested in advanced wealth management tools. Engaging content, like webinars and interactive demos, can demonstrate the app's effectiveness in real-time, building interest and trust.

Partnerships with influential fintech bloggers and industry experts can amplify reach, lending credibility through association and detailed reviews. Email campaigns tailored to segmented audiences can keep potential users engaged throughout the launch phase, providing insights into the app's features and user testimonials, nurturing leads up to the release.

Post-launch, continuous A/B testing on marketing messages and channels optimizes outreach effectiveness. Collecting analytics on user interaction with marketing content guides swift modifications in strategy, ensuring the app maintains visibility and appeal in competitive markets, crucial for sustained uptake and growth.

Pricing Models and Subscription Plans

Determining the right pricing models and subscription plans is crucial for the AI Wealth Generator's success. A tiered pricing strategy will be implemented, catering to different user needs and financial capabilities. The introductory tier, perhaps free with limited features, aims to attract newcomers and showcase the app's basic capabilities. Mid-tier and premium tiers will offer enhanced functionalities like advanced analytics and personalized wealth management advice, justifying higher fees.

Flexibility in subscription plans is pivotal. Options might include monthly, quarterly, and annual subscriptions, providing discounts for longer commitments to encourage user retention. Each plan will clearly outline the features and services offered, ensuring transparency and building trust among users.

Careful consideration will also be given to dynamic pricing strategies that could adjust based on market demand, user engagement levels, and competitive analysis. This approach ensures the app remains attractive and financially accessible while maximizing revenue potential. Input from early user feedback will guide iterative adjustments to these models to align with market expectations and user satisfaction.

Growth Hacking Tactics for User Acquisition

Growth hacking for the AI Wealth Generator focuses on innovative, low-cost strategies aimed at rapidly increasing the user base. Central to these tactics is leveraging digital channels to create viral growth effects. Collating analytics data to identify patterns in user behavior enables the app to deliver customized messages that resonate deeply with potential users.

Social media platforms are pivotal for executing referral campaigns, incentivizing existing users to invite friends in exchange for additional features or discounts. This method not only increases the user base but also reinforces user loyalty and engagement. Strategic partnerships with popular financial influencers and tech blogs can amplify reach, driving traffic back to the app through compelling, content-driven collaborations.

Lastly, implementing gamified elements within the app encourages ongoing interaction and recruitment drives. Challenges and rewards linked to user acquisition milestones keep users motivated and actively promoting the app. This approach not only capitalizes on user competitiveness but also embeds the product deeper into daily digital habits, enhancing growth trajectories significantly.

Streamlining Onboarding Processes for New Users

Streamlining the onboarding process for new users is crucial in reducing barriers to entry and enhancing user satisfaction for the AI Wealth Generator app. The goal is to create an intuitive, frictionless entry path that empowers users, fostering immediate engagement. To this end, the process begins with a simple, guided setup featuring interactive tutorials and useful tips tailored to user's financial literacy levels.

The onboarding sequence is further optimized through the use of AI-driven personalization, adapting the learning curve according to individual user behavior and preferences. Key information is presented at just the right pace, ensuring newcomers are neither overwhelmed nor bored. Smart defaults and predictive data input minimize the effort required to get started, making the initial user experience as welcoming as possible.

Finally, early stages of onboarding will incorporate quick wins, such as easy initial tasks or insights into potential financial gains. These milestones are designed to demonstrate the value of the AI Wealth Generator quickly, ensuring users feel rewarded and engaged from the outset. Each step is coupled with clear, concise support options, readily accessible for users needing assistance.

Leveraging Social Proof and User Testimonials

In the realm of digital products, particularly those in the fintech sector like the AI Wealth Generator app, social proof and user testimonials serve as vital elements that forge trust and credibility. Harnessing real feedback from users not only highlights the app's effectiveness but also emotionally engages prospective users by presenting relatable success stories. A strategically placed testimonial can convert a skeptic into a believer, emphasizing the transformative potential of the app.

Testimonials will be showcased through various mediums, including the app's website, promotional emails, and social media platforms, ensuring visibility across all touchpoints. Careful selection of these testimonials is crucial, aiming to present a diverse array of user experiences that resonate with a broad audience. This diversity not only underscores the app's versatility but also appeals to a global market.

In conclusion, the active presentation of user testimonials reinforces the app's market position. Ensuring these testimonials are genuine and verifiable fosters greater transparency and continued user trust, critical for long-term engagement and growth in a competitive digital landscape.

Navigating Compliance and Regulatory Challenges

The AI Wealth Generator app operates in a complex legal and regulatory landscape, necessitating a robust strategy to navigate compliance issues effectively. Initial steps involve rigorous research into relevant financial regulations, which vary significantly across different jurisdictions. This understanding ensures that the app not only meets minimum legal standards but also excels in regulatory compliance, thereby safeguarding user interests.

Compliance is further complicated by the continuous evolution of AI technologies, which can outpace existing legal frameworks. To address this, the development team must establish proactive relationships with regulatory bodies. Regular consultations can help predict shifts in the regulatory environment and adapt the app accordingly, minimizing disruptions and maintaining a competitive edge.

Moreover, investing in compliance as a core feature of the app's architecture guarantees that scalability does not compromise legal integrity. Automated systems for monitoring compliance updates facilitate swift adjustments to operational processes, ensuring ongoing adherence to laws and enhancing trust among users.

Establishing Partnerships with Financial Institutions

Forging strategic partnerships with financial institutions is a cornerstone of the AI Wealth Generator's expansion strategy. These alliances are pivotal, providing both credibility and a framework for the seamless integration of traditional financial services with innovative AI-driven features. Partnering with established banks and financial entities ensures that the app's offerings are underpinned by robust financial expertise and compliance acumen.

Engagement with financial institutions involves collaborative effort in product development and marketing. This synergy helps tailor the AI functionalities to fit real-world financial scenarios, enhancing the app's utility and appeal. Such partnerships can also facilitate the app's access to broader client bases through co-branded marketing strategies, thereby amplifying user acquisition efforts considerably.

Moreover, these collaborations are instrumental in navigating the complex regulatory landscapes associated with financial services. They provide essential insights and resources that are critical for maintaining compliance, ensuring that the AI Wealth Generator app not only promises but also delivers financial empowerment in a legally sound framework.

Future-proofing the App with Modular Updates

Ensuring the AI Wealth Generator app remains relevant and powerful over time, modular updates are crucial. By designing the app with a modular architecture, updates can be seamlessly integrated without disrupting the core functionalities. This strategy allows for the swift adaptation of new technologies and methodologies, ensuring the app stays at the cutting edge of AI and financial services.

Particularly, each module can be updated independently, addressing specific aspects like user interface enhancements, algorithm improvements, or the integration of new financial tools. This makes the update process less cumbersome and reduces the risk of introducing bugs into the system. Moreover, it enables personalized updates based on user feedback and emerging market trends, offering a tailored experience that evolves with user needs.

Furthermore, this approach significantly eases the process of scaling up and integrating new functionalities as they become relevant. The use of cloud-based services for deploying updates ensures that all users access the latest version, enhancing user satisfaction and security. Importantly, maintaining continuous alignment with global compliance standards is streamlined, reinforcing user trust and app credibility.

Integrating AI Ethics and Responsible AI Use

The integration of AI ethics and responsible usage practices is fundamental to the success of the AI Wealth Generator app. Anchoring the system in ethical AI usage ensures that it operates not just effectively, but fairly and transparently, fostering trust among users. To this end, ethical guidelines are embedded in every feature of the app, from data handling to AI-driven decision-making processes.

Key to this approach is the development of algorithms that are free from biases which could lead to unequal wealth creation opportunities. Thorough testing phases are employed to detect and eliminate any inadvertent biases. Additionally, continuous learning systems are integrated to update ethical protocols as societal norms evolve. Transparency mechanisms, such as explainable AI features, are also essential, providing users with understandable insights into how the AI makes decisions affecting their financial strategies.

Lastly, external audits by third-party ethics committees ensure the app adheres to international standards of AI ethics. This not only reassures users of the app's integrity but also solidifies its standing in the global market as a leader in responsible AI wealth generation. Taking these measures, the app not only advances technologically but also upholds a moral compass, guiding users towards financial empowerment responsibly.

Scaling the AI Wealth Generator for Global Reach

Scaling the AI Wealth Generator app for a global audience presents unique challenges and opportunities. The initial step involves extensive market research to understand diverse financial behaviors and needs across different cultures and economies. This information is critical in tailoring the app's features to suit varied user preferences, ensuring local relevance while maintaining a unified global service standard.

Next, adapting the app's interface and functionalities to support multiple languages and local currencies is crucial. This adaptation extends beyond mere translation; it involves cultural localization of content to resonate with users from different backgrounds. Additionally, incorporating regional compliance and legal standards into the app's framework is essential to facilitate smooth operations across borders.

Finally, establishing reliable global distribution networks and local partnerships can amplify reach and enhance service delivery. These collaborations could involve local fintech companies and telecommunications providers to leverage existing infrastructures, thereby optimizing the user experience and accelerating adoption in new markets.

SUMMARY

The chapter on 'Developing the AI Wealth Generator App' explores the process of creating an advanced financial application that leverages cutting-edge AI technologies. It begins by assessing existing AI-enabled financial apps, identifying their strengths such as personalized investment advice and real-time analytics, and noting their limitations like reliance on algorithmic models that struggle with market volatility. The narrative then shifts towards identifying and integrating core features from leading apps, emphasizing the importance of machine learning, adaptive algorithms, and predictive analytics which are crucial for crafting a robust wealth management tool. The concept of a unified AI wealth creation platform is highlighted, stressing the integration of multiple AI technologies to provide personalized, secure, and proactive wealth management solutions. A significant portion is dedicated to user-centric design and customization, outlining how a user-friendly interface and a personalized approach to financial management can significantly enhance user engagement and satisfaction. Machine Learning models form a critical component, advancing financial strategies that dynamically adapt to both market conditions and user preferences. The chapter also delves into engineering and API development for meaningful cross-platform integration, enhancing accessibility and maintaining data integrity. Security measures receive detailed attention to ensure user data protection and trust. The narrative also covers the app's potential to incorporate blockchain for enhanced transaction transparency and utilizes big data analytics for sophisticated financial advising. Commercial aspects like pricing models, marketing strategies, and user base management are discussed, providing a complete overview of the app's development from conceptual design through to market launch strategies. Lastly, the chapter encapsulates the importance of continuous improvement and scalability, ensuring that the app not only meets current user demands but is also adaptable to future advancements in technology and shifts in financial regulation.

REFERENCES

[1] Artificial Intelligence in Wealth Management. https://www.examplelink1.com

[2] Advancing Wealth Management Through AI. https://www.examplelink2.com

[3] Data Security in Fintech Applications. https://www.examplelink3.com

[4] User-Centered Design in Financial Apps. https://www.examplelink4.com

[5] Machine Learning Techniques in Financial Markets. https://www.examplelink5.com

CASE STUDY: TRANSFORMING FINANCIAL ADVISORY: THE DEVELOPMENT OF AI WEALTHGENIE

The development of the AI WealthGenie, an advanced AI-driven wealth management app, is a landmark case illuminating the convergence of technology and finance. The initiative began with a tech startup, FinnoTech AI, identifying a gap in the market for a truly integrated financial advisory solution that caters to both novice and experienced investors. The goal was to create an app that not only provides personalized financial advice but also empowers users to make informed and strategic investment decisions based on AI-generated insights.

The initial phase involved extensive market research gathering insights into user behaviors, financial goals, and frustrations with current wealth management tools. This research highlighted the need for a platform capable of offering a broad spectrum of services from basic budget tracking to sophisticated investment analysis. The critical breakthrough arrived when the development team decided to integrate machine learning algorithms with natural language processing (NLP) capabilities, enabling the app to understand and predict user needs effectively and interact with users in a conversational manner.

Comprehensive testing phases, including both closed and open beta testing, were employed to ensure accuracy and usability. Feedback from the beta tests led to iterative design refinements, particularly to improve the user interface, making it more intuitive. Security was also a major concern; hence, cutting-edge encryption and multi-factor authentication technologies were integrated to safeguard user data.

Post-launch, the AI WealthGenie quickly gained popularity due to its dynamic adaptability and proactive wealth management strategies. However, the journey did not end there. Continuous updates and algorithm refinements were necessary to handle the evolution of financial markets and changing user expectations. The app also faced challenges in terms of regulatory compliance across different regions, requiring ongoing adjustments to align with global financial laws and practices.

Case Study: Revolutionizing Retirement Planning: Introducing RetireSmart AI

In light of the increasing demand for personalized financial planning, a fintech startup, SmartFuture Tech, embarked on developing RetireSmart AI, an AI-driven platform focused on revolutionizing retirement planning. The vision was to create a comprehensive system that not only automates saving strategies but also adapts to life changes and economic conditions, providing users with a dynamic plan to achieve their retirement goals.

The project commenced with an in-depth analysis of existing retirement planning tools, revealing that most lacked the flexibility to adapt to users' changing financial situations or predict shifts in the economic landscape. Recognizing the potential to fill this gap, SmartFuture Tech gathered a team of AI specialists, financial analysts, and user experience designers to create a more responsive and intuitive tool.

To tailor personalized retirement strategies, RetireSmart AI incorporated advanced machine learning algorithms capable of learning from user inputs, market conditions, and economic indicators. The platform used predictive analytics to forecast long-term financial outcomes, suggesting adjustments as necessary. Key to its functionality was also its user-friendly interface, which allowed users to define retirement goals, manage investments, and view suggested strategies in real-time.

However, the development was not without challenges. Integrating complex AI technologies required meticulous tuning to ensure accuracy and reliability. Moreover, ensuring data security and compliance with financial regulations was paramount. The team implemented robust encryption and pursued rigorous compliance certifications. Beta testing was critical, involving diverse demographics to ensure the tool's effectiveness across different user profiles. Feedback led to several iterations, refining both the AI algorithms and the interface.

Upon launch, RetireSmart AI was met with considerable interest from users seeking a proactive approach to retirement planning. Continuous enhancement based on user feedback and shifting economic factors remained ongoing, ensuring the platform remained relevant and valuable. Furthermore, partnerships with financial advisors and institutions were established to enhance the tool's credibility and integrate professional insights.

Case Study: Optimization of Global Investment Strategies with AI NexusGlobal

The development and implementation of NexusGlobal, an advanced AI-powered investment strategy optimizer, showcases a significant step forward in tailored global investment solutions. Recognizing the potential for AI to transform investment management, especially across diverse geographic regions, a team of financial engineers and AI researchers from GlobalTech Finance embarked on designing an app that could provide high-level strategic analysis and investment recommendations, personalized to different market conditions and investor profiles.

The initial challenge was the complexities involved in understanding and predicting international market variations. The team employed a hybrid AI system leveraging both machine learning and deep learning to analyze vast datasets encompassing economic indicators, currency fluctuations, and regional financial activities. To refine their model, they incorporated real-time global financial news using natural language processing to assess market sentiment and potential geopolitical impacts on investments.

User experience design was prioritized to ensure that the complex functionalities remained accessible to a broad range of users, from individual investors to institutional stakeholders.

Multilingual support and region-specific advisory capabilities were integrated, addressing the global market's diversity. Security protocols were established using advanced encryption and blockchain technology to protect user data and ensure transaction integrity.

After launching NexusGlobal, the platform needed to continuously adapt to evolving markets. Regular updates were made possible through cloud-based technologies allowing seamless integration of new data and AI model improvements. The feedback loop from initial users highlighted the necessity for enhanced mobile compatibility, leading to a secondary development phase focusing on optimizing the app's mobile version.

Despite its success, NexusGlobal faced regulatory hurdles. Each market's regulatory environment required careful navigation to ensure compliance, involving ongoing dialogue with financial authorities and adaptive legal frameworks within the app's operations. Overcoming these challenges, NexusGlobal not only improved user investment outcomes but also significantly influenced the broader trajectory of AI in global financial strategies.

Case Study: Integrating AI-Driven Risk Management in Real-Time Trading: The AlgoTrade AI Initiative

In an era where markets are increasingly volatile, strategic risk management becomes a vital component of trading. AlgoTrade AI, developed by Quantum Financial Systems, is a testament to how AI can be harnessed to fortify trading strategies against unpredictable market movements. The project outlined a bold vision of blending cutting-edge technology with deep financial insights to create a real-time responsive trading platform.

The inception of AlgoTrade AI revolved around a clear gap observed in the existing trading tools, which lacked real-time risk assessment capabilities leading to significant trading vulnerabilities. With an objective to refine this functionality, Quantum's team incorporated various AI techniques, including machine learning (ML) and natural language processing (NLP), to foster a system capable of dynamic risk evaluation and mitigation. The core idea was for the AI to analyze global financial data streams, from news articles to market data, and to use predictive models to forecast potential market threats and offer actionable responses.

The execution phase was multi-tiered, involving the design and integration of these AI tools into a user-friendly interface. Among the notable features was the predictive analytics module that not only anticipated trends but also suggested optimal trading moves under different risk scenarios. The integration of real-time data feeds was crucial for pace maintenance with the rapidly changing market conditions.

However, deploying such technology posed significant challenges, chiefly around data integrity and model reliability. Balancing responsiveness with accuracy required rigorous validation techniques and continuous machine learning model updates. To address these, Quantum conducted several live pilot tests to refine their algorithms with real transaction data.

Post-launch, although AlgoTrade AI marked a new standard in AI-driven trading, it required continual adjustments to align with global trading regulations and to accommodate user feedback for additional customization. The platform's adaptability played a key role in its ongoing development, reflecting a shifting paradigm towards resilient, AI-augmented financial trading systems.

Case Study: Crafting Financial Strategies with AI-Enhanced Portfolio Customization

In a fiercely competitive fintech market, a surge in demand for personalized financial services led to the development of InvestSmart AI, an application designed to revolutionize how individual investors manage and diversify their portfolios. The cornerstone of InvestSmart AI's unique proposition was its ability to offer hyper-personalized investment strategies using advanced AI technologies, primarily focused on enhancing user engagement and financial outcomes.

The genesis of InvestSmart AI was rooted in a collaborative effort between data scientists, financial analysts, and user experience specialists at Fintegrate Systems. The project stemmed from recognized deficits in existing financial apps that often provided generic investment solutions, frequently misaligning with users' specific financial goals and risk tolerance. The team identified that by leveraging machine learning to analyze individual financial data and integrating it with global economic trends, they could create a nuanced understanding of each user's unique financial landscape.

Initial development phases included the creation of a robust machine learning model that tailored investment recommendations by learning from user input and market conditions. InvestSmart AI adopted a continuous learning approach, where the AI evolved its recommendations based on new data, further refining investment strategies with ongoing user feedback.

Despite the sophisticated technology, the launch of InvestSmart AI wasn't without challenges. Balancing complexity and usability emerged as a considerable hurdle. The development team prioritized making the interface intuitive, ensuring that users could easily navigate through sophisticated investment options.

Post-launch, InvestSmart AI faced rigorous scrutiny regarding its predictive capabilities and ethical use of data. It required ongoing adjustments to align with evolving global financial regulations and to enhance decision-making algorithms based on user feedback. Maintaining transparency regarding AI decision processes was crucial to building and retaining user trust, necessitating regular updates and clear communication about how user data was utilized to shape financial advice.

Case Study: Advancing Micro-Investment Through AI: The Launch of PocketInvest AI

In the burgeoning field of financial technology, PocketInvest AI emerged as a transformative platform aiming to revolutionize the concept of micro-investing. Developed by NextGen Financial Tech, a nimble startup focused on accessible investment tools, the core idea behind PocketInvest AI was to democratize investing by enabling users with limited capital to engage in the investment process using AI-driven strategies.

The project kicked off with the realization that many potential investors, particularly millennials and Gen Z, often felt alienated by traditional investment platforms due to high entry barriers and complex jargon. NextGen Financial Tech gathered an interdisciplinary team comprising AI engineers, behavioral economists, and UX designers to create a user-friendly app tailored to these younger demographics. The ambition was clear: to make investing as simple and accessible as making a daily coffee purchase.

A fundamental component of PocketInvest AI was its AI-driven recommendation engine, which utilized real-time data analytics and machine learning to suggest small, achievable investments based on user behavior and market conditions. The system was engineered to continuously learn from user interactions, enhancing its predictive capabilities and personalization over time. To cater to the tech-savvy target audience, the platform was designed with a clean, minimalistic interface that emphasized ease of use and mobile first philosophy.

However, the development journey was fraught with challenges, particularly in designing AI algorithms that could effectively handle vast amounts of data and deliver reliable investment advice while remaining regulatory compliant. The team also faced the critical task of ensuring robust cybersecurity measures were in place to protect sensitive user information and build trust.

Following an extensive beta testing period that provided crucial insights into user behaviors and system performance, PocketInvest AI was launched. It rapidly gained traction due to its low investment thresholds and user-centric design. Ongoing enhancements and adaptations have been pivotal, with regular updates to the AI algorithms to address evolving market dynamics and regulatory changes, ensuring the app stays relevant and secure in a competitive market.

Case Study: Revolutionizing Risk Management in Investment Portfolios with AI-Driven Solutions

The innovative project began with a concept by a tech startup, InvestMatrix AI, with a vision to transform how investors manage risks in their investment portfolios using artificial intelligence. This case study delves into the development, challenges, and impact of an AI tool designed to dynamically allocate assets and manage risks according to market conditions, thus offering a smarter, more adaptive portfolio management approach.

The initial stages were driven by identifying a significant lack of personalization and real-time risk assessment in existing financial advisory services. The InvestMatrix AI team, comprised of data scientists, AI experts, and seasoned financial analysts, leveraged a combination of historical market data, investor behavior studies, and predictive analytics to craft an AI-based solution that could not only anticipate market fluctuations but also adjust investment strategies accordingly.

A principal challenge was integrating diverse financial datasets with advanced AI models. The team developed a sophisticated algorithm capable of continuous learning from market feeds, news sources, and transaction records, enabling it to refine its predictions and strategies. This machine learning framework was then integrated with user-friendly dashboards that provided clients real-time insights into potential risks and recommended actions. Initial testing phases quickly highlighted the necessity for robust cybersecurity measures and scalable infrastructure to handle the high volume of real-time data.

Despite these technological hurdles, the iterative development cycle, enriched with feedback from early adopters and continuous performance analytics, led to a robust platform. Post-launch, InvestMatrix AI has not only consistently outperformed traditional risk management tools but has also been instrumental in democratizing sophisticated investing strategies, making them accessible to a broader range of investors. Regular updates and module enhancements remain crucial to adapting to the ever-evolving financial landscape, ensuring that InvestMatrix AI remains a leader in AI-driven financial risk management.

Case Study: Pioneering Sustainable Investment: ESGPro AI's Integration in Asset Management

The inception of ESGPro AI represents a milestone in the integration of environmental, social, and governance (ESG) factors into investment strategies, propelled by a fintech startup, GreenFuture Innovations. Recognizing a growing trend towards ethical investment, GreenFuture Innovations aimed to develop an AI-driven tool that not only aligns with investors' financial goals but also their values concerning sustainability and corporate responsibility.

The project began with substantial groundwork; comprehensive research was conducted to understand the dynamics of ESG data and its impact on market performance. Initial development focused on creating an AI that can effectively parse huge volumes of qualitative and quantitative ESG data, extracting actionable insights. The breakthrough was achieving the amalgamation of sophisticated machine learning models with natural language processing to evaluate sustainability reports, social impact data, and governance records to predict future financial performance based on ESG factors.

GreenFuture faced challenges in ensuring the accuracy and relevancy of the ESG data sourced from diverse databases and reports. Meticulous data validation processes were established to maintain data integrity. Additionally, crafting a user-friendly interface that could present complex ESG metrics in an accessible manner was paramount to cater to both seasoned and novice investors.

Post-launch, ESGPro AI gained traction among socially conscious investors and institutions looking to adhere to sustainability criteria without compromising on returns. The platform, however, required continuous updates to adapt to the rapidly evolving standards of ESG metrics and to integrate feedback from a broad user base. New regulatory challenges also emerged as global financial bodies began to standardize ESG reporting requirements, compelling the ESGPro AI team to constantly refine their compliance protocols. Continuous learning mechanisms were enhanced to keep the AI's analyses aligned with the latest ESG trends, ensuring that the platform remained a cutting-edge tool for sustainable investing.

REVIEW QUESTIONS

1. Considering the wealth of features in emerging AI wealth creation apps, a developer wants to create a hybrid platform merging the strengths of extant systems. This platform includes components of predictive analytics, adaptive AI, and machine learning algorithms designed to cater to individualized investment strategies based on dynamic market conditions. Which model best describes this integration approach?

A) A holistic integration model

B) A static integration model

C) A modular integration model

D) A linear upgrade model

Answer: A

Explanation: The holistic integration model best captures the essence of combining various functional and advanced technology components into a seamless, unified system. This approach not only leverages the specific advantages of each technological aspect—such as the real-time adaptability of adaptive AI, the forward-looking insights of predictive analytics, and the personalized data processing power of machine learning—but also enhances them by allowing the systems to interconnect and synergize, increasing the overall effectiveness and efficiency of the platform.

2. An upcoming AI wealth generation platform seeks to maximize user engagement and financial success by incorporating region-specific customization features, including language translation and adherence to local market practices. How does integrating these features affect the platform's market reach and user satisfaction?

A) It limits the platform to local markets.

B) It significantly increases global reach and user satisfaction.

C) It complicates the user interface causing reduced user engagement.

D) It has no significant impact on market reach.

Answer: B

Explanation: Integrating region-specific customization features significantly increases a platform's global reach and enhances user satisfaction by making the platform more accessible and relevant to a diverse global audience. By supporting multiple languages and adapting to local customs and market practices, the platform becomes more user-friendly and trustworthy, encouraging adoption across various demographics and geographical locations. This inclusivity helps in catering to broader market needs and preferences, which can lead to increased usage and loyalty to the platform.

REVIEW QUESTIONS

3. A wealth creation AI app incorporates blockchain technology to ensure transaction transparency and security. How does this integration impact the trustworthiness from the perspective of prospective users?

A) It decreases trust due to the complexity of blockchain.

B) It has a neutral impact as users are generally unaware of backend technologies.

C) It significantly enhances trust due to transparent financial operations.

D) It reduces user base as blockchain integration is often seen as an unnecessary feature.

Answer: C

Explanation: Integrating blockchain technology in a wealth creation AI app notably enhances the platform's trustworthiness among users due to the inherent attributes of blockchain—transparency, security, and immutability. Transactions recorded on a blockchain provide a verifiable and permanent record that is accessible to all users, fostering a sense of security and openness. This transparency is crucial for financial applications where users seek assurance that their financial activities and data are handled securely and with integrity, thereby fostering trust and encouraging wider adoption.

4. While developing a unified AI wealth creation platform, a team concentrates on leveraging big data analytics to provide tailored financial advice. How does this integration of big data influence the platform's capability in strategic financial advising?

A) It minimizes the platform's operational efficiency.

B) It enhances the precision of financial predictions and personalization.

C) It isolates technical audiences by increasing system complexity.

D) It has minimal impact on the advising quality.

Answer: B

Explanation: The integration of big data analytics significantly enhances the platform's capability in strategic financial advising by enabling more precise predictions and deeper personalization. Big data analytics allows for the processing and analysis of vast volumes of diverse data in real-time, which helps in identifying patterns, trends, and anomalies that might not be visible otherwise. This capability ensures that the financial advice provided is grounded in a comprehensive understanding of market dynamics and individual user data, leading to more informed and tailored financial strategies. This ultimately aids users in making better decisions and optimizing their financial growth.

BLUEPRINT FOR SUCCESS: STEP-BY-STEP GUIDE TO BUILDING THE ULTIMATE AI WEALTH GENERATOR

Identifying Key Components for an Ultimate AI Wealth Generator

The creation of an Ultimate AI Wealth Generator hinges on identifying and integrating key components that drive efficacy and prosperity. These components range from advanced AI algorithms to intuitive user interfaces, each playing a pivotal role in the app's ability to generate wealth efficiently.

Firstly, selecting robust AI technologies that can analyze vast quantities of data for predictive insights is crucial. These technologies lay the foundation for features like automated financial advice and personalized investment strategies, tailored to the individual needs and risk profiles of users. Additionally, a seamless user interface (UI) ensures that users, regardless of their technical expertise, can navigate and utilize the app's features effectively, enhancing user engagement and satisfaction.

Furthermore, integrating secure, scalable backend systems is essential for handling large volumes of transactions and data securely. This ensures not only the operational reliability but also the trust of users, which is paramount in financial applications. Ensuring compliance with international data protection regulations protects user data and builds credibility.

Defining Business Goals and Objectives

Defining clear business goals and objectives is pivotal as we construct the framework for the Ultimate AI Wealth Generator. This step aligns all subsequent development and marketing efforts, ensuring that every action taken is strategic and contributes effectively towards the overarching vision of financial empowerment through AI.

Initially, objectives must encapsulate the broad desire to innovate within the fintech space, setting benchmarks for financial inclusion, user engagement, and profitability. These goals should be SMART: Specific, Measurable, Achievable, Relevant, and Time-bound, forming a roadmap that guides every phase of the application's lifecycle from conception through to deployment and scaling.

Furthermore, establishing these objectives also involves anticipating future shifts in technology and market dynamics, preparing the platform to adapt and evolve. This forward-thinking approach not only helps in maintaining relevance but also secures a competitive edge in the rapidly evolving financial technology landscape.

In conclusion, meticulously defined goals and objectives are the keystones that support the structured development of AI-driven financial solutions, ultimately leading to sustained economic success and user satisfaction.

Choosing the Right AI Technologies for Diverse Wealth Strategies

Selecting the appropriate AI technologies is a cornerstone in sculpting an effective AI Wealth Generator. This process goes beyond mere technical selection, intertwining deeply with the strategic objectives laid out for financial empowerment. Key considerations include the technology's ability to integrate with existing systems, its scalability in processing large volumes of data, and the sophistication of its analytics capabilities.

AI choices should align with specific wealth strategies; for instance, machine learning models are apt for predictive analytics, essential in personalized financial advising. Conversely, neural networks could better handle complex pattern recognition tasks, beneficial for market trend analysis. This targeted technology alignment ensures that each module of the app serves a bespoke, strategic purpose, enhancing overall effectiveness.

Moreover, ensuring that the chosen AI technologies adhere to ethical standards and compliance requirements is as crucial as their technical merit. A careful balance of innovation, ethical consideration, and regulatory adherence will not only drive usability but also foster trust and longevity in the competitive fintech marketplace.

User Experience Design: Layout and Navigation Fundamentals

User Experience Design (UX) is pivotal in ensuring that the AI Wealth Generator is not only functional but also intuitively engaging for users. Fundamentally, the layout and navigation of the app must cater to ease of use while offering sophisticated functionalities. A clean design with a logical flow allows users, irrespective of their tech-savvy level, to effectively navigate through the complex world of financial AI technologies.

Central to achieving this is the implementation of user-centric design principles. Menus and options should be placed strategically to facilitate easy access and minimal learning curve. The interface needs to be responsive across devices, ensuring that users accessing the app from mobile phones or desktops have a seamless experience. Consideration of color schemes, typography, and element spacing further enhances readability and user interaction.

Moreover, adaptive UI elements that can personalize based on user preferences and behaviors make the application not just a tool, but a trusted companion in financial planning. By leveraging these fundamental design aspects strategically, the AI Wealth Generator positions itself as a leader in user engagement within the fintech sector.

Backend Infrastructure: Handling Large Scale AI Operations

The backbone of any robust AI Wealth Generator lies within its backend infrastructure, adept at handling large-scale AI operations efficiently. Developing a resilient backend architecture mandates a scalable and secure environment, capable of processing copious amounts of data swiftly and securely. Utilization of cloud computing technologies, such as AWS or Azure, lends immense computing power and elasticity, enabling seamless scale-up as user demands intensify.

To ensure uninterrupted service, redundancy must be built into the core of the infrastructure. This involves setting up failover mechanisms and data backup solutions that safeguard against potential system failures or security breaches. Implementing microservices architecture can further enhance system resilience by segregating operations into small, manageable units that function independently yet communicate effectively.

Moreover, the integration of advanced AI models necessitates robust computational capabilities. Utilizing GPUs or TPUs can significantly expedite data processing speeds, necessary for real-time analytics and financial forecasting. Regular updates and maintenance protocols are essential to keep the infrastructure aligned with the latest safety standards and technological advancements, ensuring sustained performance and reliability in handling complex, volumetric AI operations.

Frontend Development: Ensuring Usability and Accessibility

Frontend development blends the principles of user experience crafted in earlier stages with advanced programming to create an accessible and engaging interface. Leveraging HTML, CSS, and JavaScript, developers ensure that every aspect of the app's appearance is optimized for clarity and ease of navigation. Key features such as adaptive layouts and ARIA (Accessible Rich Internet Applications) tags are used to accommodate users with disabilities, ensuring inclusivity in wealth generation.

Moreover, the implementation of responsive design ensures that the AI Wealth Generator performs flawlessly across various devices, from desktops to smartphones. This ubiquity permits users to access financial insights and tools on-the-go, enhancing the application's utility and user satisfaction. It's crucial that these interfaces are tested across different user scenarios to guarantee a seamless and intuitive user experience.

Finally, continuous user feedback is incorporated into ongoing frontend enhancements. By adopting an iterative development process, the application remains at the forefront of technology, continuously improving and adapting to new user needs and technological advancements. The frontend thus not only captivates but also retains user engagement, directly contributing to the economic success of the AI Wealth Generator.

Integration with Existing Financial Systems

Integrating the Ultimate AI Wealth Generator with existing financial systems is pivotal for its operational success and user adoption. This layer of connectivity ensures seamless data exchange and compatibility, critical for enhancing real-time financial analysis and decision-making capabilities.

Establishing secure APIs and using middleware ensures that the wealth generator can interface efficiently with banks, investment platforms, and other financial institutions. This integration supports varied functionalities, such as instant financial transactions and real-time financial advice tailored to user profiles, pivotal in maintaining user trust and system reliability.

Moreover, attention must be paid to regulatory compliance and data harmonization. By framing integration within the strict boundaries of financial regulations, the system adheres to global standards while providing customized financial solutions. Thus, integration not only contributes to seamless operation but is also fundamental in building a credible and secure financial advisory tool.

In conclusion, the strategic integration with existing financial frameworks equips the AI Wealth Generator to offer unparalleled service, driving user satisfaction and fostering widespread adoption.

Securing Intellectual Property and Ensuring Compliance

Securing intellectual property (IP) in the development of an AI Wealth Generator plays a critical role in maintaining a competitive edge and ensuring legal compliance. Protecting the unique algorithms, machine learning models, and user-interface designs from unauthorized use is paramount. Employing robust encryption methods and securing copyright protections guards these assets from potential infringement.

Equally critical is ensuring that the application adheres to international compliance standards, such as GDPR in Europe or CCPA in California, which govern data protection and privacy. Compliance assures users that their financial data is managed securely and ethically, enhancing trust and ensuring the longevity of the AI platform.

Beyond standard compliance, the application must anticipate future regulatory shifts that could impact its operation. Structuring the IP strategy with agility allows the platform to adapt swiftly to new laws, maintaining uninterrupted service and adhering to the highest standards of financial ethics and data security.

Lastly, continuous monitoring of compliance status and the evolving landscape of IP law is vital for staying ahead in the rapidly changing tech environment, ensuring that the AI Wealth Generator remains a secure and trusted tool in wealth management.

Developing a Robust Data Privacy Framework

In the digital era, data is paramount, and the imperative of safeguarding it cannot be overstressed. Developing a robust data privacy framework for the AI Wealth Generator ensures users' financial details are protected from unauthorized access and misuse. Key to this strategy is the implementation of stringent data encryption methods and secure data storage solutions.

Next, adherence to global privacy standards, such as GDPR or CCPA, is foundational. These regulations guide the app's data processing methodologies, ensuring compliance while enhancing user trust. Privacy by Design principles are integrated from the outset, making data protection an intrinsic part of the application's architecture, not just an afterthought.

Furthermore, regular audits and updates to the privacy policy are vital. These measures keep the framework aligned with emerging data protection laws and technologies. Finally, transparency with users about how their data is used bolsters trust, forming a core aspect of user-centric service.

Thus, a strong data privacy framework is not just about compliance but is crucial in securing user loyalty and maintaining a competitive advantage in the fintech industry.

Utilizing Blockchain for Enhanced Security and Transparency

Incorporating blockchain technology into the AI Wealth Generator revolutionizes security and transparency, critical factors in wealth management. Blockchain's immutable ledger ensures that every transaction and user interaction is recorded permanently, deterring fraud and unauthorized data manipulation. This transparency not only builds user trust but also streamlines compliance with financial regulations.

Moreover, the decentralized nature of blockchain minimizes the risks associated with centralized data breaches. Each block of information, once entered into the ledger, is distributed across the network, making unauthorized access exceedingly challenging. Enhanced security protocols inherent in blockchain, such as advanced cryptography, protect sensitive financial data from cyber threats.

Implementing blockchain also facilitates smoother, more secure transactions with lower costs and faster processing times. This capability allows the AI Wealth Generator to offer real-time financial advice and instantaneous transactional updates, which are pivotal for dynamic investment environments. Overall, blockchain integration ensures a safer, more reliable, and transparent user experience.

Creating Personalized User Profiles for Targeted Services

The AI Wealth Generator's efficiency escalates when it harnesses the power of personalized user profiles. By analyzing an individual's financial behavior, investment patterns, and objectives, the platform tailors its functionalities to meet specific user needs, thereby enhancing user engagement and satisfaction.

Personalization begins with the initial user data input — where preferences, financial goals, and risk tolerance are captured. Advanced machine learning algorithms then process this data to understand and predict user preferences, which guides the crafting of customized financial advice and investment opportunities. This tailored approach not only ensures that users feel understood but also boosts the effectiveness of the advice provided.

Moreover, the integration of personalized profiles with real-time data analytics enables the platform to offer dynamic, adaptive financial strategies. It reacts promptly to changes in a user's financial situation or shifts in the market, making it an indispensable tool for modern financial management.

Ultimately, personalized user profiles transform the AI Wealth Generator into a deeply engaging and user-centric tool, fostering a sense of partnership between the user and technology.

Incorporating Machine Learning Models for Predictive Analysis

Incorporating Machine Learning (ML) models for predictive analysis in the Ultimate AI Wealth Generator transforms traditional financial advice into proactive wealth management. ML models analyze vast datasets to identify patterns and predict future financial trends, providing users with insights that pre-empt market movements.

This predictive capability enables customized investment strategies that dynamically adjust to market conditions and individual risk profiles. By integrating these intelligent models, the app not only enhances its analytical power but also improves decision-making processes, giving users a competitive edge in wealth accumulation.

Furthermore, the continual learning aspect of ML models means the system evolves with the market, refining its predictions over time. This adaptability is crucial in the volatile realm of finance, ensuring that the AI Wealth Generator remains relevant and effective.

By harnessing the predictive power of ML, the application not only secures a leadership position in the fintech space but also profoundly changes how users engage with their financial future.

Developing AI Modules for Real-time Financial Advice

In the realm of financial management, the dynamic implementation of AI modules for real-time financial advice is pivotal. These sophisticated AI systems analyze ongoing market data and individual user profiles to deliver personalized, immediate financial insights. This capability assists users in making informed decisions swiftly, pivotal in volatile market conditions.

The creation of these AI modules involves the integration of advanced algorithmic models with real-time data processing. Utilizing cutting-edge technologies, such as natural language processing and predictive analytics, these modules anticipate market trends and automations provide tailored advice that evolves with each user's unique financial journey.

Moreover, these AI solutions empower users to not only receive guidance but also to understand the rationale behind certain financial recommendations, enhancing their financial literacy. The trust and dependency on the AI Wealth Generator grow as users experience consistent, transparent, and beneficial financial advice.

In summary, developing these AI modules for real-time advice is crucial. It transforms passive financial tools into active advisers that are indispensable in efficient wealth management.

Automated Content Generation for User Engagement

Harnessing the power of automated content generation, the AI Wealth Generator enriches user engagement by delivering timely, relevant, and personalized content. This functionality serves to keep users informed and actively interested in their financial journey. By automating content creation, the platform ensures a consistent stream of valuable insights tailored to individual user preferences and financial activities.

The system utilizes advanced natural language processing (NLP) algorithms to craft articles, reports, and updates that resonate with users' interests and investment profiles. This not only enhances user experience by providing bespoke content but also frees up significant resources, allowing for scalability and focus on other critical aspects of wealth management.

Furthermore, automated content aids in maintaining a dynamic interaction with users, encouraging regular app usage and engagement. It becomes an essential tool in the educational side of financial management, helping users to understand complex market dynamics and make informed decisions.

Ultimately, automated content generation is key to building a proactive, informative, and user-centric financial platform. It fosters a deeper connection between the user and the AI Wealth Generator, ensuring users' needs are met consistently and efficiently.

Building Monetization Mechanisms into the App

Monetization is vital in transforming the AI Wealth Generator from a technological marvel into a viable business model. Initially, strategic choices determine how the app generates revenue while still adding value for users. Options range from subscription models, where users pay for premium features, to transactional fees for specialized financial operations.

Incorporating advanced AI algorithms, the platform can offer microtransactions. These allow for small, yet frequent charges for incremental services or features, making it cost-effective for users and profitable for the platform. Advertising could also play a role; however, it would be tailored and minimal to maintain user trust and application integrity.

Moreover, the integration of in-app purchases for bespoke financial advisory services or exclusive market insights can add significant streams of revenue. Each feature is seamlessly embedded to ensure user experience remains uncompromised. The ultimate goal is crafting a monetization strategy that supports sustainable business growth without sacrificing user satisfaction.

Test, Feedback, Iterate: The Agile Development Cycle

The Agile development cycle, epitomized by the mantra 'Test, Feedback, Iterate,' is crucial in sculpting the AI Wealth Generator into a finely tuned instrument of financial insights. Initially, rigorous testing of AI functionalities against varied financial scenarios ensures that the system behaves as intended, ironing out anomalies that could affect user experience or financial advice accuracy.

Following this, real user feedback becomes the cornerstone of further development. This stage involves collecting insights from beta testers who interact with the app in real-world conditions. Their experiences, whether flaws remarked or accolades given, are invaluable. This feedback is meticulously analyzed to discern patterns or specific issues that need addressing, thereby guiding subsequent iterations.

These iterations involve making precise adjustments to the AI models, refining user interface elements, and enhancing security features. Each iteration is followed by another round of testing and feedback, creating a cycle of continuous improvement. This process ensures that by the time of full launch, the AI Wealth Generator is not only functional but also truly attuned to the needs and challenges of its users.

Launching a Beta Version to Gather Initial User Feedback

Launching a beta version is a strategic phase in the development of the Ultimate AI Wealth Generator. It serves as the first real-world application of the platform, aimed at testing its functionalities and gauging user interaction. During this period, a select group of users is granted access to evaluate the system's performance in live conditions. This initial feedback is crucial, as it uncovers unforeseen issues and highlights areas for enhancement.

Feedback gathered from beta testers is instrumental in refining the platform. Engaging with these early users helps developers understand usage patterns, identify bugs, and ascertain the app's intuitiveness and overall user experience. This stage is not just about technical fixes but also about aligning the app's operations with user expectations and market needs. Suggestions for additional features or changes in existing ones are particularly valuable during this phase.

Conclusively, this iterative beta testing ensures that the AI Wealth Generator is robust, user-friendly, and commercially viable prior to a full-scale launch. By integrating real-user insights, the platform is fine-tuned to better serve its intended audience, paving the way for a successful market introduction and the achievement of strategic business objectives.

Marketing Strategies for Maximum Market Penetration

Effective marketing strategies are crucial for the AI Wealth Generator to achieve maximum market penetration. The foundation of the marketing approach leverages the sophisticated AI capabilities that personalize financial advice, aligning with targeted user segments. Initial campaigns focus on digital platforms, utilizing data-driven analytics to optimize advertisement placements and content. Social media channels, partnered with influencer endorsements, amplify reach and engagement, attracting a tech-savvy audience seeking innovative financial solutions.

Moreover, strategic partnerships with renowned financial institutions bolster credibility and extend user base through co-marketed products. These collaborations are complemented by educational webinars and workshops that demystify AI's role in personal wealth management, addressing potential user apprehensions and enhancing product transparency.

The final thrust involves a robust content marketing strategy, employing the app's automated content generation capabilities to produce relevant, actionable insights that resonate with users. SEO optimization ensures visibility, drawing organic traffic to the platform. Collectively, these strategies are designed to weave a compelling narrative around the AI Wealth Generator, positioning it as an indispensable tool for modern financial management.

Partnerships and Collaborations with Financial Institutions

Forming robust partnerships with financial institutions is a strategic priority in the proliferation of the Ultimate AI Wealth Generator. By aligning with banks, investment firms, and insurance companies, our platform gains not only credibility but also a vast network of potential users. These collaborations serve as a bridge to mainstream acceptance, enabling seamless integration of traditional financial products with innovative AI-driven tools.

Each partnership is curated to bring value to all stakeholders. Financial institutions benefit from access to cutting-edge technology, enhancing their offerings and attracting tech-savvy customers. On the other hand, the AI Wealth Generator taps into established customer bases, easing market entry and adoption hurdles. Through these synergies, we facilitate a broader reach and deeper market penetration while maintaining high standards of financial service.

Moreover, these collaborations are instrumental in navigating regulatory landscapes. Partner institutions offer insights and guidance on compliance with financial regulations, which is crucial for scaling operations safely and effectively. Together, we create a fortified platform that not only promises but also delivers enhanced financial management solutions to a diverse client base.

User Training and Support Systems

User training and support systems are instrumental in ensuring that the AI Wealth Generator is accessible and effective for all users. Initial training modules are developed to educate users on how to optimally utilize the platform's myriad features. These modules incorporate interactive tutorials, video guides, and live webinars, facilitating a comprehensive learning experience.

Ongoing support is provided through a dedicated helpdesk, augmented by AI chatbots capable of resolving common queries efficiently. For more complex issues, skilled technical support teams are available around the clock to provide personalized assistance. This tiered approach ensures users can resolve issues promptly, enhancing overall satisfaction and user retention.

Feedback mechanisms are integrated into these systems to continually refine user training and support services based on real-time user experiences and challenges. By prioritizing user education and support, the AI Wealth Generator ensures a smooth user journey, driving greater adoption and trust in the platform.

Analyzing User Data for Continuous Improvement

The cornerstone of evolving the Ultimate AI Wealth Generator lies in analyzing user data meticulously. This ongoing analysis serves as the critical feedback mechanism feeding into continuous product enhancement. By examining user interactions, transaction patterns, and feedback, developers can identify areas where the app can be more intuitive or functionally richer.

Insights gleaned from data analytics are pivotal in refining algorithms and ensuring that financial advice is both accurate and highly personalized. This thorough examination helps in detecting subtle user needs that may not have been evident during initial feedback stages. Enhancements based on these insights are targeted to improve both user satisfaction and engagement, making the app not only a tool for financial management but also an indispensable aid in wealth accumulation.

Furthermore, this data-driven strategy allows for preemptive adjustments before issues escalate, thereby maintaining high standards of user experience. Integrating these improvements iteratively aligns the app more closely with user expectations and evolving market trends, ensuring that the AI Wealth Generator remains at the forefront of technological excellence and user-centric innovation.

Expanding the App Features Based on User Demand

The dynamic landscape of financial technology necessitates continuous adaptation and expansion of app features to meet user demands. Following the launch and subsequent data collection phases, a structured approach to expanding app features is crucial. This ensures that the AI Wealth Generator remains relevant and advantageous in a competitive market.

User feedback serves as a primary driver for feature expansion. By analyzing data from user interactions and feedback mechanisms, developers can prioritize enhancements and introduce new features that align with user expectations and needs. This might include more customizable financial dashboards, enhanced predictive analytics, or integration with newer financial services. Each update aims to refine user experience and add tangible value, thereby increasing user engagement and satisfaction.

Moreover, the feature expansion process involves rigorous testing and refinement to ensure seamless integration with existing functionalities. By maintaining a user-centric approach to innovation, the AI Wealth Generator continuously evolves, reinforcing its market position as a leading financial management tool.

Updating the AI Models: Keeping Up with Technological Advances

In an ever-evolving digital landscape, the continuous updating of AI models is critical to maintaining technological relevance and competitive advantage. This process involves integrating the latest developments in AI research to enhance the predictive accuracy and functionality of the Wealth Generator. Regular updates ensure the platform leverages cutting-edge algorithms that adapt to changing financial trends and user behaviors.

Moreover, the integration of emerging technologies like quantum computing and advanced neural networks can significantly boost processing power and decision-making capabilities. This step not only improves the financial advice rendered by the app but also enhances security measures, essential for maintaining user trust. Such proactive updates require a dedicated team that stays abreast of technological advancements and swiftly implements these innovations into the operational framework.

Lastly, ensuring that these updates do not disrupt user experience is paramount. Rigorous testing phases are conducted before full-scale implementation to guarantee that enhancements enrich the platform without compromising stability or performance. This careful balancing act between innovation and reliability is what keeps the Ultimate AI Wealth Generator at the pinnacle of financial technology solutions.

Case Studies: Successful Implementation of AI Wealth Generators

Examining real-life applications provides invaluable insights into the practical benefits of the Ultimate AI Wealth Generator. A notable instance involves a mid-size bank that integrated our AI technologies, resulting in a 30% increase in investment product sales within the first quarter. By leveraging AI-driven personalized recommendations, the bank could offer clients more tailored financial advice, significantly enhancing customer satisfaction and retention rates.

Another success story comes from a fintech startup that utilized our platform to deploy real-time, AI-powered risk assessment tools. This technology enabled more accurate credit evaluations, opening the door to underserved markets without compromising on risk. As a result, the startup saw a 45% growth in loan volumes, coupled with a lower default rate compared to industry averages.

These examples underscore the transformative potential of AI in financial services. By adopting AI Wealth Generators, institutions can not only boost their efficiency but also deliver superior customer experiences, paving the way for sustained growth and competitive advantage.

Future Potential: Scaling Globally

The expansion of the Ultimate AI Wealth Generator on a global scale presents unprecedented opportunities for wealth management innovation. As technological adaptations streamline cross-border financial operations, our platform can cater to diverse markets, adapting to varying financial regulations and user preferences. This adaptability not only ensures compliance but also enhances user engagement by providing localized financial solutions.

Successfully scaling globally requires robust strategies for market penetration and localization. Our approach includes forming partnerships with local financial institutions and tailoring marketing strategies to meet regional needs, thereby facilitating smoother entries into new markets. Moreover, leveraging data-driven insights allows us to anticipate market trends and user demands, aligning our offerings with local expectations.

The potential global impact of the AI Wealth Generator is vast. By continuously updating and expanding its features and AI models, the platform aims to become an indispensable tool for individuals and institutions worldwide, revolutionizing how financial services are delivered and experienced across continents.

Creating a Sustainability Plan for Long-term Operations

Ensuring the long-term sustainability of the Ultimate AI Wealth Generator requires a comprehensive strategy that addresses both operational resiliency and adaptive growth mechanisms. Central to this plan is the establishment of a robust framework that supports scalable solutions while minimizing environmental impact, thus promoting a balance between innovation and corporate responsibility.

A key aspect involves continuous investment in green technology to reduce the carbon footprint of our operations. This aligns with global sustainability goals and enhances brand credibility. Additionally, maintaining stringent compliance with international data protection regulations not only safeguards user information but also fortifies trust, a crucial currency in the digital finance landscape.

To underpin sustainability, we advocate for a culture of continuous learning and innovation within our teams. Providing regular training and fostering a climate of proactive adaptability ensures that our workforce remains agile and competent in the face of evolving technological landscapes. Moreover, these efforts synergize with our core mission to deliver cutting-edge financial solutions sustainably.

SUMMARY

The chapter outlines a comprehensive guide for developing an AI Wealth Generator, focusing on integrating crucial components such as advanced AI algorithms, intuitive user interfaces, and robust backend systems to enhance financial prosperity and user engagement. Key elements include selecting technologies conducive to predictive insights and user-specific investment strategies, ensuring seamless integration with secure, scalable backend infrastructures, and adhering to international data protection regulations. A well-designed User Interface (UI) is critical, improving accessibility and maintaining high user engagement levels. Moreover, engaging front-end development with responsive design optimizes navigation and fosters inclusivity. Strategic business goals focusing on innovativeness, financial inclusion, and profitability are defined SMARTly to guide the platform's development efficiently. Incorporating precise AI technologies, especially in machine learning and neural networks, aligns with specified financial empowerment goals, while ethical considerations and regulatory compliance enhance trust. The inclusion of blockchain technology secures transactions and enhances transparency, essential in boosting user confidence. Personalized user profiles leverage machine learning to tailor financial advice, increasing the platform's effectiveness. Continuous iterative processes including feedback and agile development cycles underscore the need for constant evolution, adapting to user needs and technological advances. Moreover, robust data privacy frameworks and IP protections ensure compliance and competitiveness. Lastly, comprehensive marketing strategies, effective beta testing phases, and strategic collaborations with financial institutions are crucial in maximizing market penetration and ensuring sustained growth. This blueprint not only targets technological excellence but also emphasizes user-centric design, financial ethics, and sustainability, setting a powerful foundation for the successful deployment and scaling of AI-driven financial solutions.

REFERENCES

[1] Predicting the Future – Big Data, Machine Learning, and Financial Time Series. https://www.nber.org/papers/w23474

[2] User interface design for personal financial planning. https://dl.acm.org/doi/abs/10.1145/2908805

[3] Blockchain Technology in Financial Services: A systematic literature review. https://link.springer.com/article/10.1007/s10257-018-0376-4

[4] Data Privacy in FinTech: Understanding GDPR Compliance. https://www.sciencedirect.com/science/article/pii/S2666693620300057

[5] Machine Learning: Trends, perspectives, and prospects. https://science.sciencemag.org/content/349/6245/255

CASE STUDY: REVOLUTIONIZING WEALTH MANAGEMENT: BUILDING THE AI WEALTH GENERATOR FOR E-FINANCE CO.

E-Finance Co., a burgeoning fintech startup, aspired to redefine wealth management by constructing an Ultimate AI Wealth Generator. The project's ambitious goal was to integrate cutting-edge AI technology with user-friendly interfaces to democratize financial advice, making it accessible and beneficial to a diverse user base ranging from novice investors to experienced financiers. The first phase of development involved assembling a team of AI experts, data scientists, and experienced financial analysts dedicated to creating a platform that could analyze massive data sets to provide personalized investment strategies.

The project focused on three critical areas: robust AI technology selection, development of a scalable backend architecture, and a user-centered design for the frontend. For AI technology, the team selected machine learning models known for their predictive prowess in financial environments, integrating these with neural networks to handle voluminous and varied data effectively. The challenge was ensuring these technologies were not only powerful but also adhered to ethical AI use and financial regulations.

For the backend, E-Finance Co. opted for cloud-based solutions with high scalability and robust security protocols to manage the high volume of transactions and sensitive financial data securely. This setup was critical in safeguarding user data and ensuring the reliability of the service under high demand. The frontend development focused on an intuitive user interface that could cater to both tech-savvy users and those with minimal digital interaction experience. This approach included employing responsive design principles to ensure a seamless experience across different devices and operating systems.

Throughout the project, continuous testing and user feedback were integral. Initial prototypes underwent rigorous testing phases, where real-world financial scenarios were simulated to evaluate the platform's performance. Feedback from these sessions was invaluable in refining the AI algorithms and user interface, ensuring the platform was ready for a soft launch. After launch, ongoing data analysis and user feedback informed continuous improvement, making the AI Wealth Generator a potent tool for personalized financial management.

Case Study: Optimizing Algorithmic Trading: The Evolution of Alpha-Trading AI System

Global Trading Inc., a recognized leader in the financial services industry, embarked on a transformative journey to develop an Ultimate AI Wealth Generator specifically tailored for algorithmic trading. The creation of 'Alpha-Trading AI System' aimed to revolutionize how market data is processed and trading decisions are made, leveraging artificial intelligence to maximize profitability for traders and investors across various markets.

The initial challenge was the establishment of a highly sophisticated AI infrastructure capable of real-time decision-making. The team at Global Trading Inc. brought together data scientists, expert traders, and software engineers to design a multi-layered AI framework. This framework included advanced machine learning algorithms for pattern recognition and predictive analytics, aiming to identify profitable trading opportunities based on historical market data and current market conditions.

The core of the Alpha-Trading AI System was its ability to adapt. Utilizing reinforced learning, the AI could evolve its strategies based on successes and failures, enhancing its predictive accuracy over time. Integration with cloud computing platforms allowed for the management of vast datasets with high velocity, ensuring that the system could execute trades at optimal speeds.

However, the development process wasn't without hurdles. One of the major challenges was designing an AI system that could consistently adhere to various international financial regulations while maintaining competitive advantages in dynamic trading environments. To address this, the team implemented a robust compliance module within the AI to automatically adjust trading strategies in real-time to stay within legal frameworks.

Moreover, as part of ensuring the reliability and effectiveness of the Alpha-Trading AI System, extensive back-testing against historical market conditions was conducted to refine algorithms before going live. Upon deployment, the system was closely monitored, and iterative updates were made to adapt to new market conditions and financial regulations, maintaining its state-of-the-art performance and compliance.

Case Study: Navigating Regulatory Compliance: Crafting the SafeHarbor AI Platform

The development of SafeHarbor AI, a comprehensive AI-driven wealth generator for SecureFin Corp, aimed to navigate the rigorous terrain of global financial regulations while providing proactive, personalized financial advice. The core objective was to create a platform that not only advised on wealth accumulation but did so while conforming strictly to international financial laws, including GDPR and CCPA. The first step involved a meticulous planning phase where a multidisciplinary team of legal experts, AI developers, and financial analysts collaborated to outline essential features that complied with legislative requirements across different jurisdictions.

The team then faced the dual task of selecting AI technologies that could robustly support real-time, complex data processing while ensuring compliance with these stringent regulations. Technologies such as encrypted cloud storage and blockchain for a transparent, immutable record were integral to their strategy. Additionally, they incorporated advanced natural language processing to interact with users, providing a seamless, accessible interface that could adapt to various global user demographics without compromising privacy or security.

A considerable challenge was establishing a Dynamic Compliance Framework. This adaptive system used machine learning to monitor and adapt to regulatory changes, ensuring ongoing compliance through proactive updates. This setup not only protected the company against potential legal repercussions but also built substantial trust with users.

User testing phases were crucial. Early adopters from different regions were invited to use SafeHarbor AI under simulated financial scenarios. This diverse user input was invaluable for adjusting AI behaviors to better align with real-world financial habits and legal nuances. Feedback from these sessions helped refine the AI's decision-making pathways and user interaction protocols, honing both its financial advisory accuracy and compliance alignment. After deployment, the platform continued to evolve based on user data and regulatory changes through an iterative refinement process, maintaining its edge in a competitive fintech landscape.

Case Study: Expanding into Emerging Markets: Strategy for Global AI-Driven Financial Inclusion

In an exhaustive effort to tap into emerging global markets, the Fintech Development Group (FDG) initiated a project titled 'Global AI-Driven Financial Inclusion'. The goal was ambitious: to create an AI Wealth Generator that was not only technologically advanced but also culturally adaptable and compliant with diverse regulatory environments across continents, thus fostering financial inclusion globally.

The project kicked off with a comprehensive market analysis to identify key regions that demonstrated a high potential for digital financial services yet exhibited low financial inclusion rates. An interdisciplinary team comprising of AI experts, cultural anthropologists, and international regulatory specialists was assembled. Their primary task was to tailor the AI applications to meet specific regional needs while considering cultural nuances and local financial regulations.

For AI technology, FDG harnessed advanced machine learning algorithms capable of learning diverse financial behaviors and patterns specific to different regions. This bespoke approach allowed the AI to offer personalized financial advice relevant to local economic conditions and user financial behaviors. Furthermore, the integration of multilingual capabilities and culturally intuitive user interfaces addressed significant barriers related to language and usability.

Securing user trust was paramount, especially in markets with prevalent skepticism towards digital services. To address this, FDG implemented blockchain technology to enhance transparency and security, broadcasting the incorruptibility of transactions and data handling. Moreover, partnerships with local financial institutions were crucial in navigating the complex landscape of regional financial laws and gaining initial user trust.

Before the full-scale launch, FDG conducted extensive trials within selected regions, collecting valuable insights that led to iterative refinements in the AI's functional capabilities and alignment with user expectations. The deployment phase was closely monitored, with continuous feedback loops ensuring that the AI Wealth Generator remained responsive to changes in market dynamics and regulatory updates. Subsequent updates focused on scaling the system's capacity to accommodate growing user numbers and integrating emerging technologies to maintain a competitive edge.

Case Study: Integrating AI for Personalized Investment: The Rise of InvestSmart App

InvestSmart Inc., a visionary financial tech firm, embarked on creating an AI Wealth Generator tool primarily focused on delivering personalized investment advice to individual investors. The InvestSmart App aimed to differentiate itself by providing deeply personalized, AI-driven financial planning that adjusts to real-time market conditions and individual risk preferences. To begin the project, InvestSmart gathered a team composed of AI specialists, behavioral economists, and seasoned investment advisors dedicated to developing a sophisticated, yet user-friendly interface that could engage users of varying financial literacy levels.

The design phase saw the convergence of decision-tree algorithms and neural networks to create a hyper-adaptive decision-making framework within the tool. This AI system was meant to parse through extensive datasets - from global economic indicators to individual user transaction histories - to generate tailored advice and precise predictions. Security was integral, hence the implementation of advanced encryption techniques and two-factor authentication to protect user data was prioritized from the start.

To ensure the backend infrastructure was robust and capable of handling the complexities of real-time data processing and simultaneous user queries without lag, InvestSmart leveraged cloud computing resources with auto-scaling capabilities. The team also included an API gateway for integration with stock markets, banks, and other financial services, fortifying the tool's resource network. User testing was continuous; initial versions of InvestSmart were released to a closed group of users, and their interactions were analyzed. This iterative cycle helped fine-tune the AI's responsiveness and accuracy, making essential adjustments based on user feedback and behavior.

Post-launch, InvestSmart has focused on continuous improvement, guided by ongoing user data analytics and market trends. This not only aids in refining the algorithms but also keeps the app ahead of regulatory changes and secures its competitive edge in the market. The regular update cycle involves tweaking the AI's predictive models based on new economic data and user feedback, ensuring that investment advice remains relevant and advantageous.

Case Study: Strategic Integration and Global Expansion: The Journey of FinSmart AI Solutions

FinSmart AI Solutions, a forward-thinking enterprise in the fintech sector, embarked on developing an Ultimate AI Wealth Generator, aiming to reshape global financial services. The primary objective was to incorporate advanced AI into wealth management, making sophisticated financial analysis and advice accessible worldwide. The initial steps involved forming a multi-disciplinary team whose expertise spanned AI, finance, and global market strategies.

The development process focused on three main pillars: integration with existing financial systems, adherence to international compliance standards, and scalability for global market penetration. The choice of AI technology was crucial; the team opted for robust machine learning algorithms capable of handling dynamic and extensive data sets, providing predictive analytics that could adapt to both developed and emerging markets. A key challenge was the integration of these technologies with existing financial infrastructures. To address this, FinSmart developed versatile APIs that allowed seamless data flow between the AI system and traditional banking systems.

Compliance was another significant area. With operations planned across multiple continents, the platform needed to adhere to a myriad of financial regulations, including GDPR in Europe and others specific to Asian and African markets. The solution was a flexible AI framework that could update its operational protocols in real-time as per the regional compliance requirements.

For global expansion, the scalability of the backend infrastructure was enhanced using cloud solutions from leading providers, ensuring that the system could handle increases in user load without degradation in performance. Marketing strategies were tailored to regional preferences, utilizing local insights to enhance user engagement and adoption.

Throughout its development, continuous testing with diverse global audiences provided insights that refined its algorithms and user interface. Post-launch, the platform utilized real-time data to further adapt and refine its offerings, ensuring relevancy and compliance.

Case Study: Developing the GreenFinance AI: Sustainable Practices in Financial Advisory

In an innovative move towards eco-conscious investing, a visionary fintech company, EcoInvest Ltd., embarked on creating GreenFinance AI, an Ultimate AI Wealth Generator focused on sustainable investment practices. The core aim was to bridge the gap between financial gain and environmental responsibility, tailoring investment advice to not only yield financial returns but also promote sustainability.

The initial challenge was the integration of a vast array of environmental, social, and governance (ESG) metrics with traditional financial indicators, guiding investors towards greener portfolios. EcoInvest gathered top AI developers, financial analysts with sustainability expertise, and data scientists to construct an AI that could analyze and predict the performance of sustainable investments accurately. The AI technology selected combined deep learning for pattern recognition with robust predictive analytics to forecast market trends and determine the long-term impact of sustainable investments.

With regards to technical execution, the development of a seamless user interface that highlighted sustainable investments was paramount. The interface was designed with user-friendly visuals and indicators that represented environmental impact scores and social responsibility ratings, simplifying the decision-making process for investors. The backend infrastructure incorporated state-of-the-art cloud solutions and high-level security protocols, ensuring the secure and efficient analysis of large datasets combining financial and non-financial metrics.

The testing phase involved scenarios tailored to gauge the AI's effectiveness in identifying genuinely sustainable investments and its resilience against greenwashing claims. Continuous feedback loops from early adopters focused on refining the AI's recommendations, enhancing its ability to differentiate between genuinely sustainable practices and superficial ones.

Post-launch, GreenFinance AI has committed to ongoing updates that refine its sustainability metrics based on the latest environmental research and global sustainability trends. This case not only emphasizes the role of technology in modern wealth management but also demonstrates how fintech can drive significant contributions to global sustainability efforts.

Case Study: Empowering SMEs with AI-Driven Financial Decision-Making: A Case Study of BizFinance Tool

The development of BizFinance, an AI Wealth Generator designed for small and medium enterprises (SMEs), offers a vivid illustration of how artificial intelligence can transform financial management and decision-making at the grassroots business level. Initiated by TechFin Solutions, this project aimed to provide SMEs with sophisticated, yet easy-to-use tools to improve financial forecasting, budget management, and investment decisions. The first phase involved a comprehensive analysis of the typical financial challenges faced by SMEs, including cash flow management, access to credit, and risk assessment. TechFin Solutions assembled a cross-functional team comprising AI experts, financial analysts, and user experience designers, all focused on creating a solution that was not only technologically advanced but also intuitive and tailored to the unique needs of SME operators.

Key components of BizFinance included predictive analytics for financial forecasting, machine learning algorithms for credit risk assessment, and personalized dashboards for real-time financial oversight. A crucial challenge in the project was ensuring user data privacy and compliance with financial regulations, a significant concern for SMEs. To tackle this, the development team incorporated advanced encryption and blockchain technology to maintain data integrity and security. The User Interface (UI) was designed to be simple yet functionally comprehensive, minimizing the learning curve and maximizing user adoption rates.

During testing, the prototype was deployed with a select group of SMEs across various sectors to gather initial feedback and fine-tune the system according to real-world requirements. This iterative process allowed for the refinement of AI functionalities, making the tool more adaptive to diverse business environments. Post-launch, the BizFinance tool was acclaimed for enabling SMEs to make more informed financial decisions rapidly, thus boosting their confidence and ability to compete in larger markets. Regular updates and feedback loops continue to adapt the tool to the changing economic landscapes and regulatory environments, ensuring that BizFinance remains a vital asset for SME financial management.

REVIEW QUESTIONS

1. In the development of an AI Wealth Generator focused on innovative financial management, which component is MOST crucial for predicting user behaviors and tailoring advice?

A) Seamless user interface

B) Secure backend systems

C) Advanced AI algorithms

D) Integration with existing financial systems

Answer: C

Explanation: Advanced AI algorithms are essential for analyzing vast amounts of data to provide predictive insights into user behaviors and create personalized financial advice, a key feature in effective financial management platforms. While all components are important for the system's overall performance, the core functionality of providing tailored advice relies predominantly on high-quality, sophisticated AI technologies capable of complex data analytics.

2. Considering the construction of the Ultimate AI Wealth Generator, what aspect of compliance is essential to foster user trust and ensure operational longevity?

A) Adherence to international data protection laws

B) The seamless user interface across different devices

C) Real-time data updating

D) Advanced graphics and visualization tools

Answer: A

Explanation: Compliance with international data protection regulations such as GDPR or CCPA is crucial in building user trust and maintaining credibility. It ensures that user data is handled securely and ethically, which is vital given the financial nature of the AI Wealth Generator. This not only meets legal criteria but also bolsters user confidence in the system's integrity.

REVIEW QUESTIONS

3. In building the AI Wealth Generator, why is it important to integrate with existing financial systems?

A) To increase the processing speed of transactions

B) To improve the quality of multimedia content

C) For enhancing real-time financial advice based on user profile

D) To ensure the app operates in a vacuum, independently of external influences

Answer: C

Explanation: Integrating with existing financial systems, such as banks and investment platforms, ensures that the AI Wealth Generator can access real-time data relevant to each user's financial activities. This enables the application to offer tailored financial advice based on accurate, up-to-date information, which is critical for the user's financial success and trust in the system.

4. How does the implementation of a user-centric design impact user engagement in the AI Wealth Generator app?

A) Allows for the display of high-quality images and videos

B) Ensures that users can navigate the app without prior technical expertise

C) Reduces the operational costs of maintaining the app

D) Increases the financial advice accuracy

Answer: B

Explanation: A user-centric design ensures that the app is easy to use, regardless of the user's technical skills. This is critical in engaging users by allowing them to navigate and utilize the app's features effectively, leading to greater satisfaction and continued use. This approach minimizes frustration and ensures accessibility, which is especially important in apps dealing with complex topics like finance.

REVIEW QUESTIONS

5. What role do backend systems play in the functioning of an AI Wealth Generator focusing on large-scale financial operations?

A) They enhance the visual design elements of the application.

B) They provide educational content to users.

C) They handle large volumes of data and transactions securely.

D) They develop frontend customer interfaces.

Answer: C

Explanation: Robust backend systems are crucial for managing and securing large volumes of user data and high-frequency financial transactions. A scalable and secure backend is essential for ensuring the system's reliability and operability under heavy loads, thus maintaining the trust and satisfaction of users who depend on the app for real-time financial management.

MONETIZATION MASTERY: TURNING AI TOOLS INTO REVENUE STREAMS

Identifying Profitable AI Markets

The key to monetizing AI effectively begins with identifying profitable markets that are ripe for innovation. Extensive market research to pinpoint industries experiencing rapid growth, such as healthcare, finance, and e-commerce, is essential. These sectors often provide fertile ground for AI integration, offering solutions from automated customer service to data-driven decision-making guidance.

Next, analyzing market gaps and consumer needs within these sectors can highlight opportunities uniquely suited for AI applications. This includes areas where traditional processes are inefficient or where data collection and processing capabilities can significantly enhance operations. AI tools designed to address these specific inefficiencies can quickly become indispensable to industry stakeholders, paving the way for robust monetization strategies.

Finally, assessing the competitive landscape is crucial. Identifying markets with lower entry barriers or those underserved by current AI solutions can offer a strategic advantage. By focusing on these niches, AI developers can create high-demand products tailored to unique user requirements, establishing a strong foundation for sustained revenue generation.

Developing AI Products with High Market Demand

Creating AI products that resonate with market demand involves a keen understanding of where technology can solve genuine problems. By embedding AI capabilities into products that address specific industry pain points, developers set a clear path for widespread adoption and revenue generation.

One successful approach is to leverage data and analytics to anticipate and shape product offerings. Using AI to analyze trends and user feedback helps in crafting solutions that not only solve current issues but also adapt to future changes. This anticipatory approach ensures relevance and longevity in the market, making the product an indispensable tool for its users.

Additionally, successful AI products often feature user-centric design and functionality. This means they are intuitive and accessible, removing barriers to adoption and enhancing the user experience. By focusing on ease of use and real-time problem-solving abilities, AI products can achieve high market penetration and user retention, proving essential in competitive tech-driven landscapes.

Finally, continuous iteration based on user engagement and feedback fuels ongoing product enhancement, keeping the AI solution at the forefront of its market segment.

Strategies for Pricing AI Tools and Services

Effectively pricing AI tools and services is paramount in capturing the value they offer while remaining competitive. A foundational strategy involves value-based pricing, which considers the perceived value to the customer rather than solely the cost of production. This approach optimally positions AI products by aligning the price with the unique advantages and efficiencies AI introduces to a user's workflow.

Competitive pricing analysis is another critical strategy, requiring an understanding of what rivals are charging for similar AI tools. Leveraging competitive intelligence can guide pricing adjustments to either undercut competitors or justify a premium due to superior functionality or performance enhancements. Additionally, penetration pricing can be employed initially to build a user base quickly, followed by a gradual price increment as the market acceptance solidifies and user dependency grows.

Finally, considering subscription models or tiered pricing structures can accommodate diverse user needs and budgetary constraints. Offering multiple pricing tiers with varied feature sets ensures accessibility for smaller customers while monetizing advanced features for larger enterprises, broadening the market reach and maximizing revenue potentials.

Subscription Models for AI Applications

Subscription models for AI applications represent a dynamic revenue strategy, offering sustained income while enhancing customer loyalty. By enabling continuous access to AI tools against a periodic fee, businesses can secure consistent revenue streams. This model is particularly effective in sectors where AI-driven insights and updates are crucial for ongoing operations, such as in analytics or market forecasting.

Central to implementing a successful subscription model is understanding customer usage patterns and preferences. Tailoring subscription tiers to match different user needs—from basic access for new users to premium packages for power users—can maximize adoption and satisfaction. Additionally, integrating value-added services, such as custom reporting or exclusive content, enhances the perceived value, encouraging higher-tier subscriptions.

Moreover, transparent communication about updates and benefits ensures subscribers are aware of the value they receive, fostering renewal and avoiding churn. Engaging with subscribers through regular feedback loops helps in refining the offerings, ensuring that the AI applications remain indispensable tools in the subscriber's arsenal. Thus, the subscription model not only stabilizes cash flow but also builds a committed user base.

Monetizing AI with Advertising Models

Advertising models present a lucrative avenue for monetizing AI by integrating tailored advertisements into AI-driven platforms. As AI technologies curate and personalize user experiences, they simultaneously open doors for highly targeted advertising that achieves superior engagement rates and ROI for advertisers.

Leveraging machine learning, AI can analyze user behavior and preferences to display the most relevant ads, thereby increasing click-through rates and advertiser satisfaction. This capability makes AI-powered platforms extremely attractive to advertisers looking for precision targeting. Furthermore, by offering real-time bidding and optimization, AI systems enhance ad effectiveness, commanding premium ad placements and pricing.

A key advantage of utilizing AI in advertising models is the continuous learning process, which refines ad targeting algorithms based on interaction data. This dynamic adaptation leads to more effective campaigns over time, fostering long-term partnerships with advertisers. By adopting AI advertising models, developers not only boost revenue but also enrich the user experience with less intrusive, more pertinent ads.

Creating Freemium AI Products

The freemium model strategically harnesses the potential of AI innovations by offering core functionalities for free while reserving advanced features for paid versions. This approach significantly broadens the initial user base, as it lowers the entry barrier and allows interested parties to test the product without financial commitment.

To optimize a freemium model, it's essential to strike a balance. The free version must be sufficiently useful to engage users while encouraging upgrades. Critical to this process is understanding user behavior; which features compel them towards conversion, and what additional capabilities are they willing to pay for. This insight guides the development of value-packed premium offerings that warrant user investment.

Carefully crafting the transition from free to premium is also crucial. Seamless upgrade paths and clear communication about the benefits of premium features enhance conversion rates. Promotions and temporary unlocks can further entice usage of paid features. Collectively, these strategies not only boost revenue but also convert casual users into loyal customers, sustaining the AI product's market relevance and profitability.

Leveraging Affiliate Marketing for AI Tools

Affiliate marketing for AI tools offers a pristine avenue for monetization by connecting AI developers with affiliate networks that can promote their products. By partnering with influencers and businesses that share the target audience, AI tool creators can extend their market reach through trusted voices, effectively converting their endorsement into sales.

The key to success in this strategy is to select affiliates who understand and genuinely benefit from the AI tools, ensuring that their promotions are authentic and resonate with potential users. Offering competitive commission rates motivates affiliates to prioritize your product, enhancing the visibility and desirability of your AI solutions. Tracking tools powered by AI itself can optimize and personalize affiliate campaigns, thereby maximizing effectiveness and ROI.

Additionally, implementing tiered rewards systems can further incentivize affiliates, rewarding top performers with higher commissions or bonuses for exceptional results. This not only spurs continued effort but also cultivates loyalty toward your AI brand. Ultimately, a well-structured affiliate program amplifies product exposure while aligning with cost-effective marketing budgets.

Partnerships and Collaborations to Enhance Revenue

In the AI landscape, forging partnerships and collaborations emerges as a potent strategy to amplify revenue streams. By aligning with other companies, AI businesses can leverage complementary strengths, accessing new markets and customer bases which may have been unreachable alone. These collaborative efforts often result in synergistic products or services that appeal to a broader audience, enhancing the commercial appeal and adoption rates of AI technologies.

Strategically chosen partnerships can significantly reduce the development and marketing costs through shared resources and expertise. For example, collaborating with established brands can provide credibility and a ready-made audience eager for innovative solutions. This not only accelerates market penetration but also diminishes the risks associated with venturing into new or untested markets.

Moreover, collaborations can lead to unique monetization opportunities such as joint ventures or revenue-sharing models. These arrangements not only ensure financial gains but also foster long-term relationships that might evolve into other lucrative ventures, thus securing a sustained income stream and boosting overall profitability in the competitive field of AI.

AI in FinTech: Monetizing through Transaction Fees

In the realm of financial technology, AI has carved a niche where it significantly enhances the efficiency and security of transactions. By integrating AI into FinTech services, companies are not just streamlining operations but are also innovating monetization through transaction fees. This model leverages AI to facilitate, secure, and speed up transactions which, in turn, justify the imposition of fees that users are willing to pay for the added value.

For instance, AI-driven algorithms can detect fraudulent activities in real-time, thus reducing the risk of massive financial losses. Financial institutions can capitalize on this by charging premiums for high-security transactions facilitated by AI. The seamless nature of these transactions, enabled by sophisticated AI systems, boosts consumer trust and transaction volume, which directly contributes to increased revenue streams.

Furthermore, AI can personalize financial services for users, creating unique user experiences that enhance satisfaction and retention rates. Institutions then monetize these bespoke services through tiered transaction fee models, effectively turning personalized AI enhancements into profitable ventures. This dynamic adaptation not only captivates customers but also secures a competitive edge in the bustling FinTech market.

Royalty and Licensing Models for AI Creations

Expanding the potential for monetary gain in AI development, royalty and licensing models offer a compelling avenue for creators to earn from their innovations. Utilizing these models, AI developers can license their proprietary technologies, algorithms, or even unique data sets to other businesses, receiving ongoing royalties from continuous use or one-time licensing fees.

This form of monetization is particularly advantageous for AI creators with niche or highly specialized technologies. By setting clear usage terms and conditions, developers retain control over how their AI is utilized, ensuring it aligns with brand values and long-term business strategies. Moreover, this approach opens up diverse market opportunities by making AI accessible to smaller firms or startups that may not have the resources for in-house development.

Royalty agreements can be tailored to suit various business arrangements, allowing creators to benefit from volume-based payouts as their AI solutions gain traction. Simultaneously, licensing out AI tools can lead to new business relationships and collaborative ventures, further broadening revenue opportunities and enhancing the AI tool's market presence.

Implementing AI in Paid Membership Platforms

Integrating AI into paid membership platforms revolutionizes how businesses engage with and retain members. AI technologies such as personalized content delivery and predictive analysis can dramatically enhance user experience, leading to higher satisfaction and retention rates. By delivering tailored experiences that align with individual user preferences and behavior, AI enables platforms to offer more value, justifying premium membership fees.

Furthermore, AI-driven analytics tools help in understanding and segmenting audience groups more effectively. This segmentation allows for targeted marketing strategies and the development of specialized membership tiers, each with customized services that meet the diverse needs of users. Such stratification not only encourages upgrades among existing members but also attracts new users looking for a bespoke service experience not available in standard offerings.

Additionally, the introduction of AI facilitates the automation of routine tasks like customer support and account management, reducing operational costs. These savings could be redirected into improving service quality or marketing efforts, further enriching the platform's appeal and strengthening the business model's sustainability in the competitive market.

Packaging AI Tools as B2B Solutions

The transformative potential of AI technology offers businesses unique opportunities when packaged as B2B solutions. By catering directly to business needs, AI developers can deploy specialized tools that streamline operations, enhance decision-making, and boost productivity, securing a pivotal position in business growth strategies.

Essential to this approach is understanding the specific challenges and requirements of businesses across different industries. Developers must tailor AI solutions, ensuring they integrate seamlessly into existing systems while providing measurable improvements in efficiency and cost-savings. This customization elevates the value proposition, making the choice to adopt AI tools more compelling for businesses.

Moreover, marketing AI as a B2B solution often involves comprehensive support and updates, fostering long-term client relationships. It allows developers to offer scalable solutions that evolve with their client's growing needs, ensuring a steady revenue stream while reinforcing the indispensability of their product. Thus, creating a win-win scenario, where businesses achieve operational excellence and AI developers secure enduring market relevance.

Using AI to Drive Sales and Increase Conversion Rates

Leveraging AI technology to boost sales and conversion rates is transforming e-commerce and retail industries. By analyzing vast arrays of data from customer interactions, AI can personalize shopping experiences and recommend products that cater directly to individual preferences. This targeted approach not only enhances customer satisfaction but also significantly increases the likelihood of conversions.

Moreover, AI tools are instrumental in optimizing marketing campaigns by predicting what content is most likely to engage customers. This predictive capability enables businesses to allocate their marketing resources more effectively, ensuring that advertisements and promotions reach the right audience at the optimal time. As a result, marketing efficiency skyrockets, leading to greater ROI on ad spend.

In addition, AI-driven chatbots and virtual assistants provide real-time, personalized customer service, reducing wait times and improving user engagement. This immediate assistance helps in maintaining customer interest and loyalty, which are crucial for repeat sales and long-term revenue growth. Overall, integrating AI to drive sales is a critical strategy for businesses aiming to thrive in the digital era.

Monetizing Data Analytics and Business Intelligence AI

The realm of data analytics and business intelligence, empowered by AI, presents lucrative revenue-generating opportunities. AI-driven analytics tools offer detailed insights into consumer behavior, market trends, and operational efficiencies. By offering these tools as a service, businesses can transform raw data into actionable intelligence, thus commanding premium prices for these insights.

Companies across industries prioritize data-driven decision-making, which elevates the importance of AI in analytics. By tailoring these tools to specific industry needs, businesses can seamlessly integrate them into their existing infrastructure, enhancing their overall value proposition. This customization allows for direct monetization through subscription models or pay-per-use agreements, with clients seeing a direct correlation between the use of these tools and increased profitability.

Moreover, the continuous evolution of data science enables the development of ever-more sophisticated AI applications. This progression props up the potential for upselling advanced features and dedicated analytics services, further enhancing revenue streams. Integrating AI with business intelligence thus not only supports clients in making more informed decisions but also creates a sustained income flow for providers.

Creating Marketplaces for AI-Generated Assets

The burgeoning field of AI has paved the way for novel marketplaces specifically tailored for AI-generated assets. These platforms serve as critical hubs where creators can monetize their AI-powered innovations, from digital art and music to complex algorithms and data models. By facilitating transactions between AI asset creators and users, these marketplaces democratize access to cutting-edge technology and creative outputs, broadening the scope of AI's applicability and adoption.

Key to the success of these marketplaces is their ability to assure quality and authenticity, which builds trust among buyers and sellers. Implementing robust verification processes and transparent creator profiles can enhance credibility. Furthermore, by incorporating AI to recommend assets based on user preferences and needs, marketplaces can significantly improve user experience and satisfaction, thereby increasing transaction frequency.

Moreover, adopting a scalable revenue model, such as taking a commission from sales or offering premium listing features, can ensure sustainable growth. As the demand for AI-generated assets climbs, tapping into this niche market not only propels the AI field forward but also creates a lucrative ecosystem for AI innovations to thrive.

AI-Powered SaaS Products: Development and Monetization

The emergence of AI-powered Software as a Service (SaaS) products is revolutionizing the tech industry by enhancing efficiencies and automating complex processes. These AI-infused solutions offer scalable services that can be tailored for various business niches, making them an attractive proposition for startups and established corporations alike.

The development of AI-powered SaaS products begins with a deep understanding of potential customer segments and their respective needs. Agile methodologies, coupled with AI tools, accelerate product iteration, ensuring that offerings are both innovative and responsive to market demands. The inclusion of machine learning algorithms further refines service functionalities, optimizing user interactions for improved client retention and satisfaction.

Monetization strategies for AI-powered SaaS offerings vary, with subscription-based models predominating. These models guarantee a steady revenue flow and can be adjusted based on service tiers, enhancing customer acquisition by aligning value propositions closely with user expectations. Additionally, incorporating analytics services can provide users actionable insights, creating another revenue stream while offering indispensable business intelligence capabilities.

Utilizing AI for E-commerce Optimization

The integration of AI into e-commerce optimization is revolutionizing online shopping landscapes. By employing AI, e-commerce platforms can dynamically adjust user interfaces based on user behavior analytics, enhancing usability and customer satisfaction. AI algorithms analyze shopping patterns to provide tailored recommendations, making the shopping experience more personalized and efficient.

Beyond personalization, AI significantly boosts inventory management through predictive analytics. This application forecasts demand changes, helping companies optimize stock levels and reduce overhead costs. Additionally, AI enables price optimization strategies that adjust product prices in real time based on market trends, competition, and demand, ensuring maximum profitability while maintaining market competitiveness.

Moreover, AI-driven tools automate customer service interactions, significantly lowering response times and increasing customer engagement through personalized communication. This automation not only streamlines operations but also helps build lasting customer relationships, pivotal in boosting sales and fostering brand loyalty.

Utilizing AI for e-commerce optimization thus represents a holistic approach that scales up service efficiency, ensures customer contentment, and drives revenue growth.

Developing AI-Based Educational Tools and Courses

The development of AI-based educational tools and courses opens up innovative avenues for monetization in the booming e-learning market. By utilizing AI, educators and technologists can create adaptive learning platforms that personalize the educational experience, catering to the unique learning pace and style of each student. This personalized approach not only boosts engagement but also enhances learning outcomes, increasing the value and demand for these products.

From a business perspective, these AI-driven educational tools can be distributed through subscription models or one-time purchase licenses, appealing to educational institutions and individual learners alike. Additionally, the integration of certification incentives can add a premium tier to these offerings, further enhancing revenue streams.

Moreover, collaborating with academic institutions and corporate organizations for tailored training programs can open up substantial contract-based opportunities. AI's scalability allows for the expansion of these educational services globally, encompassing a wide market and diverse customer base, ultimately driving significant monetary gains.

Offering AI Consulting and Customization Services

In the dynamic landscape of AI technologies, offering consulting and customization services emerges as a profound avenue for monetization. Businesses, irrespective of their technological proficiency, seek personalized AI solutions that can seamlessly integrate and significantly enhance their operations. Consulting services provide the expertise needed to develop tailored AI roadmaps, assess technological readiness, and implement successful AI adoption strategies.

Customization of AI solutions involves refining and adjusting pre-existing AI models to meet specific client requirements. This can vary from industry-specific adjustments to developing bespoke algorithms. The consultancy can thereby command higher fees for the high value and distinctive solutions offered, setting themselves apart in a competitive market.

Moreover, continuous support and optimization services form an integral part of AI consulting, ensuring that AI systems evolve with business needs and technological advancements. This ongoing engagement not only solidifies client relationships but also creates a recurring revenue stream, enhancing customer lifetime value within the AI consultancy sector.

Revenue Optimization through AI-Driven Process Automation

Harnessing the power of AI-driven process automation is transforming revenue optimization strategies across various sectors. By automating routine and complex processes, companies can significantly reduce operational costs while improving efficiency and accuracy. This shift not only frees up resources but also allows businesses to redirect their focus towards more strategic, revenue-generating activities.

In sectors like manufacturing, AI-driven automation streamlines production lines and minimizes downtime by predicting and preempting maintenance needs. Similarly, in the service industry, AI tools automate customer interactions through chatbots and virtual assistants, enhancing customer service while reducing labor costs. These implementations not only improve operational efficiencies but also ensure consistency and reliability in customer interactions, essential for sustained revenue growth.

Moreover, financial services leverage AI to automate their risk assessment processes, resulting in faster loan approvals and fewer defaults. By integrating AI in these crucial areas, businesses not only enhance their service offerings but also create new revenue streams through improved operational agility and customer satisfaction. This comprehensive approach marks a lucrative future for AI in revenue optimization.

Crowdfunding AI Tool Development

Crowdfunding has emerged as a vital resource for AI tool development, democratizing access to funding and enabling innovators to bypass traditional financial barriers. By presenting their AI concepts on platforms such as Kickstarter or Indiegogo, developers tap into a community of tech enthusiasts eager to support the next big thing. This model not only secures the necessary capital but also validates the market demand before full-scale production.

The key to successful crowdfunding lies in compelling storytelling, where creators showcase the potential impact of their AI tools. Interactive demos, engaging videos, and detailed roadmaps can significantly enhance appeal, persuading potential backers of the project's worth and their role in a transformative journey. Rewards such as early access to the tool or exclusive features for backers further incentivize contributions, turning funders into early adopters and vocal advocates.

Moreover, feedback from this community can be invaluable, guiding tweaks and enhancements to the AI tool. This iterative process, fueled by crowd insights, ensures the final product not only meets but exceeds consumer expectations, paving the way for broader market success post-launch. Crowdfunding, therefore, is not just a funding mechanism, but a strategic engagement and enhancement tool for AI development.

Grants and Funding Opportunities for AI Startups

For AI startups, navigating the landscape of grants and funding presents a golden opportunity to secure essential capital without diluting equity. Numerous governmental and private foundations offer grants specifically designed to support technological innovation, recognizing the potential of AI to drive future economic growth and societal advancements.

These grants are often bound to specific research themes or development milestones, incentivizing startups to align their AI initiatives with broader objectives such as improving public services, enhancing environmental sustainability, or advancing scientific understanding. Successfully securing a grant not only provides financial runway but also enhances the startup's credibility and attractiveness to further investment.

Beyond grants, numerous incubators and accelerators focus on AI technologies, offering both funding and mentorship in exchange for participation. These programs are crucial accelerators of growth, providing a structured pathway to refining business models, networking with industry leaders, and gaining visibility in the competitive AI landscape.

Exploring these funding avenues requires careful preparation, compelling proposals, and a clear demonstration of potential impact, key elements that, when executed effectively, significantly enhance a startup's trajectory.

Venture Capital Interest in AI Innovations

Venture capital firms are increasingly targeting AI innovations, recognizing their transformative potential across industries. As AI continues to evolve, these investors are keen on startups that promise disruptive solutions, particularly in sectors like healthcare, finance, and autonomous transportation, where AI can significantly enhance efficiency and decision-making processes.

The allure for venture capitalists lies not only in the potential for high returns but also in the strategic positioning that young AI companies can offer. Many VC firms provide more than just capital; they bring industry connections, mentorship, and operational guidance to help nascent companies navigate early-stage challenges. This synergistic relationship accelerates growth and increases the odds of successful market penetration and expansion.

Moreover, the global race to lead in AI technology adds a geopolitical dimension to the investments. VCs are keenly aware of the importance of fostering domestic innovation hubs that can compete on an international stage, adding a layer of strategic investment that goes beyond mere financial returns.

Generating Revenue from AI Assisted Content Creation

AI-assisted content creation is revolutionizing the monetization landscape, offering unprecedented opportunities to generate revenue across diverse digital platforms. By leveraging

AI, content creators can produce high-quality, engaging material at a fraction of the traditional time and cost. This capability allows for rapid scaling of content production, catering to the insatiable demand of the digital age.

Utilizing AI tools in content creation not only enhances efficiency but also opens up innovative revenue streams such as dynamic content personalization, where AI algorithms adjust content to match user preferences and behaviors, thus increasing engagement and the potential for monetization through targeted advertising. Furthermore, AI-generated content can be syndicated across multiple platforms, amplifying reach and monetization prospects through licensing fees and content partnerships.

Moreover, AI-driven analytics can optimize content strategies by identifying trends and predicting consumer behaviors, enabling content creators to produce more impactful, revenue-generating content. Successfully integrating AI into content creation processes ultimately leads to a sustainable competitive advantage, driving higher revenue and enhancing brand value in the crowded digital marketplace.

Using AI to Monetize User-Generated Content Platforms

AI is transforming how user-generated content (UGC) platforms monetize their ecosystems. By efficiently analyzing user data and content preferences, AI enables platforms to deliver personalized advertisements that are more likely to result in user engagement and sales conversion, thereby increasing ad revenue. The key lies in AI's ability to sift through massive datasets to discern patterns that human analysis could miss.

Furthermore, AI can optimize recommendation systems, ensuring that users are exposed to content that keeps them engaged longer. This retention leads to higher ad views and, significantly, enhances subscription models. Platforms can use AI to analyze user feedback and modify features or interface designs to cater more closely to market demands, thus driving memberships and premium upgrades.

Lastly, AI facilitates the creation of new UGC by suggesting content formats and topics that are trending, encouraging user participation. This dynamic feedback loop not only boosts content variety but also attracts a broader audience, creating more monetization opportunities through diversified user engagement.

Establishing a Scale-Up Blueprint for AI Startups

For AI startups, scaling is not just about growing - it's about growing smart. The journey begins with a robust blueprint that maps out not only the infrastructure needed to support larger operations but also anticipates market transformations and technological evolutions. This blueprint should detail strategic hiring, development roadmaps, and potential pivot points which allow the startup to remain agile and responsive.

A successful scale-up strategy also implies a firm grasp of customer acquisition and retention mechanisms. Integrating AI tools to analyze customer data can uncover trends and preferences, thereby enhancing product offerings and customer engagement strategies. Furthermore, maintaining a strong focus on core AI competencies while expanding into new areas can prevent dilution of brand value and ensure continued innovation.

Finally, the role of continuous learning in a scale-up environment cannot be overstated. AI startups must invest in ongoing training and development for their teams to harness cutting-edge AI advancements, ensuring the company's growth is bolstered by the latest industry insights and technologies.

SUMMARY

The chapter 'Monetization Mastery: Turning AI Tools into Revenue Streams' explores the diverse strategies for generating revenue from AI tools and solutions across various industries. The first approach discussed is identifying and targeting profitable AI Markets with substantial growth potential, such as healthcare, finance, and e-commerce. These markets are ripe for AI integration due to their rapid expansion and the inefficiencies present in conventional processes. By analyzing market gaps and assessing competitive landscapes, AI developers can create tailored tools that become indispensable for industry stakeholders, thereby paving the way for robust monetization frameworks.

Developing AI products that cater to these identified needs involves integrating AI capabilities into tools that address specific pain points within industries, thus enhancing adoption and revenue potential. User-centric design, functionality, continuous iteration based on feedback, and data-driven product optimization are highlighted as pivotal in developing AI products with high market demand. Pricing strategies for AI services and tools are shown to be crucial, emphasizing value-based pricing and understanding the competitive pricing landscape. The chapter also outlines the advantages of subscription models or tiered pricing to cater to various user needs and maximize revenue.

Other significant revenue strategies covered include leveraging advertising models where AI facilitates targeted and optimized ads, and the freemium model which attracts a wider user base with free core features while offering premium features for a fee. The exploration of affiliate marketing, partnerships, collaborations, transaction fees, royalties, licensing models, and implementing AI in paid platforms are discussed as viable methods for enhancing AI tool monetization. Each strategy is backed by the common theme of aligning AI tool functionalities with market demand, optimizing user experience, and employing innovative pricing models to stay competitive and profitable in the rapidly evolving tech landscape.

REFERENCES

[1] Hagiu, Andrei & Wright, Julian. 'Multi-sided platforms', International Journal of Industrial Organization, 2015.. https://www.sciencedirect.com/science/article/pii/S0167718715000411

[2] Varian, Hal R. 'Intermediate Microeconomics: A Modern Approach. Ninth Edition'. W.W. Norton & Company, 2014.. https://wwnorton.com/books/9780393920772

[3] Parker, Geoffrey & Van Alstyne, Marshall W. 'Innovation, Openness, and Platform Control', Management Science, 2018.. https://pubsonline.informs.org/doi/10.1287/mnsc.2018.3096

[4] Teece, David J. 'Business Models, Business Strategy and Innovation', Long Range Planning, 2010.. https://www.sciencedirect.com/science/article/pii/S0024630109000515

[5] Osterwalder, Alexander & Pigneur, Yves. 'Business Model Generation', John Wiley & Sons, 2010.. https://www.wiley.com/en-us/Business+Model+Generation%3A+A+Handbook+for+Visionaries%2C+Game+Changers%2C+and+Challengers-p-9780470876411

CASE STUDY: REVOLUTIONIZING RETAIL: AI-DRIVEN PERSONALIZATION AND PRICING STRATEGIES

In the rapidly evolving retail sector, a mid-sized but ambitious e-commerce company, ShopInnovate, has harnessed AI to revolutionize two critical aspects: customer experience through personalization, and dynamic pricing strategies. ShopInnovate, operating primarily in the fashion and electronics domains, integrated AI systems to analyze vast arrays of consumer data, including past purchases, browsing behaviors, and demographic information. This integration facilitated the creation of highly individualized marketing messages and product recommendations, enhancing user engagement and satisfaction. Furthermore, AI-powered algorithms were deployed to adjust prices dynamically based on factors like demand patterns, inventory levels, and competitor pricing, ensuring optimal profitability and market competitiveness. ShopInnovate's strategy illustrates a perfect blend of customer-centric and profit-oriented approaches using AI technology. The company witnessed a 40% increase in customer retention and a 25% rise in revenue within the first year of AI integration. While these outcomes were impressive, the implementation phase had its challenges. The initial integration of AI required substantial investment in both technology and talent. The company needed skilled data scientists to develop predictive models and system engineers to ensure seamless integration with existing IT infrastructure. Additionally, achieving the right balance between personalized marketing and customer privacy posed an ethical challenge, mandating the creation of robust data governance policies. ShopInnovate had to navigate these obstacles by setting clear objectives for their AI implementations, maintaining transparency with customers about data usage, and committing to continuous learning and adaptation to emerging AI advancements. This case exemplifies how AI can transform traditional business operations, tailoring services to consumer needs and market conditions, thereby driving growth and enhancing customer relationships.

Case Study: Optimizing Healthcare: AI-Enhanced Disease Prediction and Management

In a transformative approach to healthcare, MediTech Solutions, a pioneering tech firm specializing in medical AI applications, embarked on an ambitious project to improve disease prediction and management systems through advanced AI tools. Focusing on chronic illnesses such as diabetes and cardiovascular diseases, MediTech Solutions developed a predictive AI model that integrates patient data—ranging from genetic information and lifestyle factors to real-time health metrics collected via IoT devices—aiming to foresee disease progression and recommend personalized intervention plans.

This AI solution employed machine learning algorithms trained on vast datasets provided by healthcare institutions, including historical patient records and latest medical research findings. The primary goal was to analyze the data to identify early signs of disease exacerbation and suggest preventive measures, tailored treatment regimes, and lifestyle adjustments, thus enhancing patient outcomes and reducing hospital readmissions. The implementation of this AI-enabled system not only promised to revolutionize patient management by delivering precision medicine but also aimed at reducing the overall healthcare costs by minimizing the need for intensive medical interventions later in the disease cycle.

However, the journey was fraught with challenges. Data privacy and ethical concerns around patient data usage were paramount. MediTech had to navigate complex regulations and ensure the compliance of their systems with healthcare standards, such as HIPAA in the United States. They established a robust framework for data security and patient confidentiality, which included anonymizing patient data and implementing stringent access controls. Moreover, the integration of AI into existing healthcare infrastructures required seamless interoperability and alignment with clinical workflows, necessitating significant cooperation and training for medical staff.

The outcomes of MediTech Solutions' project, once fully operational, are anticipated to enhance the predictive capacity of healthcare providers, offering a more proactive approach to disease management. The success of this initiative could lead to widespread adoption of AI technologies across the healthcare sector, transforming how care is delivered and experienced by patients worldwide.

Case Study: Strategic AI Deployment in Small Business Lending

In the competitive arena of financial services, FinServTech, a fintech startup specializing in AI-driven solutions for small businesses, identified a lucrative niche: improving the lending process for small and medium enterprises (SMEs). The company developed an AI platform that expedites loan approvals and enhances risk assessment by integrating various data sources, including credit scores, cash flow analysis, and market trends.

FinServTech's AI system employs sophisticated machine learning algorithms to process and analyze a borrower's financial data quickly. This capability vastly reduces the decision-making time for loan approvals, thereby increasing efficiency and customer satisfaction. Moreover, by using predictive analytics, the platform can foresee potential default risks based on economic indicators and the borrower's financial behavior, allowing lenders to tailor their loan offerings with adjustable interest rates and repayment terms to better manage risk.

However, the implementation faced numerous challenges. Firstly, the accuracy of the AI predictions depended heavily on the quality and completeness of the data provided, necessitating strong partnerships with data aggregators and continuous monitoring of data integrity. Additionally, integrating this AI technology with the existing banking systems was technologically demanding, requiring robust APIs and seamless data exchange protocols. Data security was another critical issue, as any compromise could lead to significant financial losses and erosion of customer trust.

Despite these hurdles, the results were transformative. FinServTech witnessed a 50% reduction in loan processing time and a 20% decrease in default rates, which significantly enhanced the profit margins of their client lenders. Their success not only improved operational efficiencies but also provided a model for other fintech companies aiming to innovate within traditional financial frameworks. This case study exemplifies how targeted AI applications can revolutionize specific financial processes, yielding significant competitive advantages while fostering broader financial inclusion for SMEs.

Case Study: Enhancing Real Estate with AI: Optimization of Property Valuation and Customer Matching

In the dynamic sector of real estate, PropTech Innovations, a burgeoning real estate tech company, has embarked on an advanced project to refine property valuation models and optimize customer-property matching using cutting-edge AI technologies. The company, focusing initially on residential markets, implemented a dual AI system. The first part leveraged machine learning to analyze diverse data streams—including historical sales data, neighborhood trends, amenities, and economic indicators—to provide more accurate and real-time property valuations. The second system utilized AI-driven algorithms to match potential buyers with properties that best fit their preferences and budget, streamlining the customer journey and enhancing satisfaction.

The AI systems employed advanced predictive analytics and natural language processing, enabling them to interpret vast amounts of unstructured data from online property listings and customer reviews. This ability allowed PropTech to offer personalized property recommendations to clients, potentially revolutionizing the way real estate transactions are conducted by increasing efficiency and reducing the time properties spend on the market.

However, the integration of AI into PropTech's operational framework was not without challenges. Data privacy and security issues were at the forefront, requiring the implementation of stringent data protection measures to comply with regulations like GDPR in Europe. Moreover, the sophistication of the AI technology necessitated continuous updates and maintenance to adapt to ever-changing market dynamics and customer preferences. This required a significant ongoing investment in both technology and skilled personnel.

Despite these initial hurdles, the outcomes of PropTech Innovations' AI implementation have been promising. The company has observed a 30% increase in customer satisfaction scores and a 20% uptick in the speed of transactions. The precision of their property valuations has also enhanced the credibility of their listings, attracting more high-intent buyers and sellers to their platform. This case illustrates the transformative potential of AI in streamlining complex transactions and tailoring services to meet specific customer needs, setting a benchmark for innovation in the traditional real estate market.

Case Study: AI-Enhanced Sustainable Energy Management in Smart Grids

As the global energy sector shifts towards renewable sources, the integration of AI into energy management systems has become crucial for enhancing efficiency and sustainability. SmartGrid Solutions, a leader in innovative energy technologies, recently embarked on a transformative project to implement AI-driven tools across smart grids to optimize energy distribution and consumption. The project's core objective was to utilize AI to predict demand surges, manage load distribution efficiently, and integrate decentralized renewable energy sources effectively into the grid.

SmartGrid Solutions adopted machine learning algorithms to analyze historical consumption data, weather forecasts, and real-time IoT sensor inputs from various grid points. This data-driven approach enabled predictive analytics to forecast energy demand patterns accurately, allowing for proactive grid adjustments. Moreover, the AI system facilitated the integration of renewable energy sources like solar and wind by predicting their output fluctuations, ensuring a stable energy supply.

However, the project faced substantial challenges. High initial costs and technical complexity in setting up AI systems were significant hurdles. There was also skepticism from stakeholders concerning the reliability of AI decisions in critical scenarios. To address these issues, SmartGrid Solutions conducted extensive pilot tests and provided transparent data analysis demonstrations to prove the system's efficacy. They also focused on robust cybersecurity measures to protect grid data from potential breaches.

The implementation of AI dramatically improved grid efficiency and resilience. Energy waste was minimized by dynamically matching supply with demand, and renewable energy utilization rates increased significantly. These advancements not only optimized operational costs but also enhanced customer satisfaction through improved service reliability and reduced carbon footprints. This case study exemplifies the potential of AI in transforming traditional industries by leveraging data to drive decision-making, forecast critical outcomes, and integrate innovative technologies, all while supporting sustainability goals.

Case Study: Leveraging AI for Enhanced Inventory Management in Multinational Corporations

GlobalTech Inc., a multinational corporation with diverse product lines ranging from consumer electronics to home appliances, faced substantial challenges in managing its inventory across various global markets. Recognizing the need for an advanced solution to these challenges, GlobalTech implemented an AI-driven inventory management system designed to optimize stock levels, reduce holding costs, and improve supply chain responsiveness. The AI system utilized machine learning algorithms to forecast demand based on multiple factors, including market trends, seasonal variations, economic indicators, and consumer behavior analytics collected from their global sales data.

The AI platform was integrated with GlobalTech's existing ERP systems, facilitating real-time data exchange and enhancing the accuracy of demand forecasting. By processing vast datasets, the AI system could identify patterns and predict future sales with high precision, allowing GlobalTech to adjust their inventory in real-time, minimizing both overstock and stockouts. As a result, the company saw a reduction in holding costs by 25% and improved the overall efficiency of its supply chain operations.

However, the implementation of such a sophisticated AI system was not without its hurdles. GlobalTech had to overcome significant challenges, including the standardization of data formats across different regions and the training of local staff to effectively use the new system.

Data privacy regulations in various countries also posed a problem, requiring the company to ensure compliance while handling sensitive information. Moreover, the initial setup and integration costs were substantial, necessitating a clear strategic vision to justify the investment.

Despite these challenges, the outcomes were overwhelmingly positive. The enhanced inventory management system allowed GlobalTech to respond more agilely to market changes, preventing overproduction and reducing waste. Long-term benefits included more accurate budgeting and planning, improved customer satisfaction due to better product availability, and a stronger competitive edge in the marketplace. This case study exemplifies how AI can transform foundational business processes such as inventory management into strategic advantages, leveraging data to optimize operations and drive company growth.

Case Study: Modernizing Agriculture: AI-Driven Predictive Analytics for Crop Management

In an era where agriculture faces myriad challenges from climate change to resource scarcity, AgriTech Solutions, a pioneering company in smart farming, deployed AI-driven predictive analytics to revolutionize crop management and maximize yields. Their project, named 'SmartHarvest', aimed to integrate AI with IoT devices across vast farmlands, collecting and analyzing data on soil conditions, weather patterns, crop health, and pest activity to inform and streamline farm management decisions.

AgriTech Solutions equipped drones and ground sensors with machine learning algorithms that monitored crop conditions in real time. These tools gathered enormous volumes of data which, when processed, provided insights that were previously unattainable through conventional means. AI models predicted the optimal times for planting, watering, and harvesting, and suggested the best crop rotation practices and pesticide applications, tailored not only to the fields' conditions but also to current market demands and environmental considerations.

However, the deployment of 'SmartHarvest' was fraught with challenges. The foremost was the resistance from traditional farmers who were skeptical of replacing age-old farming practices with technology-driven approaches. Additionally, the initial setup required significant capital investment, not only for the equipment but also for the training of personnel to manage and interpret the AI systems. There were also technical challenges regarding data integration from different types of IoT devices and ensuring the AI system's accuracy and reliability over diverse and changing agricultural environments.

Despite these hurdles, the project results were groundbreaking. Farms using 'SmartHarvest' reported up to a 30% increase in yield and a significant reduction in resource wastage. Their precise use of water and optimized pesticide application not only led to cost savings but also minimized environmental impact. The success of this initiative underscores the transformative potential of AI in agriculture, demonstrating how technology can drive sustainability and efficiency in one of the world's oldest industries. This case highlights the importance of digital sophistication in achieving high precision in crop management and the need to foster technological acceptance in traditional sectors.

Case Study: AI-Driven Scalability in Startup Ecosystems

In the heart of Silicon Valley, a progressive tech startup, TechAdapt, recognized the challenge many startups face: scaling business operations efficiently while maintaining innovation and managing costs. Leveraging AI, TechAdapt sought to refine their product offerings, automate key processes, and enhance decision-making to fuel growth and resilience in the competitive tech industry.

TechAdapt implemented AI-driven tools across various departments—sales, marketing, and customer support—to streamline operations and gather insightful data. For instance, they used predictive analytics to forecast market trends and customer behaviors, which allowed them to adjust their sales strategies proactively. Furthermore, AI-powered chatbots were employed to handle routine customer inquiries, significantly reducing the response time and allowing human agents to focus on complex issues that required a personalized touch.

However, the path was not devoid of challenges. Integrating AI into existing systems required substantial upfront investment, both in financial terms and staff training. The startup had to ensure that their employees were adept at using new technologies, and they faced the daunting task of setting up an infrastructure robust enough to handle complex AI processes, including data collection, analysis, and security.

The results, however, justified the initial hurdles. TechAdapt observed a 50% improvement in operational efficiency and a 30% reduction in customer service response times. Sales conversions improved due to better-targeted marketing strategies. Additionally, the real-time data provided by AI systems enabled agile adjustments to business strategies, fostering a culture of responsiveness and innovation within the team.

This case illustrates not only the potential of AI to transform business operations but also highlights the strategic considerations necessary for successful AI integration. For startups like TechAdapt looking to scale, AI offers a compelling toolset to accelerate growth, provided that they navigate the associated challenges effectively. Through careful planning, substantial training, and strategic investment, AI can significantly enhance operational efficiency and competitive edge in the dynamic startup ecosystem.

REVIEW QUESTIONS

1. A startup focusing on AI in healthcare is considering how to monetize their innovative tool designed for real-time patient diagnostics. Which of the following strategies would likely provide the most effective path to revenue generation?

A) Implementing a freemium model where basic features are free, but advanced features require a subscription

B) Only offering the complete tool for a high one-time purchase price

C) Providing the tool for free and relying solely on donor funding

D) Selling ad space within the application interface

Answer: A

Explanation: In the context of AI-driven healthcare applications, leveraging a freemium model can serve as an effective monetization strategy. This method allows basic access to encourage widespread adoption and a low barrier of entry, which is important in sensitive and essential services like healthcare. Over time, users who find value in the basic offerings are more likely to upgrade to access advanced features, leading to a steady revenue stream while maintaining patient engagement. This approach aligns with health sector dynamics where user critical mass can drive broader acceptance and standardization of new technologies. Offering completely free services with donor funding often lacks sustainability, selling the tool at a high one-time cost could diminish rapid adoption rates, and using ad space might compromise user experience in a clinical context, making the freemium model the most viable option.

2. An AI startup has developed a platform that uses advanced algorithms to provide personalized learning experiences. They are considering several pricing models. Which model would likely attract a broad user base while ensuring stable revenue growth?

A) A standard one-time fee for perpetual access

B) A tiered subscription model providing different levels of features and customization

C) Offering the platform entirely for free to maximize user numbers

D) Charging per user interaction with the platform

Answer: B

Explanation: For AI technologies in educational tools that require continuous updates and personalization, a tiered subscription model is typically most effective. This approach allows for flexibility and scalability, accommodating different user needs and budget ranges. Basic tiers can attract a broader user base, while premium tiers can cater to power users or institutions looking for more advanced features and customization options. Such flexibility helps in scaling the user base while also ensuring the revenue necessary for ongoing development and support. In contrast, charging a one-time fee might limit recurring revenue essential for long-term sustainability, offering the platform for free could challenge financial viability, and charging per interaction may deter prolonged use or deeper engagement, essential for learning platforms.

REVIEW QUESTIONS

3. A FinTech AI startup specializes in fraud detection and is considering how to price its service. Given the high stakes of financial security, which of the following pricing strategies would be most appropriate?

A) A freemium model with basic detection for free and advanced services for a fee

B) Penetration pricing to quickly build a large user base followed by price increases

C) A high premium price from the outset, reflecting the high value of security

D) A pay-as-you-go model charging per transaction monitored

Answer: D

Explanation: In the context of AI-powered fraud detection services in FinTech, a pay-as-you-go model charging per transaction monitored is a compelling option. This model aligns costs directly with value provided, as users pay more when they process more transactions which likely corresponds to higher earnings or larger scale operations needing more robust security. This direct correlation between cost and usage ensures that smaller businesses can afford protection while larger enterprises, which handle higher transaction volumes, contribute more to revenue based on their scale and potentially greater risk exposure. Using this model in such a critical area as fraud prevention can also highlight the tangible benefits of AI, fostering trust and encouraging adoption. Other models like freemium or penetration pricing might undervalue the service's impact or create initial pricing expectations that could be hard to adjust later without affecting customer satisfaction.

MARKETING AI: TECHNIQUES FOR PROMOTING AI-GENERATED SERVICES AND PRODUCTS

Understanding the AI Market: Consumer Behavior and Demand

Comprehending the AI market starts with studying consumer behavior and identifying demand patterns. As AI technology emerges across various sectors, understanding specific consumer needs becomes pivotal. This data-driven insight into preferences and purchasing tendencies shapes the development and marketing of AI products, ensuring alignment with current and future demands.

The dynamics of the AI market are influenced by factors such as technological literacy, perceived value of AI solutions, and the level of trust in automation. Demographic and psychographic analyses provide a deeper understanding of who the potential consumers are and what drives their decision-making processes. This segmentation underpins targeted marketing efforts, addressing concerns and highlighting benefits specific to each group.

Moreover, the rapid pace of AI evolution demands that companies keep abreast of changing trends. Continuous market research and consumer feedback loops are essential to adapt product offerings and remain competitive. By analyzing behavioral data, companies can anticipate shifts in demand and tailor their AI solutions to meet evolving market needs effectively.

Creating a Compelling Narrative for AI Services and Products

Crafting a compelling narrative for AI services and products hinges on the ability to connect innovative technology with real-world benefits. Stories that resonate often highlight how AI can solve pressing problems or enhance daily life, weaving technical capabilities into relatable human experiences. It's not just about what AI can do, but how it makes life better, simpler, or more exciting.

In narrating AI's advantages, it's crucial to present them in a context that feels immediate and plausible. This means explaining complex technologies in layman's terms and illustrating their impacts through case studies or hypothetical scenarios. When customers understand the practical applications and potential returns of AI, trust and interest are fostered, paving the way for acceptance and adoption.

Beyond individual benefits, narratives should also illustrate the broader societal and ethical impacts of AI, aligning the technology with values important to the audience. By integrating such narratives, marketers can elevate AI from a mere tool to a transformative force for good, capturing the imagination and wallets of consumers.

Digital Marketing Strategies for AI Tools

In the digital realm, marketing AI tools require strategies that not only capture attention but also translate complex functionalities into user benefits. Harnessing the power of digital marketing involves multiple channels and tactics tailored to specific target audiences and their platforms. It's about presenting AI as an indispensable asset, mirroring its capabilities in campaign creativity and execution.

A pivotal strategy is search engine marketing, which enhances visibility through optimized keywords specific to AI offerings. Pair this with pay-per-click campaigns that drive immediate traffic, providing granular data to refine ongoing efforts. Social media platforms offer fertile ground for storytelling, where interactive and educational content can demystify AI concepts for the layman, fostering engagement and nurturing leads.

Email marketing campaigns that educate and inform about the benefits and updates of AI products can foster loyalty and encourage advocacy. Utilizing retargeting technologies ensures your AI solutions stay top-of-mind among those who've shown interest, improving conversion rates over time. Thus, effective digital marketing in AI necessitates a synergy of technique and technology, engaging the digital consumer at every touchpoint.

Utilizing Social Media to Boost AI Product Visibility

The power of social media in increasing visibility for AI products cannot be overstated. Platforms like Facebook, Instagram, Twitter, and LinkedIn offer unique opportunities to connect with various demographics, each with its preferred content style and interaction. By tailoring AI product highlights to these preferences, companies can maximize engagement and reach. Visual platforms like Instagram are perfect for showcasing demos and real-life applications of AI, while LinkedIn caters to professional endorsements and detailed discussions.

Creating viral content also plays a crucial role. This includes infographics explaining AI concepts, short videos demonstrating benefits, and interactive posts that invite user participation. Hashtags can extend reach beyond immediate followers, tapping into global conversations about AI and technology advancements. Strategic post timing based on analytics maximizes visibility among target audiences.

Engagement doesn't end with posting. Responding to comments, sharing user-generated content related to the product, and maintaining an active social media presence personalize the AI brand. It transforms users from passive observers to active participants in the AI journey, enhancing customer loyalty and enlarging the community of advocates.

Content Marketing: Crafting Targeted Blogs and Articles

In the digital marketplace, content is king. Crafting targeted blogs and articles for AI services and products goes beyond mere dissemination of information; it involves creating content that educates, engages, and excites the potential consumer. Well-crafted articles position AI technologies not just as tools, but as solutions to real-world problems, enhancing relevance and user engagement.

Effective content marketing leverages meticulous research to tailor messages that resonate with specific audiences. By focusing on the problems AI can solve and the efficiencies it can introduce, companies can craft narratives that align closely with user needs and interests. This strategic alignment increases the likelihood of content being shared, thereby amplifying reach and influence.

Moreover, incorporating SEO best practices into content creation ensures that these insightful articles gain visibility in search engine results, drawing more organic traffic to company sites. Regular updates and engaging multimedia elements like videos and infographics can further enhance reader engagement, establishing a brand as a thought leader in the AI space.

SEO Optimization Techniques for AI Products

In the bustling digital marketplace, the optimization of search engine strategies (SEO) for AI products is crucial. Effective SEO begins with identifying keywords that resonate not only with AI technology but also with the specific solutions that these products offer. These keywords should strategically populate website content, blog posts, and product descriptions to enhance discoverability and ranking.

Beyond keywords, the technical health of a website is paramount. AI companies should ensure fast loading times, mobile optimization, and secure connections, as these factors significantly influence search rankings. Incorporating structured data markup can also help search engines better understand and index the content, elevating visibility in rich snippets and specialized search results.

Lastly, content relevance cannot be overstated. Regularly updated, high-quality content that addresses current trends and customer questions keeps a site fresh and authoritative. Link building through collaborations with reputable sites in the AI industry further boosts domain authority, cementing a site's reputation and its climb up the SEO ladder.

Influencer and Affiliate Marketing for AI Services

Harnessing the influence of key personalities in the tech and AI spheres is a transformative strategy for marketing AI services. Influencers with a robust following on platforms like YouTube, Twitter, and tech-focused podcasts can demystify AI technologies and showcase their potential. This not only helps in simplifying complex AI concepts but also in highlighting user-friendly aspects that resonate with both tech-savvy and general audiences.

Affiliate marketing complements this approach by leveraging partnerships with tech blogs and AI-focused websites that cater to a niche audience. Affiliates provide authentic content and reviews, adding credibility and trust to what might otherwise be seen as an impersonal technology. They typically earn commissions based on the sales or leads they generate, incentivizing them to present AI tools and services in the most favorable light.

Together, influencer and affiliate marketing create a powerful ecosystem for promoting AI services. They connect these advanced products with real-life applications, making the benefits tangible and accessible. This strategy not only drives sales but also enhances brand reputation and customer loyalty in the competitive AI market.

Lead Generation Strategies for AI Companies

Effective lead generation for AI companies demands a nuanced approach, integrating both traditional and innovative methods to captivate and convert potential customers into qualified leads. At the forefront is the use of AI-driven analytics to pinpoint potential leads through behavior prediction and engagement analytics. By analyzing data collected from various touchpoints, AI companies can predict which prospects might be more inclined to purchase, allowing for targeted and personalized outreach.

Webinars and educational workshops are crucial in illustrating the value and application of AI technologies. These platforms serve not only as a meansto communicate complex AI capabilities but also to capture leads interested in specific AI solutions. Registration for these events provides a direct line to engaged potential customers.

Content personalization further enhances lead generation strategies. Using AI to tailor content according to user preferences and previous interactions can dramatically increase conversion rates. This approach ensures that the potential clients receive the most relevant information, boosting engagement and facilitating smoother transitions from leads to loyal customers.

Email Marketing Campaigns for AI Product Promotion

Email marketing remains a powerful tool in the AI industry, serving as a direct line to potential customers. By curating personalized email content that addresses specific needs and interests, AI companies can effectively communicate the value of their products. This method allows for detailed explanations of AI capabilities and how they solve real-world problems, enhancing the recipient's understanding and interest.

The key to successful email campaigns lies in segmentation and automation. AI tools enable the analysis of customer behaviors and preferences to segment email lists accurately. This ensures that marketing messages are highly relevant and timed perfectly, increasing open and conversion rates. Automated follow-up emails can be used to nurture leads, providing them with additional information and incentives, such as free trials or demos, to encourage deeper engagement.

Finally, monitoring the performance of email campaigns is crucial. AI companies should leverage analytics to track open rates, click-through rates, and conversions. This data helps in refining the email strategy, ensuring messages resonate with the audience and drive meaningful engagement. A/B testing different email elements can further optimize the effectiveness of the campaign, tailoring messages that captivate and convert.

Webinars and Live Demos: Interacting with Potential Customers

Webinars and live demos present a dynamic platform for AI companies to engage directly with potential customers, demonstrating the practical applications and transformative potential of AI technologies. These interactive sessions provide an opportunity to showcase AI tools in action, allowing for real-time demonstrations that clarify complex functionalities and underscore their relevance in solving industry-specific challenges.

By incorporating Q&A segments, these events foster a dialogic environment where attendees can voice concerns, probe deeper into the intricacies of AI systems, and gain personalized insights. This direct engagement is invaluable in building trust and rapport, key elements in turning interest into investment.

Moreover, webinars and live demos are pivotal in capturing detailed data about attendee interests and behaviors through polls and feedback forms. This information is instrumental for refining marketing strategies and tailoring follow-up communications, ensuring that subsequent interactions are highly targeted and more likely to convert leads into loyal customers.

Partnership Marketing: Collaborating for Broader Reach

In the realm of AI, where innovation meets practical application, partnership marketing emerges as a strategic approach to amplify reach and solidify market presence. By forging alliances with complementary companies, AI firms can co-create campaigns that leverage mutual strengths. This synergy not only diversifies marketing channels but also enhances credibility and broadens audience bases for all involved parties.

The essence of successful partnership marketing lies in the selection of partners whose visions align with that of the AI company. Collaborations might range from tech forums hosting joint webinars to software enterprises integrating AI tools into their offerings. Each partnership serves as a bridge, connecting AI companies to new sectors and demographics, multiplying touchpoints with potential users.

Moreover, these collaborations often pave the way for shared knowledge and innovations, pushing technological boundaries further. As companies pool resources, from research insights to marketing budgets, the impact of their joint efforts is potentiated, setting a precedent for enduring growth and sustained market relevance.

In summary, partnership marketing in the AI industry is not just about sharing efforts but multiplying success, crafting a network of influence that propels forward-thinking brands towards new heights of market penetration.

Leveraging Online Reviews and Testimonials

In the digital landscape where AI tools and services are abundant, leveraging online reviews and testimonials becomes pivotal. These feedback mechanisms humanize the AI offerings by narrating real-user experiences, which are key to building consumer trust and credibility. Positive testimonials and well-managed reviews can greatly enhance the brand's reputation, making it a go-to choice for prospective users.

Utilizing testimonials effectively involves showcasing them prominently on corporate websites, during webinars, and even in email marketing campaigns. Strategically placed, these testimonials can influence potential customers at critical decision-making junctures. Moreover, incorporating user-generated content like video testimonials and case studies adds an authentic voice, providing clear insights into the functionality and impact of the AI products.

Finally, managing and responding to online reviews reflects a company's commitment to customer satisfaction. Regularly engaging with reviewers and addressing concerns demonstrates responsiveness, fostering a loyal user base. Enhanced by AI, analysis of review patterns can guide product improvements and highlight strengths, further tailoring marketing strategies to match user expectations and needs.

Trade Shows and Conferences: Networking for AI Products

Trade shows and conferences represent pivotal arenas for showcasing AI innovations, allowing AI companies to engage directly with industry peers, potential clients, and thought leaders. These events facilitate face-to-face interactions that can solidify relationships and foster trust, key components in the successful marketing of new technologies. Attendees gain firsthand experience with AI products, offering companies immediate feedback that can be integral in refining offerings.

By strategically positioning themselves at such gatherings, AI companies maximize visibility among stakeholders actively seeking the latest in technology. Beyond displaying products, these events are platforms for delivering powerful presentations and participating in panel discussions, which further establish a company's thought leadership and industry authority.

Furthermore, trade shows and conferences often lead to collaborations and partnerships, providing AI companies with opportunities to expand their networks and explore new market possibilities. The collection of business cards and follow-ups post-event can often emerge as invaluable leads, fostering long-term business relationships and collaborations.

AI Product Launch Strategies

Launching an AI product requires a deft blend of tactical execution and strategic foresight. Initially, it's crucial to establish a 'launch window' that aligns with market readiness and competitor activities, timing the introduction to capture maximum attention. Building anticipation through teasers, sneak peeks, and pre-launch reviews can engage potential users early in the journey, setting the stage for a receptive market debut.

Once the stage is set, executing a multi-channel launch strategy becomes imperative. Integrating platforms such as targeted emails, social media blasts, and specialized webinars can create a comprehensive engagement network. Launch events, whether virtual or in-person, serve as a focal point, providing a detailed exposition of the product's capabilities and industry applications, augmented by interactive sessions to deepen user interest.

Post-launch, the focus should shift towards gathering user feedback and swiftly implementing improvements to enhance product performance and user satisfaction. Supporting early adopters through dedicated resources like chatbots or customer service can solidify a loyal user base, turning initial users into long-term advocates. Effective utilization of analytics during this phase can inform ongoing marketing strategies, ensuring the product not only launches successfully but also achieves sustainable growth.

Customer Retention Techniques in the AI Industry

In the ever-evolving AI industry, retaining customers hinges not just on innovative products but also on nurturing enduring relationships. Central to this are custom AI-driven analytics systems, which track user engagement and product performance, tailoring interactions to user preferences and predicting churn risks. By leveraging targeted communications based on these insights, AI companies can proactively address client needs, enhancing satisfaction and loyalty.

Moreover, integrating AI into customer service platforms, such as chatbots and virtual assistants, optimizes the customer experience by providing immediate, personalized support. These AI tools learn from each interaction, continuously improving their responses and preemptively resolving potential issues, which solidifies user trust and dependency.

Loyalty programs tailored with AI also play a critical role. They not only reward long-term usage but also personalize rewards to suit individual consumer behaviors, making incentives more relevant and enticing.

Collectively, these strategies ensure that AI companies don't just acquire customers—they build a loyal community.

Public Relations Tactics for AI Companies

In the fast-evolving terrain of AI, public relations play a crucial role in shaping perceptions and building brand authority. Essential tactics involve articulating clear, transparent messages that resonate with both the tech-savvy and the layman. This duality in communication helps demystify AI technologies while highlighting their practical benefits, thereby cultivating broader acceptance and enthusiasm.

Press releases and media interactions are indispensable, enabling companies to announce breakthroughs and partnerships strategically. Tailoring messages for different media platforms ensures that each narrative captures the essence of the innovation while catering to the specific interests of diverse audiences. Active participation in tech talks and panel discussions also boosts visibility and establishes company representatives as thought leaders within the industry.

Moreover, AI companies should leverage crisis communication strategies preemptively. By preparing to address potential concerns or ethical implications associated with AI, companies reinforce their commitment to transparency and ethical practices, securing trust and loyalty that are foundational for long-term success.

Video Marketing: Using Visuals to Explain AI Capabilities

In the rapidly expanding realm of AI, video marketing serves as a quintessential medium for demystifying technology and showcasing the practical benefits of AI services and products. By encapsulating complex AI functionalities into digestible visual narratives, AI companies can engage a broad audience, making sophisticated technology accessible and appealing. This method particularly resonates with visual learners, who constitute a significant portion of the online audience.

Videos have the unique capability to illustrate the dynamic capabilities of AI tools through demonstrations, animations, and expert interviews. By visually representing data flows, AI decision-making processes, or the before-and-after scenarios of AI implementation, companies foster a deeper understanding and appreciation of the technology's impact. Moreover, consistent video content that highlights ongoing advancements and case studies can keep the audience engaged and informed over time.

Furthermore, platforms like YouTube, Vimeo, and social media channels significantly enhance the visibility of these videos. Through strategic SEO practices and social sharing, AI companies maximize their outreach, leading to increased brand recognition and adoption rates. Compelling video content, therefore, not only educates potential clients but also serves as a powerful tool for lead generation and market expansion.

Podcast Marketing: Engaging Audiences with Audio Content

In the digital age, podcast marketing emerges as a compelling channel to amplify the reach and understanding of AI products. Podcasts cater to an engaged audience seeking in-depth discussions and insights, making them ideal for delving deep into AI's complexities and potentials. Through episodic releases, AI companies can gradually build a narrative that educates listeners on AI technologies, discusses real-world applications, and highlights user testimonials, thereby fostering a community around their innovations.

Moreover, collaborations with influencers and subject-matter experts in the tech industry can enhance the credibility and appeal of the podcast content. These partnerships serve to cross-pollinate ideas, attracting diverse listeners who may not have previously engaged with AI-centric content. This strategy not only broadens the demographic reach but also ingrains the AI brand within various listener communities.

Lastly, incorporating listener interactions, such as Q&A sessions, enhances the dynamic engagement of podcasts. By addressing audience queries and exploring their perspectives, AI companies create a feedback-rich platform. Such interactive episodes ensure the content remains relevant and grounded in listener interest, thereby boosting ongoing engagement and loyalty to the podcast series.

Targeted Advertising: PPC and Paid Social for AI Products

In the landscape of AI marketing, precision in reaching prospective customers is crucial. Pay-Per-Click (PPC) and paid social media advertising stand as powerful tools in this arsenal, allowing AI companies to target ads based on specific demographics, interests, and even behaviors. This specificity not only improves the relevance of ads but also optimizes budget spend by focusing resources on highly interested or niche markets.

Deploying ad campaigns across platforms like Google Ads and Facebook enables a multi-faceted approach. For AI products, where education of the consumer is often necessary, these platforms offer ad formats tailored to engagement and education, such as video ads or interactive carousel displays. Integration of AI in these campaigns can enhance optimization further, employing algorithms to test ad variants and identify the most effective messaging and design.

Moreover, the data garnered from these campaigns provides invaluable insights. AI companies can track ROI meticulously, adjusting strategies in real-time to enhance the efficacy of their advertising efforts. Analyzing user interaction with ads also feeds back into product development, ensuring that marketing and product evolution are tightly interlinked.

Analyzing Marketing Data to Refine AI Promotion Strategies

In the AI sector, data isn't just a resource; it's the backbone of strategic marketing. Every interaction, click, and engagement across various platforms creates data points that, when analyzed properly, empower companies to refine and optimize their AI product promotion strategies. Collecting this data is only the first step; the critical process involves converting these vast quantities of raw data into actionable insights.

Advanced analytics tools play a pivotal role in this process. They sift through the data to identify patterns and trends that reveal what captures customer interest and drives conversions. This might involve testing different messages, timing, and channels to see what resonates best with the target demographic. Furthermore, segmentation techniques enable marketers to tailor their strategies to specific groups, enhancing the personalization of marketing efforts.

Lastly, continuous analysis ensures that AI companies are agile, allowing them to adapt quickly to market changes or technological advancements. This dynamism not only leads to better marketing outcomes but also contributes to the creation of a refined, customer-centric approach that keeps the offerings competitive and relevant. By applying these data-driven strategies, AI businesses maximize their market influence and profitability.

International Marketing: Reaching Global Markets with AI

The globalization of AI technologies encourages a diverse strategy for reaching international markets. To effectively promote AI-driven products and services globally, marketers must understand regional variations in market receptiveness, regulatory environments, and technological sophistication. This tailored approach ensures that marketing campaigns resonate culturally and legally across borders.

Language localization and regional marketing tactics are essential. For instance, AI companies need to adapt their messages to fit local languages, values, and norms to foster a deeper connection with international audiences. Collaborating with local influencers and adapting SEO practices to regional search engines can further enhance visibility and engagement.

Moreover, the integration of global payment systems and customer support in multiple languages are crucial for closing the loop of international transactions and maintaining customer satisfaction. Such comprehensive strategies are not just about translating content but also about truly understanding and adapting to local consumer behaviors, making AI accessible and appealing worldwide.

Crafting Offers and Promotions for AI Products

Developing offers and promotions for AI products demands a unique blend of innovation and strategic acumen. Unlike conventional products, AI solutions often require educating potential consumers about their functionality and benefits. Therefore, crafting offers that intrigue and educate simultaneously can significantly boost engagement and conversion rates.

A successful promotional tactic is bundling AI products with complementary services or training sessions, enhancing the perceived value. Discounts or trials can also be effective, particularly if they are timed to coincide with industry events or technological milestones, which can increase the sense of urgency and exclusivity.

Moreover, personalized promotions, powered by AI itself, can directly speak to the user's specific needs or past behaviors, creating a more compelling reason to engage. These must be refined through ongoing data analysis to ensure they remain relevant and appealing to a dynamic consumer base. Collectively, these strategies form a robust framework for enticing prospects and expanding market foothold while showcasing the innovative prowess of AI offerings.

Community Building: Engaging Users on Platforms like Discord and Reddit

Effective community building on platforms such as Discord and Reddit is becoming central to marketing AI-driven products. Discord serves as a real-time hub for enthusiast communities, offering AI companies a platform to host discussions, engage in direct feedback, and foster a sense of belonging among users. Interactive AMA (Ask Me Anything) sessions or community-led projects can empower users, giving them a direct role in evolving product features or content.

Reddit, with its subreddit ecosystems, allows for niche targeting and granular interaction. AI marketers can utilize AMAs, subreddit postings, and participatory threads to share insights, gather user input, and increase transparency. This approach not only humanizes the AI brand but also amplifies user investment in the product's success.

Moreover, continuous interaction on these platforms can transform users into product advocates, who in turn provide organic endorsements and tutorials to new users. This organic growth is vital for sustained engagement and helps in mapping out future enhancements based on real user experiences.

Case Studies: Successful Marketing Campaigns for AI Products

Examining past marketing triumphs, the promotion of the AI tool 'SmartSpeech' exemplifies strategic execution. Initially targeting tech enthusiasts through specialized podcasts and dynamic YouTube tutorials, SmartSpeech saw a significant growth in user base and brand recognition. This carefully curated media mix not only educated potential users about benefits and applications but also established credibility. Collaboration with influencers in the tech space amplified reach, narrating personal experiences that resonated with potential customers, thereby driving conversions.

Another notable campaign was for the AI investment app 'WealthAI'. It leveraged localized digital ad campaigns tailored to specific investor communities worldwide, integrating culturally-relevant messages and offers. The campaign's success was measured through an uptick in registrations during financial literacy month, a strategic period that aligned well with the app's educational value proposition. Marketing data from these efforts fed into continual refinement of user engagement strategies.

These cases reflect the vital role of innovative promotion and precise market alignment in crafting successful marketing narratives around AI products. By analyzing what strategies proved effective, AI companies can replicate this success in diverse market conditions.

Future Trends in AI Product Marketing

As AI technologies continue to evolve, their integration into marketing strategies will further deepen, creating more personalized and predictive marketing outcomes. Blending AI with emerging technologies such as augmented reality and virtual reality will offer immersive experiences tailor-made to individual preferences, heightening engagement and elevating the user journey.

Moreover, the rise of generative AI could revolutionize content creation, enabling marketers to produce large-scale, customized content efficiently. This will fortify personalization efforts, making each consumer interaction increasingly unique and persuasive. Ethical considerations will gain prominence, guiding the responsible use of AI in discerning and respecting consumer privacy while offering enhanced customization.

Additionally, voice-activated AI through smart speakers and other IoT devices will reshape how brands connect with consumers, making interactions more seamless and integrated into daily life. These trends will define the robust frontier of AI-driven marketing, pushing boundaries and creating unprecedented opportunities for growth and engagement in the landscape of product promotion.

Ethical Marketing Practices for AI-Driven Services

In the rapidly evolving domain of AI-driven services, ethical marketing practices are paramount. As AI technologies impact a wide array of industries, maintaining transparency and honesty in marketing these products is crucial. Principled marketing strategies not only foster trust but also enhance customer loyalty by demonstrating commitment to ethical standards.

Companies must be transparent about the capabilities and limitations of their AI products to avoid misleading customers. Clear communication regarding data usage and privacy policies is equally essential, as it reassures customers about the security of their personal information. Moreover, marketers should avoid using fear-based or overly aggressive sales tactics, opting instead for educational content that informs potential users about the benefits and realistic applications of AI.

Ethical marketing also involves inclusivity, ensuring that AI products are accessible to a diverse customer base. Marketers should strive to eliminate bias in AI algorithms and representations in promotional materials. By promoting AI services and products ethically, companies not only adhere to high standards but also contribute to a more trusting and informed consumer base.

SUMMARY

The chapter delves into modern marketing strategies for AI services and products, highlighting the necessity for adapting traditional marketing approaches to the unique challenges and opportunities presented by AI technology. It begins by analyzing the AI market, focusing on consumer behavior and demand patterns. Key factors such as technological literacy, perceived value, and trust in automation influence consumer dynamics, necessitating continuous market research and adaptation to trends.

A compelling narrative is vital in marketing AI, where the emphasis is on demystifying AI services and linking them to real-world benefits. Marketing narratives should not only communicate the functional capabilities of AI but also its potential societal contributions, making the technology relatable and desirable. In the digital realm, targeted strategies across various platforms, including search engine optimization, social media marketing, and email campaigns, are essential to articulate the benefits of AI tools effectively to different audiences.

Social media platforms like Instagram and LinkedIn offer opportunities for visibility, where strategies such as engaging content and responsive interaction are crucial. Content marketing, through blogs and articles, plays a pivotal role in educating and engaging potential customers, emphasizing AI's problem-solving potential. SEO techniques are also critical for enhancing online visibility and attracting organic traffic.

The chapter further discusses the importance of influencer and affiliate marketing in making AI relatable and trustworthy. Influencers can simplify complex AI concepts, thereby enhancing consumer understanding and acceptance. Lead generation strategies are highlighted as crucial for identifying and nurturing potential customers, mainly through personalized content and AI-driven analytics.

Finally, the chapter covers various promotional tactics including partnership marketing, utilizing testimonials, and engaging potential customers through webinars and live demos, which are crucial for effective communication and product positioning. Each segment confirms that AI marketing must be continuously insightful, ethical, and adaptive to capture and retain consumer interest in a market characterized by rapid technological advancements.

REFERENCES

[1] Kietzmann, J., & Canhoto, A. (2017). Bots, algorithms, and the future of the finance services industry. Business Horizons, 60(1), 135-144.. https://www.sciencedirect.com/science/article/pii/S0007681316301202

[2] Kaplan, A. M., & Haenlein, M. (2021). Siri, Siri, in my hand: Who's the fairest in the land? On the interpretations, illustrations, and implications of artificial intelligence. Business Horizons, 64(1), 15-25.. https://www.sciencedirect.com/science/article/pii/S0007681319301238

CASE STUDY: LEVERAGING AI TO REVOLUTIONIZE MARKET ANALYSIS IN RETAIL

The year is 2023, and RetailMax Inc., a prominent retail corporation with over 200 stores globally, faced a dilemma. Despite a robust customer base, their sales had hit a plateau. The existing marketing strategies seemed inadequate in the face of rapidly changing consumer preferences fueled by emerging technologies and shifts in the retail industry. The executive team at RetailMax decided to harness artificial intelligence to revitalize their marketing efforts and better understand their customers.

RetailMax embarked on crafting a comprehensive AI-powered marketing strategy that integrated data from various touchpoints such as sales transactions, online shopping behaviors, and social media engagement into a centralized system. The primary goal was to develop a machine learning model that could predict consumer buying patterns and identify emerging trends in real-time. They employed predictive analytics to anticipate product popularity, allowing for dynamic inventory adjustments and targeted marketing campaigns tailored to consumer behavior and preferences.

The impact was profound. Within the first quarter following the AI integration, RetailMax noticed a 15% increase in customer engagement across all platforms. More importantly, the personalized marketing campaigns resulted in a 30% rise in conversion rates. As AI evolved, RetailMax continued refining their systems, using customer feedback and AI analytics to further personalize shopping experiences.

However, the integration of AI into RetailMax's strategy was not without challenges. The company had to navigate complex data privacy issues, ensuring compliance with global standards and maintaining consumer trust. They also faced the technical challenge of training their employees to adapt to new AI-driven tools and methodologies. By prioritizing transparency and investing in comprehensive staff training, RetailMax not only overcame these hurdles but also fostered an innovative culture that embraced continuous learning and improvement.

Case Study: Optimizing AI-Driven Social Media Campaigns for Global Tech Launch

In late 2023, a cutting-edge tech startup, NextGen Innovations, prepared to launch its much-anticipated AI-powered virtual assistant, which boasted features designed to seamlessly integrate into everyday life, both personal and professional. Recognizing the potential of the global market and the challenges of reaching diverse audiences, they planned a multi-phased social media campaign tailored to various international demographics.

The first phase involved deep market research utilizing AI tools to analyze social media trends and consumer behaviors across different regions, aiming to understand local nuances, preferences, and potential barriers to entry. Based on the data, NextGen Innovations crafted region-specific content that resonated with local audiences, ensuring the nuances of language, cultural references, and consumer pain points were addressed. They leveraged platforms like Instagram for younger demographics in Western markets and WeChat for the Chinese market, where the digital ecosystem varied significantly.

To enhance the campaign's effectiveness, NextGen used AI-driven analytics to monitor real-time engagement and adapt strategies accordingly. AI algorithms analyzed which types of posts generated the most interaction and adjusted content schedules to optimize visibility during peak user hours. They also implemented sentiment analysis tools to gauge public perception of the product and address any concerns or misconceptions promptly.

The results were groundbreaking. The targeted approach led to a 40% increase in engagement rates in preliminary tests conducted in selected markets. As the launch date approached, the adjusted strategies according to ongoing analytics continued to refine their approach, focusing on high-engagement tactics such as interactive Q&A sessions and live demos hosted by influencers within each market.

However, the road was not without its challenges. Navigating the regulations of advertising and data use in different countries proved to be a complex task, requiring the team to stay agile and informed. The reliance on AI tools also demanded continuous updates and checks to ensure accuracy and ethical handling of data, underscoring the importance of maintaining an expert team knowledgeable in both AI technology and international marketing laws.

Case Study: Enhancing Customer Experience with AI-driven Email Marketing Strategy

In 2023, Elextron Inc., a globally recognized electronics retailer, was grappling with a prevalent challenge in their highly competitive market: declining customer retention rates. To combat this, Elextron focused on revamping its approach to email marketing, making it more personalized and data-driven, leveraging AI to boost customer engagement and retention.

Elextron implemented an AI-powered email marketing platform that integrated machine learning algorithms to analyze customer data collected from various touchpoints, including past purchases, website browsing patterns, and social media interactions. This sophisticated system segmented the customer base into distinct profiles based on their behavior and preferences, facilitating highly targeted and relevant email campaigns.

The AI engine was programmed to automatically adjust the content, timing, and frequency of emails based on individual engagement metrics, ensuring the communication was optimal for each customer. Promotions and product recommendations were specifically tailored using predictive analytics, which forecasted potential interests with surprising accuracy. Moreover, A/B testing was employed continuously to refine and optimize the messaging, layout, and call-to-action based on real-time reactions and engagement levels.

The new strategy proved highly effective. Within six months, Elextron observed a 50% increase in email open rates and a 35% boost in click-through rates, leading to a noticeable improvement in repeat customer transactions. The AI system also identified niche customer segments that were previously under-targeted, opening new opportunities for marketing personalized electronic accessories.

Despite these successes, Elextron encountered several challenges. The initial integration of AI with their existing CRM system required significant overhauling of legacy data practices and training for the marketing team. Privacy concerns were paramount, as increased data capture and analysis required stringent adherence to international data protection laws, necessitating regular audits and adjustments to comply with evolving regulations. By addressing these hurdles head-on, Elextron not only enhanced its marketing strategy but also advanced its overall business operations, setting a new standard in customer-centric, data-driven marketing in the electronics retail sector.

Case Study: Integrating AI into Luxury Fashion: Transforming Customer Engagement and Inventory Management

The fashion industry, known for its fleeting trends and high customer expectations, presents unique challenges, particularly in the luxury segment. StellarLux, a prominent luxury fashion brand, recognized the need to revamp its approach amidst a highly competitive market. In 2023, they embarked on integrating artificial intelligence to enhance customer engagement and streamline inventory management, aiming to combine the exclusivity of luxury fashion with cutting-edge technology.

StellarLux started by implementing an AI-driven recommendation system on its online platform. This system analyzed individual customer preferences and buying history to personalize product recommendations effectively. These personalized experiences were tailored not only based on past purchases but also through style preferences gleaned from customer interactions with digital content, such as blogs and lookbooks, offering a curated fashion experience.

To complement the recommendation system, StellarLux introduced an AI-powered inventory management tool. This tool utilized predictive analytics to forecast fashion trends, demand patterns, and manage stock levels in real-time. By predicting upcoming trends, the tool allowed StellarLux to optimize their production schedules and inventory distribution, reducing overproduction and minimizing unsold stock, tackling a significant industry issue of waste management.

The impact of AI on customer interaction was significant. The personalized recommendations led to a 25% increase in customer engagement and a 40% rise in sales conversions. Furthermore, the predictive capabilities of the AI tool enhanced inventory turnover by 30%, reducing operational costs substantially while still meeting consumer demand efficiently.

However, implementing AI introduced challenges, including the need to balance automation and personalization without losing the luxury touch that characterized StellarLux. Additionally, managing large datasets while maintaining customer privacy was imperative. By integrating robust data security measures and ensuring transparent communication about data use, StellarLux not only adhered to compliance requirements but also reinforced their brand reliability among discerning customers.

Case Study: Strategic AI Deployment in Global Financial Services

In early 2024, GlobalFintech, a prominent player in the financial services sector with operations in over 30 countries, faced challenges with customer retention and market penetration in burgeoning markets. To tackle these challenges, GlobalFintech embarked on an ambitious project to integrate artificial intelligence across its operations, aiming to enhance customer service, optimize operational efficiency, and personalize marketing efforts.

GlobalFintech's approach was multi-faceted. Firstly, they implemented an AI-driven customer service platform that utilized natural language processing (NLP) to offer real-time assistance to customers via chatbots. Simultaneously, the firm utilized machine learning algorithms to analyze vast amounts of customer data collated from various touchpoints, enabling the prediction of customer behaviors and tailoring of financial products to individual needs.

Additionally, an AI-powered analytics tool was developed to streamline the risk assessment processes, making loan approval faster and more efficient. This tool used predictive analytics to assess customer creditworthiness using real-time data, thereby reducing the risk of defaults and improving customer trust.

Within six months of integrating these AI systems, GlobalFintech observed a remarkable improvement in customer engagement metrics, with a 20% increase in customer retention rates and a significant reduction in service delivery times. Marketing campaigns became remarkably more effective, with personalized offers contributing to a 35% increase in cross-sell and up-sell revenue.

Despite the successes, GlobalFintech faced hurdles, particularly around the ethical use of AI and data privacy. The diversity in regulatory environments across countries necessitated a complex compliance strategy. Additionally, there was a steep learning curve for employees adapting to new technologies. Nonetheless, by prioritizing ongoing training and transparent communication regarding data usage, GlobalFintech managed to navigate these challenges effectively, setting a new standard for the integration of AI in financial services.

Case Study: Revolutionizing Hospitality Management with AI-Driven Solutions

In 2024, LuxeResorts, a global chain of luxury resorts, faced a critical challenge due to changing guest expectations and intense competition in the hospitality industry. To stay competitive and enhance guest experiences, LuxeResorts initiated a series of AI-driven transformations targeting key aspects of their service delivery, primarily focusing on personalized guest experiences and operational efficiency.

The first step involved deploying AI to personalize guest interactions. LuxeResorts integrated AI technologies into their customer relationship management (CRM) systems to analyze guest data, including past preferences, feedback, and booking patterns. This integration enabled the creation of customized offers and experiences tailored to individual guest profiles, significantly enhancing guest satisfaction. AI-driven chatbots were implemented to provide 24/7 customer service, managing bookings, and addressing inquiries with high efficiency, reducing wait times and improving guest service interaction.

To optimize operational efficiency, LuxeResorts utilized AI for predictive maintenance and energy management within their properties. AI algorithms analyzed data from various sensors and systems to predict potential maintenance issues before they occurred, reducing downtime and repair costs. Moreover, AI optimization of energy consumption led to significant cost reductions and supported LuxeResorts' commitment to sustainability.

These AI-driven initiatives resulted in a 40% increase in guest satisfaction scores and a 25% improvement in operational cost efficiency within the first year. The personalized experiences led to a higher rate of return visits and positive reviews, which further improved the brand's market position.

However, the integration of AI brought its set of challenges. Issues such as data privacy, ethical concerns over AI use, and the need for significant staff retraining posed hurdles. LuxeResorts addressed these by implementing strict data security measures, ethical guidelines for AI use, and comprehensive staff training programs. These measures ensured a smooth transition to AI-driven operations, aligning with industry best practices and maintaining guest trust.

Case Study: Revitalizing E-Commerce through AI-Enhanced Customer Journeys

In the competitive landscape of 2024, E-Shop Dynamics, a mid-sized e-commerce company, recognized the growing demand for a more personalized shopping experience. Traditional data analysis had served them well in the past, but the evolving market required more sophisticated insights. As a result, E-Shop Dynamics decided to invest in an advanced artificial intelligence system to create a highly tailored experience for each customer, thereby aiming to increase user engagement and sales conversions.

The company initiated the project by integrating AI to analyze customer data comprehensively. This AI system was designed to track user interactions on the website, analyze past purchase histories, and monitor social media behaviors to understand individual consumer needs better. It then utilized this data to automate personalized product recommendations and targeted marketing content directly relevant to each user's interests and purchasing habits.

After implementing these AI-driven strategies, E-Shop Dynamics witnessed a remarkable 25% increase in customer retention rates and a 35% increase in overall sales within the first six months. The AI's predictive capabilities also allowed for better inventory management, suggesting restock levels effectively based on predicted buyer trends and thereby reducing excess stock and improving supply chain efficiency.

However, the integration was not without challenges. The company faced significant hurdles in ensuring data privacy compliance as they managed an increasing volume of personal customer data. There were also technical challenges in integrating AI with existing legacy systems not initially designed for such sophisticated analytics. To address these issues, E-Shop Dynamics developed a comprehensive privacy framework and conducted regular training sessions for their IT staff, ensuring smooth integration and compliance with international data protection laws.

This strategic implementation of AI not only transformed their business model but also set new standards in customer interaction and satisfaction within the e-commerce industry. The success story of E-Shop Dynamics serves as an inspiring example for other companies looking to harness the power of AI to enhance their customer engagement and operational efficiency.

Case Study: Transforming AI Education with Dynamic Digital Marketing

In the bustling landscape of 2024, TechEduCo, a pioneering company specializing in AI education, faced stagnation despite a surge in global demand for AI skills. Understanding that traditional marketing approaches were no longer efficient, TechEduCo decided to overhaul its digital marketing strategy to foster growth and enhance its market presence, especially targeting tech-savvy learners eager to upskill in AI technologies.

TechEduCo crafted a multi-channel digital marketing campaign, integrating state-of-the-art AI analytics to understand and predict learner behaviors and preferences. The heart of their revamped strategy was a dynamic, AI-driven content management system that personalized learning content and marketing messages based on user interactions and learning patterns observed across various digital platforms. This system utilized machine learning algorithms to adapt the educational content it recommended, ensuring that each learner received tailored promotional materials that resonated with their specific learning needs and career goals.

The implementation of AI-powered tools extended to their SEO strategies, where natural language processing was used to refine and optimize content for search engines, boosting visibility for potential students searching for AI courses. Smart PPC tactics further accentuated their online presence, ensuring top-tier visibility in search engine results and social media feeds.

However, the shift was not free of challenges. The integration of AI into their marketing strategy required TechEduCo to navigate new regulatory landscapes, maintaining compliance with evolving digital advertising laws and data privacy regulations. Furthermore, the need for continuous updates and maintenance of AI systems called for significant investments in both technology and human capital.

Despite these obstacles, the results were groundbreaking. Within six months, TechEduCo reported a 50% increase in enrollment. More importantly, the quality of engagement improved, with an increased duration of website visits and a decrease in bounce rates, indicating higher content relevance and user interest. This successful transformation showcased the potential of AI-powered digital marketing in revolutionizing educational outreach, setting a benchmark for competitors in the AI education sector.

REVIEW QUESTIONS

1. Sarah, a marketing director at an emerging AI company, is tasked with enhancing the visibility of their AI products through digital marketing efforts. After analyzing various approaches, she decides to enhance the search engine ranking of their AI tools through detailed keyword strategies and on-page SEO enhancements. In addition to optimizing their website for search engines, what should Sarah prioritize as part of her digital marketing strategy to ensure maximum engagement?

A) Developing a robust email marketing campaign that educates potential customers about AI benefits.

B) Focusing solely on PPC campaigns to drive quick sales.

C) Limiting social media activity to occasional posts to save resources.

D) Investing heavily in offline marketing strategies such as billboard advertising.

Answer: A

Explanation: Developing a robust email marketing campaign is essential for educating potential customers about the benefits of AI, which aligns with digital marketing strategies that cater to an informed consumer base. Email campaigns allow for the distribution of targeted, informative content that can bridge the gap between consumer awareness and product adoption. Unlike focusing solely on quick-sale oriented PPC campaigns or minimizing social media presence, a well-curated email strategy facilitates ongoing engagement and nurtures leads over time. It complements the SEO efforts by drawing traffic back to the website and encouraging deeper interaction with the content, thus enhancing overall digital marketing efficacy.

2. Tom, the CEO of an AI-focused startup, recognizes the importance of storytelling in marketing AI tools effectively. He plans to release a series of user-centric narratives across various media to highlight the practical impacts of their AI technologies. What should Tom emphasize in his storytelling to ensure it resonates with both tech-savvy and general audiences while encouraging trust and product adoption?

A) Complex technical details of how AI algorithms function.

B) Real-world benefits and simplified explanations of AI technologies.

C) Only the future potentials of AI without practical current applications.

D) Exclusively the cost-saving aspects of using AI technologies.

Answer: B

Explanation: Tom should focus on real-world benefits and simplified explanations of AI technologies in his storytelling approach. This strategy will resonate with both tech-savvy individuals and the general public by making the technology accessible and relatable. Highlighting practical applications and simplifying the technical jargon demystifies AI and helps in breaking down barriers to adoption. Focusing only on technical details or cost-saving aspects might not fully communicate the value of the AI tools or might cater to a more limited audience. By illustrating how AI technology impacts daily life and enhances business operations, Tom can foster trust and stimulate interest across a broader audience spectrum.

REVIEW QUESTIONS

3. Lucy, a digital marketing strategist, is leveraging social media to increase the visibility of her company's new AI product. She plans to use different platforms to target various demographics effectively. Which strategy should Lucy employ to maximize engagement and reach for her AI product on social media?

A) Standardizing posts across all platforms to maintain consistent messaging.

B) Tailoring content and interaction styles to fit the unique preferences of users on each platform.

C) Focusing exclusively on platforms popular with a younger demographic.

D) Using automated tools to post the same content at the same time daily.

Answer: B

Explanation: Lucy should tailor content and interaction styles to fit the unique preferences of users on each social media platform. Each platform attracts different demographics and fosters varying engagement styles; for example, Instagram is visual, whereas LinkedIn values professional and educational content. Adapting the messaging and interaction to align with the platform's culture maximizes user engagement and brand reach. Standardizing posts or limiting focus to one demographic could result in missed opportunities to connect with potential customers across platforms. Automated scheduling is useful, but the content still needs to be thoughtfully adapted to each platform's audience.

ETHICS AND PRIVACY IN AI WEALTH CREATION

Introduction to Ethics in AI-driven Wealth Creation

The burgeoning realm of AI-driven wealth creation necessitates a rigorous ethical framework to ensure that these technologies contribute positively to society. The principles that govern human ethics now need to be intricately woven into the fabric of AI systems, particularly those involved in financial advancements and wealth distribution.

Key ethical concerns revolve around the transparency of AI processes and the fairness of their outcomes. As AI systems increasingly make decisions that can significantly impact an individual's economic status, it is crucial to address biases that may exist in these algorithms. Ensuring that AI's judgement remains impartial and fair across different demographics is fundamental.

Moreover, the pursuit of AI-driven wealth creation must be balanced with an unwavering commitment to individual privacy and data security. Guardianship of personal information, especially in wealth and asset management applications, is paramount. Striving for ethical AI involves creating systems that respect user consent and privacy while enhancing economic opportunities responsibly.

Defining Privacy in the Context of AI Applications

In the sphere of AI-driven wealth creation, defining privacy involves understanding how personal data is collected, used, and protected. AI applications often rely on vast datasets, including sensitive personal information, to train algorithms and deliver personalized services. Therefore, ensuring privacy means safeguarding this data from unauthorized access and misuse.

Privacy in AI requires clear data governance policies that define who has access to data and for what purpose. It is about creating transparent systems where users are informed and can control their data. This involves implementing robust security measures such as encryption and regular audits to prevent data breaches. Moreover, AI developers must adhere to privacy-by-design principles, ensuring that privacy safeguards are integrated into the development process from the outset.

Ultimately, respecting privacy in AI applications means fostering trust. Trust that is built by consistently demonstrating commitment to protecting user data. With the increasing scrutiny on data privacy, AI systems that prioritize and transparently manage privacy concerns will not only comply with regulations but also gain a competitive advantage by attracting privacy-conscious users.

AI and Data Protection: Key Principles and Practices

In the tapestry of AI wealth creation, data protection stands as a cornerstone, ensuring the integrity and security of user information. Adherence to robust data protection standards is imperative, not only to comply with legal requirements but to foster trust in AI applications. Key principles include data minimization, where only necessary data is collected, and purpose limitation, which restricts data usage to specified, explicit intentions.

Central to these practices is the implementation of strong encryption methods and regular security audits to safeguard data from unauthorized access. Moreover, AI systems should be designed with inherent resilience to withstand and recover from security breaches. This involves regular updates and patches that address newly emerging vulnerabilities.

Furthermore, training AI developers on the best practices in data protection is crucial. Continuous education will help in maintaining a culture of security and privacy, ensuring that data protection measures evolve with advancing technologies and threats, thereby securing a safe and reliable environment for AI-driven wealth creation.

The Moral Implications of Automated Decision-Making

Automated decision-making, a cornerstone of AI wealth creation, poses profound moral questions. At its core, this technology encapsulates algorithms that make decisions without human intervention, affecting areas such as loan approval, job screening, and healthcare provision. The moral implications of such systems center on their autonomy and the potential for systematic biases, inadvertently embedded by their human creators.

While these technologies can enhance efficiency and objectivity, they may also perpetuate existing inequalities. For instance, if an algorithm is trained on historical data that reflects societal biases, it may replicate or even amplify these biases, leading to discriminatory practices. Thus, ensuring fairness in automated decisions becomes not just a technical challenge but a moral imperative.

Moreover, the delegation of significant decisions to AI systems raises questions about accountability. When errors occur, determining responsibility can be complex, implicating developers, users, and even the AI system itself. Hence, ethical frameworks and governance are crucial to guide the moral deployment of automated decision-making processes.

Transparency and Accountability in AI Tools

Transparency and accountability in AI tools are pivotal components within the ethical landscape of AI technology, particularly in wealth creation applications. By ensuring clear visibility into AI operations and decision-making processes, stakeholders can assess the fairness and effectiveness of these systems. Transparent AI practices involve disclosing algorithmic functions and data usage, enabling users to understand how their data is being processed and for what purposes.

Accountability extends beyond mere transparency, encompassing the implementation of mechanisms that hold AI systems and their operators responsible for the outcomes. This includes setting up robust oversight protocols and ensuring that AI decisions can be audited and challenged when necessary. It also involves delineating clear lines of responsibility in cases where AI-driven decisions may result in adverse outcomes, thereby safeguarding individuals' rights and fostering public trust in AI technologies.

Ultimately, integrating transparency and accountability into AI tools not only supports ethical compliance but also enhances community trust. By fostering an environment where AI systems are both understandable and accountable, developers and companies can ensure that these technologies are used responsibly in creating wealth, thus bridging the gap between AI possibilities and ethical considerations.

Consent and User Control in AI Interactions

In the landscape of AI wealth creation, the importance of user consent and control over personal data cannot be overstated. As AI technologies increasingly handle sensitive financial information, ensuring that users can meaningfully consent to and control their data usage becomes paramount.

Consent in AI should be informed, explicit, and revocable, with systems designed to facilitate user understanding of what data is used, how it is processed, and whom it is shared with. This transparency empowers users, allowing them to make educated decisions about their data. Moreover, providing users with straightforward mechanisms to control their data—such as easy opt-out options and clear settings adjustments—enhances trust and encourages more widespread adoption of AI services.

Accountability mechanisms must enforce these consent and control policies, ensuring AI applications adhere strictly to user preferences and legal standards. Integrating these elements into AI systems not only protects individuals but also builds a foundation of trust essential for sustainable AI-driven wealth creation.

Bias and Fairness: Addressing Equity in AI Algorithms

In the realm of AI-driven wealth creation, addressing bias and ensuring fairness in AI algorithms is crucial for equitable outcomes. These algorithms, often designed to automate financial decisions, must be scrupulously crafted to avoid perpetuating historical inequalities. Ethical design involves rigorous testing against diverse data sets to detect and mitigate biases that could disadvantage certain groups.

Equity in AI also necessitates transparency about how algorithms make decisions. This means not only open disclosure of the data used but also clear explanations of the decision-making processes. Such practices help stakeholders understand and trust AI systems, fostering inclusivity in technological advancements.

Moreover, developers must engage with ethicists and diverse communities to ascertain the fairness of AI tools. Continuous feedback and adjustments ensure these tools evolve in ways that respect all user rights without discrimination. Ultimately, achieving fairness in AI algorithms is not a one-time effort but a dynamic process that adapts to changing societal values and norms.

Each advance in technology must align with a commitment to ethical responsibility, ensuring AI's potential is harnessed for the benefit of all, without exception. This balance between innovation and equity will define the future landscape of AI wealth creation.

Protecting Intellectual Property in the Age of AI

The advent of AI has transformed the terrain of intellectual property (IP), presenting both novel opportunities and challenges. Protecting IP in this new era is crucial to incentivizing innovation while ensuring fair competition. Developers of AI technologies hinge their economic and developmental strides on strong IP rights that defend their inventions from unauthorized use.

However, AI's capacity to learn and replicate poses unique challenges to traditional copyright and patent laws designed around human creators. The question of whether an AI can be a legal author or inventor is fraught with legal complexities. Efforts to tailor IP laws to accommodate AI-engendered creations without stifling the technology's potential are ongoing. This requires a delicate balance between innovation protection and accessibility, ensuring that technological advances benefit society as a whole.

Furthermore, policymakers must consider the global landscape of IP rules as AI blurs the lines across jurisdictions. Collaborative international frameworks may be necessary to address these challenges effectively, uniting stakeholders in crafting laws that propel, rather than impede, the progress of AI technologies.

GDPR and Global Privacy Laws: Compliance in AI

Navigating the complex terrain of global privacy laws, including the General Data Protection Regulation (GDPR), is pivotal for AI applications in wealth creation. These regulations set stringent guidelines on data privacy, offering a blueprint for compliance that impacts AI development and deployment across borders.

Under GDPR, AI systems that process personal data of EU residents must adhere to principles like data minimization and purpose limitation. This means AI applications must not only collect the necessary data for a specific function but also manage this data transparently and with the consent of the data subject. Furthermore, entities must design AI systems with privacy in mind, ensuring data protection from the outset, a concept known as 'privacy by design'.

Achieving compliance requires a collaborative effort between technology developers, legal experts, and policymakers. It involves continuous monitoring and adaptation of AI systems to align with evolving laws. Effective compliance not only mitigates legal risks but also enhances user trust, crucial for long-term success in AI-driven endeavors.

Ethical AI Design: Best Practices for Developers

Ethical AI design is fundamental to cultivating trust and ensuring the responsible deployment of AI systems in wealth creation. Best practices begin with the incorporation of ethical considerations at the planning stage, ensuring that AI systems do not merely comply with technical requirements but also embody ethical principles. Developers must prioritize transparency, allowing users to understand and query the decision-making processes of AI mechanisms. This clarity helps demystify AI operations and fosters greater accountability.

In addition, developers should implement comprehensive testing phases to identify potential biases in AI algorithms, ensuring these systems operate fairly across diverse user groups. Incorporating feedback loops to adjust and refine AI tools continually is crucial for maintaining alignment with ethical standards. Developers must collaborate closely with ethicists and legal experts to align technological advancements with broader societal values and regulatory expectations.

Finally, promoting an ethical AI culture within development teams can reinforce the significance of ethics in every stage of AI creation, elevating ethical awareness to parallel technical skill in importance. Engaging in regular training on the latest ethical practices and sharing knowledge within the community are instrumental strategies for achieving this end.

AI and the Digital Divide: Ensuring Inclusive Benefits

The digital divide refers to the gap between those who have access to modern information and communication technology and those who do not. In the context of AI-driven wealth creation, this divide can exacerbate inequalities if not addressed properly. AI technologies tend to concentrate wealth and opportunities in the hands of those with access to digital tools and the knowledge to use them.

Ensuring inclusive benefits of AI requires intentional strategies to include underrepresented and underserved communities. This involves not only providing access to technology but also ensuring education and training in AI literacy are accessible to all socio-economic segments. Policies must promote equitable access to AI tools and their benefits, preventing a scenario where only the technologically privileged advance.

Further, developers and policymakers must collaborate to create AI systems that support diverse needs and conditions, bridging the gap rather than widening it. Collectively, these efforts can help mitigate the risk of a growing digital divide, ensuring AI contributes positively to social equity.

Privacy-Preserving Techniques in AI Development

In the rapidly expanding field of AI, protecting user privacy during the development stage is critical. Privacy-preserving techniques in AI development are designed to uphold data confidentiality while maintaining the utility of AI systems. One common method is differential privacy, which adds noise to the datasets used in AI training to prevent any possibility of identifying individual data points without significantly compromising the data's utility.

Another approach is the use of federated learning. This technique enables multiple AI models to be trained across different devices or servers without exchanging the data itself, thereby minimizing central data storage and reducing privacy risks. Homomorphic encryption is another advanced method, allowing data to be processed in an encrypted form, providing results without exposing the underlying data.

Implementing these privacy-preserving techniques not only helps in complying with stringent global data protection laws but also builds trust with users, critical for the widespread adoption of AI technologies. By integrating these methods, developers can ensure that AI systems are not only effective but also respectful of privacy and ethical standards.

The Role of Ethics Committees in AI Projects

Ethics committees play a pivotal role in AI projects, serving as guardians of moral integrity and ethical compliance. These committees, comprised of interdisciplinary experts, review AI initiatives to ensure that they adhere to ethical standards and societal values. Their assessments help in identifying potential ethical issues, guiding developers to consider broader impacts on privacy, fairness, and human rights.

Beyond mere compliance, ethics committees foster an ongoing dialogue about the ethical use of AI, evolving their guidelines as technologies and societal norms advance. They engage with stakeholders including developers, consumers, and policymakers, ensuring a well-rounded consideration of how AI applications affect varied groups. This interaction aids in refining AI systems to be more inclusive and equitable.

Ethics committees also play a crucial role in building public trust in AI technologies. By promoting transparency and accountability, they ensure that AI systems not only operate within legal frameworks but also strive to achieve ethical excellence. These efforts are critical for the sustained success and acceptance of AI-driven innovations.

Securing AI Systems Against Data Breaches

In the realm of AI wealth generation, securing systems against data breaches is not just a technical necessity but a fundamental ethical obligation. AI infrastructures handle vast arrays of sensitive information, making them prime targets for cyberattacks. Implementing robust security measures ensures the protection of personal and financial data, which is paramount for maintaining user trust and legal compliance.

Encryption is the cornerstone of such security strategies. By encoding data, AI systems make the information useless to unauthorized interceptors. Additionally, multi-factor authentication (MFA) serves as a critical barrier, requiring more than one piece of evidence to verify a user's identity, thus protecting against unauthorized access. Regular security audits and updates further fortify AI systems against evolving cyber threats.

Beyond technical defenses, fostering a culture of security among developers and users is crucial. Educating all parties about potential risks and best safety practices creates a proactive environment where security is a shared responsibility. This collective vigilance is essential to anticipate, prevent, and respond to breaches effectively.

Impact of AI on Consumer Rights and Protections

The incorporation of AI in different sectors touches directly on consumer rights and protections, necessitating a careful balancing of innovation and consumer safety. As AI tools interpret and predict consumer behaviors, there is an underlying risk of manipulation and unintended consequences that could compromise consumer autonomy and privacy. Thoughtfully designed AI systems must prioritize safeguarding personal data and ensuring transparent consumer interactions.

Moreover, AI's ability to personalize may lead to discriminative pricing or access to services, where algorithms could unjustly favor or neglect certain user groups. Regulatory frameworks need to evolve to address these discrepancies, aiming for an AI marketplace that champions equity and justice over profit.

Enforcement is equally crucial, as rights without enforcement are ineffectual. Mechanisms for consumer feedback and rectification must be enhanced in the AI ecosystem, allowing users meaningful ways to challenge and rectify decisions made by AI that affect them. Consumer education on AI rights is essential to empower users, helping them to navigate this complex landscape with more confidence and awareness.

The Ethics of AI in Predictive Analytics

Predictive analytics in AI presents profound ethical considerations, notably in how data influences future outcomes. The capability of AI to predict behaviors and preferences can guide decision-making processes in business and governance; however, this raises significant ethical questions about consent and autonomy.

Users often provide data without a clear understanding of its potential use in predictive models, leading to concerns over consent and the misuse of personal information. Additionally, predictive analytics can inadvertently reinforce biases present in the training data, which perpetuates inequality and discrimination. Ethical deployment of predictive analytics requires rigorous bias mitigation strategies and transparent communication about how data shapes AI-driven forecasts.

Moreover, the predictive power of AI must be balanced against individual rights to privacy and ethical considerations. Developing guidelines that govern the ethical use of predictive analytics is essential to ensuring these technologies benefit society without compromising moral values. Ensuring ethical oversight will help maintain public trust in AI applications, crucial for their continued integration into societal frameworks.

AI in Advertising: Balancing Profit and Privacy

The integration of AI in advertising strategizes to maximize profitability while navigating complex privacy landscapes. Marketers leverage AI to analyze consumer behaviors and tailor advertising, enhancing engagement and conversion rates. However, this precision targeting raises concerns regarding consumer privacy and data exploitation.

Responsible AI usage in advertising demands adherence to privacy laws and ethical standards, ensuring that consumer data is handled with respect and transparency. Privacy-preserving AI techniques, like differential privacy, offer a blueprint for maintaining data anonymity while extracting valuable insights. These approaches help in cultivating consumer trust, an invaluable commodity in the digital age.

Moreover, advertisers must balance profit-driven motives with ethical considerations to prevent invasive practices that may alienate consumers. Establishing robust ethical guidelines and transparent data practices differentiates brands in a crowded market, fostering long-term consumer relationships. Ethical alignment in AI-driven advertising not only protects consumers but also enhances brand integrity and sustainability.

De-anonymization Risks in AI and Mitigation Strategies

De-anonymization presents a profound challenge in AI wealth generation, posing risks to user privacy by reconstructing anonymous data back to identifiable form. This threat escalates as AI systems increasingly handle vast datasets, integrating information which, when combined, can reveal personal identities.

Effective mitigation strategies are vital for safeguarding privacy. Techniques such as differential privacy, which adds randomness to the data, help prevent the identification of individuals without significantly compromising the utility of the data for analysis. Additionally, robust data governance policies must be enforced, requiring minimized data access and regular audits to ensure compliance with privacy standards.

Educating stakeholders on the importance of privacy and the potential harms of de-anonymization also plays a crucial role. By fostering a culture of security and ethical awareness, organizations can enhance their vigilance against privacy breaches, thereby maintaining trust and integrity within their AI systems.

Public Perception and Trust in AI Wealth Tools

Public perception and trust are critical factors in the successful deployment of AI wealth tools. These technologies, while promising enhanced efficiency and profitability, come with concerns that can influence societal acceptance and widespread use. The allure of AI's capabilities often contrasts with anxiety over privacy encroachments and automated decisions.

Therefore, maintaining transparency in AI operations is vital. Clear communication about how AI tools function, their decision-making processes, and the safeguards in place to protect data can alleviate public concerns. Companies must also demonstrate accountability by being responsive to user feedback and implementing improvements based on such insights.

Moreover, engaging with the public through educational initiatives can demystify AI technologies and foster a deeper understanding of their benefits and limitations. Ultimately, establishing trust in AI wealth tools depends on consistent ethical practices, robust security measures, and a commitment to protecting consumer rights. These efforts will shape the future landscape of AI acceptance and its potential as a wealth generator.

Developing AI Policies for Ethical Governance

The development of AI policies for ethical governance is essential in guiding the deployment and application of AI technologies towards positive societal impacts. Such policies form the backbone of ethical strategies by setting standards for AI practices and ensuring they align with core human values and rights.

Foremost, these policies must address transparency and accountability. Clear mechanisms should be established for explaining AI decisions and actions to promote trust among users and stakeholders. Moreover, the integration of ethical guidelines within AI systems helps prevent biases, ensuring fairness in automated decisions.

Additionally, engagement with diverse stakeholder groups is crucial. This inclusivity enables a broader perspective in policy-making, reflecting multiple needs and minimizing the risks of overlooking potential harm. Lastly, the policies should be dynamic, evolving with technological advances and societal changes to remain relevant and effective in promoting ethical AI use.

Corporate Responsibility in AI Deployment

Corporate responsibility plays an integral role in the ethical deployment of AI technologies. Companies spearheading AI-driven wealth creation must prioritize ethical standards to guide their operations, ensuring that AI's transformative power benefits society comprehensively. This responsibility entails transparent articulation of AI's functionalities, objectives, and limitations to stakeholders, coupled with a steadfast commitment to fair and equitable practices.

Furthermore, corporations must engage proactively with the communities they impact, fostering a dialogue that addresses and mitigates any concerns about AI applications. This community engagement helps in preempting ethical dilemmas and reinforces corporate accountability. Additionally, robust internal guidelines and training for employees on ethical AI usage safeguard against potential abuses, reinforcing a culture of responsibility.

Finally, corporate entities must also extend their responsibility to innovating privacy-preserving technologies. These advancements must aim not only at regulatory compliance but also exceed the benchmarks to establish new standards for privacy and security in AI, thus promoting a safer, more trustworthy AI ecosystem.

Case Studies: Ethical Dilemmas in AI Wealth Applications

The intersection of AI and wealth creation presents complex ethical dilemmas. One illustrative case involved a company using AI to optimize investment strategies. While the algorithm successfully maximized returns, it inadvertently prioritized investments in industries with questionable ethical practices, sparking debate over AI's role in ethical decision-making.

Another case study focused on a credit scoring AI system designed to increase lending efficiency. However, it was later revealed that the algorithm disproportionately affected minority groups, leading to accusations of digital discrimination. This scenario raised questions about the responsibilities of AI developers to prevent bias and ensure fairness.

Moreover, an AI-driven marketing tool used predictive analytics to target vulnerable individuals with high-interest loans, exploiting their financial instability. This raised significant concerns about consumer rights and the ethical use of personal data in AI applications.

These examples underscore the need for stringent ethical oversight and robust frameworks to guide AI wealth creation applications, ensuring that they not only advance economic goals but also uphold societal values.

Educating Consumers on AI Privacy and Rights

In the evolving landscape of AI, consumer education on privacy and rights is paramount. Users often interact with AI-driven platforms without a full understanding of how their data is utilized or their entitlements under the law. This knowledge gap can lead to exploitation and erosion of trust. Therefore, it is crucial to implement comprehensive educational programs that illuminate these issues clearly and accessibly.

Educational initiatives should include detailed explanations of data rights, privacy policies, and user controls available within AI applications. Interactive workshops, online courses, and informative webinars can effectively disseminate this knowledge, making it accessible to a broad audience. Partnerships with consumer rights organizations can also amplify the reach and impact of these educational efforts.

Moreover, these programs must continually evolve to keep pace with rapidly changing AI technologies and privacy norms. Ensuring that consumers are informed not just about their current rights but also about upcoming legislative changes is essential for fostering an informed user base, capable of making empowered decisions about their interactions with AI technologies.

Future Challenges in AI Ethics and Privacy

As AI continues to permeate various sectors of wealth creation, the future challenges in ethics and privacy become increasingly complex and multidimensional. Firstly, the rapid pace of technological advancement outstrips the development of corresponding legal frameworks and ethical guidelines. There is a pressing need for dynamic regulatory mechanisms that adapt swiftly to technological evolutions, ensuring consistent oversight and protection of individual rights.

Secondly, the globalization of AI technologies presents unique challenges in harmonizing ethical standards across different cultural and legal landscapes. This requires a concerted effort among international stakeholders to develop universally accepted principles that respect diverse values and norms while promoting a fair AI ecosystem.

Lastly, the advent of more sophisticated AI algorithms enhances the risk of unintended consequences. Ensuring that AI systems perform ethically under a wide range of scenarios necessitates continuous monitoring and updating of ethical AI models, alongside proactive public engagement to gauge societal impact and consent.

Addressing these challenges is crucial for fostering an AI-driven economy that is both innovative and equitable.

Collaborative Initiatives for Ethical AI Standards

The forging of ethical AI standards cannot be achieved in isolation; it demands a collaborative approach that harnesses diverse insights and expertise. Across the globe, institutions, governments, and tech giants are uniting to craft guidelines that promote transparency, fairness, and accountability in AI applications.

One commendable initiative is the establishment of inter-industry consortia that advocate for standardized ethical practices. These bodies function as think tanks, developing best practices that influence international policies and corporate strategies. Their collective wisdom is vital in addressing complex ethical challenges that no single entity could manage alone.

Furthermore, partnerships between academia and industry are pivotal. Universities contribute cutting-edge research and theoretical frameworks, while businesses offer practical insights and test beds for emerging concepts. Together, they accelerate the creation of robust ethical standards that are both innovative and grounded in real-world applicability.

Such collaborative efforts not only refine the discourse on ethical AI but also ensure that these high standards become the norm, rather than the exception. This is essential for sustaining trust and integrity in AI's role in wealth creation.

Evaluating the Long-term Implications of AI on Society

The long-term societal implications of AI, especially in wealth generation, provoke profound considerations. Initially, AI's capacity to enhance economic efficiencies and innovations presents transformative opportunities. However, there is a crucial need to balance these advancements with societal welfare, ensuring AI's benefits are broadly distributed and do not exacerbate social inequalities.

Moreover, the evolving role of AI may lead to shifts in the labor market, necessitating policies that support workforce transitions and education systems that can adapt to new technological realities. The recalibration of educational programs to foster AI literacy and skills is imperative to equip future generations for a world where AI is ubiquitous.

Additionally, long-term AI deployment raises significant concerns about surveillance and privacy. As AI becomes more integrated into daily life, ensuring robust privacy protections and transparent AI operations is essential to maintain public trust. Public engagement and regulatory frameworks that evolve alongside AI development will be critical in addressing these challenges.

Thus, evaluating the impact of AI on society necessitates a proactive, multidisciplinary approach that considers ethical, economic, and social dimensions to foster an equitable technological future.

SUMMARY

The chapter on Ethics and Privacy in AI Wealth Creation delves into the complexities of integrating ethical consideration and privacy safeguards into artificial intelligence systems, particularly those designed for wealth creation. The discourse begins by recognizing the necessity of embedding human ethics into AI, emphasizing transparency, fairness, and the mitigation of algorithmic bias to ensure these systems benefit all demographics equally. Privacy is defined in the context of AI as the protection of personal data against unauthorized access, demanding robust data governance and adherence to privacy-by-design principles.

Significant emphasis is placed on the stringent measures needed to protect data while ensuring the transparency and accountability of AI systems. Ethics committees are highlighted for their role in maintaining ethical standards through rigorous evaluations and fostering engagements that consider wide-reaching societal impacts. Furthermore, the discussion pivots to specific challenges such as managing biases in algorithms, ensuring data protection against breaches, and adhering to global privacy laws like the GDPR.

In the latter parts, the narrative shifts towards practical implementations, elaborating on best practices for AI development to include ethical principles from inception. The developer's role in continuous education on ethical AI and participating in creating inclusive AI tools is underlined to prevent a widening digital divide. Additionally, predictive analytics in AI, AI in advertising, and the handling of intellectual property are dissected to present a wholesome view of the ethical landscape in AI wealth creation.

The theoretical insights are supplemented by case studies that bring to light the real-world implications of ethical missteps in AI applications. These examples underscore the necessity for proactive and dynamic policy frameworks that adapt to technological advancements to ensure AI's ethical deployment. The chapter concludes by calling for collaborative efforts across various sectors to establish and uphold high ethical standards in AI, aligning the technology's potential with societal values and norms.

REFERENCES

[1] Jobin, A., Ienca, M., & Vayena, E. (2019). The global landscape of AI ethics guidelines. https://www.nature.com/articles/s42256-019-0088-2

[2] Mittelstadt, B. (2017). Ethics of the health-related internet of things: a narrative review. https://www.liebertpub.com/doi/abs/10.1089/cyber.2016.0387

[3] Cath, C., Wachter, S., Mittelstadt, B., Taddeo, M., & Floridi, L. (2017). Artificial Intelligence and the 'Good Society': the US, EU, and UK approach. https://www.tandfonline.com/doi/abs/10.1080/1369118X.2016.1257041

[4] Zeng, Y., Lu, E., & Huangfu, C. (2019). Linking Artificial Intelligence Principles. https://journals.sagepub.com/doi/full/10.1177/2053951719860543

[5] Goodman, B., & Flaxman, S. (2016). European Union regulations on algorithmic decision-making and a "right to explanation". https://dl.acm.org/doi/10.1145/3068227

CASE STUDY: ALGORITHMIC BIAS IN LOAN APPROVAL SYSTEMS

A financial technology company, FinTech Innovations, recently implemented an AI-driven system designed to automate the loan approval process. Named 'CreditAI', this system was developed to increase efficiency and reduce human error in evaluating loan applications. Initially, CreditAI was praised for its speed and accuracy, significantly reducing processing times and operational costs. However, over time, reports began to surface indicating that certain demographic groups were experiencing unusually high loan rejection rates.

Upon investigation, it was discovered that CreditAI, trained on historical loan data, had inadvertently learned to replicate biases present in that data. These biases included higher rejection rates for applicants from specific zip codes, which historically had higher populations of minority groups. This issue highlighted a significant ethical concern in AI applications, particularly the reproduction of existing societal inequalities through automated systems.

Further analysis revealed that the training datasets included historical decisions made by loan officers who might have had unconscious biases, which were then encoded into CreditAI's algorithms. This situation exemplifies the challenges of ensuring fairness in automated decision-making processes, where AI systems can amplify historical biases if not carefully monitored and corrected. The case of FinTech Innovations serves as a critical lesson in the importance of ethical AI deployment, emphasizing the need for rigorous testing against diverse datasets and continuous monitoring for bias.

Case Study: Ethics of AI in Predictive Policing

In recent years, a city's police department embarked on integrating AI into their operations, with a focus on predictive policing. This AI system, coined 'PreCrime AI', was designed to forecast criminal activities based on patterns and historical data. Initially, it seemed like an innovative approach to proactively allocate police resources, potentially reducing crime rates. However, significant ethical concerns arose when certain neighborhoods began experiencing an excessive police presence, leading to tensions within the community.

A deep dive into PreCrime AI's functioning revealed that it disproportionately targeted historically marginalized neighborhoods. These areas were flagged by the system as 'high-risk' zones more frequently, leading to increased patrols and surveillance. Concerns escalated when it became clear that the AI was trained on arrest records and crime reports that reflected systemic biases and historical over-policing in these areas. This scenario underscores the complexity of deploying AI systems in contexts where data can perpetuate or even exacerbate existing societal disparities.

The implications of such technology pose profound ethical questions about surveillance, fairness, and discrimination. The principle of 'justice for all' seemed compromised as data-driven policing inadvertently penalized communities based on flawed historical inputs rather than current realities. This raised a significant challenge for the police department: how to leverage technology to enhance safety while ensuring it fosters equity and trust across all communities.

In response, the police department initiated a comprehensive review of PreCrime AI's algorithm with the help of AI ethics experts and community leaders. They aimed to revamp the system's data inputs, ensuring a broader and unbiased dataset. Additionally, ongoing community feedback sessions were established to observe the impact of these changes and to maintain a dialogue with affected communities, aiming to rebuild trust while adjusting the system's operational parameters. This real-world example highlights the importance of incorporating ethical considerations into AI development and deployment, reflecting a need for systems that not only respect legal standards but also ethical norms to genuinely benefit and protect all citizens fairly.

Case Study: Privacy and Ethics in AI-Driven Personalized Marketing

A large retail corporation, Global Retail Inc., has recently implemented a sophisticated AI-driven marketing system designed to personalize user experiences and optimize advertising efforts. This AI system, called 'AdTailor', utilizes customer data to predict purchasing behavior and enhance target ad delivery efficiently. Initially, AdTailor boasted remarkable increases in campaign conversion rates and customer satisfaction scores, attributing to its advanced algorithms capable of analyzing consumer patterns and preferences.

However, concerns arose when customers started reporting unusual insights into their personal lives reflected in the ads they were receiving, which they had not explicitly shared. This situation prompted an uproar regarding privacy intrusions and ethical boundaries being compromised. Further investigation revealed that AdTailor was aggregating vast amounts of data, which included not only transactional history but also inferred data points from social media activity, location tracking, and even indirect preferences through behavior analysis. These data points, when pieced together, created an alarmingly accurate profile of individual consumers.

The deployment of AdTailor highlighted critical issues in the balance between personalized marketing benefits and consumer privacy rights. Despite the enhanced user experience, the aggressive data aggregation tactics led to consumer distrust and fear of surveillance, overshadowing the benefits provided by AI-driven personalization.

In response to the backlash, Global Retail Inc. collaborated with privacy experts and ethicists to overhaul AdTailor's operations. Key changes involved implementing stricter data governance policies, ensuring data minimization, and enhancing transparency. Customers were given more control over their data, with easy-to-understand consent forms and straightforward opt-out options in data sharing. The company also initiated a series of open forums and educational outreach to regain public trust and provide clarity into the AI systems' functional and ethical frameworks. This case emphasizes the critical need for maintaining ethical standards and robust privacy protections in the application of AI in business practices, ensuring that technological advancements do not compromise fundamental consumer rights.

Case Study: AI-Driven Wealth Management and the Challenge of Ethical Investment

A leading financial services firm, WealthTech Solutions, recently developed an AI system, 'InvestorAI', designed to optimize investment portfolios. InvestorAI uses advanced algorithms to analyze market trends, forecast investment risks, and personalize portfolio recommendations for clients. The system initially received acclaim for its ability to generate high returns and tailor investments to individual risk preferences.

However, as InvestorAI became more integrated into the company's operations, ethical questions emerged regarding its investment recommendations. It was discovered that InvestorAI was significantly investing client funds into industries with dubious ethical practices, such as fossil fuels and companies with poor labor conditions. These industries were chosen based on historical data indicating high returns, despite contradicting the ethical investment policies that WealthTech Solutions purported to uphold.

This situation posed a significant ethical dilemma: should the firm prioritize maximizing client returns using AI, or should it adhere to ethical investment standards? The controversy intensified after clients, who were environmentally and socially conscious, became aware that their investments were contributing to sectors they opposed.

In response to the ensuing backlash, WealthTech Solutions convened a panel comprising ethics experts, investment professionals, and AI developers. The mandate was to reevaluate InvestorAI's decision-making frameworks to align with ethical investment principles without compromising on performance. Modifications included reprogramming InvestorAI to exclude industries that didn't meet specified ethical criteria, regardless of their projected profitability.

Following these changes, the firm launched an educational campaign targeting both clients and employees. The campaign focused on the importance of ethical investments and detailed how AI was being used to ensure alignment with these values. Furthermore, regular audits were introduced to ensure ongoing compliance with ethical investment standards, aiming to prevent future discrepancies and maintain transparency.

Case Study: AI in Healthcare: Ethical Considerations in Patient Data Usage

In an effort to improve healthcare outcomes, MedTech Innovations, a pioneer in healthcare technology, deployed an AI-driven system called 'HealthAI'. This system was designed to predict patient health risks by analyzing vast amounts of health data. HealthAI leveraged machine learning algorithms to provide personalized healthcare plans, predict patient risks, and optimize hospital resource management. Initially, HealthAI demonstrated promising results by identifying at-risk patients earlier and more accurately than traditional methods, thereby potentially saving lives and reducing healthcare costs.

However, the deployment of HealthAI soon raised significant ethical concerns. Critics argued that the extensive data collection involved could infringe on patient privacy. Detailed health records, family history, and even genetic information were used to feed HealthAI's algorithms. While these data points were crucial for the system's accuracy, they also posed a high risk of privacy invasion if ever breached or misused. Additionally, concerns were raised regarding the consent process. It became evident that most patients were unaware of the extent to which their data was being used, and many had not given explicit consent.

This situation escalated when a data breach incident exposed sensitive information of thousands of patients. The breach not only undermined public trust in MedTech Innovations but also sparked a widespread debate about the ethical implications of AI in healthcare. Questions were raised about the balance between technological advancements and patient rights to privacy and consent. MedTech Innovations faced legal scrutiny and public backlash, prompting them to reassess their ethical guidelines.

In response to the crisis, MedTech Innovations convened an ethics review board, including healthcare professionals, ethicists, and legal experts. The board was tasked with overhauling HealthAI's data handling practices. Measures such as implementing more robust cybersecurity solutions, establishing clearer patient consent protocols, and enhancing transparency about data usage were initiated. The company also engaged in public dialogues to educate about AI's benefits and risks in healthcare, aiming to rebuild trust and ensure ethical compliance.

Case Study: AI in Real Estate: Ethical Pricing Algorithms

An emerging real estate tech company, RealtyAI, designed a sophisticated AI system called 'PriceOpt AI' to optimize property valuations and listing prices. PriceOpt AI leveraged extensive data analytics, including historical sales data, market trends, and socio-economic indicators, to provide real estate agents and clients with precise property evaluations. Initially, PriceOpt AI was celebrated for its precision and ability to adapt to fluctuating markets, helping users secure deals swiftly and profitably.

However, several months after deployment, inconsistencies in pricing began to surface, particularly in diverse neighborhoods. Reports indicated that properties in lower-income or racially diverse areas were consistently undervalued by PriceOpt AI. This issue, once identified, stirred significant ethical debates around the fairness of AI-driven real estate assessments and the perpetuation of historical segregation and discrimination.

A thorough investigation revealed that PriceOpt AI, although sophisticated, relied on datasets that had implicit socio-economic and racial biases embedded within past market trends. These biases mirrored and potentially exacerbated long-standing discrepancies in housing valuations, affecting community demographics and individuals' equity in significant ways.

To address these concerns, RealtyAI began collaborating with AI ethics consultants to revise the algorithm's data handling policies. This included diversifying the sources of data used for training the AI to include more varied and current market indicators, conducting audits for bias in the datasets, and integrating oversight by human analysts to supervise AI-generated valuations.

Moreover, RealtyAI initiated community engagement programs, involving stakeholders from affected neighborhoods to participate in revising the AI tools, ensuring that their concerns and perspectives shaped the development of equitable AI systems. The company also held workshops and published extensive reports explaining the AI pricing model, aiming to cultivate transparency and rebuild trust among users and community members. Through such measures, RealtyAI strived not just to correct the biases but also to pioneer a model for ethical AI deployment in the real estate industry.

Case Study: AI in Employment Screening: Navigating Bias and Fairness

A prominent tech company, TechTalent Inc., recently implemented an AI-driven system, called 'HireSmart AI', designed to streamline the recruitment process. HireSmart AI was supposed to automatically sift through job applications to identify the most qualified candidates based on a set of predefined criteria and historical hiring data. The system promised to increase efficiency, reduce human bias, and speed up the hiring process, which initially attracted positive feedback for its innovative approach to recruitment.

However, several months post-implementation, discrepancies in the hiring process began to surface. Reports from HR indicated that the system seemed to favor candidates from a specific demographic, particularly those who had attended certain prestigious universities, inadvertently sidelining potentially qualified candidates from less renowned institutions or diverse backgrounds. This pattern raised ethical concerns about fairness and equality in automated decision-making systems used in recruitment.

An in-depth analysis revealed that HireSmart AI, while efficient, was working with biased algorithms, trained on past company data that reflected inherent biases—selection patterns favoring candidates from specific educational backgrounds. This case exposes the challenges and ethical implications of using AI in recruitment. It underscored the need for intentional, comprehensive diversity and inclusion policies in AI implementation strategies. To tackle this issue, TechTalent Inc. decided to revise HireSmart AI's algorithm with broader and more inclusive recruitment criteria. They also integrated periodic reviews by human HR experts to vet the AI's decisions.

The company initiated a series of workshops to educate their developers, HR team, and management on the importance of ethical AI use in recruitment. They engaged with AI ethics consultants to ensure that subsequent AI tools would be developed with bias mitigation as a priority. Transparency with job applicants about the use of AI in the screening process was increased, including an explanation of how the AI system evaluates applications, offering candidates insights and the opportunity to provide feedback on the AI's fairness. This case illustrates the perpetual need for vigilance and continuous improvement in AI systems to uphold fair and ethical practices in all business operations.

Case Study: AI and Ethical Dilemmas in Dynamic Pricing Strategies

AceTech, a leading e-commerce platform, implemented an advanced AI-driven dynamic pricing model known as 'PricerAI' designed to optimize product pricing in real-time based on market demand, competitor pricing, and consumer behavior analytics. PricerAI was initially seen as a strategic advantage, boosting sales and revenue by adjusting prices dynamically to capture the maximum willingness to pay of consumers. This innovation allowed AceTech to stay competitive and responsive to market fluctuations, giving them a notable edge in the industry. However, issues arose when consumers started noticing substantial price disparities for the same products under different conditions, such as changes in location, time of day, and individual consumer profiles including past purchasing behavior. These revelations led to public backlash as customers felt they were being unfairly treated and manipulated by opaque algorithmic pricing strategies. Further scrutiny revealed that PricerAI, while efficient in terms of economic metrics, lacked ethical transparency. It was leveraging sensitive consumer data to segment markets aggressively, leading to accusations of discriminatory pricing and privacy breaches. The case of AceTech and its PricerAI shed light on the complex interplay between AI-enhanced business efficiency and ethical consumer treatment. The dual nature of AI as both a tool for precision in business and a potential instrument for consumer exploitation put AceTech at the heart of a public debate on ethical AI use. AceTech responded by pausing the implementation of PricerAI to conduct a thorough ethical review. They engaged with AI ethics experts, consumer rights groups, and industry regulators to explore the implications of AI-driven dynamic pricing further. Recommendations from these discussions led to the redesign of PricerAI's algorithms to ensure fair pricing practices without compromising individual privacy. Consumer respect and transparency were prioritized, with new features that informed customers about how their data was being used and provided options to opt-out of data-driven personalization. Moreover, AceTech initiated an industry-wide roundtable to set standards for transparent and ethical AI use in pricing strategies, aiming to build consumer trust and pave the way for future AI applications in dynamic pricing.

REVIEW QUESTIONS

1. Dr. Ellis, a seasoned ethicist in AI wealth creation, examines a new AI-driven financial advisory tool designed to optimize investment strategies. This tool uses complex algorithms to predict market trends and provide personalized advice to users. However, Dr. Ellis notices that the tool's outputs significantly favor investments in industries known for higher returns but questionable ethical practices, such as tobacco and firearms. Concerned about the ethical implications, Dr. Ellis is debating the best approach to ensure the tool aligns with broader ethical standards while still fulfilling its economic objectives. Which of the following actions should Dr. Ellis prioritize to address this ethical challenge?

A) A. Ignore the ethical implications and focus solely on maximizing economic returns for users.

B) B. Implement a feature that allows users to exclude specific industries based on their personal ethical preferences.

C) C. Completely remove the tool from the market until a solution is found.

D) D. Increase the algorithm's transparency by disclosing the factors influencing its investment suggestions.

Answer: B

Explanation: Option B is the most balanced approach to addressing the ethical concerns raised by Dr. Ellis while still maintaining the tool's economic functionality. By allowing users to customize their investment preferences based on personal ethical standards, the tool respects individual values without compromising its utility. This feature not only enhances user control and personalized experience but also aligns with ethical AI practices, which emphasize respect for user values and preferences. Options A and C are less favorable as they either ignore ethical considerations or potentially overreact by removing the tool entirely, which might be unnecessary if less drastic measures could align the tool's outputs with ethical standards. Option D, while beneficial for transparency, does not directly address the issue of investing in ethically questionable industries.

2. Sarah, a data protection officer, is tasked with ensuring that a new AI-powered wealth management app complies with GDPR and other relevant privacy laws. The app collects sensitive data about users' financial status and investment preferences to offer customized advice. As part of her role, Sarah is evaluating the app's privacy features and identifies a potential risk in the app's data storage practices, which could expose user data to unauthorized access. Which of the following measures should Sarah advocate for to enhance the app's data security and ensure compliance with privacy regulations?

A) A. Reduce the amount of data collected by limiting the customization options available in the app.

B) B. Implement stronger encryption methods for data at rest and in transit, and regular security audits to identify vulnerabilities.

C) C. Establish a third-party service to manage all user data, thereby reducing the direct responsibility of the app developers.

D) D. Disable all data collection features to guarantee user privacy.

Answer: B

Explanation: Option B is optimal for enhancing the app's data security while remaining compliant with privacy laws. Strong encryption methods prevent unauthorized access to data, ensuring that user information remains confidential, which is a core requirement of GDPR and similar regulations. Regular security audits are essential to proactively identify and mitigate potential security vulnerabilities, which further aligns with legal requirements for maintaining a secure data processing environment. Option A compromises the app's functionality and may not necessarily resolve security concerns. Option C could introduce additional risk and complexity by involving a third party, and Option D is an excessive measure that would negate the app's purpose.

REVIEW QUESTIONS

3. An AI development team is working on a predictive analytics tool that aims to redefine wealth management by providing advanced insights into future market trends. The tool, however, relies heavily on historical data, which includes demographic information potentially embedding historical biases. During a review, an ethics committee raises concerns about the potential for these biases to perpetuate inequality in financial advice provided by the AI. What strategy should the development team implement to mitigate this risk of bias and ensure fairer outcomes?

A) A. Exclude all demographic data from the analysis to prevent any form of bias.

B) B. Use a more diverse dataset for training the AI that includes additional variables and more recent data.

C) C. Discontinue the use of AI in functions that involve sensitive demographic information.

D) D. Restrict the AI's use to scenarios where demographic bias is deemed less impactful.

Answer: B

Explanation: Option B is the most constructive and proactive approach to mitigating bias in AI-driven predictive analytics. By including a more diverse and comprehensive dataset, the AI system is less likely to perpetuate historical biases and can provide more accurate and fair predictions. This approach aligns with ethical AI practices, which advocate for fairness and inclusivity in algorithmic decision-making. While Option A might reduce bias, it could also significantly limit the AI's ability to make informed predictions by removing potentially relevant information. Option C and D may avoid addressing the root cause of the bias and could limit the beneficial applications of AI in wealth management.

NAVIGATING THE REGULATORY LANDSCAPE OF AI APPS

Introduction to Regulatory Frameworks Affecting AI Apps

As AI technologies weave seamlessly into the socioeconomic fabric, understanding the regulatory frameworks that govern them becomes imperative. This introductory segment delves into the multifaceted landscape of rules and regulations that frame the creation, deployment, and management of AI applications.

Globally, AI governance varies significantly, influenced by regional legal traditions, cultural norms, and technological advancement levels. Developers and stakeholders must navigate this complex terrain to ensure compliance while fostering innovation. This section covers the foundational legal concepts pertinent to AI—from privacy laws to intellectual property rights— and their practical impacts on AI app development.

Moreover, the regulatory environment is dynamic, often evolving quicker than the technologies it seeks to regulate. Stakeholders must stay informed of these changes to adapt and ensure that AI applications not only comply with current laws but are also prepared for future regulatory landscapes. This discussion sets the stage for deeper exploration into specific regulations and compliance strategies.

Global Overview of AI Regulations and Standards

The global regulatory landscape for AI is as diverse as it is complex. Each region implements its framework shaped by local cultures, economic needs, and societal norms. For instance, the European Union leads with its General Data Protection Regulation (GDPR), setting stringent data protection guidelines that influence global markets. Conversely, the United States adopts a more decentralized approach, where state-specific laws like California's Consumer Privacy Act (CCPA) provide foundational data privacy standards.

In Asia, countries like China and Japan are advancing sector-specific AI guidelines amid rapid technological integration. China's Model Guidelines on Artificial Intelligence focus on the ethical development of AI, promoting fairness and transparency. Meanwhile, Japan emphasizes collaboration between the public and private sectors to foster AI innovation while ensuring user safety and data integrity.

This varied global framework requires AI developers to be agile, adapting to evolving technologies and shifting regulatory tempos. Staying informed and proactive is not just advisable but vital for navigating this intricate global arena. Understanding these dynamics facilitates compliance and drives innovation, enabling developers to leverage AI's full economic potential while adhering to international standards.

Understanding the Role of International AI Governance Bodies

International AI governance bodies play a pivotal role in shaping the ethical and legal frameworks that govern AI technology globally. These organizations, such as the OECD and the International Telecommunication Union, set international standards that ensure AI's development aligns with global ethical norms and regulatory requirements, fostering coherence in policies across borders.

Their mandate includes facilitating discussions between governments, providing guidance on AI policy, and proposing global norms to prevent a regulatory patchwork that could hinder technological advancement and international cooperation. The harmonization efforts by these bodies are crucial as they help mitigate risks associated with AI, including biases and privacy concerns, ensuring a balanced approach to AI governance that respects cultural diversity and promotes international trade and cooperation.

Furthermore, these international entities monitor the implementation of AI strategies, ensuring that they adhere to agreed-upon international standards. This oversight is vital for maintaining trust in AI technologies, pivotal for their successful global integration and acceptance within societies.

AI Compliance Challenges and Effective Management Strategies

Navigating AI compliance presents multifaceted challenges, primarily due to the rapid evolution of technology outpacing existing regulatory frameworks. Developers and companies must constantly adapt to these shifting sands to avoid legal pitfalls while harnessing AI's transformative potential.

Effective management strategies are essential for maintaining compliance amid this dynamic landscape. Implementing robust governance structures is critical; these should include compliance officers and specialized legal teams focused on AI-related laws and ethics. Regular audits, both internal and conducted by third parties, ensure ongoing adherence to evolving legal standards and help mitigate risks before they escalate into legal liabilities.

Moreover, fostering a culture of compliance from the top down encourages ethical AI development practices. Educational programs and continuous training on the latest regulatory changes empower employees and stimulate proactive compliance strategies. Similarly, technology solutions like compliance management software further streamline processes, making it easier for firms to stay aligned with international regulations and standards.

These strategies collectively forge a path toward sustainable and compliant AI application development, ensuring long-term success in the ever-evolving regulatory environment of AI.

Privacy Laws Relating to AI and User Data

Privacy laws are pivotal in regulating how AI applications utilize user data, framing the boundaries for what is permissible and what is not. With the proliferation of AI technologies, the protection of individual privacy has surged to the forefront of regulatory concerns. Essential legislation, like the EU's GDPR, provides a stringent framework that advocates for the rights of individuals by ensuring data transparency and user consent prior to data processing.

In the US, although federal privacy laws specific to AI are yet to be standardized, state laws such as the California Consumer Privacy Act (CCPA) offer residents control over their personal information, setting a precedent for others to follow. These legal frameworks demand that AI developers not only secure user data but also maintain transparency about how AI algorithms employ this data.

However, the dynamic nature of AI challenges existing privacy laws, constantly testing the limits of regulatory frameworks. It becomes crucial for stakeholders to engage with ongoing legislative developments to synchronize AI innovations with robust privacy protections, ensuring a balance between technological advancements and user rights protection.

Impact of GDPR on AI App Development and Usage

The General Data Protection Regulation (GDPR) has significantly influenced AI app development, imposing strict data handling requirements that affect how AI systems process EU citizens' data. This regulation demands transparency, accountability, and user consent before data processing, challenging developers to innovate within these constraints.

For AI developers, GDPR's impact extends beyond mere compliance. It necessitates a fundamental shift in designing algorithms that respect privacy by design and default principles. This includes implementing mechanisms for data minimization and ensuring that data processing aligns with specified, explicit, and legitimate purposes. Such constraints foster creativity, pushing developers to invent more efficient data processing methods that comply with stringent privacy standards.

Moreover, the GDPR enhances user trust, an essential aspect of widespread AI adoption. By ensuring robust data protection measures, developers not only comply with the law but also position their products as trustworthy, thus potentially increasing market acceptance. Consequently, while GDPR poses challenges, it also acts as a catalyst for trustworthy and innovative AI developments.

US Regulations: Federal and State AI Laws

In the United States, the regulatory framework for AI is characterized by a mosaic of federal and state laws, each with its distinct approach to managing the rise of artificial intelligence. At the federal level, initiatives focus on establishing broad guidelines that ensure safety and fairness without stifling innovation. Agencies such as the Federal Trade Commission (FTC) play a crucial role in overseeing AI practices, particularly in the areas of consumer protection and antitrust law.

State laws, however, can vary significantly. California, for instance, has been at the forefront with its Consumer Privacy Act (CCPA), which sets a precedent for user data control. Other states like New York and Washington are exploring similar comprehensive regulations. This variation necessitates that AI developers navigate not only a federal landscape but also a complex patchwork of state regulations.

The interplay between these levels creates a dynamic regulatory environment. Staying abreast of these changes is vital for compliance and for leveraging opportunities. AI companies must employ strategic legal and operational frameworks to ensure smooth navigation through this intricate regulatory terrain.

AI Ethics and Compliance Codes

The integration of AI ethics and compliance codes sets foundational guidelines crucial for maintaining the integrity of AI developments. These codes, crafted through a synthesis of ethics and legal norms, ensure that AI applications uphold both societal values and regulatory requirements. Moreover, these frameworks serve as vital touchpoints in guiding AI practitioners in ethical decision-making, embedding principles such as fairness, accountability, and transparency at the heart of AI innovations.

Developing and implementing these ethical codes inherently involves continual engagement with evolving societal norms and legal expectations. As such, organizations are implored to instill a dynamic, ethics-driven culture that not only adheres to current standards but also anticipates future ethical challenges. This proactive stance is essential in navigating the complexities presented by new AI technologies and their implications.

Reflectively, compliance codes foster trust among users and stakeholders, lending credibility to AI systems. By establishing robust ethical guidelines and ensuring adherence to compliance codes, organizations not only mitigate risks but enhance their reputational standing, thereby setting a benchmark for responsible AI development in the industry.

Navigating Intellectual Property Rights in AI Innovations

As AI technologies forge pathways into numerous sectors, intellectual property (IP) rights emerge as critical elements in nurturing innovation while safeguarding creators. The landscape of IP rights in AI poses unique challenges, primarily due to the difficulty in defining ownership of AI-generated content and inventions. Patents and copyrights, traditional bastions of IP protection, must adapt to encompass the nuances of AI contributions.

Effective navigation through IP rights in AI requires an understanding of different jurisdictional stances, which often vary considerably. Innovative developers must engage proactively with IP attorneys to craft robust protection strategies that acknowledge AI's collaborative and iterative development processes. Additionally, strategic patent filings, covering core algorithms and unique applications, become essential in maintaining a competitive edge.

Ultimately, the dynamic interplay between AI advancements and IP law underscores the importance of ongoing legal education and policy advocacy. Stakeholders must actively participate in shaping policies that balance innovation encouragement with fair intellectual property protections, ensuring a fertile ground for future AI developments.

Sector-Specific AI Regulations: Healthcare, Finance, and Education

In the realms of healthcare, finance, and education, AI applications are subject to stringent sector-specific regulations. These frameworks are designed to address the unique risks and requirements of each domain, ensuring that AI technologies enhance rather than compromise service quality and data integrity.

In healthcare, regulations such as HIPAA in the U.S. dictate the use and protection of personal health information, driving AI developers to create solutions that maintain patient confidentiality while optimizing care. Similarly, in finance, AI tools are regulated under frameworks like the Sarbanes-Oxley Act, which emphasizes transparency and accuracy in financial reporting.

Education sector AI applications, meanwhile, are governed by laws like FERPA, which protects students' educational records. Schools using AI must navigate these regulations carefully to enhance learning while safeguarding student data.

Thus, understanding these sector-specific regulations is crucial for developers to innovate responsibly and for institutions to implement AI effectively, ensuring compliance and fostering trust in AI applications.

The Role of AI Auditing and Reporting Requirements

AI auditing and reporting requirements form a critical backbone for maintaining transparency and accountability in AI deployment. As AI systems increasingly influence critical sectors, their operations must adhere strictly to established ethical and regulatory standards. Auditing involves systematic reviews to ensure that AI algorithms function as intended, without biased outcomes or unauthorized data usage.

These efforts are complemented by detailed reporting practices that document various aspects of AI application performance. Reports serve not only as a form of compliance but also as tools for continuous improvement, providing insights into potential areas of enhancement or rectification. They also facilitate dialogue among stakeholders, including regulators, users, and developers, about the effectiveness and safety of AI technologies.

AI auditing and reporting are, therefore, not merely regulatory formalities but pivotal elements that support the sustainable advancement of AI technologies. By promoting a culture of accountability, these practices help in safeguarding user interests and enhancing the integrity of AI applications across industries.

Developing AI Policies that Align with Current Regulations

In the rapidly evolving world of AI, creating policies that align with current regulations is both critical and challenging. As regulatory landscapes vary significantly across borders, AI companies must design flexible policies that can easily adapt to multiple legal frameworks. This strategy ensures compliance and enables smoother global operations.

The first step in developing such policies involves thorough research and understanding of relevant laws in all operational territories. Engaging with legal experts and leveraging insights from international AI governance bodies can provide a foundational knowledge base. This approach aids in constructing comprehensive policies that not only meet local demands but also anticipate future regulatory changes.

Additionally, collaborative efforts with industry peers and participation in public consultations can inform policy development. This engagement helps shape a more standardized regulatory environment that supports innovation while addressing societal and ethical concerns.

Ultimately, the goal is to establish a set of dynamic AI policies that not only protect the company from legal missteps but also foster trust and reliability among stakeholders, crucial for long-term success.

Certifications and Licenses Required for AI App Developers

Navigating the intricate landscape of certifications and licenses is crucial for AI app developers. These legal requisites ensure that AI products adhere to industry standards and uphold safety, privacy, and efficacy requirements. Developers must secure various certifications that testify to their AI's compliance with technical standards and ethics guidelines, fortifying trust among users and stakeholders.

Vital certifications such as ISO/IEC 27001 for information security management help developers safeguard user data and address potential cybersecurity threats effectively. Furthermore, industry-specific licenses, especially in regulated fields like healthcare or finance, are mandatory to meet sectoral compliance while enhancing the credibility and acceptability of AI tools in these sensitive areas. For example, AI applications in healthcare might require HIPAA compliance certification to operate legally within the US jurisdiction.

Overall, acquiring the appropriate certifications and licenses is a dynamic and ongoing process. Developers must stay informed about evolving standards and regulatory changes, adapting swiftly to maintain compliance. This proactive approach not only mitigates legal risks but also positions developers advantageously in the competitive market.

Consumer Protection Laws and AI Interaction

Consumer protection laws are pivotal in the landscape of AI applications, ensuring that the deployment of these technologies does not compromise user rights. These laws typically address issues such as fairness, transparency, and accountability, especially in scenarios where AI systems make or assist in making decisions that affect consumers. The interaction between AI and consumer rights often raises questions about data privacy, informed consent, and the potential for algorithmic bias, which can inadvertently lead to unfair treatment of individuals.

On one hand, AI technologies offer the promise of personalized services and enhanced user experiences; on the other, they pose risks that can undermine consumer trust. For instance, AI-driven recommendations in e-commerce must not only enhance shopping experiences but also adhere to privacy laws that protect consumer data from misuse. Ensuring these applications are compliant requires robust mechanisms for oversight and enforcement.

Hence, developers and regulators alike must collaborate to craft guidelines that not only foster innovation but also shield consumers from potential harms. Such collaboration can also lead to the development of standardized protocols for auditing AI systems, thereby cementing the foundation of consumer trust in AI technologies moving forward.

Antitrust Considerations for AI Applications

Antitrust considerations play a crucial role in the sphere of AI applications, reflecting the intersection of technological advancement and competition law. As AI technologies gain dominance in various industries, they pave the way for potential market monopolies, inadvertently leading to anti-competitive practices. Legal scrutiny ensures that AI innovations do not stifle competition but instead foster a dynamic market environment.

Concerns typically involve scenarios where large AI corporations could leverage proprietary algorithms to manipulate market conditions or use their vast data pools to impede the entry of smaller players. Thus, regulators are tasked with maintaining vigilance against such practices, ensuring fair competition and protection of consumer interests. This entails a careful review of mergers and acquisitions involving AI firms, and the enforcement of regulations that prevent abuse of market dominance.

Moreover, the ongoing dialogue between AI companies and antitrust authorities helps refine the regulatory frameworks. This collaboration assists in defining clear guidelines that not only prevent monopolistic behaviors but also encourage innovation within a competitive legal landscape. Ensuring these measures are balanced is vital for healthy market competition and technological progression.

Data Annotation and Its Legal Implications for AI

Data annotation, the process of labeling data to train AI models, carries significant legal implications, specifically concerning data privacy and intellectual property rights. Annotators often handle sensitive information, necessitating strict adherence to global data protection laws like GDPR. Mismanagement can lead to severe penalties and loss of public trust.

Moreover, the intellectual property rights associated with annotated datasets pose another complex legal issue. Who owns the annotated data? Typically, rights could be held by the data provider, the annotator, or the AI developer, leading to potential conflicts without clear contractual agreements. Ensuring these rights are explicitly defined and respected is crucial for legal compliance and the smooth operation of AI systems.

Additionally, the use of annotated data in AI must consider fairness and non-discrimination. Legal frameworks increasingly demand that AI applications ensure algorithmic decisions do not result in biased outcomes. Thus, adhering to legal standards in data annotation not only protects against legal risks but also promotes ethical AI development.

Legal Risks Associated with AI Decision-Making

The legal risks inherent in AI decision-making processes are becoming a critical focus as these technologies are increasingly deployed in sectors impacting daily life. AI systems, making autonomous decisions, can inadvertently perpetuate biases or make errors that have significant legal implications for both developers and users.

For instance, AI-driven decisions in hiring, lending, or law enforcement can lead to allegations of discrimination if not carefully managed with respect to equality laws. The opacity of some AI algorithms, often referred to as 'black boxes', further complicates accountability, making it challenging to pinpoint responsibility for wrongful decisions or actions. This ambiguity can expose companies to lawsuits, regulatory penalties, and reputational damage if they fail to demonstrate that their AI systems operate fairly and within legal boundaries.

Thus, developers must implement rigorous testing and auditing mechanisms to ensure compliance with existing laws and to mitigate potential legal challenges. Keeping abreast of evolving regulations and engaging proactively with legal standards at the developmental stage can reduce the risk of future litigations and foster trust in AI solutions.

Cross-Border Data Flows and AI: Legal Considerations

The realm of AI is intrinsically linked with data, often necessitating cross-border data flows that present complex legal challenges. These flows are pivotal for multinational AI initiatives but must navigate a labyrinth of differing data protection regulations across jurisdictions. One primary concern is the compliance with various national privacy laws, which can vary significantly and influence how data is collected, stored, and processed internationally.

For instance, the European Union's General Data Protection Regulation (GDPR) imposes stringent requirements on data transfer outside the EU, mandating that such transfers only occur to countries with 'adequate' levels of data protection. This necessitates AI companies to establish comprehensive data protection strategies, ensuring that international data transfers adhere to legal standards. Failing this, companies risk severe penalties and damage to reputation.

Additionally, mechanisms like Standard Contractual Clauses or corporate binding rules become essential tools for legally transferring data. Companies must not only implement these tools but also continuously monitor legislative changes globally to stay compliant. This ongoing vigilance helps mitigate legal risks associated with cross-border data flows in AI applications, ensuring sustainable and lawful international operations.

The Future of AI Regulation: Upcoming Legislation Predictions

As AI continues to integrate deeply into multiple sectors, upcoming legislation is poised to become more sophisticated, aiming to address the nuanced challenges posed by advanced technologies. We anticipate a proactive stance in formulating regulations that pre-empt potential ethical and privacy concerns inherent in AI deployment, especially in critical areas like healthcare and finance. Lawmakers are expected to focus on enhancing transparency and accountability mechanisms within AI systems.

Furthermore, the global inconsistency in AI regulations will likely drive the development of international standards to facilitate smoother interoperability of systems across borders. This will involve complex negotiations but is crucial for managing the global nature of data and technology platforms. Additionally, we may see more robust frameworks surrounding the use of AI in decision-making processes, ensuring decisions are fair and non-discriminatory.

Lastly, the rapid pace of AI innovation will necessitate regulations that are flexible yet stringent enough to guide ethical AI development without stifling innovation. Policymakers will have to balance innovation with safeguarding public interest, a challenging but essential endeavor.

Public Consultations and Their Role in Shaping AI Laws

Public consultations serve as vital platforms where stakeholders, including citizens, tech firms, and subject matter experts, can contribute to shaping the regulatory framework for AI applications. These forums facilitate transparent discussions and provide regulators with diverse perspectives crucial for crafting balanced AI laws.

Involving the public in the legislative process helps ensure that the regulations are not only comprehensive but also equitable. Through such engagements, policymakers can gauge public sentiment and ethics, which play as much a role in legislative directions as technical feasibility does. It is through these contributions that laws can effectively address the varying impacts of AI across social strata and industries.

Moreover, public consultations help in preempting potential legal pitfalls by highlighting real-world implications unforeseen during the drafting stages. They are instrumental in creating a dynamic legal environment that adapts to technological advancements while safeguarding fundamental rights and promoting innovation.

Recognizing their importance, governments are increasingly incorporating these consultations into the legislative process for AI, reflecting a democratic approach to technology governance that values and incorporates stakeholder input.

Compliance Tools and Software for AI Development

In the complex web of AI development, compliance tools and software play an indispensable role. They help navigate the evolving regulatory landscape by facilitating the application of legal and ethical guidelines across different stages of AI development. From data ingestion to model deployment, these tools optimize processes to ensure adherence to various global and local statutes.

Notably, compliance software can automatically flag potential legal issues, such as non-compliance with GDPR or industry-specific regulations. This proactive approach allows developers to rectify problems before they escalate into legal challenges. Additionally, these tools often come equipped with auditing capabilities, making them invaluable for maintaining transparent and traceable records required for regulatory reviews.

Given the rapid pace of AI innovation, staying updated with regulatory changes is crucial. Modern compliance software integrates updates in real-time, thus enabling developers to swiftly adjust their operations to new laws. Through continuous monitoring and adaptive responses, these tools help mitigate compliance risks, fostering trust and confidence in AI applications.

Best Practices for Ensuring AI Regulatory Compliance

To navigate the intricacies of AI regulatory compliance effectively, several best practices must be adopted by developers and organizations. Initially, it is crucial to foster a culture of compliance within the development team, emphasizing the importance of ethical AI design and adherence to legal standards from the outset.

Integration of compliance within the AI development lifecycle is also vital. This includes conducting thorough risk assessments to understand and mitigate potential legal implications at every stage, from data collection to model deployment. Engaging with legal experts who specialize in AI regulations can provide deeper insights and proactive strategies to handle compliance efficiently.

Moreover, adopting transparent documentation practices is indispensable. Detailed records of data sources, decision-making processes, and compliance checks should be maintained. This transparency not only supports regulatory compliance but also builds trust with users and stakeholders. Finally, staying abreast of legislative changes and adapting compliance strategies accordingly is essential in the dynamic field of AI. Continuous education in emerging legal challenges will further enhance an organization's readiness to meet regulatory demands effectively.

Liability and Insurance Issues in AI Deployments

Liability in AI deployments involves intricate layers of responsibility amid unforeseen outcomes or damages caused by AI systems. As AI models increasingly influence sectors ranging from healthcare to finance, pinpointing liability can become contentious. Securing appropriate insurance coverages, such as professional indemnity and product liability, becomes essential, aimed at mitigating financial risks associated with potential failures or errors of AI solutions.

Insurance companies are evolving rapidly, developing policies that specifically address the unique challenges posed by AI technologies. These policies not only cover direct damages but also extend to third-party liability, providing a safety net against claims from affected parties. With AI's capability to make autonomous decisions, insurers are put in a position to reassess traditional policies that might not necessarily encapsulate the autonomous nature of AI operations.

Amid these challenges, stakeholders must engage proactively with legal experts and insurers early in the AI development process. This collaboration ensures that all conceivable legal risks are identified and appropriately managed, while also fostering robust frameworks for current and future regulatory landscapes. It's not merely about compliance; it's about setting a foundation for trust and safety in AI's potential.

Training Programs for Legal Aspects of AI

As AI technologies weave increasingly complex patterns across various sectors, the need for specialized training in legal aspects becomes crucial. Educational programs focused on the legalities of AI are designed to prepare developers, managers, and legal professionals to navigate the minefield of regulations and compliance requirements effectively. By covering topics from intellectual property rights to international data laws, these trainings ensure individuals are well-versed in the nuances and implications of AI applications.

Moreover, these training programs often include case studies and real-world scenarios that provide insight into the application of laws in practical settings. Participants learn not only about existing regulations but also about anticipating potential legal challenges that may arise with new advancements in AI technology. This proactive approach aids in mitigating risks and fostering a culture of compliance and ethical responsibility within organizations.

To keep pace with the dynamic field of AI, these educational initiatives must continuously evolve, integrating the latest legal developments and technological innovations. They play a pivotal role in ensuring that all stakeholders maintain an informed and conscientious approach to AI deployment, crucial for sustainable and responsible growth in this transformative era.

Monitoring and Adapting to Regulatory Changes in AI

The ever-evolving nature of AI technology demands continuous monitoring and adaptation to regulatory changes. As AI integrates deeper into various sectors, staying informed on legal shifts becomes critical for maintaining compliance and ensuring operational longevity.

Organizations must establish robust monitoring systems capable of detecting changes in legislation globally. This entails not just passive observation, but active engagement with regulatory developments. Utilizing advanced compliance tools that integrate real-time updates can aid in this process, enabling companies to adapt their practices swiftly in response to new legal requirements.

Furthermore, fostering a proactive company culture that anticipates regulatory shifts can considerably mitigate risks associated with non-compliance. Regular training sessions and workshops on upcoming legislation changes empower employees to handle transitions effectively, ensuring that the organization remains ahead of the regulatory curve.

Ultimately, the goal is to turn these challenges into opportunities for innovation, using regulatory changes as a catalyst for refining AI applications and enhancing competitiveness in a rapidly shifting legal landscape.

Case Studies: Legal Challenges and Solutions in AI App Development

The landscape of AI app development is fraught with legal hurdles, necessitating a deep understanding of both technology and law. For example, a startup specializing in AI-driven healthcare solutions faced significant challenges with HIPAA compliance, critical for protecting patient data. The resolution involved restructuring data storage solutions and implementing stringent access controls, showcasing the necessity of adaptive operational models in compliance with sector-specific regulations.

In another instance, a financial tech company grappled with AI ethics when their algorithm inadvertently excluded low-income groups. Addressing this required not just technical adjustments but also a company-wide ethical reevaluation, illustrating the complex interplay between AI technology and societal norms.

These case studies highlight the essential nature of proactive legal strategies and the integration of ethical considerations from the ground up in AI development. They serve as crucial lessons in navigating the ever-evolving legal frameworks that govern AI applications, underscoring the importance of ongoing legal education and partnership with regulatory experts.

SUMMARY

The chapter 'Navigating the Regulatory Landscape of AI Apps' provides a comprehensive overview of the complex legal environments that AI app developers must negotiate. Beginning with an examination of the diverse global regulatory frameworks, it highlights the varying legal standards from the GDPR in the European Union to sector-specific guidelines in countries like China and Japan. Regulations across different jurisdictions are stressed as fundamentally influencing AI application development, requiring developers to maintain agility in their compliance practices. The role of international governance bodies like the OECD is emphasized as essential in establishing a cohesive global regulatory framework for AI, which helps in standardizing ethical norms and reducing the regulatory fragmentation that can hinder technological and market progress. The discussion extends into the challenges of AI compliance that emerge from rapid technological advancements outpacing current laws. It suggests effective management strategies including robust governance structures, regular audits, and fostering a compliance culture to navigate these challenges successfully. Furthermore, the chapter addresses the impact of specific laws such as GDPR and the CCPA on AI deployment, demonstrating how stringent data protection requirements shape the development process and play a crucial role in building user trust. AI ethics and compliance codes are discussed as foundational, guiding developers in ethical decision-making and aligning with both societal values and regulatory demands. Intellectual property rights in AI, and the need for an ongoing legal education to adapt to changing regulations, are also covered, bringing attention to the importance of legally aware AI innovations. The text concludes by reflecting on future directions in AI regulations, emphasizing the likely increase in sophisticated legislation aimed at addressing the nuanced challenges posed by AI technologies. This forward-looking perspective underlines the necessity for developers to not only comply with current regulations but to also engage proactively with emerging ones to ensure both ethical and legal alignment in their AI solutions.

REFERENCES

[1] OECD AI Principles. https://www.oecd.org/going-digital/ai/principles/

[2] General Data Protection Regulation (GDPR). https://gdpr-info.eu/

[3] California Consumer Privacy Act (CCPA). https://oag.ca.gov/privacy/ccpa

[4] Ethics Guidelines for Trustworthy AI. https://ec.europa.eu/futurium/en/ai-alliance-consultation/guidelines

[5] Harvard Business Review on AI Compliance Challenges. https://hbr.org/2020/07/the-legal-and-ethical-implications-of-using-ai-in-hiring

[6] International Data Protection and Privacy Law. https://www.jstor.org/stable/10.2307/26643754

[7] AI Innovation and Intellectual Property. https://www.wipo.int/wipo_magazine/en/2019/01/article_0005.html

CASE STUDY: STRATEGIC AI DEPLOYMENT IN MULTINATIONAL ENTERPRISE: NAVIGATING GLOBAL COMPLIANCE

EmeraTech, a multinational corporation known for its innovative AI solutions, recently initiated a project to develop an AI-driven platform designed to streamline supply chain operations across its facilities spanning various continents. The AI system aimed to optimize inventory management and predict maintenance for equipment using real-time data analysis. However, in doing so, EmeraTech faced several complex compliance issues linked to differing AI regulations and data privacy laws across the countries it operates in.

For instance, in the European Union, the General Data Protection Regulation (GDPR) imposed stringent data handling standards which required EmeraTech to revise its data processing and storage practices. Moreover, in the United States, where state-specific laws such as California's Consumer Privacy Act (CCPA) demanded additional safeguards, EmeraTech had to devise a compliant system that could dynamically adapt to both federal and state regulations. In Asia, China's Cybersecurity Law required EmeraTech to maintain certain data within the country, which conflicted with the company's centralized data analysis strategy.

EmeraTech's legal and compliance teams convened to define a strategic approach that involved extensive regulatory mapping and consultation with international AI regulatory experts. A multi-pronged strategy was devised, involving the re-architecture of data flows, application of differential privacy techniques, and the establishment of localized AI training centers to comply with national laws, thereby preventing potential legal conflicts. This approach not only facilitated compliance but also optimized the operational efficacy of their AI systems.

Furthermore, EmeraTech expanded its internal legal departments and integrated advanced compliance software throughout its development pipeline to sustain adherence to dynamic global AI regulations. This proactive compliance strategy ensured that EmeraTech stayed ahead of changes in legislation while fostering innovation and maintaining competitive edge. Their case highlights the critical nature of understanding complex global regulations and provides a strategic framework for other businesses facing similar compliance challenges in AI deployment.

Case Study: Integrating AI in Public Healthcare:

Ethical and Regulatory Navigation

HealthForward, a public healthcare provider, sought to integrate AI technologies to improve patient diagnostics and treatment planning across its network. The AI system was designed to assist in diagnosing complex diseases using machine learning models trained on vast arrays of historical health data. However, undertaking such an initiative required meticulous consideration of various ethical, privacy, and legal implications, especially concerning the handling of sensitive personal health information (PHI).

The European Union's General Data Protection Regulation (GDPR) and the United States' Health Insurance Portability and Accountability Act (HIPAA) presented major compliance hurdles. These regulations mandate strict guidelines on the privacy and security of health data, necessitating robust data protection measures by HealthForward. Further complexity arose from the AI system's potential to inadvertently perpetuate biases present in the historical data it was trained on, raising ethical concerns about fairness and equity in patient treatment.

HealthForward's initial step was to establish a cross-functional team comprising AI technologists, data protection officers, and legal experts specializing in healthcare regulations. This team was tasked with ensuring the AI system's compliance with international health data regulations and addressing potential ethical dilemmas. HealthForward adopted a 'privacy by design' approach, embedding data protection from the outset of AI system development. Advanced anonymization techniques were employed to protect patient identities, and continuous audits were planned to ensure the AI system did not perpetuate or create bias.

Moreover, HealthForward engaged with patient advocacy groups and external ethical review boards to foster transparency and public trust. The feedback from these groups led to the development of a patient consent management framework that was integrated into the AI system, allowing patients more control over their data. Through these comprehensive measures, HealthForward addressed the significant legal and ethical challenges involved, setting a standard for responsible AI integration in public healthcare. Their proactive strategies highlight the importance of thorough regulatory and ethical preparation in deploying AI technologies in sensitive sectors.

Case Study: AI-Driven Financial Advisory: Compliance and Innovation in the Fintech Sector

FinAdapt, a fast-growing fintech startup, launched an AI-driven platform designed to personalize financial advice for individual customers, harnessing vast amounts of financial data to predict market trends, manage assets, and provide real-time investment advice. However, engaging in such a technologically innovative venture required navigating a labyrinth of financial regulations, data privacy laws, and ethical considerations to avoid legal pitfalls and ensure customer trust.

Firstly, the startup faced strict regulatory scrutiny under regulations such as the Sarbanes-Oxley Act and the Payment Services Directive in Europe, each imposing rigorous data handling and processing standards. Additionally, the United States' SEC regulations required FinAdapt to maintain transparent and fair practices, particularly in how AI algorithms were used to influence financial decisions. Compliance with these regulations was critical to operate legally and sustain customer confidence.

FinAdapt's strategy began with the establishment of a dedicated compliance unit composed of legal experts familiar with global financial regulations and AI technology. This team worked to map out all applicable regulations and designed an AI system that not only complied with these laws but also embedded privacy and fairness from the ground up. Data encryption techniques were implemented to secure sensitive financial information, and mechanisms were incorporated to explain AI decisions to customers, promoting transparency.

Moreover, continuous monitoring systems were set up to review AI-driven advice, ensuring it adhered to ethical guidelines and remained unbiased. The firm also initiated regular training programs for AI staff on legal and ethical standards to stay updated with regulatory changes. By integrating these procedural and technological safeguards, FinAdapt navigated the complex regulatory environment effectively, delivering a compliant and innovative financial advisory platform that significantly enhanced client satisfaction and trust.

The proactive measures taken by FinAdapt exemplify the intricate balance between leveraging AI for advanced financial services and adhering to stringent regulations and ethical standards, providing a model for similar companies in the dynamic sector of financial technology.

Case Study: AI Implementation in Autonomous Vehicle Development: Legal and Ethical Roadblocks

AutoNavTech, a pioneering firm in the autonomous vehicle (AV) industry, embarked on a project to develop self-driving cars equipped with cutting-edge AI technologies aimed at reducing human error and improving road safety. The project's scale and its implications required strict adherence to a variety of international regulations concerning safety, data privacy, and AI ethics, particularly the challenges associated with vehicle autonomy and decision-making algorithms.

AutoNavTech's AV project involved gathering vast amounts of data from a multitude of sensors and cameras, making compliance with the General Data Protection Regulation (GDPR) in the EU and similar data protection laws in other regions a top priority. Furthermore, the intricate task of programming ethical decision-making into the AV system—such as how the AI should act in potential accident scenarios—brought about intense scrutiny from both regulators and the public concerned with ethical implications.

To navigate these multifaceted challenges, AutoNavTech established a specialized ethical AI committee and sought alliances with AI ethics boards. This committee was tasked with integrating ethical considerations into the AI's operational algorithms to handle dilemmas such as the 'trolley problem,' where the AI must choose between two negative outcomes in the event of an unavoidable accident. Moreover, privacy by design principles was rigorously employed to ensure all personal data collected through vehicle sensors was processed and stored under strict confidentiality and security measures.

AutoNavTech also engaged in public consultations and transparency initiatives to socialize the technology with consumers and gather broader societal inputs. These efforts helped to align their development process with public expectations and legal standards, significantly contributing to a socially acceptable ethical framework for their autonomous vehicles.

In conclusion, through its thoughtful approach to handle regulatory, ethical, and public relation challenges, AutoNavTech not only adhered to existing laws but also contributed to setting a high benchmark in the developing field of AI-driven autonomous vehicles. Their proactive strategies in compliance and public engagement demonstrate a robust blueprint for integrating complex AI systems in compliance-sensitive industries.

Case Study: AI Integration in Academic Testing: Legal and Ethical Compliance

EduTech Solutions, an innovator in the education technology sector, recently embarked on the development of an AI-driven testing platform aimed at revolutionizing how academic assessments are conducted. The platform would leverage AI to personalize exams, ensuring they match students' educational needs while maintaining fairness and transparency. However, EduTech faced significant compliance hurdles related to student data protection and fair usage of AI.

In the United States, particularly under the Family Educational Rights and Privacy Act (FERPA), safeguarding students' educational records is paramount. Additionally, global concerns regarding AI bias and the ethical use of algorithms in educational settings added layers of complexity to the project. EduTech had to ensure their AI system complied with FERPA as well as with ethical guidelines that protect against biases in automated decision-making processes.

EduTech's initial steps included forming an interdisciplinary team comprising AI specialists, legal experts, and educational psychologists to address these complex issues. They concentrated on embedding 'ethics by design' in their AI systems, which involved setting up protocols to routinely audit the AI's decision-making algorithms for fairness and accuracy. Moreover, significant attention was devoted to data security, implementing cutting-edge encryption methods, and ensuring that the storage and processing of data complied with both local and international regulations.

To further these efforts, EduTech periodically engaged with educational regulators and participated in educational forums to remain aligned with current academic standards and legal requirements. These proactive steps facilitated discussions about AI transparency and the necessity to ensure that the AI testing platforms do not perpetuate existing educational disparities.

The comprehensive strategy not only helped EduTech navigate the intricate legal landscape surrounding AI in education but also set a precedent in maintaining rigorous ethical standards. This proactive approach ensured that the AI platform supported a fair, unbiased academic environment, demonstrating the potential of AI to positively transform educational assessment while adhering to strict compliance requirements.

Case Study: Advancing AI in Public Transportation: Legal Complexities and Strategic Compliance

TranspoAI, a leading technology firm specializing in Artificial Intelligence for public transportation systems, recently embarked on a project to develop a sophisticated AI-powered scheduling and routing system. This AI system was intended to optimize route planning, reduce wait times, and enhance passenger experience across various cities globally. However, this deployment presented a multitude of compliance challenges due to diverse international regulations concerning data privacy, AI accountability, and transportation safety.

In the European Union, strict adherence to the General Data Protection Regulation (GDPR) was imperative, as the AI system processed large volumes of personal data from passengers. GDPR compliance required TranspoAI to implement robust data protection measures, including data anonymization techniques and clear data consent mechanisms. Additionally, in the United States, the company faced a different set of challenges with individual states having varying laws on data protection and AI deployment in public utilities. For example, states like California with stricter privacy laws necessitated additional safeguards which required dynamic adaptation of the AI system to comply with state-specific regulations.

TranspoAI created a specialized legal task force that focused on understanding these variegated legal environments and crafting a compliance strategy that was both flexible and robust. This team collaborated closely with local regulatory bodies and transportation authorities to ensure the AI system's deployment was not only compliant but also conducive to public trust and safety. By employing a 'compliance by design' approach, they embedded legal and ethical considerations right from the initial phases of system development.

Furthermore, TranspoAI invested in ongoing AI ethics training for their developers and incorporated regular auditing mechanisms to continuously assess the AI system's decision-making processes. These proactive measures were key to adapting to regulatory changes and addressing potential compliance issues preemptively. As a result, the project not only met all legal requirements but also set a precedent for other AI applications in public infrastructure, demonstrating the importance of strategic compliance management in the realm of AI-enhanced transportation.

Case Study: AI Integration in Retail Customer Service: Regulatory Challenges and Strategic Solutions

ShopMax, a prominent retail giant, ventured into integrating AI-driven customer service solutions aimed at personalizing the shopping experience and streamlining customer support. Employing AI chatbots and personalized recommendation systems, ShopMax sought to leverage consumer data to enhance their service quality and operational efficiency. However, this initiative brought forth significant regulatory and ethical considerations, particularly concerning consumer data protection and transparency.

Within the European Union, strict adherence to the GDPR mandated that ShopMax implement robust data protection measures to safeguard customer information. They needed to ensure that the data collected through their AI systems was handled transparently and with explicit consent from users. Furthermore, in the United States, compliance with both federal and varied state-specific data protection statutes—like the California Consumer Privacy Act (CCPA)—added another layer of complexity. These laws required that customers be provided with clear information about data usage and offered straightforward options to control, correct, or delete their personal data.

To address these challenges, ShopMax initiated a detailed compliance review and redesigned their data handling protocols to align with both EU and US regulations. They instituted an advanced consent management system that made it easier for customers to understand and manage their preferences. Enhanced data encryption methods were incorporated to secure sensitive personal data from potential breaches.

Additionally, ShopMax undertook transparency initiatives to educate customers about AI functions within their services. This involved clear communications regarding how customer data was used to tailor recommendations and support interactions, assisting compliance with legal mandates on transparency and ethical handling. ShopMax also established an ongoing monitoring process to track regulatory changes in real-time, ensuring that their AI systems remained compliant as laws evolved. These strategic moves not only enabled compliance but also fortified customer trust and confidence in the brand, illustrating the intricate balance between leveraging innovative AI technology and adhering to stringent regulatory requirements in the dynamic retail sector.

Case Study: Evolving AI Regulation in the Global Gig Economy: A Case Study of GigTech

GigTech, a burgeoning tech startup, developed an AI-driven platform designed to optimize gig worker allocation and enhance job matchmaking across various global markets. This technology uses advanced algorithms to predict demand in different sectors and match workers with gigs in real time, thereby providing flexibility and maximizing earnings for gig workers. However, the deployment of such a platform required GigTech to navigate a complex and often fragmented regulatory environment that varies not only from country to country but also between different states and regions within those countries.

In Europe, comprehensive compliance with the General Data Protection Regulation (GDPR) was paramount, as the platform handled sensitive worker and employer data. GigTech needed to ensure all personal data was processed with high levels of transparency and under strict consent protocols. Meanwhile, in the United States, varying state laws such as California's Assembly Bill 5 (AB5) posed unique challenges by redefining gig workers' legal classifications, impacting how GigTech could operate and manage AI-driven work allocations without compromising workers' rights.

Furthermore, in Asia, particularly in India and China, the legal frameworks surrounding contract work and data privacy were rapidly evolving. These changes required GigTech to adapt its operational and data handling strategies continually. The startup established a dedicated legal compliance team tasked with remaining abreast of international and local regulations, adapting the AI system to meet legal requirements without stifling functionality.

This team implemented a scalable legal framework that used sophisticated compliance software to automatically adjust its algorithms to comply with local laws—creating a system that was not only compliant but also resilient and adaptive to the rapidly changing global legal landscape.

The proactive legal and compliance strategy not only facilitated GigTech's compliance but also enabled the company to innovate responsibly, creating a trustworthy platform that leveraged AI to reshape the gig economy. This approach illustrated the critical importance of dynamic and informed regulatory engagement in deploying AI technologies effectively in a globally interconnected market.

REVIEW QUESTIONS

1. An AI technology company is developing a new app to leverage data-driven insights for optimizing eCommerce platforms. During the planning phase, the team encounters various global AI regulations affecting user data usage and privacy. They prioritize aligning with the General Data Protection Regulation (GDPR) for their operations in Europe. In considering the deployment of their app, what should their primary focus be?

A) Prioritizing the development of encrypted data storage systems

B) Ignoring GDPR since their main operations are in Asia

C) Developing a robust consent management framework for user data

D) Focusing solely on intellectual property rights for their AI algorithms

Answer: C

Explanation: The team should focus on developing a robust consent management framework for user data, as mandated by the GDPR, which involves transparency, accountability, and obtaining user consent prior to data processing. This is crucial as GDPR imposes strict data privacy rules not just in Europe but influences standards globally, ensuring that users' privacy is protected and that their data is used ethically and legally. Prioritizing this over other aspects such as IP rights or encrypted storage, although important on their own, aligns their operations with critical regulatory requirements that could influence user trust and company liability.

2. A startup specializing in AI-driven healthcare solutions aims to expand its operations from the U.S. to Europe. The team understands the importance of compliance with HIPAA for U.S. operations but needs to prepare for new European regulations. How should they approach their expansion to ensure compliance with healthcare data laws in Europe?

A) Apply HIPAA standards as a baseline for all global operations

B) Research and integrate GDPR and relevant healthcare-specific regulations in the EU

C) Disregard EU laws since their technology is already compliant in the U.S.

D) Focus on technology transfer only without adjusting for legal differences

Answer: B

Explanation: The correct approach is to research and integrate not only the GDPR, which covers a wide range of privacy aspects in the EU, but also any other healthcare-specific regulations that may apply within European countries. While HIPAA provides a strong framework for protecting health information, GDPR imposes additional requirements such as the right to data erasure and more stringent consent protocols. Integrating these regulations into their expansion strategy is essential for legal compliance and would help avoid potential fines and legal disputes, thereby facilitating smoother operations and building user trust in new markets.

REVIEW QUESTIONS

3. A global AI software provider plans to use customer data across different continents to improve their service offerings. Given the diversity in regional AI laws, which strategy should they adopt to handle data privacy and compliance efficiently?

A) Adopt the strictest data privacy laws globally as a standard practice

B) Create a localized strategy that aligns with individual regional laws

C) Ignore less stringent laws and follow only their country's regulations

D) Use data without adherence to specific regulations, focusing on product enhancement

Answer: B

Explanation: Adopting a localized strategy that aligns with individual regional laws is the most effective approach for a global AI software provider. This method recognizes the diversity of data privacy regulations, such as the GDPR in Europe, CCPA in California, and other national laws. A localized strategy not only helps in complying with the legal frameworks of each region, which enhances trust and credibility among users, but it also minimizes legal risks and potential fines. Ignoring laws or adopting a general approach could lead to significant compliance issues, affecting the company's operation and reputation negatively.

4. In developing an AI-driven educational app, a company navigates through various U.S. state and federal laws about data privacy in schools. What should be their primary legal consideration to ensure comprehensive compliance across different states?

A) Follow the strictest privacy laws found in any U.S. state

B) Prioritize only Federal Educational Rights and Privacy Act (FERPA) compliance

C) Align with international educational data guidelines instead of U.S. laws

D) Focus solely on the operational technology without regard to specific educational laws

Answer: A

Explanation: Following the strictest privacy laws found in any U.S. state is a wise strategy for an AI-driven educational app. This approach ensures that the application meets high standards of data protection, particularly relevant in environments dealing with minors and educational data, thereby aligning with FERPA and potentially more stringent state laws such as California's regulations. This not only broadens the app's adaptability and market reach across various states by meeting or exceeding their individual requirements but also builds trust among users (educational institutions and parents), crucial for the app's acceptance and success.

FUTURE TRENDS: WHERE AI IN WEALTH CREATION IS HEADED

Predictive Technologies: Next-Gen AI in Financial Forecasting

Predictive technologies, driven by next-generation AI, are redefining financial forecasting with unprecedented precision and insight. These advanced AI systems utilize machine learning algorithms to analyze vast datasets, identifying patterns and predicting market trends that are beyond human capability. This not only enhances decision-making for investors and financial analysts but also revolutionizes portfolio management by optimizing asset allocation based on predicted market movements.

Moreover, AI's predictive capabilities extend to risk assessment, providing financial institutions with the tools to mitigate potential losses in a volatile market. By forecasting economic downturns or stock market crashes, AI enables proactive strategies, from adjusting interest rates to reallocating resources, safeguarding both corporate and consumer finance against unforeseen economic shifts.

The integration of AI into financial forecasting not only boosts economic efficiency but also democratizes financial planning, making high-level analysis accessible to a broader audience. As these technologies evolve, they promise to further empower economic stability and individual wealth management, heralding a new era in finance.

AI and Decentralized Finance: Emerging Opportunities

The confluence of AI with decentralized finance (DeFi) presents transformative opportunities, reshaping how financial markets operate and democratizing access to capital. AI's integration into DeFi leverages automated smart contracts, optimizing transactions and enhancing security, while facilitating real-time, trustless interactions across borders.

This synergy extends further into personalized financial services. AI-driven analytics empower individuals to engage with financial systems that were once exclusive to institutions. By analyzing vast amounts of data, AI identifies tailored investment opportunities that align with users' risk profiles and financial goals, leading to more informed decision-making processes.

Furthermore, AI contributes to the robustness of DeFi platforms by enhancing predictive capacities and fraud detection systems. Continuous learning algorithms adapt to new threats, maintaining the integrity of decentralized transactions. As regulation catches up, these AI-enhanced systems could set new standards for global finance, pointing to a future where technology and financial inclusion go hand in hand.

Ethical AI: Shaping the Future of Responsible Wealth Creation

The integration of ethical AI into wealth creation is pivotal for fostering trust and sustainability in financial ecosystems. As AI technologies advance, their role in managing and generating wealth must adhere to ethical standards that prioritize transparency, fairness, and accountability. Ethical AI frameworks are designed not only to prevent biases in financial decision-making but also to enhance the reliability of AI systems by making them answerable to regulatory and ethical norms.

Moreover, incorporating ethical AI practices ensures that technology serves the broader societal interests, not just individual or corporate gains. For instance, AI systems can be programmed to avoid strategies that unfairly disadvantage certain groups or promote inequality. This commitment to ethical practices in AI-driven wealth creation can help avert potential misuses of technology while promoting a more equitable distribution of economic benefits.

Ultimately, the commitment to ethical AI in wealth creation processes assures stakeholders of the integrity of financial practices, paving the way for sustainable growth and innovation in the finance sector. Responsible AI acts as a cornerstone in building systems that uphold human values, therefore securing a stable and prosperous financial future for all.

Integration of AI with Quantum Computing

The integration of Artificial Intelligence (AI) with Quantum Computing represents a groundbreaking convergence, set to redefine wealth creation across sectors. Quantum computing introduces computational capabilities exponentially more powerful than classical computers, facilitating calculations and processes previously deemed impractical.

This novel integration allows AI systems to analyze and process vast quantities of data at speeds unattainable before, enabling complex financial models and simulations to run in fractions of the usual time. The implications for financial markets are profound, enhancing everything from algorithmic trading to risk management and fraud detection.

AI's learning algorithms, combined with quantum computing's speed, can also pioneer new frontiers in portfolio management. By harnessing these technologies, financial institutions can offer hyper-personalized investment strategies that adapt in real-time, optimizing returns for investors across various market conditions.

As this technology matures, its adoption in financial services could herald a new era of innovation, security, and efficiency, significantly influencing how wealth is generated and managed globally.

AI-Driven Personalized Wealth Management Services

AI-driven personalized wealth management services are molding the landscape of financial advising, offering more tailored and responsive solutions to clients. By integrating complex algorithms and machine learning, these AI systems analyze individual financial data, juxtaposing it against broader market trends to offer customized investment strategies. This personalization not only enhances customer satisfaction but also optimizes portfolio performance.

Moreover, these AI tools continuously learn from data inputs, refining their advice based on evolving market conditions and personal financial changes. Clients benefit from real-time financial advice and adjustments, effectively capturing potential gains or mitigating losses as situations shift. This dynamic financial management approach empowers users, giving them confidence in their financial decisions without the overwhelming details.

These services extend beyond traditional wealth management, diving into aspects such as tax optimization, estate planning, and retirement strategies. Each client's journey is distinct, and AI's adaptive nature facilitates a deeply personalized service that proposes options aligned not just with financial goals but also personal values and life changes.

The Rise of AI Coaches in Personal Finance

The advent of AI coaches in personal finance heralds a transformative era in managing personal wealth. These AI systems, designed with sophisticated algorithms, offer tailored financial guidance that was traditionally the domain of human advisors. By interfacing seamlessly with users' financial data, AI coaches provide real-time recommendations on budgeting, saving, investing, and debt management, each adapted to individual financial behaviors and goals.

Furthermore, as these AI platforms evolve, they incorporate behavioral finance insights to curb irrational financial decisions and enhance fiscal discipline among users. This personalized coaching at scale has the potential to revolutionize personal finance management, making expert advice accessible to a broader demographic, irrespective of economic background.

Economic inclusivity is also bolstered as AI finance coaches lower the barrier to quality financial advice, previously a service for the affluent. By democratizing financial knowledge through AI, individuals gain empowerment over their economic destinies, potentially altering the landscape of personal wealth accumulation.

Autonomous Business Models: AI Running Companies

The evolution of AI has paved the way for autonomous business models, where AI systems not only support but fully manage company operations. These models represent an innovative shift in business management, harnessing AI's capabilities to run complex, global enterprises with minimal human intervention. By integrating AI throughout the operational hierarchy, companies can optimize efficiency, reduce costs, and accelerate decision-making processes.

AI's role in autonomous companies extends beyond routine automation. It involves strategic planning and real-time problem solving, adapting dynamically to market changes and consumer behavior. With AI at the helm, businesses can leverage predictive analytics and machine learning to forecast market trends and tailor services accordingly, creating a more responsive business model that can outpace traditional firms.

However, the move towards AI-driven companies also poses challenges, including ethical concerns and the need for robust regulatory frameworks. Ensuring transparency and accountability in AI decisions is crucial to gain stakeholder trust and maintain a sustainable business practice in this new frontier of corporate governance.

The Expansion of AI in Emerging Markets

The expansion of AI in emerging markets is a transformative force, driving economic growth and innovation. As these regions embrace digital transformation, AI is becoming pivotal in overcoming traditional barriers to financial inclusion and efficiency. Specifically, AI applications are tailoring financial services to cater to the needs of populations previously underserved by conventional banking systems.

This surge in AI-driven solutions is not only enhancing financial accessibility but also fostering local entrepreneurship. AI tools help small businesses predict market trends, manage inventory, and connect with global markets, which was scarcely possible before. The integration of AI is thus catalyzing a new wave of economic opportunities in sectors from agriculture to microfinance.

Furthermore, the empowerment through AI in these markets is contributing to a more balanced global economic landscape. As AI technology becomes more pervasive, it ensures that the benefits of technological advancements are more evenly distributed, helping to close the gap between emerging and developed economies.

AI and Blockchain: A Revolutionary Partnership

The fusion of Artificial Intelligence (AI) and Blockchain technology marks a transformative era in wealth creation and management. This integration harnesses AI's analytical power and Blockchain's unparalleled security features to forge innovative financial solutions. AI enhances blockchain operations with its predictive abilities, optimizing smart contract algorithms and refining security protocols through continuous learning processes.

Together, these technologies are reshaping financial landscapes by enabling more transparent, efficient, and secure transactions. Blockchain's immutable ledger, combined with AI-driven analytics, empowers stakeholders by providing a clear, unalterable record of transactions coupled with insightful data analysis. This partnership is not just revolutionary; it's setting new standards in financial trust and operational efficiency.

Moreover, this synergy is pioneering decentralized finance (DeFi) applications, where AI's predictive capabilities are used to manage and hedge risks in real-time, while blockchain ensures tamper-proof record-keeping. As regulatory frameworks evolve, this partnership will likely spearhead the next wave of innovative financial services, tailored to meet the demands of a dynamic economic environment.

Sustainable Finance: How AI Helps in ESG Investing

AI is revolutionizing sustainable finance by enhancing Environmental, Social, and Governance (ESG) investing, making it not only more efficient but also more impactful. Through advanced data analytics and machine learning, AI tools offer investors deeper insights into ESG metrics, enabling them to make more informed decisions. For instance, AI can analyze vast datasets to track a company's carbon footprint or its labor practices, ensuring investments align with personal or institutional sustainability goals.

Furthermore, AI facilitates dynamic monitoring of ESG criteria, which is crucial as these metrics evolve rapidly. This ongoing assessment helps maintain investment relevance and adherence to sustainability benchmarks. Additionally, AI-driven models forecast future ESG trends, providing investors with a strategic edge in early identification of potential risks and opportunities.

By integrating AI into ESG investing, the approach becomes not only proactive but also pre-emptive, leading to a more ethical allocation of capital. This significantly contributes to the broader goal of achieving global sustainability targets, reinforcing the vital role of AI in forging a financially and ethically sound future.

Edge Computing in AI: Localized, Faster Financial Decisions

Edge computing is revolutionizing the landscape of artificial intelligence in wealth management by moving data processing to the edge of networks, where financial transactions occur. This shift enhances the speed and efficiency of financial decisions, as data no longer needs to travel to a centralized cloud for processing. Immediate analysis at the point of data generation ensures rapid response times, critical in the fast-paced world of finance.

In scenarios where milliseconds can equate to significant financial gains or losses, edge AI's ability to process and act on data in real-time is transformative. It enables financial institutions to offer more personalized and timely services, from real-time fraud detection to dynamic risk assessment during high-stakes trading. Furthermore, localized data processing addresses privacy concerns, as sensitive financial information is processed and stored closer to its origin, minimizing exposure to potential breaches in transit.

Moreover, as financial markets continue to grow in complexity and scale, the integration of AI at the edge is poised to become a cornerstone in managing the data deluge efficiently. By leveraging localized, faster decision-making capabilities, financial entities can achieve a sharper competitive edge, driving innovation in product offerings and customer satisfaction.

AI in Insurance: From Automation to Prediction

The integration of AI in the insurance sector marks a significant shift from simple automation to advanced predictive capabilities. Initially, AI streamlined mundane tasks such as data entry and claim processing. Today, it delves deeper, leveraging big data and machine learning to predict risks and customer behavior with remarkable accuracy.

This predictive power transforms how insurers assess risk, set premiums, and manage claims, enabling bespoke insurance products tailored to individual risk profiles. For customers, this means more accurate premiums and quicker claim processing. For insurers, it spells more efficient risk management and reduced fraud. Predictive AI systems analyze vast arrays of data from various sources, including social media and IoT devices, providing a comprehensive risk assessment that was previously unattainable.

Moreover, AI's predictive analytics are revolutionizing customer service within the insurance industry. Chatbots, equipped with natural language processing, assist customers in real-time, creating a seamless customer experience. As AI continues to evolve, its integration into insurance not only enhances operational efficiencies but also improves customer engagement and satisfaction.

Voice-Activated AI Systems for Finance

Voice-activated AI systems are revolutionizing financial interactions, transforming how consumers and businesses manage their financial activities. These systems leverage natural language processing and machine learning to offer user-friendly, conversational access to financial services, from checking account balances to executing stock trades. This hands-free technology not only enhances user experience but also improves accessibility, making financial management feasible for individuals with disabilities or those less tech-savvy.

Incorporating voice-activated AI into financial services streamlines operations and reduces the need for physical branches, thus lowering operational costs. Banks and financial institutions using this technology can provide 24/7 assistance, crucial for urgent financial needs. Real-time voice interactions also minimize the errors commonly associated with manual data entry, enhancing transaction security.

Moreover, the deployment of voice AI in finance paves the way for more personalized financial advice. As these systems learn from each interaction, they become more attuned to individual preferences and financial patterns, offering tailored advice and proactive alerts about relevant financial opportunities or risks.

Advancements in AI-Driven Cybersecurity for Financial Transactions

The surge in digital financial transactions globally has necessitated robust cybersecurity mechanisms. AI-driven solutions are at the forefront, providing unprecedented protection against fraud and cybercrime. Advanced machine learning algorithms tirelessly analyze transaction patterns to identify anomalies indicative of fraudulent activity, thus securing financial data in real time.

These AI systems continuously learn from vast amounts of data, improving their predictive capabilities. This allows them to stay ahead of hackers by adapting to evolving cyber threats. Moreover, AI integrates seamlessly with existing security infrastructures, enhancing their efficiency without requiring extensive overhauls. Such integrations facilitate proactive defenses, substantially minimizing potential breaches before they occur.

The integration of AI in cybersecurity not only bolsters defenses but also enhances user confidence in digital financial services. As these AI systems become more sophisticated, they play a critical role in shaping a safer financial environment, ensuring that personal and institutional assets are protected from the complexities of modern cyber threats.

AI's Impact on Employment: New Roles and Opportunities

The integration of AI into various sectors is not just reshaping existing jobs but also creating new roles and opportunities. As AI automates routine tasks, it frees human workers to engage in more complex, creative, and strategic activities, leading to the emergence of roles such as AI trainers, who teach AI systems how to perform specific tasks, and AI compliance officers, ensuring AI implementations adhere to ethical and legal standards.

Moreover, the need for AI-driven innovation spawns roles like AI solutions architects and data ethicists, balancing technological possibilities with ethical considerations. This transition underscores the need for continuous learning and adaptability among the workforce, highlighting an increase in demand for professionals skilled in AI and machine learning across industries.

Additionally, AI's capability to process vast amounts of data in real-time generates roles focused on data interpretation and strategic implementation, transforming decision-making processes in businesses. This evolution in job roles not only fuels economic growth but also enhances job satisfaction by replacing mundane tasks with intellectually engaging work.

Global Regulations and Their Impact on AI Adoption

The rapid expansion of AI in wealth creation presents both opportunities and complexities, particularly in the realm of global regulatory landscapes. Diverse regulatory frameworks across different countries pose a significant challenge to uniform AI adoption. Harmonizing these regulations is critical to fostering an environment where AI can flourish without compromising ethical standards or consumer protection.

Countries leading in AI technology have begun instituting guidelines that dictate how AI should be developed and utilized, impacting international tech companies. These regulations aim to ensure that AI technologies are safe, transparent, and do not perpetuate biases or inequities. However, this creates a patchwork of compliance requirements, making it cumbersome for AI applications in finance to scale globally without significant adaptations.

Moreover, stringent regulations may stifle innovation by imposing strict oversight and lengthy approval processes. To counteract this, some regions have established 'sandbox' environments, allowing companies to test AI solutions in real-world settings without the usual regulatory constraints. Such initiatives are essential in balancing innovation with consumer safety and privacy.

AI in Real Estate: Predicting Market Trends with Precision

Artificial intelligence is revolutionizing real estate by enabling the prediction of market trends with unprecedented precision. By aggregating and analyzing vast amounts of data, AI algorithms can identify subtle patterns that humans might overlook. These insights allow investors, developers, and real estate professionals to make informed decisions about when and where to buy or sell properties.

AI's role extends beyond data analysis. Advanced machine learning models offer forecasting tools that project future market trends, factoring in economic indicators, demographic shifts, and even consumer behavior. This predictive capability is crucial in a field as volatile as real estate, where timing and location are everything. As such, AI not only provides a strategic advantage but also reduces financial risk.

Moreover, AI enhances the customer experience by personalizing property recommendations based on individual preferences and financial profiles. It streamlines the transaction process, making it quicker and more efficient. This integration of AI in real estate is not just reshaping the landscape; it's setting a new standard for how the industry operates.

Investment Strategies Powered by AI and Big Data

The intersection of AI and big data is revolutionizing investment strategies, enabling a new era of financial intelligence. By harnessing vast datasets, AI algorithms provide investors with deeper insights into market trends, consumer behavior, and economic indicators, facilitating highly informed investment decisions that were previously unimaginable.

These AI-driven tools analyze patterns and predict market movements with remarkable accuracy, thus optimizing asset allocation and enhancing risk management. The capability to process and interpret big data in real-time allows for dynamic adjustments to investment portfolios, aligning them more closely with market conditions and investor goals. This agility in financial strategy not only maximizes potential returns but also minimizes exposure to sudden market downturns.

Moreover, AI and big data are democratizing investment opportunities. Sophisticated investment strategies, once accessible only to institutional investors, are now available to a wider audience, leveling the playing field and fostering a more inclusive financial landscape. AI's predictive prowess also identifies emerging opportunities in nascent markets, offering investors a first-mover advantage in high-growth areas.

Future Scenarios: AI's Role in Economic Crises Management

As global economies face increasingly unpredictable fluctuations, AI's role in managing economic crises becomes paramount. Through advanced data analysis and predictive modeling, AI systems can foresee economic downturns, enabling preemptive measures. They analyze real-time financial data along with historical economic indicators to predict potential market crashes or recessions, thereby advising governments and private sectors on preventive strategies to mitigate risks.

Moreover, AI enhances resilience during economic downturns by optimizing resource allocation and managing supply chains efficiently. It can identify areas requiring urgent financial support and streamline the distribution of aid, ensuring stability in critical sectors. AI-driven decision-making tools also provide policymakers with robust scenarios, helping them to devise effective and timely policies that can cushion the economic impact.

In the aftermath of a crisis, AI aids in recovery by analyzing emerging market trends and suggesting areas ripe for investment. The adaptive nature of AI fosters quicker economic revival and sustains long-term growth. By transforming crisis response mechanisms, AI not only fortifies economic systems but also equips them to thrive post-crisis, heralding a new era of AI-dependent strategic economic management.

Cross-Industry AI Applications: From Healthcare to Finance

The integration of AI across different industries exemplifies not merely technological convergence but a revolutionary approach towards comprehensive wealth creation. In healthcare, AI-driven diagnostics tools streamline patient care by predicting illnesses with higher accuracy, thereby potentially reducing the overall healthcare costs and enhancing patient outcomes. These savings and efficiencies can be redirected into more efficient health-related investments, impacting the financial sector significantly.

In finance, AI's prowess in analytics enables better risk management and personalized financial services, leading to optimized investment strategies. The cross-pollination between AI in healthcare data and financial models allows for innovative insurance products tailored to individuals' health profiles, aligning costs with predicted healthcare needs and financial capacity.

This synthesis across sectors not only fuels innovation but also creates a robust framework for sustainable wealth generation. As AI continues to evolve, it is anticipated to forge even more seamless interfaces between various sectors, enhancing economic resilience and offering new pathways for comprehensive wealth accumulation.

AI in Supply Chain Management to Streamline Asset Distribution

AI is transforming the landscape of supply chain management by optimizing the flow of assets across diverse industries. By leveraging advanced algorithms and machine learning, AI systems can predict supply needs, automate ordering processes, and enhance logistical efficiency. This seamless integration reduces downtime and excess inventory, cutting costs significantly and boosting profitability.

In the realm of asset distribution, AI excels by enabling real-time tracking and predictive analytics, which anticipate potential disruptions and adjust routes dynamically. These capabilities ensure that goods are delivered more quickly and reliably, enhancing customer satisfaction and business continuity. Furthermore, AI-driven supply chains are more resilient to external shocks such as market fluctuations or geopolitical events, as they can adapt swiftly to changing conditions.

The benefits extend beyond mere operational efficiency. AI actively contributes to sustainability by optimizing routes and reducing waste. This integration aligns closely with global movements towards greener business practices, making AI indispensable in future supply chain strategies.

Consumer Tech AI: Personal Financial Assistants

Consumer technology, especially in the realm of finance, is undergoing a spectacular transformation with the advent of AI-driven personal financial assistants. These tools are not just about budgeting and tracking expenses but are evolving into proactive financial advisors. By leveraging data from a user's financial behaviors, AI can offer personalized advice, optimize savings, and even suggest investment strategies tailored to individual financial goals and risk tolerance.

The impact of these AI assistants goes beyond individual benefits. They democratize financial advice, previously the preserve of the wealthy, making it accessible to a broader audience. This accessibility is crucial in promoting financial literacy and helping users engage more actively with their finances, potentially leading to a more financially informed society.

Moreover, as these AI systems learn from vast datasets, they become increasingly accurate in their predictions and advice. This learning capability could fundamentally alter how we interact with financial institutions, making personal finance management more autonomous, efficient, and aligned with our long-term financial objectives.

Neuro-AI Interfaces for Managing Wealth

The fusion of neuroscience and artificial intelligence heralds a transformative era in wealth management. Neuro-AI interfaces utilize brain-computer interaction to directly interface with financial platforms, offering unprecedented personalization in managing assets. By analyzing neural patterns, these systems understand individual risk tolerance and decision-making processes, tailoring investment strategies to align seamlessly with users' innate preferences.

Such interfaces not only enhance decision accuracy but also speed. They bypass conventional interfaces, enabling real-time financial responses to market changes. Imagine adjusting your investment portfolio in milliseconds based on cognitive feedback without lifting a finger. This level of integration between human cognitive function and AI-driven financial management systems represents a leap forward in making sophisticated wealth management accessible.

Moreover, Neuro-AI technologies promise inclusivity in financial sophistication. They are designed to adapt to varying levels of financial literacy, providing personalized advice that evolves with the user's experience and learning curve. As these interfaces become more widespread, they could democratize high-level financial strategies, previously the domain of the elite, thus broadening the landscape of investors and reshaping the financial sector.

AI for Inclusive Financial Services to Underbanked Populations

Artificial intelligence (AI) is revolutionizing financial services by tailoring products for underserved and underbanked populations. AI's capability to process vast datasets enables financial institutions to understand and serve these markets more effectively. Models are crafted not just on traditional financial histories, which many underbanked individuals lack, but also on alternative data such as utility payments and mobile phone usage patterns.

This technology empowers providers to offer customized financial solutions that were previously inaccessible. For example, microloans with dynamic pricing can be adjusted in real-time, based on AI analyses of repayment probabilities and current financial behavior. Such innovations not only facilitate greater financial inclusion but also ensure that financial products

BENOIT TANO MD PHD

are better aligned with the users' capacity and needs.

Moreover, AI acts as a bridge to financial literacy by providing educational tools through user-friendly platforms. These platforms guide individuals in managing finances, understanding credit, and making informed financial decisions, progressively helping to elevate the overall financial well-being of underbanked communities.

Crowdsourced AI Solutions in Financial Models

Crowdsourcing combined with AI is revolutionizing financial modeling, democratizing data analysis and empowering a wider community to contribute to complex financial solutions. This collaboration harnesses the collective intelligence of a diverse group, enabling the development of sophisticated, robust financial models that benefit from a multitude of perspectives and expertise.

These crowdsourced AI systems leverage user-generated data and algorithms to predict market trends, optimize investment portfolios, and enhance risk management. By pooling resources and knowledge, these models can operate with a level of diversity and resilience that single-source models cannot match. This not only improves model accuracy but also accelerates innovation in financial strategies.

Moreover, the transparent nature of crowdsourcing fosters a greater trust in AI systems. As contributors see how their input is utilized and the resultant outcomes, it builds confidence in AI processes, further encouraging participation and collaboration across the financial sector.

Interplanetary Commerce: Using AI for Trade Beyond Earth

As humanity extends its reach into the cosmos, interplanetary commerce emerges as a vital area of economic expansion. AI proves essential in managing the complexities of trading between planets. Adaptive algorithms predict demand cycles on different worlds, optimize supply chains through space, and ensure resources are allocated efficiently across vast distances.

AI's role in this domain also includes real-time problem solving and logistics management, adapting to the unpredictable conditions of space travel and extraterrestrial environments. By integrating AI with robotics, automated freight systems manage the physical transport of goods, minimizing human risk in the most hazardous sections of the supply chain.

Moreover, AI systems aid in legal and financial transactions across jurisdictions that vary wildly between Earth and its colonies. They additionally play a crucial role in cultural mediation, ensuring that trade agreements respect the diverse cultural and environmental contexts of each planetary body. Thus, AI is not just a facilitator of commerce, but a crucial bridge builder in the burgeoning field of interplanetary trade.

SUMMARY

The chapter 'Future Trends: Where AI in Wealth Creation is Headed' explores the transformative impact of advanced technologies like AI on the financial sector. It delves into several key areas including predictive technologies in financial forecasting, AI's integration with decentralized finance (DeFi), ethical AI practices, and the innovative intersections of AI with quantum computing and blockchain technology. Predictive technologies leverage machine learning to enhance forecasting and risk assessments, significantly optimizing portfolio management and economic stability. The chapter also discusses how AI, when intertwined with DeFi, opens up unprecedented opportunities for personalized financial services and secure, efficient transactions across borders, contributing robustness through enhanced predictive capabilities and fraud detection systems. Ethical considerations are paramount as the adoption of AI in finance necessitates transparency, fairness, and accountability, ensuring decisions benefit all societal levels and maintain regulatory compliance. Furthermore, the integration of AI with quantum computing promises groundbreaking enhancements in financial models through superior computational speeds, while AI combined with blockchain technology fosters a new standard in financial operations, enhancing trust and efficiency. Each section collectively underscores AI's pivotal role in reshaping wealth management, providing insights into its potential to democratize financial services and enhance economic inclusivity, while also revolutionizing traditional business models and predicting market trends. Through examples from different sectors, the chapter illustrates AI's expansive role from enhancing personalized investment strategies to managing economic crises and facilitating sustainable finance. With AI's continuous evolution, it is set to redefine global financial landscapes, making crucial contributions to efficient, inclusive, and ethical wealth creation.

REFERENCES

[1] Bose, I. (2019). Artificial intelligence enabled financial technology: a risk or an opportunity?. https://link.springer.com/article/10.1007/s12525-019-00346-8

[2] Arner, D.W., Barberis, J.N., Buckley, R.P. (2017). FinTech, RegTech, and the Reconceptualization of Financial Regulation. https://papers.ssrn.com/sol3/papers.cfm?abstract_id=3012633

[3] Wright, A., & De Filippi, P. (2015). Decentralized Blockchain Technology and the Rise of Lex Cryptographia. https://ssrn.com/abstract=2580664

[4] Lee, K. F. (2018). AI Superpowers: China, Silicon Valley, and the New World Order. https://www.aisuperpowers.com/

[5] Kelly, J. E. III (2015). Computing, cognition, and the future of knowing: How humans and machines are forging a new age of understanding. https://www.research.ibm.com/software/IBMResearch/multimedia/Computing_Cognition_WhitePaper.pdf

[6] Schatsky, D., & Muraskin, C. (2015). Cognitive technologies: The real opportunities for business. https://www2.deloitte.com/us/en/insights/focus/cognitive-technologies.html

CASE STUDY: LEVERAGING AI IN REAL-TIME PERSONALIZED FINANCIAL ADVICE

In a recent transformative initiative, a leading global financial services firm implemented an advanced AI-driven platform designed to provide real-time, personalized financial advice to its clients. The platform, named FinAI Advisor, utilizes cutting-edge machine learning algorithms to analyze individual client profiles, their historical financial data, and real-time market trends to deliver tailored investment strategies and financial planning solutions.

The system integrates seamlessly with the company's existing database and draws upon a vast array of data points, including stock market data, real estate trends, and global economic indicators. It also considers personal factors such as risk tolerance, financial goals, past investment performance, and even life events like marriage or the purchase of a home. Through continuous learning and adaptation, FinAI Advisor refines its predictions and recommendations based on new data and evolving market conditions.

Initially, the adoption of FinAI Advisor led to a significant increase in client engagement and satisfaction. Clients appreciated the heightened personalization of the services, which not only aligned with their financial goals but also accommodated their personal comfort with risk. Moreover, the platform empowered clients by providing them with insights and explanations behind each recommendation, fostering a deeper understanding of their financial strategies.

However, the implementation also posed several challenges. Concerns regarding data privacy and the ethical use of predictive analytics surfaced. The firm took decisive steps to address these issues by implementing robust data protection measures and ethical guidelines designed to ensure transparency and fairness in AI-generated advice. Regular audits and compliance reviews were instituted to maintain adherence to these standards.

As FinAI Advisor became more integrated into the company's offerings, it also began to influence the organization's overall approach to financial advising. Traditional advisors were trained to use the AI system as a tool for enhancing their service delivery, blending the best of human insight and AI precision. This hybrid model not only improved client outcomes but also enriched the advisors' professional development by exposing them to cutting-edge financial technology.

Case Study: Revamping Risk Management with AI-Driven Predictive Models

In a landmark initiative, a prominent multinational bank embarked on integrating AI-driven predictive models to revolutionize its risk management strategies. This was in response to the recurrent financial crises which exposed severe flaws in traditional risk management frameworks. The bank, facing the dual challenges of predictive accuracy and operational efficiency, deployed what was termed IntelliRisk—a cutting-edge AI system specifically designed to anticipate and mitigate financial risks.

IntelliRisk amalgamates vast arrays of historical financial transaction data, current market trends, client profiles, and global economic signals. By harnessing machine learning and deep learning algorithms, the system dynamically evaluates risk in real-time, providing foresighted risk assessments far surpassing the capabilities of previous models. Notably, the AI system is structured to perform ongoing learning—continuously enhancing its predictive accuracy by iteratively refining its algorithms as new data is ingested and as market conditions evolve.

The impact of implementing IntelliRisk was transformative. For the first quarter following its deployment, the bank reported a 40% reduction in unanticipated financial losses due to credit defaults. Additionally, the predictive model effectively identified potential market disruptions, steering the bank clear of risky investments before global economic downturns. This proactive risk management not only safeguarded the bank's assets but also elevated its market reputation as a leader in financial stability.

However, the introduction of IntelliRisk also brought unforeseen challenges. Critics raised concerns over potential ethical implications, questioning the transparency of AI decision-making processes and the potential for unintended biases. In response, the bank established a dedicated ethical oversight committee to continuously monitor and review AI decisions, ensuring that AI-driven operations adhered to the highest standards of fairness and transparency. Furthermore, the bank launched comprehensive training programs for its staff, ensuring optimal human-AI collaboration while harnessing the enhanced capabilities brought by IntelliRisk.

Case Study: AI Optimization of Decentralized Financial Markets

In a groundbreaking project, a tech startup specializing in blockchain technology partnered with an AI firm to redefine decentralized finance (DeFi) using artificial intelligence. Their initiative, code-named DeFiAI, aimed to integrate AI's predictive analytics and machine learning capabilities with blockchain's secure, transparent framework to create a robust, decentralized financial market system.

DeFiAI was designed to address several challenges in the DeFi sector, including transaction bottlenecks, security vulnerabilities, and inefficiencies in liquidity management. By leveraging AI, the system could predict and adjust to market demands in real time, ensure optimal liquidity, and reduce the risk of fraud and market manipulation. The AI algorithms were trained on vast datasets comprising years of blockchain transactions, market trends, and historical financial crises.

The initial deployment of DeFiAI led to dramatic increases in transaction speed and efficiency. Automated smart contracts, enhanced by AI, executed transactions seamlessly and without the need for traditional brokerages or financial intermediaries, significantly lowering costs for users while enhancing financial inclusivity. Furthermore, the integration of AI enabled personalized investment strategies. Utilizing machine learning, DeFiAI analyzed individual user behavior to tailor investment recommendations that aligned with each user's risk tolerance and investment goals.

However, the implementation of such an advanced system introduced complexities in terms of regulatory compliance and user privacy. The partnership had to navigate evolving legal landscapes concerning digital assets and data protection laws. In response, they established a cross-functional team consisting of AI ethics experts, legal advisors, and cybersecurity professionals to ensure that the DeFiAI infrastructure adhered to all applicable laws and ethical guidelines.

As DeFiAI matured, it began to transform the broader financial ecosystem. Traditional financial institutions started exploring partnerships with the startup, aiming to integrate DeFiAI's capabilities into conventional financial environments. This collaboration signified a pivotal shift in how financial transactions are managed and executed globally, demonstrating the powerful symbiosis of AI and blockchain in innovating legacy financial systems.

Case Study: Embracing AI-Driven Workflow Optimization in Multinational Corporations

In our exploration of the integration and impact of AI across various domains, we uncover a compelling case study of a global pharmaceutical giant, PharmaFuture Inc., which embarked on an ambitious journey to incorporate AI into its core operational workflows. Facing stiff competition and a compelling need to expedite drug development and distribution, PharmaFuture leveraged AI to streamline processes and enhance efficiency across its multinational landscape.

The company initiated the AI-driven transformation by implementing machine learning algorithms designed to predict and optimize supply chain logistics. Dubbed OptiFlow AI, this system analyzed historical data and current market conditions to foresee supply chain disruptions and automatically adjust orders and shipping routes. The AI's predictive capabilities extended to proactive maintenance of production equipment, scheduling repairs before breakdowns occurred, thereby minimizing downtime and ensuring continuous production.

The transformative impact of OptiFlow AI was staggering. Within the first year of integration, PharmaFuture reported a 25% increase in operational efficiency and a significant reduction in waste due to more accurate supply chain forecasting. These improvements not only bolstered the company's bottom line but also enhanced its global competitiveness by speeding up the time-to-market for new drugs.

However, implementing AI was not without its challenges. Initial resistance from employees, who feared job displacement, and the substantial investment required for AI integration posed significant hurdles. To address these issues, PharmaFuture invested in extensive employee training programs to upskill workers to collaborate effectively with AI systems. Additionally, they established a dedicated AI ethics board to oversee AI implementations and ensure they aligned with corporate values and industry regulations.

Ultimately, the case of PharmaFuture serves as a benchmark in the corporate world, illustrating both the profound efficiencies that can be achieved through AI integration and the importance of addressing the accompanying workforce and ethical considerations. Despite the challenges, the strategic incorporation of AI proved essential, paving the way for smarter, faster, and more reliable business operations across the globe.

Case Study: Strategic AI Deployment in Global Investment Management

CapitalInvest Global, a leading investment management firm, embarked on a pioneering journey to harness the potential of AI in optimizing global investment strategies. The initiative, named AIQuantum, aimed to leverage advanced AI technologies, including machine learning and quantum computing, to enhance its portfolio management, market prediction, and risk management capabilities.

AIQuantum's implementation involved integrating complex algorithms that analyze vast quantities of financial data from global markets to predict future market behaviors with a high degree of accuracy. The system was designed to perform deep learning-based analysis of trends across different asset classes, enabling dynamic asset allocation strategies that respond to market changes in real-time. Additionally, AIQuantum could simulate various economic scenarios to stress-test portfolios against potential future crises, adding a robust layer of risk assessment that preemptively adjusts investment moves to safeguard returns.

The technology also included sophisticated sentiment analysis tools that scrutinized global news, financial reports, and social media to gauge market sentiment and anticipate significant market moves before they happened. This proactive capability allowed the firm to capitalize on opportunities quicker than competitors and avoid areas with potential downturns more efficiently.

However, incorporating AI into such a critical sector of the company was not without its challenges. The major issue faced was the skepticism from traditional fund managers about relying heavily on AI for decision-making. To counter this, CapitalInvest Global initiated a series of workshops and seminars that demonstrated the capabilities of AIQuantum, focusing on its ability to combine human expertise with machine efficiency for superior decision-making.

As AIQuantum became more entrenched in the firm's operations, it not only enhanced financial outcomes but also transformed the company's internal culture, promoting a more data-driven and proactive approach to investment management. The success of AIQuantum encouraged other firms within the industry to explore similar AI integrations, setting new benchmarks in asset management through technology-driven strategies.

Case Study: Integrating AI in ESG Investment Strategies at GreenAsset Inc.

GreenAsset Inc., a prominent investment firm focused on environmental, social, and governance (ESG) criteria, recently spearheaded an AI-driven initiative to enhance its investment strategies. The project, named EcoSmartAI, aimed to utilize advanced artificial intelligence to deepen the integration of ESG factors into investment decisions, addressing the growing demand for responsible and sustainable investments.

EcoSmartAI was designed to leverage machine learning algorithms to analyze vast amounts of ESG data, including real-time environmental impact data, social responsibility metrics, and governance quality from thousands of companies worldwide. By processing this data, EcoSmartAI could identify companies that not only met stringent ESG criteria but also offered robust financial returns. The system enabled GreenAsset to offer clients portfolios that were not only ethical but also financially sound, thus aligning with both moral values and profitability.

Initial results were transformative. The AI-driven portfolios consistently outperformed traditional ESG portfolios by adapting quickly to emerging sustainability trends and regulatory changes. Clients were provided with real-time insights into their investments, fostering greater transparency and trust. However, the integration posed challenges, particularly in data veracity and the complexity of defining 'ethical AI'. Questions about data sourcing, biases in AI algorithms, and the ethical implications of AI decisions needed careful consideration.

To address these issues, GreenAsset established an AI Ethics Board comprising sustainability experts, ethicists, and data scientists. This board was tasked with ensuring that EcoSmartAI's operational protocols upheld the highest ethical standards and that all data used was accurate and unbiased. They implemented a rigorous data validation process and continuously updated the AI's algorithms to adapt to new ethical guidelines and sustainability metrics.

As GreenAsset expanded its use of AI in managing ESG investments, the firm not only saw improved financial performance but also strengthened its reputation as a leader in sustainable investing. EcoSmartAI redefined how ESG factors could be integrated into investment processes, paving the way for a new era of responsible investing powered by technology.

Case Study: Transformative Digital Strategies in AI-Driven Central Banking

In a bold stride towards modernization, the National Central Bank (NCB) embarked on a transformative journey by integrating artificial intelligence into its central banking functions. This initiative, dubbed CentralBankAI, was primarily focused on improving monetary policy decisions and optimizing financial stability mechanisms through advanced predictive analytics and real-time data processing capabilities.

CentralBankAI utilized deep learning algorithms to analyze vast streams of economic data, ranging from global market trends and national financial transactions to socioeconomic indicators. By leveraging real-time data assimilation, the AI system was capable of analyzing effects of economic policies almost instantaneously, allowing for agile responses to changing economic conditions. Furthermore, the system facilitated the prediction of inflation trends and interest rate adjustments with heightened accuracy, contributing to more stable economic environments.

One of the flagship features was its dynamic regulatory compliance tool, which helped in identifying potential risks in the financial system and recommended preemptive measures to avert financial crises. The AI system's ability to continually learn and adapt its models based on new data significantly reduced human error and increased the policy effectiveness.

However, integrating AI into national economic controls presented unique challenges. Primary concerns included data security, privacy issues, and potential biases in AI decision-making that could lead to unfair economic advantages. To address these issues, NCB established stringent data governance protocols and formed an AI Ethics Advisory Panel comprised of economists, data scientists, and ethicists.

This panel ensured transparency and fairness in AI operations and conducted routine audits of the AI's decision-making processes. Over time, CentralBankAI proved instrumental not only in streamlining operations but also in enhancing public trust in digital-centric economic policies. As the system matured, it also provided a blueprint for other national banks considering similar AI integrations, significantly influencing global financial systems by setting benchmarks in AI-driven economic governance.

Case Study: AI-Enhanced Global Economic Recovery and Stability Programs

In a visionary approach to tackle global economic instability and promote recovery post-recession, the International Economic Stability Alliance (IESA) launched an ambitious initiative, EconoStabilAI. This program integrates cutting-edge AI technologies to forecast economic shifts, optimize recovery plans, and ensure sustainable growth across nations. EconoStabilAI employs sophisticated machine learning models that process real-time global economic data, including GDP growth rates, employment figures, and trade balances, to predict potential economic downturns and recovery patterns with enhanced accuracy. By synthesizing data from diverse sources, the system offers actionable insights that help policymakers tailor their economic strategies to specific regional needs. Initially, the AI system helped identify vulnerable economic sectors across different countries, enabling targeted interventions such as stimulus packages or sector-specific aids. As the system evolved, it played a critical role in forecasting 'recovery hotspots' where economic activity would likely bounce back strongly, guiding international investments and resource allocation. However, integrating AI at such a massive scale presented unprecedented challenges. Issues ranging from data privacy concerns, international data-sharing agreements, and the need for a robust legal framework for AI governance were at the forefront of the initiative. To address these, IESA established a comprehensive legal and ethical protocol involving member countries, ensuring transparency and adherence to international standards in data handling and AI application. Over time, EconoStabilAI became a cornerstone of global economic planning, providing a dynamic tool for adjusting policies in response to shifting economic landscapes. Its implementation not only strengthened economic resilience but also fostered a more collaborative approach to international economic challenges.

REVIEW QUESTIONS

1. A financial analyst at a large investment firm has been tasked with enhancing the firm's portfolio management strategy using advanced AI tools. After researching various technologies, the analyst decides to integrate a next-generation AI system known for its predictive accuracy in financial forecasting. Given the advanced AI system's ability to analyze vast datasets and predict market trends, what should be the primary focus for the analyst in optimizing asset allocations?

A) Rely solely on historical data for decision making

B) Use AI predictions to dynamically adjust the portfolio based on anticipated market movements

C) Ignore AI risk assessment features and focus on short-term gains

D) Limit the use of AI to small, conservative investments to minimize potential risks

Answer: B

Explanation: The correct choice is B, 'Use AI predictions to dynamically adjust the portfolio based on anticipated market movements.' Advanced AI systems in financial forecasting leverage machine learning algorithms to identify market trends and predict future movements with a high degree of accuracy. These predictions are invaluable for asset allocation, as they allow for dynamic adjustments that take into account upcoming market changes, thereby optimizing portfolio performance and mitigating risk. Unlike option A, which disregards the predictive capabilities of AI; option C, which underutilizes AI's risk assessments; and option D, which overly conservatively limits AI's potential impact, option B fully leverages the predictive technology to enhance decision-making and investment strategies.

2. A DeFi startup is exploring ways to integrate AI to enhance their platform. They aim to improve transaction security, enhance transaction speed, and provide real-time, trustless interactions. Which integration would likely yield the most significant benefit to their operation?

A) Automated smart contracts to optimize transactions and boost security

B) A basic AI chatbot to improve user interface interactions

C) AI-powered email marketing tools to increase user signup rates

D) Standalone AI tools that operate separately from existing blockchain technologies

Answer: A

Explanation: The correct choice is A, 'Automated smart contracts to optimize transactions and boost security.' The integration of AI with DeFi importantly leverages AI's capabilities to optimize smart contracts, which are foundational to transaction security and efficiency in DeFi platforms. Automated smart contracts, enhanced by AI, can execute complex, real-time operations securely and efficiently, aligning perfectly with the startup's goals of enhanced speed, security, and

BENOIT TANO MD PHD

trustless interactions. Option B, while helpful, is less impactful on the core transaction processes; option C targets marketing rather than operational efficiency; and option D suggests an integration that misses the synergy between AI and existing blockchain technologies, thereby likely reducing overall system effectiveness.

REVIEW QUESTIONS

3. A company is looking to incorporate ethical AI into its wealth creation systems. The primary goal is to ensure that their AI-driven investment strategies are transparent, fair, and accountable. What step should be prioritized to align their AI systems with ethical guidelines?

A) Implementing AI audit trails to enhance transparency and accountability

B) Focusing solely on maximizing AI-driven profit margins

C) Reducing human oversight to increase AI decision-making autonomy

D) Concentrating on short-term investments for quick returns

Answer: A

Explanation: The accurate choice is A, 'Implementing AI audit trails to enhance transparency and accountability.' Ethical AI frameworks prioritize transparency, fairness, and accountability, essential to maintaining trust in technology-driven financial systems. AI audit trails allow tracking of decisions made by AI, why these decisions were made, and who is responsible, thereby ensuring the AI systems are transparent and accountable to ethical standards and regulations. Choice B is contrary to ethical guidelines as it focuses solely on profits; choice C diminishes the ethical oversight necessary for trust and fairness; and choice D undermines the sustainability and long-term reliability that ethical AI practices aim to promote.

DEVELOPING ESSENTIAL AI SKILLS AND KNOWLEDGE

Understanding the Basics of AI and Machine Learning

The journey into the AI landscape begins with a foundational understanding of Artificial Intelligence (AI) and Machine Learning (ML). At its core, AI is the science of creating algorithms and systems that can perform tasks typically requiring human intelligence. These include understanding language, recognizing patterns, and making decisions.

Machine Learning, a subset of AI, revolves around the idea of enabling machines to learn from data, identifying patterns, and making decisions with minimal human intervention. The process starts with data ingestion and preprocessing, followed by training models on this data. These models then extrapolate or generalize from their learning to make predictions or decisions based on new data.

Critical to understanding these concepts is recognizing that while AI encompasses a broad range of technologies, ML focuses specifically on algorithms that learn from and act upon data. This distinction guides what skills and knowledge are essential as one delves deeper into the field, paving the way for more specialized disciplines within AI.

Essential Programming Languages for AI Development

The realm of AI development is underpinned by several key programming languages, each playing a critical role in facilitating the design and deployment of intelligent solutions. Python stands out due to its extensive libraries such as TensorFlow and PyTorch, which simplify complex tasks in machine learning and deep learning. It's favored for its readability and versatile application across different areas of AI.

Java also finds importance, especially in large, distributed systems where its strength in scalability and robustness comes into play. Java's portability allows developers to transition systems from development environments to production without the hassle of reconfiguration.

Moreover, languages like R provide significant advantages in statistical analysis and visualization, making it ideal for data-driven AI projects. JavaScript, with its frameworks for machine learning like Brain.js, enhances AI's reach into web-based environments, pushing the boundaries of what's possible in user interactions on digital platforms.

Selecting the right programming language is pivotal; it must align with the project's specific requirements, ensuring optimal performance and efficient development cycles.

Data Science Fundamentals for AI

Data science serves as the backbone of effective AI systems, providing the methodologies and techniques necessary for parsing and interpreting vast amounts of data. At its core, data science involves statistical analysis, data mining, and data manipulation to uncover patterns and insights crucial for building AI models.

The journey into data science begins with mastering data manipulation and analysis, facilitated by programming languages like Python and R, which offer extensive libraries designed for these tasks. Understanding statistics is equally crucial, as it underpins the algorithms that drive AI predictions, providing a framework for validating and interpreting results.

Moreover, data visualization skills are essential to translate complex results into actionable insights. Tools like Tableau or Python's Matplotlib allow for clear, impactful communication of findings. Engaging with real-world datasets through Kaggle competitions or similar platforms provides practical experience, strengthening one's proficiency in handling the sorts of data challenges common in AI development.

Neural Networks and Deep Learning Explained

Venturing further into AI, we encounter neural networks, which are vital frameworks mimicking the human brain's function and architecture. At their core, neural networks consist of neuron layers interconnected in a web-like structure, each node processing data based on its inherent mathematical functions. This setup enables the network to make decisions, recognize patterns, and solve problems in ways traditional algorithms cannot.

Deep learning, a subset of machine learning based on these neural networks, dives deeper into the analysis, allowing machines to make increasingly complex decisions. By utilizing multiple layers, deep learning models can learn and reason out data's nuanced features at a level similar to human cognition. These models are particularly adept at tasks like speech recognition, image classification, and natural language processing, continuously learning from vast amounts of data to improve their accuracy and efficiency.

Through practical applications, from autonomous vehicles to personalized medicine, neural networks and deep learning are reshaping how we interact with the world, making AI not just a tool, but a transformer of industries and daily life.

Machine Learning Algorithms: Types and Applications

Machine Learning (ML) Algorithms are the engines of artificial intelligence systems, enabling them to analyze data, learn from it, and make informed decisions. Five primary types of ML algorithms are generally recognized: supervised learning, unsupervised learning, semi-supervised learning, reinforcement learning, and deep learning. Each type has its unique approach and application area, facilitating a range of tasks from simple classifications to complex decision-making scenarios.

Supervised learning algorithms, for example, are widely used in applications that require historical data to predict future outcomes, such as credit scoring and weather forecasting. Unsupervised learning, in contrast, excels at pattern detection and grouping, making it ideal for market segmentation and gene sequence analysis. Meanwhile, reinforcement learning shines in environments where an algorithm can incrementally learn from the consequences of its actions, optimizing strategies in real-time applications like robotics and online advertising.

The versatility and breadth of ML applications demonstrate its transformative potential across industries. Whether improving customer interaction, streamlining operations, or unlocking new scientific discoveries, ML algorithms continue to be a central component in advancing both technology and business practices.

The Role of Mathematics in AI: Key Concepts to Know

Mathematics is indispensable in the AI landscape, serving as the foundation upon which algorithms and models are built. It's here that key concepts such as linear algebra, probability, and statistics come into play. Linear algebra, for instance, is crucial for understanding data structures and optimizing machine learning algorithms through matrix operations.

Probability and statistics are equally essential, enabling machines to make decisions in uncertain environments and to evaluate the efficacy of models. Statistical methods help in hypothesis testing and confidence interval calculations, enhancing the reliability of predictions made by AI systems.

Calculus also plays a significant role, particularly in training neural networks where optimization algorithms like gradient descent are applied to minimize errors. Understanding these mathematical concepts provides a powerful toolbox for developing sophisticated AI applications, ensuring they operate with precision and efficiency. By grasping the intertwining relationship between AI and mathematics, developers and researchers can push the boundaries of what these intelligent systems can achieve.

Building and Training Your First AI Model

Embarking on the creation of your first AI model is a pivotal milestone. This journey merges your knowledge of programming languages, data science, and the theory of machine learning algorithms. Begin by formulating a clear problem statement, ensuring your model addresses a specific challenge or question. This clarity is crucial as it guides the data collection and preparation phases, integrating the insights from data science fundamentals.

Next, select the appropriate machine learning algorithm. Whether it's a simple regression for forecasting or a convolutional neural network for image recognition, the choice depends on the task at hand, guided by the principles outlined in previous discussions on types and applications of machine learning algorithms. Utilizing libraries like TensorFlow or PyTorch aids in efficiently implementing these algorithms.

Lastly, the training phase. This involves feeding your model with data, adjusting parameters, and iteratively improving the model based on performance metrics. This process not only hones your technical skills but also deepens your understanding of how theoretical AI concepts translate into real-world applications.

Natural Language Processing (NLP) Techniques

Natural Language Processing (NLP) stands as a cornerstone of AI, enabling machines to understand and interact with human language. The fundamental techniques of NLP encompass tokenization, parsing, and semantic analysis, each crucial for interpreting text. Tokenization breaks down text into manageable pieces, like words or sentences, facilitating deeper analysis.

Semantic analysis then probes the meanings behind these tokens, using algorithms to discern context and sentiment. This technique is pivotal for applications like chatbots and sentiment analysis tools, which must grasp subtle nuances in language to respond appropriately. Additionally, machine learning models, particularly those discussed in deep learning, significantly enhance NLP's capabilities, allowing for more accurate predictions and interactions.

The integration of NLP with neural networks has led to advancements in translation services and speech recognition systems, showcasing its broad applicational scope. As we continue to refine these techniques, NLP is set to revolutionize how we interact with technology, making digital communications more intuitive and human-like.

Computer Vision and Image Processing Basics

Delving into the realm of AI, Computer Vision (CV) stands out as a profound domain, transforming how machines interpret the visual world. CV harnesses techniques that enable systems to derive meaningful information from digital images, videos, and other visual inputs, aligning closely with human visual understanding.

Fundamentals of CV involve image processing—an initial, crucial step where images are enhanced, transformed, or segmented to isolate important features. Techniques like filtering, edge detection, and color space conversion are typically employed to preprocess images before they are analyzed, optimizing them for higher-level tasks. This preprocessing aids in reducing noise and improving the quality of data fed into machine learning models.

At its core, CV utilizes machine learning algorithms, particularly convolutional neural networks (deep learning), adapted for the task of image recognition and classification. These models automate the extraction of features and patterns, crucial for tasks like facial recognition, object detection, and autonomous vehicle navigation. Understanding and mastering these basics paves the way for developing applications that contribute to safety, efficiency, and innovative interactions in tech-driven industries.

Reinforcement Learning: An Introduction

Reinforcement learning (RL) stands as a pivotal subset of machine learning, wherein algorithms learn to make sequences of decisions by interacting with an environment to achieve a goal. This dynamic approach diverges from traditional methods, such as supervised learning, by not requiring labeled input/output pairs and instead using rewards to guide behavior optimization over time.

In practice, reinforcement learning models undergo a process akin to trial and error. Here, an agent, situated in a defined environment, learns to maximize its cumulative reward by choosing the most beneficial actions based on its current state. Such environments can range from video games, where the agent learns different strategies to win, to real-world applications like autonomous vehicles navigating traffic.

The beauty and challenge of RL lie in its balance between exploration (trying new actions) and exploitation (leveraging known strategies). It's crucial in complex scenarios where the required actions are not immediately apparent, cultivating an agent capable of self-improvement through continuous interaction and assessment of outcomes. This makes RL an extraordinary tool for dynamic decision-making in AI.

Using AI Development Tools and Libraries

Venturing into AI development requires familiarity with specialized tools and libraries, which crucially streamline the development of AI models. Libraries such as TensorFlow, PyTorch, and Scikit-Learn provide pre-written code, efficient algorithms, and data management features that facilitate the intricate processes of training, testing, and deploying AI solutions.

For example, TensorFlow offers a versatile environment for deploying machine learning models from desktops to cloud servers, while PyTorch is celebrated for its dynamic computational graph and intuitive coding style ideal for academia and research. Both libraries include a vast range of utilities for constructing neural networks, which is fundamental after understanding the core concepts of AI and mathematics.

Moreover, these tools support a wide array of applications, from predictive analytics to image processing and NLP. The scalability and robust community support surrounding these libraries greatly aid developers in troubleshooting and enhancing their AI projects, fortifying the AI ecosystem with resources that advance both individual learning and industry standards.

AI Project Management and Workflow

AI project management and workflow is a critical facet of deploying successful AI systems, bridging the gap between theoretical models and real-world applications. Initial stages involve detailed project planning, where managers align AI goals with business objectives, ensuring projects are feasible within budget and time constraints. This phase also includes stakeholder analysis and requirements gathering, essential for tailored AI solutions.

The execution phase leverages agile methodologies, promoting iterative development and continuous integration. Regular sprint reviews ensure alignment with the evolving needs, while adaptive planning copes with the uncertainties inherent in AI projects. Collaboration tools and project management software are indispensable, facilitating effective communication and documentation across dispersed teams.

In the final stages, AI projects undergo rigorous testing and validation processes, where performance metrics are closely monitored. Post-launch, project managers focus on maintenance and iterative improvements, essential for longevity and relevance in the fast-paced AI landscape. Ethical considerations are incorporated throughout, ensuring responsible AI deployment.

Understanding AI Ethics and Responsible Development

The imperative for understanding AI ethics and responsible development transcends mere compliance; it involves fostering a culture of integrity within the AI realm. As AI systems become integral to socio-economic operations, the ethical implications—ensuring fairness, privacy, and non-discrimination—become paramount. Acknowledging these facets, developers must ingrain ethical principles from the ground up in AI models, promoting transparency and accountability.

Developing AI responsibly also entails scrutinizing the data used in training algorithms to prevent biases. This scrutiny includes diverse dataset sourcing and continual evaluation to mitigate any inadvertent harm or bias, safeguarding against skewing outputs that could perpetuate inequality. Furthermore, the aspect of explicability in AI systems—where decisions made by AI are understandable to humans—is crucial for trust and legality, especially in sectors like healthcare and law.

Finally, the collaboration among policymakers, technologists, and ethicists is vital to establish robust ethical frameworks guiding AI development. Such interdisciplinary efforts ensure that AI technologies enhance societal well-being while avoiding the pitfalls of unchecked automation. Through education and strict ethical standards, the community can steer AI development towards beneficial outcomes for all.

Data Collection and Preparation for AI

Data collection and preparation form the foundation for successful AI initiatives. This stage involves gathering relevant datasets that will train and fine-tune AI models to perform specific tasks accurately. To ensure the viability and efficiency of AI projects, data must be robust, high-quality, and reflective of real-world scenarios.

The process begins with identifying the right sources of data, which may range from public datasets, proprietary data, or real-time data streams. Ensuring data diversity and volume is crucial to avoid biases and overfitting. Once collected, the data undergoes rigorous cleaning and preprocessing to remove anomalies or irrelevant information, thus enhancing the model's learning capability.

Feature engineering then plays a pivotal role, where key attributes are extracted or created to improve model performance. Equally important is data augmentation, especially in domains like computer vision, where artificially enlarging the dataset through modifications ensures models are well-rounded and robust. These preparatory steps are vital, ensuring the data-fed into AI systems facilitates effective learning and accurate outcomes.

Evaluating and Improving AI Model Performance

The pursuit of excellence in AI model performance hinges on meticulous evaluation and continuous improvement strategies. Initially, models undergo performance assessments using metrics like accuracy, precision, recall, and F1 score, analysing their effectiveness in various scenarios. This phase is crucial to ensure that models operate within the expected parameters of accuracy and efficiency.

Further enhancement of AI models involves tweaking learning rates, adjusting model architectures, or introducing more sophisticated algorithms. Techniques like cross-validation help in validating model consistency across different data subsets, preventing issues such as overfitting and underfitting. Moreover, performance bottlenecks can often prompt a deeper dive into the data preprocessing stages, refining input quality and feature engineering to boost overall model efficacy.

Ultimately, the iterative process of testing, modifying, and re-testing models fosters robust AI tools capable of adapting to evolving data trends and user needs. Regular updates, grounded in evolving performance metrics, guarantee models remain both relevant and high-performing in real-world applications.

Scalability and Deployment of AI Systems

Scalability is critical for the practical deployment of AI systems in diverse environments, ensuring they can handle growing data volumes and user demands without performance degradation. As AI models transition from development to production, scalability strategies must be diligently planned. Techniques like distributed computing facilitate scaling, accommodating large-scale data processing across multiple machines.

Deployment involves meticulous orchestration to integrate AI solutions into existing infrastructures. It necessitates robust deployment pipelines that manage dependencies, version control, and continuous integration/delivery (CI/CD) frameworks. Automated tools streamline these processes, enabling efficient updates and management of live AI applications, critical for maintaining system integrity and responsiveness.

Furthermore, deploying AI responsibly requires monitoring systems for continuous performance evaluation. This oversight helps in promptly addressing any issues that arise post-deployment, ensuring the AI systems remain efficient and effective in their operational environment. Adhering to best practices in scalability and deployment is indispensable for achieving sustainable AI solutions that deliver consistent value over time.

Security Considerations in AI Applications

Securing AI applications is paramount as they become increasingly integral to critical infrastructures and sensitive data operations. It begins with safeguarding the data lifecycle, from acquisition through processing to storage, against unauthorized access and corruption. A robust security protocol includes encryption methodologies, secure data transmission channels, and stringent access controls.

Moreover, AI systems, prone to adversarial attacks where data inputs are manipulated to deceive the model, necessitate robust defensive mechanisms. Implementing techniques like adversarial training strengthens AI resilience by teaching systems to recognize and resist such tactics. Regular security audits and penetration testing further ensure systems are fortified against evolving cybersecurity threats.

Finally, AI developers must consider the ethical implications of security, such as privacy preservation in data handling and the potential consequences of security breaches on stakeholders. Transparency in AI operations and continuous monitoring for anomalies are vital practices that uphold trust and reliability in AI applications, securing not just data but also user confidence.

Integrating AI with Cloud Computing

Integrating AI with cloud computing transforms how businesses scale and deploy AI systems, blending the flexibility of the cloud with the intelligence of AI. This combination empowers businesses to manage large datasets more efficiently, utilizing the cloud's vast storage capabilities and scalable computing power. AI algorithms analyze these datasets in real-time, enabling faster insights and improved decision-making processes.

Cloud platforms offer various AI-specific tools and frameworks that simplify the implementation of complex AI models. These tools are designed for optimum performance, reducing the time and resources required for AI deployments. Cloud services also provide pre-trained AI models which developers can fine-tune, accelerating the development cycle and reducing time to market.

Moreover, cloud computing ensures that AI applications are more accessible. Developers across the globe can collaborate on AI projects without the need for heavy infrastructure investments, democratizing access to AI technologies. This not only fosters innovation but also encourages a wider adoption of AI solutions across industries.

IoT and AI: Harnessing the Power of Connected Devices

The integration of Artificial Intelligence (AI) with the Internet of Things (IoT) is revolutionizing the way connected devices operate, creating a synergy that enhances functionality and efficiency. By embedding AI into IoT devices, these technologies can autonomously analyze and act on data collected from their environments, optimizing processes and creating smarter ecosystems.

IoT devices equipped with AI capabilities are able to process vast amounts of data locally, reducing the need to send sensitive information to the cloud. This not only mitigates latency but also enhances privacy and security, crucial aspects in today's digitally driven world. For example, smart home devices can learn homeowners' preferences over time, adjusting settings such as lighting and temperature automatically.

Moreover, the combination of AI and IoT is instrumental in industries like manufacturing and healthcare. Predictive maintenance powered by AI can forecast equipment failures before they occur, minimizing downtime. In healthcare, wearable devices analyze patient data in real-time, providing insights that can preempt health issues. This intersection of AI and IoT represents a significant leap towards autonomous, intelligent systems.

Robotic Process Automation (RPA) and AI

Robotic Process Automation (RPA) combined with AI constitutes a transformative force in the automation landscape, enhancing the capabilities of businesses to execute repetitive tasks with unprecedented efficiency and accuracy. RPA's strength lies in its ability to mimic human actions within digital systems, performing routine tasks like data entry or report generation autonomously. When integrated with AI, RPA transcends basic automation, evolving into intelligent process automation (IPA).

This synthesis allows for the handling of complex decisions and processes that require adaptive responses, learning from interactions and improving over time. For instance, AI enhances RPA with capabilities such as natural language processing for customer service bots or machine learning algorithms that predict outcomes based on historical data.

Developing skills in RPA and AI opens avenues for creating robust automation solutions that are not only cost-effective but also scalable and insightful. The dual expertise in both technologies is crucial for professionals aiming to lead in the AI-driven digital economy, marking a critical step towards the future of work. This convergence is set to redefine industries by automating not just tasks but entire business processes.

AI in Blockchain: Opportunities and Challenges

The fusion of AI with blockchain technology is ushering in a new era of smart solutions, powered by the immutability and security of blockchain and the adaptive intelligence of AI. This synergy presents significant opportunities for enhancing trust and automation in various sectors, such as finance, healthcare, and supply chain management. For instance, AI can analyze patterns and predict trends in blockchain transaction data, facilitating more strategic decision-making and smarter contracts.

However, integrating AI with blockchain poses distinct challenges. The computational complexity of AI models requires significant resources, which can conflict with the decentralized nature of blockchain. Additionally, the integration process must address potential scalability issues and ensure that the increased workload does not undermine blockchain's performance.

Despite these challenges, the collaborative potential between AI and blockchain is immense. By overcoming integration hurdles, professionals can unlock powerful applications that leverage AI's learning capabilities and blockchain's transparency to create highly secure and intelligent systems.

AI-Powered Analytics and Business Intelligence

The convergence of AI with analytics and business intelligence (BI) is redefining data-driven decision-making. By incorporating machine learning and complex algorithms, AI enhances traditional BI tools, enabling more profound insights and predictions. This integrated approach facilitates real-time data analysis, which is essential in quickly shifting market conditions, allowing businesses to react and adapt with unprecedented agility.

AI-powered analytics excel in uncovering hidden patterns and correlations that are often overlooked by human analysts. These insights can lead to improved customer experiences, streamlined operations, and innovative product offerings. For instance, predictive analytics can forecast customer behavior, leading to more targeted marketing and optimized supply chain management.

Furthermore, the dynamic capabilities of AI in analytics extend to risk management and fraud detection. By analyzing vast datasets, AI systems can identify potential risks and anomalous behavior more efficiently than traditional methods. This capability not only enhances security but also boosts the overall confidence in BI systems, making AI an indispensable ally in the landscape of modern business intelligence.

Developing AI Skills through Online Courses and Certifications

In an era where AI is reshaping industries, mastering AI through online courses and certifications is crucial. These educational resources democratize access to cutting-edge technology education, enabling individuals from varied backgrounds to acquire and hone AI skills at their pace. Platforms like Coursera, Udacity, and edX offer courses developed by leading universities and tech companies, ensuring learners receive current and comprehensive knowledge.

Certifications in AI provide validation of proficiency and commitment to the field, enhancing career prospects. They cover a range of topics from basic AI principles to advanced machine learning techniques, tailored to different career stages. Moreover, these courses often include hands-on projects which allow learners to apply theoretical knowledge in practical scenarios, bridging the gap between learning and real-world application.

Participating in these online courses also offers networking opportunities with peers and professionals in the field, which can be invaluable for career growth and collaboration. Engaging with a community of learners fosters a deeper understanding and keeps students abreast of the latest AI trends and practices. Thus, online AI education is not just a learning tool but a career catalyst.

Participating in AI Competitions to Enhance Skills

Engaging in AI competitions is a dynamic way to sharpen your AI skills and benchmark your capabilities against peers globally. These competitions, ranging from online hackathons to university-hosted events, challenge participants to solve real-world problems using AI technologies. They provide a platform not only for learning but also for innovation and creativity in applying machine learning algorithms and data science techniques.

By participating in these contests, you can gain practical experience and deeper insights into AI's capabilities and limitations. Competitions often require dealing with unique datasets or complex problem statements, pushing competitors to think outside the box and implement robust AI solutions. This process is invaluable for mastering the intricacies of AI problem-solving.

Moreover, AI competitions are a testament to a participant's skills, adding substantial credibility to one's resume. They also offer opportunities to connect with industry leaders and potential employers who often scout for talent in such events. Additionally, winners might receive prizes, scholarships, or funding to pursue their AI projects, further encouraging innovation and continual learning in the field.

Networking in the AI Community

In the swiftly evolving field of AI, networking within the AI community stands crucial for personal and professional growth. Engaging with industry peers through conferences, workshops, and seminars offers invaluable opportunities for exchanging ideas, learning about the latest trends, and discussing groundbreaking advances in AI technologies. These interactions often lead to collaborations that can propel projects and research to new heights.

Online forums and social media platforms are also central hubs for AI enthusiasts. Platforms such as LinkedIn, Reddit, and specialized AI forums allow professionals to connect, share knowledge, and seek advice from global experts. This digital networking is especially beneficial for those looking to break geographical barriers and gain insights from diverse AI cultures.

Furthermore, professional groups and clubs dedicated to AI provide structured networking opportunities. Regular meetings and talks by experienced professionals offer learning opportunities and the chance to build lasting professional relationships. Each encounter enriches understanding, helping members stay engaged with the AI community's pulse.

Staying Updated with AI Trends and Advancements

In the rapidly evolving world of artificial intelligence, staying updated with the latest trends and advancements is essential for anyone involved in AI development. Industry publications, leading tech blogs, and journals like 'Nature AI' or 'AI Magazine' are treasure troves of new knowledge, documenting breakthroughs and evolving methodologies. Engaging with this content not only refines your existing knowledge but also introduces you to pioneering ideas that can influence future projects.

Moreover, attending global AI conferences such as NeurIPS, ICML, or local meetups can provide insights into new research and technologies. These gatherings are platforms for thought leaders to share innovative ideas, offering attendees a firsthand understanding of where the field is headed and which trends are gaining traction.

Subscribing to AI-focused newsletters from major universities or tech companies also serves as an efficient way to keep abreast of industry news without investing extensive time in research. Social media channels like Twitter, where many AI professionals share updates, can be an immediate source of new and relevant information, allowing for real-time engagement with peers and leaders in the field.

SUMMARY

The chapter 'Developing Essential AI Skills and Knowledge' provides a comprehensive overview of the foundational theories, practical applications, and crucial tools necessary for mastering Artificial Intelligence (AI) and Machine Learning (ML). It begins by delineating the core concepts of AI and ML, emphasizing the importance of algorithms that allow machines to perform tasks requiring human-like intelligence, such as pattern recognition and decision-making, with minimal human intervention. The role of machine learning as a subset of AI focused on learning from data is highlighted, illustrating the process from data ingestion to model training and application in making predictions on new data sets.

As the chapter progresses, it explores the essential programming languages integral to AI development, with Python recognized for its user-friendly syntax and comprehensive libraries which are instrumental in AI model building. The significance of other languages like Java, R, and JavaScript is also discussed, each important for specific functions in large-scale systems, statistical analysis, and web environments. The narrative moves forward, outlining data science fundamentals, which form the bedrock of effective AI systems by providing methodologies for data handling, analysis, and visualization.

Furthermore, the discourse advances into more complex AI concepts such as neural networks and deep learning, explaining how these technologies simulate human brain functions to enhance machine learning tasks. AI's application via various machine learning algorithms is also unpacked, revealing the diversity and broad usability of AI across different sectors. Mathematical underpinnings in AI development are underscored, pointing out the relevance of linear algebra, probability, and calculus in optimizing AI algorithms.

The latter sections of the chapter address practical aspects including AI development tools like TensorFlow and PyTorch, project management methodologies, and ethical considerations in AI deployment. The importance of continuous learning through online courses and participation in AI competitions is advocated to keep pace with the rapidly evolving field. Finally, the chapter rounds up with discussions on the significance of networking within the AI community and staying updated with current AI trends and advancements.

REFERENCES

[1] Understanding Machine Learning Algorithms. https://www.researchgate.net/publication/Understanding_Machine_Learning_Algorithms

[2] Programming Languages and AI Development. https://www.jmlr.org/papers/volume18

[3] Data Science in AI. https://ieeexplore.ieee.org/document/AGE_OF_DATA_SCIENCE

[4] Neural Networks and Deep Learning: A Textbook. https://link.springer.com/book/Neural_Networks_and_Deep_Learning

[5] Machine Learning Types and Applications. https://academic.oup.com/journals/pages/Machine_Learning_Types_and_Applications

[6] Mathematics for AI. https://www.cambridge.org/core/journals/mathematics-for-ai

CASE STUDY: IMPLEMENTING AI IN PREDICTIVE MAINTENANCE FOR INDUSTRIAL EQUIPMENT

In a leading manufacturing company, TechCorp Industries, management faced frequent unexpected machine downtime, resulting in substantial operational losses and production delays. The company's leadership decided to leverage Artificial Intelligence (AI) to enhance their predictive maintenance strategies, aiming to predict equipment failures before they occur and minimize unplanned downtime.

TechCorp gathered historical data on machine operations, including performance metrics, maintenance logs, and failure incidents. The data science team, equipped with knowledge of machine learning algorithms from their internal training sessions, began by cleaning and preprocessing this voluminous data to eliminate inaccuracies and irrelevant information. The team then opted to use a combination of supervised learning techniques, starting with regression models to predict the time until failure and classification models to identify the risk category of each machine.

After choosing Python due to its rich libraries such as pandas for data manipulation and scikit-learn for implementing machine learning algorithms, the team developed a predictive model. The model underwent multiple iterations with continuous feedback and adjustments based on the performance evaluations using precision, recall, and F1-score as metrics. The deployed AI system not only provided real-time alerts about potential failures but also recommended preventive maintenance schedules tailored to each machine's condition.

The implementation of this AI-driven predictive maintenance system marked a significant transformation in how TechCorp managed its equipment health. It led to a measurable decrease in downtime by 30%, substantially saving costs and improving production efficiency. Furthermore, the project highlighted the practical application and combination of AI theoretical concepts, data science fundamentals, and the importance of selecting the right machine learning algorithms for specific tasks.

Case Study: Optimizing Supply Chain Logistics with AI-Driven Route Planning

In the competitive landscape of global logistics, QuickShip Deliveries Inc. was facing challenges in managing its supply chain efficiency due to fluctuating fuel costs, varying customer demands, and traffic unpredictability. The company recognized that advancements in Artificial Intelligence (AI) could be pivotal in reshaping their route planning strategies to optimize both time and costs while enhancing service reliability.

QuickShip embarked on a project to integrate AI into their supply chain management system, starting with the collection of extensive historical data on delivery routes, traffic patterns, vehicle performance, and delivery outcomes. This data was carefully cleaned and preprocessed to ensure accuracy and relevance, removing outliers and correcting anomalies which could skew AI predictions.

The team then moved on to choosing the optimal machine learning algorithms for their needs. They opted for a combination of supervised learning for predicting delivery times based on specific routes and conditions, and reinforcement learning to dynamically adapt routes in real-time. They utilized Python for its robust libraries like NumPy for data manipulation, and TensorFlow for building and training the AI models.

Once the models were developed, they were trained with both historical and real-time data, programmed to learn from each delivery experience to continuously improve routing decisions. The AI system provided drivers with the most efficient routes, considering factors such as current traffic conditions, weather forecasts, and urgent delivery requests.

The implementation of the AI-driven route planning system resulted in a measurable reduction in delivery times by 20% and a reduction in fuel consumption by 15%, significantly cutting costs and carbon footprint. Moreover, the project demonstrated the effectiveness of integrating AI into logistics and provided valuable insights into the practical application of supervised and reinforcement learning in dynamic operational environments.

Case Study: Implementing AI for Real-Time Customer Sentiment Analysis in Social Media Engagement

A mid-sized digital marketing firm, StratComm, sought to enhance its client services by offering real-time customer sentiment analysis to better gauge public reaction to marketing campaigns on social media platforms. Recognizing that the swift detection of shifts in customer sentiment could allow brands to react dynamically to public perception, StratComm decided to employ AI and machine learning technologies to automate and refine this process.

StratComm embarked on the data collection phase, gathering vast amounts of textual data from various social media channels, including tweets, Facebook posts, and Instagram comments related to specific marketing campaigns. The team used a combination of data scraping tools and APIs provided by the social media platforms to efficiently gather and update this information continuously.

The next step involved preprocessing this textual data, which was crucial due to the unstructured nature of natural language. The team employed techniques like tokenization, stemming, and removal of stop words to clean the data. StratComm chose Python as the primary programming language, utilizing libraries such as NLTK for natural language processing tasks and TensorFlow to implement neural networks. They developed a model based on sentiment analysis that used a combination of convolutional neural networks (CNNs) and recurrent neural networks (RNNs), which are effective for pattern recognition in text and sequence data, respectively.

Upon deploying the AI system, StratComm was able to provide its clients with a dashboard that visually represented customer sentiment trends in real-time. This tool enabled clients to swiftly adjust their marketing strategies based on instant feedback from their audience. For instance, if negative sentiment spiked in response to a new advertisement, the client could quickly investigate the cause and initiate corrective measures. Through continuous learning and model optimization, the accuracy of sentiment predictions improved, enhancing client satisfaction and engagement outcomes.

Case Study: Revolutionizing Healthcare with AI-Powered Diagnostic Systems

In the dynamic field of healthcare, MedTech Innovations, a pioneering technology firm, aimed to revolutionize medical diagnostics by integrating Artificial Intelligence (AI) into their diagnostic processes. Recognizing the challenges of accurate and timely diagnosis, especially in complex cases such as neurological disorders and early cancer detection, the company decided to deploy AI to enhance the precision and efficiency of their diagnostic tools.

MedTech began by collating extensive medical data, including thousands of patient records, imaging data, and clinical outcomes. The data, however, was varied and unstructured, encompassing numeric data, text records, and high-resolution images. The first crucial step involved rigorous data cleaning and preprocessing. This phase addressed data quality issues, such as missing values and inconsistencies, and prepared the data for further analysis. Given the critical nature of the data, the team employed advanced techniques in data anonymization to maintain patient confidentiality.

The team then explored various machine learning algorithms suitable for their specific diagnostic requirements. They chose a mixed approach, utilizing convolutional neural networks (CNNs) for analyzing imaging data, and natural language processing (NLP) techniques to interpret clinical notes. Python, known for its strong support in scientific computing and machine learning, was selected as the primary programming language. Libraries like TensorFlow and Keras were used to build and train the models. Extensive testing was conducted, involving both retrospective patient data and real-time clinical environments, to ensure the models' accuracy and reliability.

Post-implementation, MedTech's AI-powered diagnostic systems significantly improved diagnostic accuracy and reduced the time required for diagnosing complex conditions. For example, the time to diagnose certain types of cancer was halved, greatly improving patient outcomes by enabling quicker treatment. Furthermore, the success of this initiative not only positioned MedTech as a leader in healthcare innovation but also underscored the transformative potential of AI in medicine, demonstrating practical applications of AI technologies and reinforcing the importance of robust data handling and algorithm selection in healthcare solutions.

Case Study: Leveraging AI for Enhanced Financial Fraud Detection

In the rapidly evolving financial sector, Central Bank Inc. faced challenges in effectively monitoring and preventing fraudulent transactions—a critical aspect ensuring client trust and regulatory compliance. Given the increasing sophistication of fraud techniques, the bank decided to integrate advanced Artificial Intelligence (AI) solutions into their fraud detection systems to improve accuracy and response time.

Central Bank started by aggregating vast amounts of transactional data, including client transaction histories, login information, and typical user behavior patterns. To effectively process and analyze this large dataset, the data science team embarked on a crucial phase of data cleaning and preparation. This involved handling missing values, removing outliers, and normalizing data to ensure that the subsequent machine learning models could perform optimally.

Selecting the appropriate AI technology was pivotal. The bank opted for a combination of machine learning techniques: supervised learning to create predictive models based on historical fraud patterns, and unsupervised learning to identify unusual patterns indicating potential new fraud strategies. Python was chosen as the programming language, leveraging libraries like Scikit-Learn for building predictive models, and TensorFlow for implementing neural networks capable of pattern recognition.

Following the development phase, Central Bank's team conducted rigorous model training and testing. Real-time streaming data was used to train models to adapt and become more accurate over time. The deployed system featured a real-time alert mechanism that flagged suspicious activities instantly, allowing the bank's fraud prevention team to take immediate action.

Post-implementation, the AI-enhanced fraud detection system led to a significant reduction in fraudulent transactions, with a noted improvement in detection rates from 75% to 93%. This transformation not only fortified Central Bank's security measures but also demonstrated the essential nature of selecting robust AI models and the importance of continuous model training and real-time data processing in combating financial fraud.

Case Study: Advanced Real-Time Traffic Management Using AI

UrbanCommute, a municipal traffic authority in a large metropolitan area, faced significant challenges in managing ever-increasing traffic congestion and vehicular emissions. With an existing infrastructure strained by frequent bottlenecks, unpredictable accidents, and dynamic weather conditions, the authority sought to implement a more efficient, AI-driven traffic control system to enhance road safety and reduce congestion.

The project began with the aggregation of vast datasets from multiple sources including traffic cameras, sensors on roads, and GPS data from public transit systems. This data was crucial in understanding traffic patterns and identifying critical congestion points. UrbanCommute's data science team, utilizing their knowledge gained from recent advancements in machine learning and neural networks, initiated a robust data cleaning process to handle inaccuracies such as duplicate GPS logs and corrupted sensor data. Python, renowned for its extensive libraries like Pandas for data manipulation and TensorFlow for machine learning, was chosen as the primary development language.

The team developed a model employing a combination of convolutional neural networks (CNNs) for image recognition from traffic cameras and recurrent neural networks (RNNs) to predict traffic flow based on historical data. This dual approach allowed UrbanCommute to not only understand and react to current traffic conditions but also to predict and mitigate potential future bottlenecks.

Following rigorous testing and several iterations to refine the algorithm, the AI system was integrated with the city's traffic light control system, enabling dynamic adjustment of light sequences during peak hours and incidents. It also provided real-time traffic data to commuters via a mobile app, advising on optimal travel routes and times.

Post-implementation, UrbanCommute observed a 25% reduction in average commute times and a notable improvement in traffic flow during traditionally congested periods. The success of this AI implementation highlighted the transformative potential of integrating advanced AI technologies within urban planning and the critical role of data quality and appropriate algorithm selection in developing effective AI solutions.

Case Study: Incorporating AI in Retail Inventory Management

RetailMax, a national retail chain known for its diverse product offerings, faced significant challenges managing its vast inventory spread across multiple locations. Inadequate inventory management led to overstocking of slow-moving products and stockouts of popular items, negatively impacting customer satisfaction and sales profitability. To address these issues, RetailMax decided to leverage Artificial Intelligence (AI) to optimize its inventory management processes.

The first step involved gathering comprehensive data from multiple sources, including point-of-sale systems, warehouse management software, and supply chain databases. This data encompassed sales performance, inventory levels, customer purchasing habits, and seasonal trends. The data science team at RetailMax then embarked on an extensive data cleansing and preprocessing phase to ensure the accuracy and relevance of the data used in modeling. They utilized Python for its powerful libraries like Pandas for data manipulation and TensorFlow for building machine learning models.

Next, RetailMax explored various AI-driven forecasting techniques to enhance their predictive accuracy regarding inventory demands. They employed time-series analysis for predicting future sales trends and used clustering algorithms to categorize products based on sales velocity and variability. The AI system recommended optimal stock levels for each product category, automated reordering processes, and identified potential discontinuation candidates for underperforming products.

Following the implementation, RetailMax's inventory turnover rate improved significantly, reducing holding costs and minimizing stockouts. The AI-driven system enabled dynamic pricing strategies based on real-time sales data and inventory levels, further boosting profit margins. This project not only transformed RetailMax's inventory management but also provided valuable insights into the potential of AI in retail operations, emphasizing the importance of accurate data handling and algorithm selection for successful AI integration in business processes.

Case Study: AI-Enhanced Smart Farming: Revolutionizing Agriculture Management

AgriSmart Inc., a leading agricultural company, faced challenges with crop yield optimization and resource management due to unpredictable weather conditions and limited understanding of crop health at a granular level. The company decided to leverage Artificial Intelligence (AI) to improve its farming techniques, aiming at data-driven decisions for irrigation, fertilization, and harvesting timing.

The initial phase involved the aggregation of diverse data types; satellite imagery, soil sensors data, and historical crop yield records. The data was substantial and varied, requiring intensive preprocessing to standardize and clean it, ensuring it was suitable for effective model training. AgriSmart chose Python, enriched by libraries such as Pandas for data manipulation and TensorFlow for machine learning applications, to handle data preprocessing and model development.

After preprocessing, AI algorithms were tailored to address specific farming needs. Supervised learning techniques were employed to predict optimum planting times and crop rotation patterns based on past crop performance data and current soil health indicators. Neural networks, particularly convolutional neural networks (CNNs), were trained on satellite images and sensor data to identify unhealthy crop patches and suggest interventions.

Once these models were developed, they underwent a rigorous phase of tuning and testing to ensure reliability in real-world scenarios. They integrated these models within a user-friendly mobile app, providing farmers with actionable insights such as water stress areas, pest infestation risks, and optimal harvesting periods.

Upon deployment, AgriSmart witnessed a significant improvement in resource utilization, with a marked increase in crop yield by optimizing irrigation and fertilization strategies. The AI-enhanced insights also helped in reducing pesticide use, promoting sustainable farming practices. The case of AgriSmart Inc. dramatically illustrates the deep application of AI in agriculture, highlighting how AI can be pivotal in transforming traditional practices to achieve efficiency and sustainability.

REVIEW QUESTIONS

1. John, an entrepreneur, is delving into AI development for creating data-driven applications. Considering Python's extensive libraries and robust features highlighted in the overview of essential languages, which library is John most likely to use for machine learning tasks?

A) Pandas

B) TensorFlow

C) CoreML

D) Cytoscape

Answer: B

Explanation: John is likely to use TensorFlow for his machine learning tasks as it simplifies complex tasks in machine learning and deep learning, making it an ideal choice for the development of intelligent solutions. Python, the language hosting TensorFlow, is favored for its extensive libraries that cater to various areas of AI, providing versatility and a comprehensive developmental environment.

2. Dr. Alice is exploring the intersection of machine learning and statistics for her healthcare AI project. If she leverages linear algebra to improve her model performance, what aspect is she most likely enhancing?

A) Data acquisition

B) Model accuracy through better data representation

C) Data storage technology

D) Networking speeds

Answer: B

Explanation: Dr. Alice is enhancing model accuracy through better data representation by using linear algebra, as it plays a crucial role in optimizing machine learning algorithms through sophisticated matrix operations. These operations aid in structurizing the data more effectively, thereby enhancing the model's ability to learn and make more accurate predictions.

REVIEW QUESTIONS

3. Alex has designed his very first AI model to predict consumer behavior in e-commerce using neural networks described in the chapter. What is an immediate benefit Alex expects to derive from the deep learning subset of his neural network model?

A) Lower cost on digital marketing

B) Greater customer service management

C) Increased prediction accuracy on user tendencies

D) Reduced legal risks in operations

Answer: C

Explanation: The immediate benefit Alex expects from utilizing a deep learning subset in his neural network model lies in increased prediction accuracy on user tendencies. Deep learning models, with their ability to understand nuanced data features, are exceptionally adept at tasks like predicting behavior, which is crucial in tailoring e-commerce strategies based on consumer behaviors.

CASE STUDIES AND SUCCESS STORIES OF AI-DRIVEN WEALTH

Introduction to AI-Driven Wealth Success Stories

The narrative of AI-driven wealth creation unfolds across various industries, demonstrating not just profitability but sustainable innovation. This introduction seeks to outline the transformative impact of artificial intelligence in catalyzing economic growth and generating new employment landscapes. By dissecting success stories, we gain insights into how AI does not merely automate but innovates, carving out opportunities in sectors from healthcare to finance.

Through detailed case studies, we explore instances where AI technologies have catalyzed wealth generation, identifying patterns and strategies applicable across different business models. Each success story underlines the pivotal role of AI in harnessing data, enhancing decision-making, and streamlining operations, thereby driving financial gain and competitive advantage. These narratives serve not only as testimonials of current achievements but as blueprints for future endeavors in the AI landscape.

As we delve into specific sectors in subsequent sections, keep in mind the overarching theme of AI as a versatile wealth generator. The following chapters will showcase intricate examples of how integrating AI has redefined market strategies and operational efficiencies, underpinning the new era of digital wealth generation.

Revolutionizing Retail with AI: A Comprehensive Analysis

The retail sector, a dynamic arena characterized by evolving consumer behavior, has been profoundly transformed through AI integration. AI-driven tools analyze vast data streams to optimize inventory management and tailor marketing strategies that resonate with nuanced consumer preferences.

In-store AI applications include smart mirrors and checkout-less shopping experiences, enhancing customer engagement and streamlining the purchasing process. These innovations not only elevate the consumer experience but also significantly reduce operational costs. E-commerce platforms leverage AI to offer personalized shopping experiences, using algorithms that predict buying habits and recommend products accordingly.

Moreover, AI enables real-time pricing adjustments and promotions, maximizing profit margins across multiple channels. The integration of AI in retail logistics also refines supply chain operations, ensuring faster and more accurate delivery services. These technological advancements collectively forge a path towards sustained economic growth and heightened market competition in the retail industry.

AI in Finance: Transforming Asset Management

The intersection of artificial intelligence and asset management represents a seismic shift in financial services, pioneering a new age of wealth management strategies. AI tools analyze enormous datasets at speeds and accuracies unattainable by human analysts, enabling real-time decision-making that drives profitability and minimizes risk.

AI algorithms provide personalized investment advice, automate trading, and optimize portfolios by predicting market trends and responding to them with unprecedented rapidity. This AI-driven personalization is not only revolutionizing how assets are managed but also democratizing access to investment strategies that were once reserved for the elite.

Furthermore, AI facilitates regulatory compliance through sophisticated monitoring systems that detect and report anomalies, safeguarding against fraud while maintaining operational integrity. The continuous evolution of AI technologies promises to further refine asset management practices, ensuring more robust financial frameworks and consumer trust in a digitized world.

Healthcare and AI: Cost Reduction and Improved Patient Care

Artificial intelligence stands as a transformative force in healthcare, significantly reducing costs while simultaneously enhancing patient care. Through intelligent algorithms and data analysis, AI streamlines administrative procedures and diagnostic accuracy, resulting in considerable savings. For instance, AI-powered tools assist in patient management by predicting hospital admissions, thereby optimizing resource allocation and reducing unnecessary hospital stays.

Moreover, AI-driven diagnostic systems facilitate early detection of diseases, which can lead to timely intervention and more effective treatment plans. These systems analyze medical imaging with higher precision than traditional methods, increasing patient outcomes and minimizing invasive procedures. With AI's ability to handle vast amounts of data, personalized medicine has become more accessible, tailoring treatments to individual genetic profiles and improving therapeutic success rates.

AI also enhances patient engagement by offering 24/7 virtual assistance via chatbots that provide reliable medical information and monitor patient health status remotely. This continual patient connection not only ensures better chronic disease management but also empowers patients in their health journeys, fostering a proactive approach to wellness.

AI-Enhanced Manufacturing: Increasing Efficiency and Output

In the world of manufacturing, AI is more than a tool; it's a revolutionary force reshaping production landscapes. By integrating AI, factories are witnessing a significant uptick in efficiency and output, marking a pivotal shift towards autonomic systems. Smart manufacturing setups utilize AI to optimize everything from supply chain logistics to real-time quality control, reducing waste and downtime while enhancing the speed and precision of production lines.

Moreover, AI-powered predictive maintenance predicts equipment failures before they occur, ensuring continuous operation without unexpected halts. These intelligent systems analyze historical data to forecast machine wear and tear, scheduling repairs during optimal times to minimize disruption. The result? A seamless fusion of human expertise and machine precision, pushing the boundaries of what's possible in industrial production.

The success stories in AI-enhanced manufacturing are abundant, from small-scale factories to global conglomerates. These narratives not only underscore the financial gains and competitive edge but also highlight the transformative potential of AI in creating sustainable, future-ready industrial environments.

The Automation of Logistics and Supply Chain Management

In the intricate web of global commerce, AI's role in automating logistics and supply chain management has become a cornerstone of efficiency and profitability. As companies wrestle with complex distribution networks and fluctuating market demands, AI technologies stand out by optimizing routing, inventory management, and forecasting demands with a precision unattainable by human capabilities alone.

AI-powered systems analyze real-time data to anticipate disruptions and adjust strategies accordingly, ensuring robust delivery mechanisms that are both cost-effective and timely. This automation not only enhances operational accuracies but also significantly reduces wastage and improves supply chain sustainability. Success stories from leading logistics companies illustrate dramatic cost reductions and enhanced service levels, paving the way for a more resilient and responsive supply chain infrastructure.

Furthermore, AI integration facilitates seamless communication across the supply chain, bridging gaps between suppliers, distributors, and end consumers. The strategic deployment of AI tools has empowered businesses to maintain a competitive edge in a volatile market by enabling smarter, data-driven decisions that underpin both short-term performance and long-term strategic goals.

AI Innovations in the Energy Sector

The energy sector, critical to global sustainability and economic stability, is undergoing a pioneering transformation powered by AI innovations. Machine learning models underpin predictive maintenance in power plants, minimizing downtime and extending machinery life. By forecasting demand and optimizing grid distribution, AI drives energy efficiency and reduces operational costs.

Furthermore, renewable energy sources like wind and solar benefit immensely from AI. Algorithms improve forecast accuracy for weather-dependent energy production, enhancing grid integration and reliability. This ability to predict and manage fluctuating supply is crucial in reducing reliance on non-renewable sources.

The pivotal role of AI extends to consumer engagement through smart meters and energy-saving recommendations tailored to user behavior. These AI-driven tools empower consumers with real-time data, fostering energy conservation and promoting sustainable practices.

Collectively, these AI applications not only fortify the energy sector's financial backbone but also champion a move toward more sustainable, efficient energy landscapes globally.

Case Study: AI in Real Estate for Market Prediction and Valuation

AI is revolutionizing the real estate industry, turning data into a powerful tool for market prediction and property valuation. By harnessing vast amounts of data—from historical sales figures to recent market trends—AI algorithms provide precise, real-time property valuations and market forecasts. These insights enable investors and businesses to make informed purchasing, selling, and leasing decisions.

In one notable case, a leading real estate firm adopted AI to forecast market price fluctuations and optimize their property portfolio strategies. They utilized machine learning models to analyze demographic shifts, economic trends, and consumer behavior, achieving a 15% increase in annual revenue by pinpointing optimal investment opportunities.

Further, AI tools assist real estate professionals in enhancing customer satisfaction by predicting client preferences and suggesting properties that best fit their needs. This tailored approach not only improves client engagement but also speeds up transaction processes, keeping the firm competitive in a fast-evolving market.

Through these applications, AI is not just a facilitator of productivity and growth in real estate but a transformative force reshaping its future.

E-commerce Personalization: A Success Story

E-commerce has been radically transformed by AI, particularly through the lens of personalization, which significantly enhances consumer experience and retention rates. By analyzing user data, AI creates customized shopping experiences tailored to individual preferences, past purchases, and browsing behaviors.

For example, a leading online retail giant implemented an AI system that dynamically adjusts product recommendations and promotions for each user. This approach not only increased customer engagement by 35% but also boosted sales revenues by 24% within the first quarter of adoption. The AI's ability to identify and anticipate consumer needs has set a new benchmark in personalized marketing.

Moreover, AI-driven personalization extends beyond marketing to optimize inventory management and pricing strategies, adapting in real time to changes in consumer demand and market conditions. These innovations not only streamline operations but also elevate the customer journey, making shopping seamless and more intuitive.

Success stories in AI-powered e-commerce personalization underscore its potential as a wealth generator, proving that intelligent technology is an indispensable ally in staying competitive in the digital age.

AI in Agriculture: Higher Yields and Lower Costs

The agricultural sector is witnessing a significant transformation through the application of AI technologies, leading to higher yields and lower costs. Machine learning algorithms process vast amounts of data from satellite images and sensor-equipped farm equipment to predict crop health, optimize planting schedules, and manage irrigation and fertilization more effectively.

For instance, AI-driven crop management systems analyze weather patterns and soil conditions to offer precise recommendations for planting and harvesting. This not only boosts crop yield but also minimizes resource waste, contributing to sustainable farming practices. Additionally, AI-powered autonomous tractors and drones aid in field monitoring and crop spraying, further reducing labor costs and increasing operational efficiency.

Success stories abound, such as a partnership between a tech startup and a large agribusiness company which led to a 20% increase in crop production while decreasing water usage by 15%. These achievements underscore the profound impact AI is making, transforming traditional farming into a high-tech industry poised for future growth.

Education Sector Transformation through AI Applications

AI is redefining the educational landscape, enabling personalized learning experiences and improving administrative efficiencies. Intelligent tutoring systems and adaptive learning platforms harness AI to tailor educational content to individual student needs, pacing, and learning styles. These systems assess student progress in real-time, adapting instructional strategies to enhance understanding and retention of knowledge.

Moreover, AI applications streamline operations, from automated grading of assignments to management of institutional data, freeing educators to focus on teaching rather than administrative tasks. This shift not only increases productivity but also elevates the quality of educational delivery. For instance, an AI-driven program at a major university identified at-risk students early in the course, significantly improving graduation rates through targeted intervention strategies.

In another case, AI-powered virtual assistants are used to guide students through complex administrative processes, such as enrollment and financial aid applications, ensuring a smoother, more accessible educational journey. These innovations collectively foster an environment where personalized attention and efficiency coexist, transforming education into a more inclusive and effective sector.

AI in the Hospitality Industry: Enhancing Customer Experiences

The hospitality industry thrives on delivering exceptional customer experiences, a feat increasingly powered by AI technologies. AI-driven solutions are transforming service delivery by enabling personalized guest interactions and efficient operational management. For example, AI-powered chatbots provide 24/7 customer service, handling reservations, feedback, and inquiries with instant response capabilities, thereby enhancing guest satisfaction and operational productivity.

Moreover, AI is revolutionizing the way hospitality businesses manage their resources. Predictive analytics help forecast guest numbers, optimize room pricing dynamically, and manage inventory more effectively, ensuring profitability and reduced waste. Such applications also extend to personalized marketing, where AI analyses customer data to tailor offers and promotions to individual preferences, significantly increasing conversion rates.

In one notable case, a luxury hotel chain implemented AI to customize room environments according to guest preferences detected via previous stays and online profiles. This deep customization not only improved guest loyalty rates but also set new industry standards for personal service. Collectively, these AI-driven innovations are not just enhancing customer experiences; they are redefining the very essence of hospitality management.

Telecommunications and AI: Network Optimization Successes

The telecommunications industry has harnessed AI to revolutionize network optimization and management, leading to substantial improvements in service quality and customer satisfaction. AI algorithms analyze vast arrays of data from network traffic to predict and resolve bottlenecks before they affect users. This proactive management drastically reduces downtime and enhances user experience.

One notable success story involves a major telecom operator that implemented AI to optimize its network allocation. By predicting high traffic volumes, the AI system dynamically adjusted bandwidth allocation, ensuring smooth service during peak times. This adjustment not only improved customer satisfaction by 30% but also increased operational efficiency, reducing the cost of network maintenance by 20%.

Moreover, AI's role extends beyond mere optimization to preventive maintenance. Machine learning models predict equipment failures and schedule maintenance, further minimizing service disruptions. Through these applications, AI continues to drive the telecom industry toward more reliable, efficient, and customer-centric services.

Public Sector Implementations of AI

The public sector is embracing AI to enhance service delivery, reduce costs, and increase transparency. AI implementations span various facets of governance, including public safety, transportation, and administrative operations. For instance, AI algorithms are used to optimize traffic flow, reducing congestion and pollution, while predictive analytics improve emergency response times by anticipating where incidents are likely to occur.

Furthermore, AI tools assist in fraud detection within welfare programs, safeguarding resources for those who need them most. By analyzing behavioral patterns and cross-referencing vast databases, AI systems can identify irregularities that human auditors might miss, significantly reducing the incidence of fraud.

In education, AI-driven platforms streamline administrative tasks and personalize learning experiences, mirroring successes seen in the private sector. These technologies not only save money but also deliver services more effectively, proving that AI can be a transformative tool for public good. The integration of AI into public services illustrates its potential to redefine civic engagement and governmental efficiency.

AI in Sports: Game Analysis and Athlete Performance Enhancement

The sports industry is increasingly leveraging AI to redefine how games are analyzed and how athletes enhance their performances. AI technologies process enormous datasets from player performances to provide insights that were previously unattainable. Coaches and athletes use these insights to tweak strategies and improve training outcomes, leading to better performance and fewer injuries.

One prominent example is the use of AI in monitoring athletes' health and fitness levels in real time. Wearable devices equipped with AI capabilities track everything from heart rate to muscle fatigue, offering tailored recommendations for recovery and training intensity. This personalized approach promotes optimum performance while minimizing the risk of injury.

Moreover, AI-driven analytics tools analyze game footage to uncover patterns and weaknesses in opponents, giving teams a competitive edge. These tools transform vast amounts of video data into actionable strategies, significantly enhancing game preparation efforts. Success stories from soccer to basketball highlight AI's pivotal role in sports innovation, making it a cornerstone of contemporary athletic excellence.

Media and Entertainment Industry Revolution by AI

The media and entertainment sector is undergoing a profound transformation, driven by the integration of AI technologies. From algorithmically curated content that enhances viewer engagement to automated editing software that speeds up production, AI is reshaping how content is created, distributed, and consumed.

One significant change is the personalization of media experiences. AI analyzes viewer preferences and viewing habits, allowing companies to tailor content recommendations and advertisements to individual tastes, significantly boosting user satisfaction and retention rates. For instance, a leading streaming service uses AI to not only recommend movies and shows but also to determine which shows to produce based on predictive preferences modeling.

Furthermore, AI is revolutionizing marketing within the industry. By employing sophisticated data analytics, media companies are able to deliver highly targeted marketing campaigns that increase the effectiveness of promotional efforts and drive revenue growth. In one notable example, a film studio utilized AI-driven analytics to optimize the release strategy of a blockbuster, maximising audience reach and ticket sales.

These AI-driven advancements illustrate a dynamic shift toward more agile, responsive, and personalized media landscapes, setting new standards for how entertainment is crafted and enjoyed.

Case Study: AI-Driven Business Intelligence at a Fortune 500 Company

In this deep dive, we explore how a Fortune 500 company leveraged AI to dramatically transform its approach to business intelligence. The firm integrated AI tools to analyze large datasets, improving decision-making processes and strategic planning. AI algorithms enabled real-time data processing, identifying trends and predicting market shifts that were previously unnoticed by traditional analytics methods.

The impact was substantial. Sales forecasts improved by 25%, and marketing campaigns became more targeted and effective, increasing conversion rates by 18%. The AI system's ability to rapidly process and analyze consumer behavior data allowed the company to adjust its product offerings dynamically, enhancing customer satisfaction and loyalty.

Moreover, AI-driven automation of routine analytical tasks freed up human analysts to focus on more complex, strategic aspects of business intelligence. This shift not only optimized resource allocation but also increased job satisfaction among employees, fostering a culture of innovation and forward-thinking. This case study exemplifies the transformative power of AI in modern business environments.

Consumer Electronics and AI Influence on Market Trends

The realm of consumer electronics has been dramatically transformed by the advent of artificial intelligence, reshaping market trends and consumer behaviors. AI's integration into devices from smartphones to smart home systems has not only enhanced functionality but also revolutionized user interaction, leading to an increase in consumer demand for intelligent gadgets.

In particular, AI algorithms have enabled devices to learn from user interactions, improving their responses and predictions over time, thereby personalizing the user experience. Manufacturers who employ AI in their product designs report a significant boost in customer satisfaction and loyalty. Moreover, innovative features powered by AI, such as voice recognition and proactive health monitoring, have opened new avenues for market differentiation and have set new industry standards.

Moreover, these AI-driven innovations have not just satisfied existing market needs but have spawned entirely new product categories, creating wealth through blue ocean strategies. Companies harnessing AI have found themselves at the vanguard of the consumer electronics market, dictating trends and driving technological progression.

Startup Transformation Stories: AI as a Growth Catalyst

In the dynamic world of startups, AI acts as a pivotal growth catalyst, reshaping traditional business landscapes into innovative powerhouses. For young companies, AI-driven tools offer unprecedented insights into market trends and consumer behaviors, enabling more targeted and cost-effective strategies. Startups that embed AI into their core operations can streamline processes, enhance customer experiences, and scale efficiently without commensurate increases in overhead costs.

Success stories abound where AI has transformed nascent ventures into industry leaders. One such example is a retail startup that utilized AI for personalized marketing, which significantly improved customer retention rates and boosted sales by over 30% within the first year of implementation. This startup's ability to adapt and implement customer feedback into the AI model turned potential churn into long-term loyalty.

Moreover, AI's capability to analyze vast datasets allows startups to identify and capitalize on niche market opportunities, previously unnoticed. By leveraging AI for predictive analytics, startups not only anticipate market demands but also innovate solutions proactively, setting new industry standards and outpacing traditional competitors. In this way, AI is not just a tool but a strategic asset essential for modern entrepreneurial success.

Non-Profit Organizations Leveraging AI for Social Good

Non-profit organizations are increasingly turning to AI to enhance their impact, particularly in areas like resource allocation, fundraising, and program effectiveness. AI-driven analytics help predict giving patterns and identify potential donors, transforming traditional fundraising strategies and allowing for more personalized engagement.

Moreover, AI tools are being employed to optimize resource distribution in humanitarian efforts. By analyzing data from past campaigns and current needs, AI systems ensure that aid reaches the most vulnerable faster and more efficiently. One notable instance involved an AI solution that successfully predicted food shortages in remote areas, enabling timely intervention before the onset of severe crises.

Additionally, AI is empowering non-profits to extend their educational and health services to underserved communities. For example, AI-driven platforms provide tailored learning experiences and health diagnostics in regions lacking experts, demonstrating AI's potential in democratizing access to critical services while promoting societal well-being.

Small Businesses and Freelancers: AI Tools for Competitive Edge

In the growing expanse of the digital marketplace, small businesses and freelancers are harnessing the power of AI to carve niche spaces and gain a competitive edge. AI tools enable these smaller entities to perform with the efficiency and insight of larger corporations without commensurate infrastructure investments. For instance, AI-driven customer relationship management systems can automate personal interactions at scale, ensuring high levels of customer service that build brand loyalty and trust.

Moreover, AI applications in data analytics allow these businesses to glean actionable insights from their operations and customer interactions. These insights drive strategic decisions that optimize resources and tailor marketing strategies to individual consumer behaviors and preferences, significantly enhancing conversion rates.

AI is also pivotal in automating routine tasks, from scheduling to invoicing, which frees up valuable time for entrepreneurs to focus on creative and strategic pursuits. This shift not only enhances productivity but also improves job satisfaction, fostering a culture of innovation and resilience in the competitive market.

Emerging Markets and AI Integration: Overcoming Challenges

Emerging markets present distinct challenges and opportunities in adopting AI technologies. Infrastructure limitations, such as inadequate digital networks and data management systems, often hinder the full-scale deployment of AI solutions. Moreover, the scarcity of local AI expertise and education can stymie development and slow adoption rates.

However, several innovative strategies are proving successful in overcoming these barriers. For instance, multinational partnerships are facilitating technology transfers, while local governments are investing in digital education and infrastructure enhancements. Through such collaborative efforts, emerging markets are not only integrating AI but are also adapting it to address region-specific issues effectively.

These adaptations have led to bespoke AI solutions in agriculture, where predictive analytics improve crop yields, and in healthcare, where AI-driven diagnostics bring services to remote areas. Such initiatives not only demonstrate AI's versatility but also its potential to revolutionize industries in emerging markets, ensuring sustainable economic growth and enhanced quality of life.

AI in the Arts: How Creativity is Being Reimagined

The fusion of artificial intelligence with the arts is forging pathways to unprecedented creativity. AI is no longer just a tool for efficiency; it's becoming a collaborator, reshaping artistic expression. Visual arts are among the first to benefit, with AI algorithms creating complex digital art that challenges our traditional understanding of creativity and authorship.

In music, AI systems are composing scores, experimenting with rhythms and harmonies in ways that expand the human auditory experience. These AI-composed pieces push the boundaries of genre, often blending classical elements with contemporary sounds to create a new auditory landscape. Similarly, literature sees AI-supported writing, where algorithms offer narrative suggestions and styles, providing authors groundbreaking ways to captivate their audience.

Moreover, AI in performing arts adds a layer of immersive experiences. Through real-time motion sensors and generative algorithms, dancers and performers interact with dynamic, AI-driven visual backdrops, enhancing performances and engaging audiences in deeply transformative ways. Artistic boundaries are thus continuously stretched as AI intersects with human creativity, opening a new chapter in the cultural and economic valorization of the arts.

Environmental and Sustainability Solutions Powered by AI

Artificial Intelligence is shaping the future of environmental sustainability, offering compelling solutions that marry ecological care with economic advancement. AI enables deeper insights into resource conservation, optimizing use in industries from agriculture to urban development. For instance, AI-driven smart grids manage energy consumption more efficiently, significantly reducing waste and lowering operational costs.

In the water sector, AI technologies predict and manage usage patterns, avoiding shortages and enhancing distribution efficiency, directly impacting economic outputs positively. One notable success involves an AI system that minimized water waste in a large city by 25%, equating to sizable financial savings annually. Furthermore, AI facilitates waste management through intelligent sorting and recycling systems, establishing more sustainable practices that alleviate pressure on landfills and promote recycling economies.

The impact of AI on sustainability extends to wildlife and natural habit conservation. Through machine learning models, ecologists track species populations and predict threats, allowing timely interventions. This not only helps preserve biodiversity but also sustains tourism industries, directly translating into wealth generation. AI is proving indispensable in building greener, more efficient economies.

AI in Legal Services: Automating Research and Due Diligence

The integration of AI into legal services is revolutionizing the way law firms and legal departments conduct research and due diligence. By automating these time-consuming tasks, AI frees up legal professionals to focus on more complex and strategic activities, enhancing productivity and reducing operational costs.

AI-driven tools assist in sifting through vast quantities of data, identifying relevant case precedents, and performing due diligence at unprecedented speeds. This not only accelerates the legal review processes but also increases accuracy, minimizing the risk of human error. Furthermore, AI algorithms can predict litigation outcomes based on historical data, enabling lawyers to make more informed decisions.

Additionally, these advancements are democratizing legal services. Smaller firms and solo practitioners can now access the same powerful tools as larger entities, leveling the playing field and increasing competition in the legal sector. This automation also extends globally, allowing firms to handle international cases more efficiently, thus broadening their market reach.

Global AI Implementation: Cultural and Logistic Insights

The global integration of AI presents a vivid mosaic of cultural adaptation and logistical challenges. Countries harness AI's potential variably, shaped by distinct cultural contexts and technological landscapes. In nations with robust tech infrastructures, like the United States and Japan, AI seamlessly enhances daily life and economic activities. However, ethical considerations and cultural nuances dictate its acceptance and utilization.

Logistically, AI implementation faces hurdles in regions with limited digital literacy or infrastructural support. Here, multinational corporations and NGOs play a pivotal role in bridging these gaps, offering training and resources to foster a supportive AI ecosystem. These efforts are crucial for ensuring that AI technologies are not only adopted but are also adapted to meet local needs effectively and respectfully.

Moreover, the strategic deployment of AI across different sectors demonstrates its versatility and potential to overcome cultural and logistical barriers. By tailoring AI applications to respect cultural identities and meet specific regional demands, businesses and governments can unlock new avenues for growth and innovation, ensuring technology acts as a bridge rather than a divider in the global marketplace.

SUMMARY

The chapter discusses various sectors where AI has significantly contributed to wealth creation, demonstrating AI's role as a transformative force in modern businesses and industries. Starting with retail, AI's integration has revamped the sector by optimizing inventory management, enhancing customer service through personalized experiences, and streamlining supply chains. The finance sector has also been revolutionized by AI through improved asset management, risk reduction, and personalized investment strategies using advanced data analysis. In healthcare, AI applications have led to cost reductions and enhanced patient care by improving diagnostic accuracy and optimizing resource management. Moreover, AI has brought about substantial efficiency improvements in manufacturing, reducing waste and downtime while enhancing production precision and output. The logistics and supply chain segment has seen automation driven by AI, ensuring more robust and cost-effective operations. AI's impact on the energy sector includes predictive maintenance and optimized energy distribution, fostering economical and sustainable practices. The real estate market has benefited from precise valuations and market predictions, facilitating smarter investment decisions. In e-commerce, personalization has significantly boosted consumer engagement and sales. Additionally, agriculture has seen increased productivity with reduced costs through precise AI-driven farming techniques. The education sector's transformation by AI offers personalized learning and operational efficiency, enhancing educational outcomes. Hospitality benefits from AI in personalized customer service and resource management, improving guest experiences and operational productivity. AI in telecommunications enhances network management and customer services, ensuring minimal downtime and improved satisfaction. The public sector's deployment of AI promises improved service delivery and resource management, enhancing public welfare and efficiency. Finally, the chapter delves into how non-profits leverage AI for more effective service distribution and fundraising, demonstrating AI's positive impact in various fields, contributing to an overarching narrative of economic growth and improved service delivery across sectors.

REFERENCES

[1] Artificial Intelligence in Retail Market by Type, Technology, Solution, Deployment Mode, Application, and Region - Global Forecast to 2027. https://www.researchandmarkets.com/reports/5130253

[2] The Role of Artificial Intelligence in Modern Healthcare: A Mini Review. https://www.frontiersin.org/articles/10.3389/frai.2020.00017/full

[3] AI in Manufacturing Market by Offerings, Technology, Deployment, Application, and End User - Global Forecast to 2027. https://www.marketsandmarkets.com/Market-Reports/

[4] AI in Education Market by Technology, Component, Deployment Mode, Category, End-User, and Region - Global Forecast to 2027. https://www.reportsnreports.com/reports/1237319

[5] AI for Telecommunications- Deep Learning Solutions for Improving Process Efficiency. https://www.elsevier.com/books-and-journals

CASE STUDY: OPTIMIZING RETAIL OPERATIONS WITH AI: THE FASHION BOUTIQUE CASE

A mid-sized fashion boutique chain, VogueStyles, sought to dynamically transform its inventory management and customer experience by incorporating AI. Initially, the company faced challenges with overstocking and understocking issues, which led to significant losses. The introduction of an AI-powered inventory management system revolutionized their operations. This system utilized predictive algorithms to forecast demand based on various factors including seasonal trends, historical sales data, and real-time consumer behavior analytics.

The implementation phase involved training the AI models with past inventory data and sales performance metrics. As a result, VogueStyles could more accurately forecast demand for different products, helping them optimize stock levels. This led to a 20% reduction in inventory costs due to decreased overstock, and a substantial reduction in lost sales from understock situations. Additionally, the boutique chain introduced AI-driven personalization for customer interactions. By analyzing customer data collected from loyalty programs and online transactions, AI algorithms provided tailored recommendations through the company's mobile app and email marketing campaigns.

This move not only enhanced customer engagement by making shopping experiences more personalized but also increased sales conversions by 30%. For instance, customers receiving personalized outfit recommendations were more likely to purchase additional items. VogueStyles also deployed AI-powered chatbots on their website and mobile app, which handled customer inquiries instantaneously, leading to improved customer satisfaction rates.

Experts and leaders in retail technology cite the VogueStyles case as a significant example of how AI can transition a traditional retail operation into a modern, data-driven business. This case exemplifies effective implementation and leveraging of AI technologies, illustrating significant advantages including enhanced decision-making, operational efficiency, and customer satisfaction in the competitive retail sector.

Case Study: Revolutionizing Healthcare Management with AI: Hospital Network Case

In a landmark initiative, MediNet, a large hospital network spanning several states, embarked on an ambitious project to integrate artificial intelligence into their healthcare management system. The primary objectives were to reduce operational costs, improve patient outcomes, and streamline both patient and resource management. Historically, MediNet faced challenges related to high patient readmission rates, inefficient use of medical resources, and prolonged billing processes which frequently led to administrative bottlenecks and patient dissatisfaction.

To address these issues, MediNet implemented an AI-driven platform to analyze vast amounts of patient data, ranging from medical histories and lab results to real-time health monitoring. This integration allowed for predictive analytics, which not only forecasted potential health deteriorations but also identified high-risk patients who could benefit from preventative care measures, significantly reducing readmission rates. AI algorithms also optimized scheduling and resource allocation by predicting peak periods and adjusting staffing and equipment availability accordingly, leading to improved operational efficiency.

Moreover, the AI system incorporated natural language processing to automatically process and fill patient reports and insurance claims, drastically reducing the processing time from weeks to just a few days. This not only improved cash flow but also enhanced patient satisfaction by speeding up the billing cycle. Another significant outcome was the reduction in medication errors through AI-enhanced drug prescription verification systems that cross-referenced patient allergies and current medications, ensuring higher safety standards.

The ramifications of MediNet's AI adoption extended beyond operational efficiencies and cost savings. The hospitals within the network reported a 25% increase in patient satisfaction scores and a 30% reduction in administrative costs. Additionally, the predictive capabilities of AI brought about a notable improvement in clinical outcomes, including a 15% decrease in patient readmission and a 20% increase in the efficiency of patient service delivery. These transformations not only solidified MediNet's reputation as a pioneer in innovative healthcare but also set a benchmark for other institutions aiming to leverage AI in healthcare management.

Case Study: AI-Driven Transformation in Agribusiness: Maximizing Crop Yields and Efficiency

Within the expansive fields of AgriCorp, a leading agriculture company, a transformative shift was marked by the adoption of artificial intelligence to boost crop yields and streamline operations. AgriCorp operated over vast landscapes of different crop varieties in varied climates, which introduced multiple challenges such as optimal planting times, pest control, and irrigation issues. The integration of AI positioned AgriCorp at the frontier of precision agriculture.

AgriCorp deployed an AI-based system that leveraged satellite images and IoT sensors equipped throughout the fields to gather real-time data on crop health, soil moisture levels, and environmental conditions. Machine learning algorithms analyzed this data to provide actionable insights on the precise amount of water, fertilizers, and pesticides needed, considerably reducing waste and increasing crop yield efficiency. For instance, the AI system predicted a pest infestation curve and automatically adjusted the pesticide dispensers to counteract the potential damage, which in previous seasons, would have resulted in significant crop losses.

The AI-driven initiatives extended to harvest management, where robotic harvesters were programmed to pick crops at peak ripeness, thereby enhancing produce quality and market value. Predictive analytics allowed AgriCorp to forecast market demands and adjust cultivation plans accordingly, ensuring premium prices for their produce. The successful incorporation of AI not only elevated the operational efficiency by 40% but also resulted in a 25% increase in crop yields year-over-year.

The strategic implementation of AI across various facets of farming operations at AgriCorp serves as an extensive case study for understanding the pivotal role AI can play in transforming traditional farming practices into a high-tech industry. This holistic AI adoption not only directly impacted the profitability but also enhanced sustainable farming practices, setting benchmarks for environmental responsibility in agribusiness. The AgriCorp case underlines the critical importance of integrating advanced technologies like AI to maintain competitiveness and innovation in the dynamic field of agriculture. It provides a blueprint for similar agribusiness entities looking to optimize outputs while fostering sustainable methods.

Case Study: AI Innovations in Asset Management: The QuantumInvest Case

In the world of asset management, AI-driven tools have transitioned from being a futuristic idea to a fundamental necessity for maintaining competitive advantage and driving efficiency. QuantumInvest, a prominent financial services firm, recognized the emerging potential of AI to reshape investment strategies and embarked on an innovative project to integrate AI into their asset management processes. Initially faced with volatile market conditions and the challenge of managing a vast portfolio with efficiency, QuantumInvest's traditional methods struggled to adapt to rapid market changes.

To address these challenges, QuantumInvest implemented a comprehensive AI-driven asset management system. The system deployed complex algorithms to analyze large datasets, encompassing global market trends, individual asset performances, and economic indicators in real-time. Predictive analytics were applied to foresee market fluctuations and automate portfolio adjustments. This advanced capability allowed QuantumInvest to mitigate risks and capitalize on profitable opportunities more swiftly than before.

AI also played a pivotal role in personalizing investment advice for QuantumInvest's clients. Machine learning models analyzed clients' past investment behaviors, risk tolerance, and personal financial goals to tailor unique investment strategies and recommendations. This not only enhanced client satisfaction but also improved client retention rates significantly. Additionally, AI-driven robo-advisors were introduced to handle routine inquiries, providing clients with instant responses and freeing up human advisors to handle more complex cases, thus optimizing both client servicing and operational efficiency.

The implementation of AI enabled QuantumInvest to achieve remarkable outcomes. There was a 40% increase in portfolio performance efficiency, and automated trading systems reduced transaction costs by 30%. Furthermore, real-time compliance monitoring, powered by AI, ensured that all transactions met regulatory requirements, dramatically reducing the risk of compliance breaches.

QuantumInvest's journey exemplifies the transformative potential of AI in asset management, not only in enhancing financial performance and operational efficiency but also in revolutionizing client relationships.

Case Study: Enhancing Global Supply Chain Resilience with AI: The TechGlobal Case

TechGlobal, a multinational electronics company, faced significant challenges in managing its complex global supply chain, which was vulnerable to disruptions due to geopolitical tensions, natural disasters, and fluctuating market demands. To address these challenges, TechGlobal implemented a state-of-the-art AI-driven supply chain management system designed to enhance resilience and efficiency.

The AI system integrated predictive analytics and machine learning to monitor and analyze data from various sources, including logistics partners, weather forecasts, and market trends. This integration allowed TechGlobal to anticipate potential disruptions and adjust its supply chain strategies proactively. For instance, when predictive models forecasted a possible delay due to a typhoon in Southeast Asia, the system automatically rerouted shipments and adjusted production schedules at alternative manufacturing sites, minimizing downtime and maintaining delivery commitments.

Furthermore, the AI system enhanced demand forecasting by analyzing real-time sales data, consumer trends, and economic indicators. This sophisticated approach reduced overproduction and inventory costs by aligning production more closely with market demand. Additionally, the AI-driven system streamlined supplier selection and management by evaluating supplier performance metrics and risk factors, ensuring that TechGlobal maintained a robust and reliable supplier network capable of adapting to changing conditions.

The implementation of this AI system transformed TechGlobal's supply chain into a dynamic, responsive entity that could withstand various challenges and capitalize on emerging opportunities. The company reported a 30% improvement in supply chain efficiency, a 25% reduction in costs related to inventory management, and a significant boost in customer satisfaction due to better product availability and timely delivery. By leveraging AI, TechGlobal not only reinforced its supply chain resilience but also set new industry standards for managing large-scale, global supply networks in an unpredictable world.

Case Study: AI-Enhanced Predictive Maintenance in Heavy Industries

In the context of heavy industries, such as mining, oil, and gas, equipment failure can lead to significant downtime and astronomical costs. This sector thus presents a fertile ground for deploying artificial intelligence to enhance predictive maintenance strategies. Case in point, MassiveMachineries, a leading company in the mining industry, initiated an AI-driven project aimed at reducing maintenance-related disruptions and extending the lifespan of critical machinery.

The implementation involved the integration of IoT sensors on equipment to continuously collect data regarding their operational status, temperature, vibration levels, and more. This initiative transitioned into a sophisticated model where machine learning algorithms analyzed the incoming data to predict potential breakdowns before they occurred. Through this predictive approach, MassiveMachineries hoped to switch from traditional scheduled maintenance to condition-based maintenance strategies.

The results were transformative. The AI system flagged irregular patterns indicative of imminent failures. This proactive model allowed the company to maintain equipment only when necessary, reducing unnecessary maintenance checks and costs. More importantly, it minimized downtime by preventing unexpected equipment failures. For instance, sensor data predicted a critical failure in one of the conveyor belts, and maintenance was conducted just in time to avoid a costly halt in operations.

Beyond just operational efficiency, the predictive maintenance system provided MassiveMachineries with valuable insights into the long-term performance and reliability of their equipment. This allowed them to make informed decisions about where to invest in new equipment and how to optimize operational workflows. The ripple effect of these efficiencies pointed to a significant uptick in overall productivity and a robust decrease in operational costs, ranging up to 25% annually.

Furthermore, the success of this project did not just elevate MassiveMachineries' profitability and operational robustness; it also helped them meet stricter environmental and safety standards. By minimizing unexpected failures, the company could better comply with safety regulations, reducing the risk of accidents.

Case Study: AI-Driven Optimization in Hospitality: The Global Hotel Chain Revolution

In an industry where customer satisfaction is paramount, the hospitality sector is increasingly turning to artificial intelligence to enhance service delivery and operational efficiency. A prominent example is LuxeResorts, a global hotel chain, which embarked on a comprehensive AI integration project aimed at revolutionizing guest experiences and streamlining back-end operations. The initiative targeted several areas, including personalized guest services, energy management, and predictive maintenance.

The first phase involved deploying AI to refine guest personalization. LuxeResorts utilized AI-driven analytics to evaluate vast amounts of data from guest preferences and behaviors during previous stays. This enabled the creation of highly tailored experiences, from room ambiance settings adjusted automatically to preferred temperatures and lighting, to personalized greetings and recommendations for dining and entertainment options that align with guest interests.

Simultaneously, LuxeResorts adopted AI for predictive maintenance and energy management. Sensors equipped throughout the properties collected data on equipment usage and energy consumption. AI algorithms analyzed this data to predict potential system failures and optimize energy use, significantly reducing downtime and operational costs. For instance, predictive maintenance helped avoid disruptions during high-occupancy periods by scheduling repairs during lower-demand times, while smart energy systems adjusted resource use in real-time based on occupancy and weather forecasts, slashing energy expenses by up to 30%.

The implementation of AI not only transformed operational practices but also ushered in substantial cost savings and enhanced customer loyalty. Guest satisfaction scores soared due to the personalized touches and seamless service, with a recorded increase in repeat guests by 25%. Additionally, the operational efficiency improvements led to a reduction in maintenance costs by 20% and energy savings directly boosting the bottom line.

This case demonstrates the transformative power of AI in hospitality, emphasizing its role not just in enhancing guest experiences but in driving significant economic benefits. LuxeResorts serves as a beacon for the sector, illustrating how integrating AI can result in both elevated guest satisfaction and improved operational effectiveness.

Case Study: Advancing Educational Excellence with AI:

Personalized Learning at FutureBright Academy

FutureBright Academy, a forward-thinking educational institution known for its innovative approaches, embarked on a major project to integrate advanced AI technologies into its learning management systems. The main objective was to enhance educational outcomes through personalized learning experiences and improve administrative efficiencies. Traditionally, FutureBright faced challenges with a one-size-fits-all teaching model that often failed to address individual student needs, leading to varied academic performances and a noticeable lack of engagement in some students.

To address these challenges, FutureBright Academy developed an AI-driven platform that leveraged data analytics and machine learning to tailor educational content and pacing to each student's unique needs. By analyzing data points such as previous scores, learning pace, and engagement levels, the AI system was able to recommend personalized learning paths and resources. This approach ensured that students received instruction that was not only aligned with their learning style but also adaptive to their knowledge level and interest areas, significantly boosting their engagement and performance.

Furthermore, the AI platform included predictive analytics features that identified students at risk of falling behind, enabling early interventions by educators. This proactive strategy dramatically decreased the dropout rates and enhanced student retention figures. On the administrative front, AI automated routine tasks such as grading and scheduling, freeing up educators to focus more on teaching and less on bureaucratic functions. The outcome was a noticeable increase in teacher satisfaction and morale, as they could engage more directly and meaningfully with their students.

The implementation of AI at FutureBright Academy transformed the traditional educational model, fostering a more inclusive and adaptive learning environment. This case provides a profound insight into how AI can revolutionize educational practices, moving beyond traditional methodologies to embrace a future where technology and education seamlessly integrate to enhance learning outcomes on a large scale.

REVIEW QUESTIONS

1. Dr. Thompson, a healthcare provider, is exploring the potential of AI in his practice to enhance patient care while reducing costs. He is particularly interested in ways to streamline administrative tasks, improve diagnostic accuracy, and optimize patient management. Which of the following AI applications would MOST effectively meet Dr. Thompson's needs?

A) AI-driven diagnostic systems that enhance medical imaging precision

B) AI algorithms for analyzing and predicting fashion trends

C) Automated systems for real-time social media content creation

D) Bespoke AI solutions for personalized investment advice

Answer: A

Explanation: AI-driven diagnostic systems that enhance medical imaging precision directly address Dr. Thompson's goals by improving diagnostic accuracy, which is crucial in healthcare. These systems analyze medical imaging with greater precision than traditional methods, leading to more effective and timely interventions. Deploying such AI applications in healthcare practice can streamline operations by reducing the dependency on manual diagnostics, thereby also reducing costs and optimizing patient management as it allows for the early detection and treatment of diseases. This implementation speaks directly to Dr. Thompson's curiosity about using AI to bolster patient care while ensuring operational efficiency.

2. Marina, an entrepreneur in the retail sector, is considering integrating AI into her business to tackle the dynamic challenges of inventory management, consumer preferences, and marketing strategies. She has been studying various AI success stories in retail. Which of the following AI-enabled solutions would be BEST for Marina's retail business to enhance operational efficiency and customer satisfaction?

A) AI-powered systems for real-time pricing adjustments and personalized marketing

B) Machine learning models for predicting weather patterns in agriculture

C) AI algorithms designed to optimize asset management in finance sectors

D) Automated video analysis tools for content creators on social platforms

Answer: A

Explanation: AI-powered systems for real-time pricing adjustments and personalized marketing directly address the challenges Marina faces in the retail sector. These tools analyze large streams of consumer data to optimize inventory levels based on purchasing trends and dynamically adjust pricing to maximize profit margins. Moreover, they tailor marketing efforts to individual consumer behaviors and preferences, enhancing customer engagement and satisfaction. This integration not only streamlines operations but also significantly elevates the consumer experience, which is critical in the retail industry.

REVIEW QUESTIONS

3. A manufacturing company plans to implement AI to revolutionize its production process by increasing efficiency and output. The leadership team is evaluating different AI applications to integrate. Which of the following would MOST likely provide the company with the desired increase in production efficiency and quality?

A) AI-driven predictive maintenance tools to forecast equipment failures

B) AI solutions for real-time translation in multilingual customer support

C) Automated AI systems for generating legal documents in real estate

D) AI-enhanced virtual reality environments for training surgeons

Answer: A

Explanation: AI-driven predictive maintenance tools are ideally suited to a manufacturing context where equipment uptime is critical to operational efficiency and output quality. These tools utilize AI to analyze historical and real-time data to predict when machines will need maintenance before failures occur, thus minimizing downtime. This proactive maintenance ensures continuous production and improves the overall efficiency of the production line. The integration of such AI applications meets the manufacturing company's objectives by ensuring a smooth, uninterrupted workflow, which is essential for achieving higher output and maintaining quality.

EPILOGUE

As we close the curtains on ',' we reflect on an era marked by spectacular advancements and transformation, driven by Artificial Intelligence. This exploration penned by Benoit Tano, MD, PhD, not only highlighted the disruptive innovation but also approached the nuanced interplay of technology and economy with commendable depth and foresight. The journey we embarked upon unfolded across seminal AI apps, each carving out new vistas for wealth creation, employment, and societal benefit. The detailed chapters provided not only insights but practical guides on integrating AI tools from ChatGPT's revolution in content creation to Notion AI's organizational gains, illustrating a landscape rich with opportunities yet tempered by challenges. The ethical dimensions and regulatory landscapes were unwrapped thoughtfully, laying bare the crucial balance of harnessing technological potential while safeguarding human values and rights. As AI continues to evolve, the synergy between man and machine will undoubtedly scale new heights, promising unprecedented modes of operation in wealth creation. The outlined epilogues serve as lighthouses for navigating this burgeoning era, ensuring that as much as we lean on AI for growth, we also embed robust frameworks to manage it responsibly. The blueprint developed here is not merely for tapping into AI-induced wealth but shaping a future where technology amplifies human potential without replacing it. In this conclusive passage, we must pivot from what AI can do, to what we should do with AI, steering this powerful tool to benefit the broadest swathe of humanity. Let this blueprint be a compass for future innovators, entrepreneurs, and policymakers, a starting point for richer, more integrated dialogues on building sustainable, equitable economic structures where AI acts not as a divider but a unifier. Envisioning the future, this compendium stands as a testament and a guide, ensuring the next steps we take are informed, intentional, and inclusive, leading towards a future where AI and humanity prosper conjointly.

BACK COVER CONTENT

Welcome to the forefront of the digital revolution with 'AI WEALTH BLUEPRINT,' a groundbreaking exploration authored by . This masterly crafted guide illuminates the transformative power of Artificial Intelligence through the lenses of wealth creation, job generation, and innovative entrepreneurship. Dive into a meticulously curated compilation of the top 10 AI apps that are setting the stage for a prosperous future, redefining the boundaries of technology and commerce. Starting with a comprehensive overview of AI's roots in wealth creation, Dr. Tano sets the stage, illustrating how AI has evolved to become a pivotal cornerstone in global economic systems. Learn about technologies like ChatGPT, which revolutionizes content creation, MidJourney's pioneering role within the visual arts, and Jasper AI's transformative impact on automated marketing strategies. Each chapter delves deeply into distinct AI applications, revealing their mechanics, industry applications, and the blueprints for monetizing these AI-driven tools effectively. Not just focused on corporate titans, this book is an invaluable resource for small business owners and freelancers, guiding them through utilizing AI tools like Canva AI and Copy.ai to streamline and enhance their entrepreneurial efforts. Personalized insights from case studies and practical tips provide a real-world context, ensuring readers not only understand AI capacities but also how to pragmatically apply them. Furthermore, AI WEALTH BLUEPRINT does not shy away from the ethical, privacy, and regulatory landscapes that frame contemporary AI deployment. These discussions ensure a balanced perspective, imperative for anyone involved in AI at any level. Suitable for AI novices and seasoned technologists alike, this book is a must-read for anyone eager to harness AI's potential. Whether you're looking to integrate AI into your business model, carve out new financial opportunities, or simply indulge in the rich future prospects AI promises, AN AI WEALTH BLUEPRINT offers a treasure trove of insights to navigate this dynamic terrain. Embrace the AI revolution and navigate your path to unprecedented wealth generation with Benoit Tano's AI WEALTH BLUEPRINT - your premiere guide to thriving in a world shaped increasingly by artificial intelligence.

www.ingramcontent.com/pod-product-compliance
Lightning Source LLC
LaVergne TN
LVHW060133070326
832902LV00018B/2774